ARMOUR AGAINST FATE

Michael Occleshaw

ARMOUR AGAINST FATE

British Military Intelligence in the First World War

COLUMBUS BOOKS
LONDON

First published in Great Britain in 1989 by
COLUMBUS BOOKS LIMITED
19-23 Ludgate Hill, London, EC4M 7PD

British Library Cataloguing in Publication Data
Occleshaw, Michael
Armour against fate: British military intelligence
in the twentieth century.
1. British Army intelligence services,
1914-1987
I. Title
335.3'432

ISBN 0-86287-407-6

Designed by Fred Price
Set in Linotype Plantin

Printed and bound in Great Britain
by MacKays of Chatham, plc

TO BETTY

The glories of our blood and state
Are shadows, not substantial things.
There is no armour against fate –
Death lays his icy hand on Kings;
  Sceptre and Crown
  Must tumble down
And in the dust be equal made
With the poor crooked scythe and spade.

'The Contention of Ajax and Ulysses for the Armour of Achilles', I.iii.

James Shirley, 1659

Contents

Illustrations

(All photographs, unless otherwise indicated, are reproduced courtesy of the Imperial War Museum.)

Maps and Tables

Foreword

ONE of the greatest obstacles in writing any sort of book on Intelligence, at least in the United Kingdom, is the fact that very nearly all documentary evidence relating to the subject is either destroyed or withheld from the researcher. In the case of the First World War, this is plainly ridiculous after seventy years, for what was done then can hardly have any bearing on national security in an age of satellites, computers and electronic wizardry, nor can it affect the reputation of any living person. Yet secrecy still clings to the subject like a limpet to a rock and in recent years the Official Secrets Act has been subjected to much well-justified criticism. The present (1989) Government's proposed reforms will go some way to clarify the situation, but hold out little prospect of the release of documents which might aid the historian.

The policy regarding Intelligence documents is due to be reviewed in 1992, when, perhaps, the more absurd reaches of secrecy just might be relaxed. Documents more than 50 years old cannot threaten the State in a rapidly changing world and it is high time the Act was modified accordingly. This book has been composed largely from research amongst unpublished private papers (which would probably have been seized had governments known of their existence), and from recorded interviews with veterans, as well as from a great deal of research amongst the less well-known documents in the Public Record Office.

When extracts from any source are quoted, whether it is from a diary, a private letter, an official document or anything else, most original spelling has been retained and sentence construction, especially in interviews, only altered to avoid repetition. All my recorded interviews are available for scrutiny and will shortly be donated to the Imperial War Museum.

The words Military Intelligence are intended, for the purposes of this book, to be interpreted in their narrowest sense, referring to the collection and evaluation of information by and for the Army alone both before and during the Great War.

I must stress that this is not a book about spies; these gentry do appear from time to time, but only to the extent to which they had a bearing on the wider field of Military Intelligence. My narrative develops continuously and broadly rather than dwelling on selected occurrences or ventures. Only by following that development through its various stages, beginning with the opening discussion about how the First World War became the kind of war it was, can we hope to comprehend the difficulties which dictated the way Intelligence had to operate and why its progress followed the course it did. In this way the reader can measure my understanding of Intelligence, the men who worked in it, and the value of its contribution to final victory.

Acknowledgements

I WOULD like to record my grateful thanks to a number of people whose help was vital to the research and writing of this book. I would particularly like to acknowledge the unstinted assistance and encouragement of Trevor Jones MA (Cantab.) of the University of Keele and of Colonel Felix Robson (Retd.) formerly of the Intelligence Corps and, until recently, curator of the Intelligence Corps Museum. Joseph Murray, veteran of the Hood Battalion of the Royal Naval Division deserves special mention for his interest and criticisms and for sharing his memories with me. Special thanks are also due to the Earl Haig of Bemersyde and to Lieutenant-Colonel John Charteris MC for permission to study the papers of Field-Marshal Earl Haig and of Brigadier-General John Charteris; to Edith Gilchrist, Hon. Archivist of the Royal Free Hospital, Hampstead; Colonel Richard Kirke CBE; John Terraine; Martin Middlebrook; and Anthony Summers. Thanks are also owed to Curtis Brown Group Ltd., for permission to quote from R. S. Churchill's *Lord Derby: 'King of Lancashire'* on behalf of the estate of R. S. Churchill; Miss Doris Topley for permitting me to quote from the papers of A. E. Thompson; L. W. Galer and Mrs S. M. Simpson for the same facility with the papers of Guy Buckridge and Sir Vernon Kell respectively; and Lady Ravensdale and the County Archivist, Hertfordshire, for permission to publish extracts from the correspondence of Sir William Pulteney and Lady Desborough.

Acknowledgement is also due to Mr Richard Randle Meinertzhagen and the Trustees of the estate of Colonel Richard Meinertzhagen; the Trustees of the Liddell Hart Centre for Military Archives, King's College, London; and the National Library of Scotland. Crown-copyright material in the Public Record Office is reproduced by permission of the Controller of Her Majesty's Stationery Office, as are extracts from *The Official History of the Great War: Mesopotamia Campaign (Vol. 1); The Official History of the Great War: Military*

Operations France and Belgium; and *The Eye in the Air: History of Air Observation and Reconnaissance for the Army 1785–1945* by P. Mead. Quotations from the King George V Archives at Windsor Castle are reproduced by the gracious permission of Her Majesty the Queen. Extracts from the papers of Lord Trenchard are reproduced by kind permission of the Royal Air Force Museum, Hendon. I wish also to thank Times Newspapers Ltd for permission to quote from two articles published in *The Times* and Macmillan Publishers for permission to use material from Alistair Horne's masterly *The Price of Glory*. Thanks are also due to Harrap Books Ltd for permission to quote from General Sir Archibald Wavell's *Allenby: A Study in Greatness,* published by George G. Harrap and Co. Ltd.

Two museums are worthy of very special mention: the Imperial War Museum, London, and the Intelligence Corps Museum, Ashford. My most grateful thanks, therefore, to the Trustees and staff of both foundations for their unfailing courtesy and attention.

Michael Edward Occleshaw
December 1988

Abbreviations

THE following abbreviations have been used throughout the book. Military abbreviations are in accordance with the usage of the First World War.

BCI	Bureau Central Interallié.
BEF	British Expeditionary Force, France and Belgium.
BGGS (I)	Brigadier-General, General Staff (Intelligence).
BGI	Brigadier-General Intelligence.
C	Commander Mansfield Smith-Cumming, Chief of the Secret Service.
C/E	Counter-Espionage.
CID	Committee of Imperial Defence.
CIGS	Chief of the Imperial General Staff.
CRA	Commander, Royal Artillery.
CRE	Commander, Royal Engineers.
DAS	Director Army Signals.
DMI	Director (Directorate) of Military Intelligence.
DMO	Director (Directorate) of Military Operations.
DMRS	Department of Munitions Requirements and Statistics.
DSI	Director (Directorate) of Special Intelligence.
EEF	Egyptian Expeditionary Force.
FO	Foreign Office.
GHQ	General Headquarters.
GOC	General Officer Commanding.
GSO	General Staff Officer. Where a number succeeds the initials it represents the grade of the officer.
GQG	Grand Quartier Général.
I	Intelligence (branch or head of).
ICMA	Intelligence Corps Museum, Ashford.
IWM	Imperial War Museum.
KCL	Liddell Hart Military Archives, King's College, London.
MA	Military Attaché.
MED	Mediterranean Expeditionary Force.
MI	Section of the Military Intelligence Directorate.

MID	Munitions Inventions Department.
NLS	National Library of Scotland, Edinburgh.
O	Operations (branch or head of).
OC	Officer Commanding.
OHL	Oberste Heeres Leitung.
PRO	Public Record Office, Kew.
RA	Royal Artillery.
RFC	Royal Flying Corps.
RHL	Rhodes House Library, Oxford.
RN	Royal Navy.
SS	Secret Service.
WO	War Office.
WTID	War Trade Intelligence Department.

ONE

The Nature of the Beast

NAPOLEON Bonaparte cast a very long shadow indeed. One hundred years after his final overthrow on the bloody and cataclysmic field of Waterloo, his example still dominated the thinking of European generals like some latter-day Gulliver amidst the Lilliputians, serving at once as an inspiration, a model and a bogeyman. Yet his most profound legacy lay less in the naïve cult of Napoleon-worship or the inclination to imitate him, more in a school of thought which attempted to reduce the art of war at its highest level to a systematic and almost mathematical rhythm conducted through the medium of a General Staff.

The concept of a General Staff, a body of highly professional officers holding a strategic and tactical doctrine in common, who were charged with responsibility for the smooth command and control of the army in the field and the dissemination of the commander's will throughout its ranks, was a direct response to one of Napoleon's most complete victories, the crushing of the Russo-Prussian Armies in the whirlwind campaign of 1806-7. He not only shattered the old Prussian Army, the legacy of Frederick the Great, but placed the whole Prussian state in wretched subjugation. Two things rapidly became clear to the Prussians: they had to destroy Napoleon in order effectively to re-establish their independence and, in the absence of a Napoleon of their own, they had to evolve a means to take on and beat the grand master at his own game.

The method which was chosen, or rather forced upon the Prussians, under the guiding hand of David von Scharnhorst, the first chief of the new General Staff, was to train an élite corps of officers who would present an identical correct solution to any given military problem even when acting independently. It was, in effect, an attempt to institutionalize military genius[1] and make it the common property of the army by attaching members of the elite to all levels of command,

1 The phrase is T. N. Dupuy's. See T. N. Dupuy, *A Genius for War*, London, 1977, p. 24 ff.

thus endowing every formation with a common doctrine and all-pervasive standard of excellence. Had not the French Emperor 'rightly said in this connection that many of the problems faced by the Commander-in-Chief resemble mathematical problems worthy of the gifts of a Newton or an Euler'?[1] Elsewhere, too, Napoleon had stated that one day, if he could ever find the time, he would codify his practice of war into a formula which could be studied by anybody.[2]

By the end of the Napoleonic Wars the new concept still had to justify itself. Although Napoleon had been irretrievably defeated, his genius, even when on the wane, had still proved only too capable of inflicting grievous reverses on his opponents, and he had in the end been brought low by a combination of circumstances in which the new Prussian General Staff had figured not at all prominently. The infant had shown promise, but had not proved itself to be a prodigy or even remarkably precocious. Many of the existing senior Prussian officers had had no Staff training, some resented the imposition of the new blue-eyed boys on their commands, but most of all time had been too short, a mere eight years, to inculcate the new approach to the required depth.

By the end of the nineteenth century, however, the infant had grown to maturity and bestowed tremendous victories upon Prussian arms, winning world-shaking political rewards and establishing Prussia at the head of a mighty German Empire exuding power and confidence in the centre of Europe, to the concern of its neighbours and the obliteration of the old balance of power. Bismarck's political genius would have counted for naught but for the Prussian Army: it was through the army that Bismarck's goals were realized and the new German Empire established, and the Germans were never allowed to forget it. Militarization was seen as creator and saviour and, during the Second Reich, its supremacy over every other idea was a major cause of the nervous instability of the rest of Europe in the years leading to the outbreak of the First World War. One of the problems which had undone Napoleon was his inability to oversee and co-ordinate the enormous forces of his *Grande Armée* over the vast tracts of territory involved in the great campaigns of 1812-15; with hundreds of thousands of men spread over thousands of square miles, it was a task beyond the capacity of any one man, even though he were a

1 Carl von Clausewitz, *On War*, Book 1, New Jersey, 1976, p. 112.

2 Marshal Saint-Cyr, *Mémoires pour servir à l'Histoire Militaire sous la Directoire, le Consulat et l'Empire*, Vol. IV, p. 149.

genius. Napoleon had been forced to delegate more and more and to give his marshals independent commands, and his marshals didn't measure up to the task. Had he had at his disposal a modern (i.e. Prussian) General Staff, with subordinates possessing a common doctrine and training, how very different would have been the course of those campaigns.

The crushing victories won by the Prussians against the Austrians in 1866 and the French in 1870-1 enthroned their General Staff as the very apogee of military excellence. No army could now dare take the field without a General Staff cast in the Prussian mould. With armies growing ever larger through conscription – another profound legacy of the Napoleonic Wars – and theatres of war spanning several provinces at a time, a General Staff promised an efficient and flexible remedy to the problems of command and control. The armies of the later nineteenth and early twentieth centuries went Prussian-mad in consequence, adopting everything they could from the seemingly all-powerful Teutons, down to the minutiae of drill and style of uniform. The British Army adopted the *pickelhaube* (the spiked helmet of the Prussians, from which today's police helmets are descended) and, after the sequence of humiliating reverses sustained at the hands of untrained Boer farmers in the South African War of 1899-1902, began rather more usefully to introduce some Prussian-style professionalism.

The General Staff outlook steeped its protégés in a detached and intellectual frame of mind in which feelings had small place, something which can reasonably be termed the General Staff Mentality, hereinafter GSM. It set them apart from the run-of-the-mill soldiery, almost as if they were a sect of cloistered ascetics divorced from the rude and painful realities of life and death at the sharp end of war. This was no accident: the training of these budding generals demanded that they keep clear heads capable of analysis and reason when under the greatest stress and distraction. Command, in an age of rapid and far-reaching technological and social change, demanded calmness and clear-thinking.

Animated by these values and the assumptions they sanctioned, the General Staffs expected to steer their armies to quick victory and the politicians expected then to reap the harvest of victory. The plan was seductive in its simplicity and the armies of Europe fell victim to its seduction one after the other. But in the process something was lost, for war is a social activity conducted by organized groups of people and as such it involves living and moral forces which the theoretical emphasis of the GSM effectively tried to suppress. Napoleon's genius had not been founded on dry theory or even entirely on the thorough preparations he made before embarking on a campaign, but embraced the unpredictable and very human attributes of inspiration and intuition. Such wayward qualities were anathema to the GSM, which sought to deal in clear principles and well-defined responses, 'correct' according to the dominating Staff doctrine. Consequently, the factors which motivate men to transcend seemingly impossible obstacles and serve as an inspiration to all, were left behind. So narrowly technical was the GSM that it effectively blinkered the commands of armies, something perhaps most easily demonstrated by Ludendorff's comment that he had read nothing but military books for thirty years. The General Staff approach was to cast aside anything but the particularly, or purely, military. Its adherents lost sight of the fact that great wars between great industrial powers belong to other provinces of life as well. I do not mean to be taken as saying that intuition and inspiration are in themselves acceptable substitutes for a professional and technically competent General Staff, but the absence of flexibility certainly exerted a baneful influence on generalship in the First World War through the attitudes it encouraged in many senior officers.

Theory was, of course, essential to their profession – to a greater extent than in any other, since great wars are infrequent and there can be little other opportunity for putting theory to the test; and theory is only a guide to judgement, not a substitute for it. But men of the second rank in all walks of life prefer that which is sound and methodical, which does not require them to expose their inadequacies by making decisions which take them onto unfamiliar ground, ground which is fraught with danger. Men of lesser talents are by nature inclined to prudence and tradition; they do what is accepted as right without having to exercise any creative talent or thought. Under the General Staff régime, men of such character could, or so they thought, tie the art of war to a disciplined approach, hence theory and method came in large part to replace insight and judgement in leadership.

This does not mean that theory should be cast aside as an irrelevancy, but it needs to be balanced by individual judgement, by the ability to weigh ends against means and apply the brake to the more absurd reaches of concept and logic, preventing actions which are eminently justifiable in concept but deadly in practice.

This almost platonic approach is depicted with superb precision in the British Official History of the First World War. Written by a Staff officer, Brigadier-General Sir James E. Edmonds, for other Staff officers, the *History* is a very scholarly work, but one in which events of great moment are reduced to a tidy, well-ordered analysis in which the confusion and terror felt by the men on the receiving end is completely lost. The first day of the great Somme offensive, 1 July 1916, ranks as one of the great disasters of British military history, comparable in scale only to the surrender of Singapore a generation later. This grand tragedy was made up of countless small tragedies along the length of the 25,000 yards of rural Picardy attacked on that day, but the *History* recounts these disasters with the same monotonous exactitude. Take, for instance, the account of the attack of the 11th Battalion of the Border Regiment near the Leipzig Salient below the Thiepval Ridge:

> At 8.30 a.m., according to the time-table, the 11/Border Regiment, in reserve, moved out from Authuille Wood. Unable, in the smoke and dust, to see the actual situation, and believing the advance to be going according to plan, the battalion expected to find the southern face of the salient in British hands. It came at once under heavy enfilade machine-gun fire from the Nord Werk sector to the south. In spite of this fire which caused devastating casualties, including Lieut.-Colonel P. W. Machell, killed, with practically all the officers, the lines of companies continued their efforts to cross No-Man's-Land. Small parties on the left succeeded in reaching Leipzig Redoubt, where they joined the 17/Highland L.I., but the majority were unable to get forward, and the survivors were reassembled during the day in Authuille Wood.[1]

It is a model of its kind – bland, ponderous, didactic and remorseless. There is nothing here to give the reader any impression of the difficulties in persuading nearly 1,000 heavily encumbered and frightened men to enter the unknown. They merely 'moved out from Authuille Wood' like clockwork, apparently unhindered by fallen trees, barbed wire, dead bodies, shell craters or loss of nerve. Only one man, the commanding officer, is mentioned by name. He is briefly noted to have been killed – but, the reader might well ask, what effect did this have on the men under his command? These men

1 Brigadier-General Sir James E. Edmonds, *The Official History of The Great War: Military Operations France and Belgium* December 1915–July 1, 1916. Originally published 1932, reprinted Woking, 1986, p. 401.

are reduced to 'lines of companies', 'small parties' or 'survivors'. Admittedly, Edmonds had a great deal of ground to cover with a lot happening in it, and certainly one could not expect emotional outpourings, but the result is so far removed from human reality that one wonders whether the Official Historian was writing about the same battle described vividly by Basil Liddell Hart or Martin Middlebrook.

Britain had gone to war to prevent the domination of Europe by a militaristic German Empire; any peace which left Europe under German hegemony would have spelled ruin for Britain and her people, so the stakes were enormous. The war had to be fought through to a victorious conclusion and that could not be done without accepting severe losses. Acceptance of that fact and carelessness of it, however, are very different things. There were officers who went overboard in their dedication to dispassionate General Staff methods and, intoxicated by the vision of the great Moltke lounging on a couch reading a novel as the Prussian Army went to war in 1870, considered this style to be the epitome of ambition, just as Drake's cool continuation of his game of bowls had fired the imaginations of earlier generations of Englishmen. However, both Moltke and Drake knew their adversaries and were experienced men of action, not of planning alone; and experience of the sort necessary in 1914, the experience of total war, was non-existent.

Instead the GSM found a ready receptacle in the minds of young men who entered the army straight from school, and in late nineteenth and early twentieth century Britain that usually meant the public schools and those which aped them. Forcibly endowed with an outlook described as 'muscular Christianity', they were called upon to cultivate an unbending approach to the vicissitudes of life and to suppress their emotions, any display of which incurred the derision of a boy's peers as unmanly and effeminate. They were taught and expected to 'play up, play up and play the game' regardless of circumstances, and to strive to overcome obstacles by an unflinching display of team spirit. Individual enterprise and independence of mind were frowned upon. The group was all that mattered, whether team, house or school, and members who broke this code were speedily brought to heel by the collective displeasure of schoolmasters, prefects and companions. This code, to which several generations of schoolboys found themselves bound, is perhaps best exemplified in Sir Henry Newbolt's 'Vitaï Lampada':

There's a breathless hush in the Close tonight –
  Ten to make and the match to win –
A bumping pitch and a blinding light,
  An hour to play and the last man in.
And it's not for the sake of a ribboned coat,
  Or the selfish hope of a season's fame,
But his Captain's hand on his shoulder smote –
  'Play up! play up! and play the game!'

The sand of the desert is sodden red, –
  Red with the wreck of a square that broke; –
The Gatling's jammed and the Colonel dead,
  And the regiment blind with dust and smoke.
The river of death has brimmed his banks,
  And England's far, and Honour a name,
But the voice of a schoolboy rallies the ranks:
  'Play up! play up! and play the game!'

This is the word that year by year,
  While in her place the School is set,
Every one of her sons must hear,
  And none that hears it dare forget.
This they all with a joyful mind
  Bear through life like a torch in flame,
And falling fling to the host behind –
  'Play up! play up! and play the game!'[1]

Newbolt's starched lines are resonant with stoicism and solid, immovable courage in the face of impossible odds. Here it is not individual skill and ability which turn either the cricket match or the battle, but a frame of mind in which team-work and sportsmanship reign supreme. Of course team-work is an essential in all human social endeavour, but in the Newboltian ambit there is no room for the equally human attributes of individual genius or imagination. This attitude indelibly impressed its recipients with a devotion to what has come to be taken for the typically British mien of the 'stiff upper lip', a care to remain unruffled in the face of calamity and do the 'right thing', whatever the cost. It might give strength to those not blessed with brains or sensibility but inextricably allied to this was an uncritical moral tone. One of its central tenets was the belief, or more accurately, the casual

1 *The Selected Poems of Henry Newbolt*, edited and with an introduction by Patric Dickinson, London, 1981, pp. 38-9. See also 'The School At War', p. 79.

acceptance that the British and especially the officer class were morally superior to all others in any and all circumstances, and that Britain was the natural repository for the world's moral wisdom. Men brought up in this tradition and then soused in General Staff techniques could no more question their attitudes than they could shed their skins, and the pernicious side of this influence can readily be seen in the decisions of too many of the generals of the First World War. It was, for example, seriously expected that mere Turks would never stand against a resolute landing on the Gallipoli Peninsula by British forces, an opinion which remained unshaken even after the events of 25 April 1915 proved otherwise.

Their detachment from the realities of life and death at the front inspired bitter resentment amongst many of the men in the ranks whose fates they controlled, and the tone of many of the memoirs and private diaries of ordinary soldiers bears ample witness both to the degree of animosity felt and the great gulf that existed between the two worlds. When one adds to this detachment an apparent ignorance of a technological revolution which had equipped an enemy, in this case the Turks, with formidable power, and a consequent failure to provide the means to overcome it, the stage is indeed set for a repetitive tragedy of epic proportions.

Today it is commonplace to condemn all First World War generals as equally guilty of callous indifference to the fate of the ranks, of stubborn pig-headedness and of a disinclination to listen – one might almost say a determination not to listen – to alternative advice which on some occasions could have achieved the same military goals at much less cost. But new examples come to light. Consider for a moment the case of Lieutenant-General Sir Aylmer Hunter-Weston, GOC of VIII Corps, which acquired an unenviable reputation for excessively heavy casualties in a war where heavy losses were the norm. In April 1934, veterans from the Royal Naval Division (RND) made a pilgrimage to the Dardanelles where many of them had been first-blooded in battle. Major-General Sir Archibald Paris, commander of the division at Gallipoli, joined the ship *(The Duchess of Richmond)* at Naples. He invited the veterans to his cabin where all his maps and papers were laid out and, during the wide-ranging discussions there, Paris recalled a conversation with Hunter-Weston, his then Corps commander, on board HMS *Queen Elizabeth*, the mighty new super-dreadnought which served as flagship during the first months of the ill-fated campaign. According to Paris, Hunter-Weston had outlined his plans for a battle in the immediate future when Paris interjected, 'But, General, won't this idea be very costly in casualties?' To Paris's astonishment Hunter-Weston replied shortly, 'What the hell do I care for casualties!' Paris got up to walk out but as he reached the cabin door, Hunter-Weston said, 'You'll stay to dinner, won't you, General?'

'I was so disgusted that I didn't even answer him,' said Paris.[1]

Hunter-Weston later led his battered VIII Corps through the prolonged horrors of the Somme campaign where once again it sustained dreadful losses. Such actions continued to enjoy general support at home. In October 1916 whilst the blood-letting continued, Hunter-Weston stood for Parliament in a bye-election at North Ayrshire in Scotland. His opponent, the Reverend Chelmers, stood on a pacifist platform and Hunter-Weston won the resounding victory which he had so signally failed to win in the field.[2]

General Staff experience was a necessity for any officer with career ambitions in the pre-1914 Army, an experience which all too often meant that aspiring officers had consciously to distance themselves from the troops carrying out their plans.

Sir James Edmonds, the impassive Official Historian of military operations during the First World War, noted that when he left the embryonic Intelligence section of the Staff he had the choice of becoming Commandant of the School of Military Engineering, a safe desk job, or taking an active post with the 4th Division. Edmonds favoured the active command and said so to General Sir Herbert Miles while they were walking in St James's Park. Miles, then Quarter Master General, promptly disillusioned the young Edmonds by telling him, 'My dear boy, if you want to get on in the army, don't go near troops, don't go near troops.'[3]

But not all the generals reflected such complacency. Personal ambition might prompt some to adopt G S M habits of thought and the need for professional survival (promotion) could harden others; that is

1 Leading Seaman Joseph Murray, Hood Battalion, 63rd (Royal Naval) Division. Interview with author, 15 June 1982 [hereinafter Murray interview].

2 Hunter-Weston received 7,419 votes, his opponent a mere 1,300. *See* Martin Middlebrook, *The First Day On The Somme*, London, 1971, pp. 295-6.

3 Papers of Brigadier-General Sir James Edmonds [hereinafter Edmonds Papers], III/5/30, Liddell Hart Centre for Military Archives, King's College, London [hereinafter KCL].

unless a budding general wanted the reputation of a heretic, a reputation which would most surely blight his prospects. But some did escape the straitjacket of the GSM and accept responsibility for the lives of the men entrusted to their care. The much-maligned Field-Marshal Haig is a case in point; his reputation has been extensively calumniated by many writers – both soldiers and historians – over many years, writers who level accusations of blind incompetence, outright stupidity, wilful ignorance and cold indifference against him. Haig was never a free agent, having to trim his plans to the politicians and the often conflicting demands of the French, and in that he was as much a victim of circumstances as the meanest private in the army he led, circumstances that deprived him of the opportunity to display his ability to the full. Lord Trenchard, when commander of the RFC in France, had better chances to observe Haig and the pressures under which he had to operate than any of Haig's critics, and he summed up the position in a masterly manner. Referring to an incident in the Boer War, in which he had served as an officer in the Royal Scots, he wrote:

> In the afternoon, I was sent for by the General who told me to recapture the hill which we had captured in the morning, but I was not to have casualties. And I remember I replied, did he want the hill captured or not?
>
> That remark of the General's has remained with me all my life. It has always seemed to me that the hardest thing in any war is to have Commanding Officers of sufficient calibre who will not mind, when the object is important, losing casualties. All Englishmen are brave, but what it is hard to find is the men for responsible positions who will fight and order others to fight and get killed. It is the hardest thing in life. Douglas Haig once told me it was the greatest strain of any man always to be planning how others were to get killed. How very true it is.[1]

How similar to those now levelled at Haig were the criticisms that greeted the great Duke of Marlborough after the successful but expensive storming of the Schellenberg in the famous Blenheim campaign, and Harley's scathing rhetorical question in the House of Commons: 'But are there not many such hills in Germany?' How similar to Haig's strain was the reaction of Wellington after the Waterloo campaign of 1815, a victory whose cost reduced the 'Iron Duke' to tears and made him wish never to see another general

1 Papers of the Viscount Trenchard [hereinafter Trenchard Papers], MFC 76/61, 'Autobiographical Notes', RAF Museum, Hendon.

engagement. Since Wellington's time, indeed since Marlborough's, the British have been shielded from experiencing the full horrors and the real cost of total war at first hand.

The literature of the Napoleonic period is revealing for the way in which it shows how little the wars in Europe impinged on British consciousness, other than as an awareness of the increase in the price of bread and the portrayal of hopeful officers in His Majesty's forces as little more than convenient altar-fodder for marriage-hungry young ladies.

It was not so for the rest of Europe; the victories Napoleon won in his dazzling, meteoric career were only won at great cost, and in the campaigns of 1812 and 1813 the butcher's bill was being counted in hundreds of thousands. The British had been fortuitously protected from this realization by having their small army ignominiously pushed from the continental mainland, and back behind their naval shield, years earlier, notwithstanding their engagement in the Peninsular War.

Total war has to be recognized for what it is; and to understand that, it is essential to compare it to a limited war. A limited war is fought for specific goals in which only a proportion of the state's total strength in men and money is fielded. In a limited war, or so classical military theory teaches us, peace is reached easily through one or other of the combatants discovering that the expenditure in men and money outweighs any likely political gain. Therefore, as the state's vital interests are in no way threatened, there is little except some face to be lost in negotiating a peace in which political changes of small denominations are made – such as the transfer of a frontier province or far-off colony. One may cite as examples the wars of the Italian principalities during the Renaissance, or most of the conflicts of the eighteenth century, or even the Austro-Prussian War of 1866. More recently still, the Falklands conflict of 1982 can be seen as a virtually tailor-made example. In short, a limited war seeks to persuade a hostile government to change its policy in a specific instance. It does not seek to overthrow the government, the policy maker, or the society it represents.

Total war presents a devastating contrast, for total war is the heavy collision of the survival values of whole societies – survival itself is at stake and such stakes cause the societies playing for them to summon up every last residue of their strength in pursuit of their goals. Pitting the whole fabric of their societies against each other, neither party can afford to compromise, for to do so would be to write off a considerable and perhaps vital part of the national investment in the war, an investment measured not in so many millions of money, so many thousands of expendable men, but in terms of Gross National Product, a whole way of life and a generation of young men. Those few governments which have decided to cut their losses in a total war and shown themselves weak enough (or, arguably, strong-willed enough) to throw in the towel have not survived the wave of popular anger, bitterness and frustration which inevitably rose to sweep them away.

Both popular feeling and the fear engendered by it were real enough and expressed themselves on different occasions in all the countries engaged in the war; but in the end, total war served to bring out the very worst in all peoples, just as it has always done. In years of peace when questions of outright survival are far from mind, people have the time and luxury to pursue higher standards in the many different spheres of their civilizations. Total war rends this complacency asunder and forces people to do things they do not want to do, throwing into disarray the accepted conventions and moral standards of civilized life. This dreadful ferment unlocks a violent fanaticism which, it seems, can only be sated by prodigious quantities of blood, by the cry that the end *does* justify the means, however cruel they might be. Bald expediency is the ruling force. Human nature has repeatedly shown itself ready and willing to outrage the laws of civilized society in what Paul Fussell described as 'the universal fantasy – the Huckleberry Finn daydream – of flagrant disobedience to authority'.[1] The very aspects of that nature which are ordinarily frowned upon within a society are now lauded and encouraged, so long as they are directed against the enemy.

As war is a social activity it follows that in total war every fibre of society is committed willy-nilly to the struggle, thus every fibre of society is a legitimate target and, as part of the whole war effort, is open to exposure to violence: starvation through blockade, aerial bombardment ('strategic bombing') or propaganda – and other modern refinements beyond these.

The vital importance of people might appear to be an obvious starting point for any study of military history, but surprisingly most military historians confine their art to biographies of great leaders or to

1 Paul Fussell, *The Great War and Modern Memory*, Oxford, 1975, p. 124.

more or less accurate accounts of the operations of armies in the field. But not only does war influence society; society can dictate how wars are fought and often why.

Contrary to Marxist belief, feudalism was neither an economic nor a social system but was founded upon the need to have properly trained and armed men (the knights) available for military service under trustworthy leaders (the barons). Although feudal society gave all the trappings of wealth and power to the nobility, that was not its object; it was a society built upon military need and designed for war, and it only perished when it no longer served that end. Armies do not operate in some sort of vacuum, divorced from the normal course of life and politics. They are instruments used in the political struggle for power: at its strongest, power is the ability to force people to do what they otherwise would not do. Nowhere is the deeply woven intermeshing of war and society more apparent than it is in a total war, a war in which all members of society are affected whether they will it or not. We are missing something fundamental if we insist upon regarding victory in the First World War solely as the result of operational prowess. We would, in fact, be making precisely the same mistake as the 1914 vintage General Staffs made. This was a war not to be won on the battlefields alone, but in the hearts and minds of millions of perfectly ordinary people who never went within a mile of the bloodbath at the front.

The transformation from agricultural to industrial society added grist to the mill of changes in society and warfare wrought by the French Revolution and Napoleon. Gone were the limited wars that were such a feature of the eighteenth century. Military historians are fond of arguing whether the heady tempo of the Napoleonic Wars was the offspring of technical and scientific change, or the spawn of new ideas and new attitudes to government which sought to bring power to the people.

Technical changes there were in the latter half of the eighteenth century: new roads, canals, railways and embryonic industry altered the social and demographic map of Europe. However, these changes were characteristic of just a portion of the continent, for while France, the Low Countries and Northern Italy certainly benefited, other areas, like Eastern Europe, Russia and Spain, slumbered on as heretofore. Yet in these places Napoleonic war attained a speed and savagery just as great as in the more developed provinces to the west, and on that basis we must acknowledge that there was something greater than technical progress at work which spread the new military gospel of total war.

The key to the answer lies in the advent of conscription which, introduced in Revolutionary France in 1792 and copied by her victims, made warfare the business of all adult males and thereby lent wings to making the populations of countries the final arbiters of their destinies. But before considering that, we should regard the effect of conscription on the handling of warfare.

The Napoleonic wars spanned two decades. We speak of the series of struggles, against Austria, Russia, Prussia, Spain and Britain, as being parts of one continuous war in which these component conflicts were really campaigns. Napoleon's enemies were able to rise and return to the struggle because his victories never crushed their spirit; after making the political concessions demanded of them at the conference table, they immediately set about restoring their forces with the full intention of overturning the offending political settlement at the earliest opportunity.

Armies were used to defend, attack or outflank. The pure defensive never really exists outside of a temporary need to gain time or wear an enemy down, and every successful act of defence in history has had as its accompaniment a resolute counter-stroke to drive the broken enemy pell-mell before it. As Napoleon put it, 'The whole art of war consists in a well-reasoned and circumspect defensive, followed by a rapid and audacious attack.' Armies which squat on their haunches let the initiative pass unresistingly to the enemy who will eventually use it to destroy the static defender. Wellington's retirement to the famous Lines of Torres Vedras was planned with eventual attack firmly in mind. He knew only too well that he would never drive the French from the Peninsula by sitting in his fastness, the product of geography, skilled engineering and months of back-breaking labour. The Lines of Torres Vedras served the designs of the British commander superbly by wearing out his opponents until they were ripe for the inevitable counter-stroke, but they were never more than a well-thought-out stop-gap to counter French numerical superiority. Even the battle which brought the great Napoleon's career to an end, Waterloo, was fought by Wellington's army from a defensive posture for only as long as the Duke was forced to fight that way; victory was won by Wellington's counter-attack in conjunction with the Prussians.

Moltke the Elder, the model for Staff officers of 1914, had

consistently advocated the envelopment of the enemy's flank. All his greatest victories had been won this way and any doubts about the futility of frontal attacks should have been settled at Gravelotte-St Privat in 1870. Here, the elite Prussian Guard advanced to the assault up the glacis-like slope leading to St Privat, there to be brought to an untidy and shuddering halt by the withering fire of the chassepots of Canrobert's Corps. The attack failed and cost the Guard over a quarter of its strength; ironically, the battle was only won when the despised Saxons fell upon the French flank, to turn Canrobert's men out of their positions like a fleeing mob. The ill-judged Prussian attack meant the victory was a pyrrhic one which, in terms of casualties, bore all the hallmarks of a defeat.

In his wars, however, Moltke had not had to contend with mass conscript armies backed by modern industry. By 1914 the major military powers of Europe could all match the conscript masses of Germany with conscript masses of their own. Armies had swollen to enormous sizes, so much so that large groups called armies had supplanted the smaller corps as the essential unit of independent manoeuvre; in 1914, remember, the Germans alone deployed a mass of seven complete armies on the Western front. These huge numbers of men straddled whole theatres of war, and the ability to move reserves rapidly through the common use of railways meant effectively that there was no opportunity for manoeuvre on a large scale. The resulting picture is a familiar one – armies equipped with rapid-fire weapons stretching across whole continents and offering no flanks against which Moltke's favourite gambit could be employed. If armies were to attack, as in the end they had to, then the only way they could do so was by frontal assault. Looking for victory in the field, the options available were already hopelessly restricted from the very beginning and no skilful generalship or subtle strategem could alter that terrible fact.

Operations in the First World War have frequently been likened to siege warfare and writers fond of pushing this analogy invariably demand to know why the techniques of siege warfare were not used to overcome the difficulties presented by what might be termed the Constant Tactical Problem (CTP for convenience) – how to steal the edge from the all-conquering defensive. Tanks, gas, smoke, open-order infantry formations and ground-attack aircraft were eventually all used in this, but before them were those very siege techniques. Mining, starvation by blockade, battering a breach with guns followed by a full-scale storm were all siege techniques and all were fully employed. Attempts were even made to gain ground by sapping towards the enemy's lines, but this was brought to naught by the enemy promptly driving counter-saps forward, so the whole exercise only served to bring the opposing lines to close quarters where conditions became far worse.

Those writers fond of employing this analogy imply that through the systematic and deliberate use of siegecraft the problems would be broken soon enough. As is so often the case with people who are anxious to press an idea home, they push the analogy too far. In siege warfare, the garrison of a city is none too large and certainly not blessed with a national reserve of millions of men, and then again the lines of the besieging army are continuous around the object of their attentions. Nor is there in fact any inevitability about the march of a siege, for history is replete with examples of sensibly and resolutely defended cities which have defied their opponents completely, or at least for years – Ostend (1601-4) and Gibraltar (1779-82) are just two examples.

Sieges were notably chancy affairs until the arrival on the scene in the seventeenth century of Sébastien le Prestre de Vauban. Urban geographers studying the traditional city descend in droves upon Vauban, whose clearly delineated defensive designs gave the traditional fortified city its characteristic shape and exercised a profound influence on the lives of the city-dwellers. So far as Vauban's military career is concerned, however, this emphasis is misplaced. The ability which rightly won him his gilded laurels was less the defence of cities than the taking of them by carefully contrived lines of parallels which promised to reduce any fortress, however spirited the opposition.

Following the birth of the artillery attack against city walls, retrenchments – which could fairly be described as improvised interior defences – sprang into prominence at the great siege of Padua in 1509, where they presented the apparently successful storming parties with an unlooked-for and insuperable obstacle, barring their further progress just as effectively as barbed wire and trenches deployed in depth did four hundred years later. Once the new lines were reached, the whole laborious process of bringing up the guns to open a new breach had to run its bloody course again. Siege techniques in the tactical dimension could enable an army to establish a foothold in the enceinte of trench lines in the First World War, but further lines behind that and the enemy's ability to rush reserves to the threatened point by rail would quickly stop the breach, rendering anything gained as little more than a minor incursion in baldly tactical terms. So siegecraft provides an analogy limited to certain respects, notably in the tactical sphere and within the psychological framework, with all which that implies in terms of siege mentality. Beyond that it is downright misleading to apply it to the trench warfare of the First World War.

Leaders who are called upon to wage such titanic wars need particular qualities of resolution. They must have the dedication and hardness of character to drive the effort home without being intimidated either by the cost or the responsibility, without being forced to mirror rather than initiate. Men without this character trait can never be leaders in a total war for they would quail at every hurdle. As Napoleon was wont to say, 'An army of lions led by a stag will never be an army of lions.' Thus it was that the Soviet Union would suffer the loss of twenty millions of its people in the Second World War, and thus it was that commanders of the stamp of Grant, Haig and Zhukov rose to the fore. Similarly in the political field. The men of straw, the Asquiths, Briands and Bethmann-Hollwegs of this world, were mown down by decisive hardliners in the shape of Lloyd George, Clemenceau and Ludendorff.

The frame of mind required to fight through total war is pungently illustrated in the words of Admiral of the Fleet Lord Fisher of Kilverstone, the man who had dragged a complacent Royal Navy into the twentieth century. As First Sea Lord, Fisher had prepared and equipped the unwilling Navy both materially and spiritually to fight the Great War. A fierce and vigorous man, Fisher had been in uneasy retirement in 1914 when he was recalled to the Admiralty at the behest of Winston Churchill, then First Lord of the Admiralty, following the disgraceful public campaign which had forced the resignation of Prince Louis of Battenberg as First Sea Lord because of his German family connections. By 1919 Fisher was out in the cold again, one of yesterday's men after his resignation over the Dardanelles campaign, and engaged in writing his fiery memoirs. His view of modern warfare was typically uncompromising. He likened the idea of fighting with restraint to 'fighting using only one fist against the other man with two; the other fist damn soon comes out! The ancient who formulated that "All's fair in love and war" enunciated a great principle:

War is the essence of violence.
Moderation in war is imbecility.
HIT FIRST. HIT HARD. KEEP ON HITTING.'[1]

The ruthless, unyielding nature of both the man and of total war breathes forth from those words. Total war is violence stretched to its uttermost point, where compromise is shut out and defeat unthinkable, a view echoed more recently by General Douglas MacArthur with his 'There is no substitute for victory.'

At the onset of the First World War, each of the great powers was still in the throes of coming to terms with the phenomenally rapid industrialization which had been the salient feature of development in the late nineteenth century, transforming essentially agricultural societies generally characterized by a slow and relatively passive outlook. For the most part the population had lived in isolated rural communities that were largely self-sufficient and bounded by static horizons; communication, especially the communication of ideas, was a slow and awkward process. The industrial revolution had shaken this style of life to its foundations, notably through the arrival of the railway, and rendered society far more volatile and susceptible to the idea of change. Factories, mines, mills and railways required great concentrations of people to service them and, ideally, to form a home market. The impoverished rural populations had flocked to the centres of industry in the hope of bettering their condition and giving security to their lives, but instead found themselves exploited, almost irrelevant, jammed cheek by jowl into sordid and insanitary slums where life was so plentiful as to be as cheap as the dirt amidst which they lived. Factory and mine regulations governed their lives: the only purpose of the new industrial working class seemed to be endless and unremitting toil. As individuals they had ceased to have any significance or purpose.

It is no accident that new political and philosophical theories thrust their way to the surface of this benighted régime; the latter half of the nineteenth century witnessed the birth of Communism, Socialism, Anarchy and Nihilism, theories whose growth took their time from the rapid beat of industry. The conditions of life for the industrial masses provided a fertile seed-bed for resentment. When great numbers of people live so closely together, communication is both

1 Lord Fisher, special article 'Memories' (Part IV), *The Times*, 15 October 1919, p. 14. © Times Newspapers Ltd, 1919.

easy and natural. The deplorable conditions in which these people had to live and work made them a ready and receptive audience for those thinkers who preferred a path out of the industrial slough of despond. Revolutions need inspiration and leadership – they do not 'just happen'. The 'oppressed' population can be seen as a pile of firewood complete with kindling. Some, like the Webbs, sought to dampen it by encouraging change from above, but there were others trying very hard to ignite it. Marxists, Anarchists and Nihilists strove to do just that and their lack of success may be attributed to the fact that trade unionism and democratic socialism also promised easier and more persuasive roads to change. War and conscription had not yet removed many standard inhibitions or given the ratchet of resentment yet another sharp twist. Nevertheless, industrialization had been matched, step by step, by enormous strides made in movements for social and political change. By 1914 in most of Western Europe the various Socialist parties were serious contenders for government in countries with democratic institutions.

War had to be made to seem almost attractive, certainly a necessity. Conscripts, however, are often in armies against their will and, having little enough reason to fight men who have done them no wrong and even less reason to be killed, their passions need to be inflamed to drive them to the dizzy heights of heroism. Brutality and violence must be harnessed to the pursuit of defined political goals; and for these to be reached, the inclination towards violence must never be allowed to falter. It must be motivated constantly and there is no better way of supplying this motivation than to excite men's passions. The conscript must believe he is fighting for great ideals. The enemy must be depicted as unutterably evil, embodying something so wicked and oppressive, so base and perverse that nothing less than his total submission will suffice to safeguard civilized society from his evil designs.

The fierce and persuasive propaganda needed to instil these convictions into the hearts of the soldiers was directed towards the whole of society, for total war demands the mobilization of every particle of national strength in the common effort. But making the people conscious participants also involves them in common retribution, in suffering all the hardships and privations of war as well as many of its dangers. In this way a sovereign right passes almost unnoticed into the hands of the people, for if their wholehearted support and effort is needed to fight such a war then equally they have the option of withdrawing their support, and so making the continuation of war a physical and moral impossibility. As individual citizens they can exert only a derisory influence upon the war but *en masse*, in their hundreds of thousands and millions, their influence is something neither governments nor armies can afford to disregard. The transfer of this sovereign right in decisions of war and peace has been imperceptible and governments are loath to grant it formal recognition; but recognize it they have had to.

Where does Intelligence come into the picture? Intelligence does not operate in a vacuum. It is one cog in the mighty machine of command, an accessory to help the commander make decisions by which he expects to win the desired victory. It is but common sense to observe that plans are more certain of success if the planners have sound information upon which to base their decisions, for only in this way can they consciously direct the forces at their disposal against the points where the decision can be gained. In short, Intelligence is about the direction of force and how to apply it with the greatest economy to achieve the greatest effect. In general terms, military Intelligence is charged with gathering and evaluating information about the enemy whilst preventing him from discovering what your own forces are doing, a simple enough theory but in practice a vexatious, frustrating, onerous and often painstakingly boring task, akin to assembling a jigsaw with no picture to serve as guide and with numbers of pieces missing. Be that as it may, the character of the war will inevitably determine the character of the information sought, and in a total war the information needed transcends the narrow bounds of operations of armies in the field by virtue of the fact that it is a social conflict rather than an exclusively military one.

The mass participation of contending populations in the wide variety of effort which underpins the ability of a modern state to conduct a great war had transformed the character of war. Intelligence could no longer rest content with concentrating on the strength and deployment of armed forces but had to expand its horizons to assess larger factors: the supply of recruits, the provision of money, the industrial production of *matériel*, the manufacture of munitions, the provision of foodstuffs, the maintenance of transport, the very will to continue to make the effort, the rifts and jealousies between members of the opposing state. All were sucked into the Intelligence spectrum as draughts are drawn to chimneys.

The extension of political rights during the nineteenth century in the shape of the right to vote and to stand for election had been one recognition of the new facts of political life, but it was a recognition which of itself sharpened political awareness and made public opinion a legitimate target in both peace and war. The growth of the twin giants, mass conscription and mass industrialized electorates, and the power they were capable of wielding, was not lost upon the Intelligence services in Britain. Sir Vernon Kell, the first and greatest head of the counter-espionage service, MI5, conceded this influence in total war when he wrote:

> However high, to commence with, may have been the state of public opinion with regard to the uprightness of the cause of the war, nothing fails so rapidly as the failure to maintain the temperature of that opinion well above shooting point, until victory is achieved.[1]

He was even more explicit in his acknowledgement of this truth when he observed that 'much depends on whether the civil population wishes you to win or lose the war'.[2]

Unless this salient fact is clearly grasped we will go sadly astray in our understanding of a war which in its social and political implications represents a major watershed in history, one whose reverberations echo down the decades to our own times. The search for Napoleonic-style victory in the field was the pursuit of a phantom, the commanders who sought it founding their vision on the triumph of the Prussian General Staff in 1870-1, a war in which the classical terms of flanks to be enveloped, centres pierced and communications cut still held good. As they saw it, the war of 1914 was to be a war of short duration, 'over by Christmas', a struggle between armies rather than societies, where one army won one round and another the next, where there was no thought of a desperate fight to the finish with massive social forces set in motion. Little heed was paid to the prospect of a vicious and prolonged life-and-death struggle between whole peoples. Only the increasing agony of the prolonged conflict and the social stresses and strains it evoked wrought a gradual change in General Staff outlook, and central to that change was a slow-dawning realization that Intelligence had a key role to play.

To be most effective, Intelligence must relate its aims and activities

1 Papers of Sir Vernon Kell [hereinafter Kell Papers], PP/MCR/120, 'The Control of Civil Populations in War', The Imperial War Museum, London [hereinafter IWM].
2 Ibid.

to the command decisions which govern the where and when of the purpose of armies – fighting. It must be anchored firmly in the province of Operations as an aid to directing the fight to a triumphant conclusion: the central aim of Intelligence is action. But in 1914 that realization was, literally, years away. The commanders regarded it as little as they regarded the effects of industrialization and growing political awareness on their society. In extenuation, it has to be said that these did not present a dramatic and predictable process but an untidy one which required time for people gradually to adapt their way of life. Although the General Staffs had adapted to changes which bore directly upon their profession, in the shape of weapons like machine guns, quick-firing artillery and, to some limited extent, entirely novel and potentially revolutionary features like aeroplanes, they had not perceived the social context of the coming struggle and were woefully ill-prepared to cope with it. In this respect neither the British General Staff nor the British Intelligence Services differed from their European counterparts.

When Britain went to war in 1914, the Asquith Government resigned responsibility for its conduct into the hands of Field-Marshal Lord Kitchener, military hero of late Victorian and Edwardian times who stepped into the breach as Secretary of State for War. By this act the Government virtually abdicated from direction of the country's military effort. This was a grave error and they spent much of the ensuing four years trying to reclaim the authority they had so blithely surrendered. The ever-growing national effort conjured forth to meet the demands of industrialized total war was too great for any single man to control, even as it had proved for a man of Napoleon's stamp. How Kitchener could be expected to shoulder this burden and haul it home over the long and winding trail is beyond belief – unless one is alert to the attitudes towards warfare which were in vogue at the time. Even the mighty German Army, the military trend-setter of the time, marched firmly to the tempo of 1870 with a marvellous plan which would crush the French in a matter of months. This was carried to quite absurd lengths, with the Kaiser and his *Grosshauptquartier* taking pains to occupy exactly the same hotel in Cologne which had berthed Wilhelm I in 1870; there was even another Moltke in the saddle as Chief of Staff.

Are we being unjust to the General Staffs in expecting them to have been able to see beyond the technical horizons of their art? How many people ever manage to bring a visionary foresight to the fields in which they work? There was, however, an awesome monument to the war of the future in the shape of the American Civil War, in which total war in all its sordid and unfettered brutality had been loosed amongst civilized and industrious peoples. That war had been fought with stakes so high they precluded all thought of mutual concessions reached over a negotiating table. The Union simply could not afford to acknowledge the secession of a number of its component States, since to do so would have been to sign the death warrant of the United States and all it stood for. Unable to come to a *modus vivendi*, the Union had no alternative but to destroy the Confederacy root and branch by the military occupation of its territories and the complete subjugation of its citizens, along with the annihilation of its Government. Yet the Confederacy was no more able passively to submit to destruction than was the Union. There being no grounds for compromise, war to the death was the only solution. The solution took more than four years to run its bloody course, during which upwards of 600,000 Americans were killed in the field – more than the United States lost in either of the two World Wars. It ended with the triumph of the big battalions and big industry of the Union and the complete destruction of the Confederacy.

For all its modernity in both aim and conduct (it was a war of conscripted armies using railways, digging entrenchments and employing modern weapons like the machine gun and the submarine) the American Civil War was pooh-poohed by European soldiers and those few statesmen who turned their attention to military matters. It was arrogantly regarded as an ill-directed scrap between unsophisticated and culturally backward peoples from which Europeans could learn little. Besides, in the course of the same decade could not Europe boast better examples of how a war *should* be fought in the Austro-Prussian and Franco-Prussian Wars? Moltke's opinion that the American Civil War consisted of armed mobs chasing each other around the countryside found wide acceptance in nineteenth-century Europe, a continent which barely fifty years later would be conscripting its own armed mobs to replace the slaughtered professional soldiers in an even more momentous struggle.

Where the General Staffs floundered, a Jewish banker from Warsaw showed the way. Mr I. S. Bloch had no military training but that was actually an advantage, since being an outsider often helps make observation keener and perspective more proportional. His enormous study, *The War Of The Future In Its Technical, Economic and Political Relations*, was approached with an open mind unfettered by theory or by past and inapplicable experiences. It took years of solid, painstaking devotion to write and was based entirely upon independent research, receiving neither encouragement nor financial support from any official quarter. Of this monumental labour, only the sixth volume was ever translated into English.[1]

Neither the full version nor the single-volume translation ever seems to have gained any currency amongst the British military hierarchy, although in Russia the Tsar went so far as to make it recommended (but not required) reading for his Staff officers. What the General Staffs would have found was hardly calculated to inspire acceptance, for Bloch's hypothesis was that the war of the future would not be a replay of the Napoleonic Wars or even of 1870-1, to be decided in a matter of hours or days in a single clash on some obscure field of which no one had ever heard. On the contrary, Bloch argued, the array of fearsome modern weapons and the nature of modern society made such an outcome wishful thinking, since the armies would be unable to press their attacks to a conclusion. Instead he foresaw, with an icy logic based on an intensive study of contemporary weaponry, industry and society, a prolonged and devastating struggle which would drag on through ponderous and pitiless years, years in which no ravishingly clever stratagem, or splendidly timed and executed manoeuvre, could ever yield the victory so earnestly sought. The next great war, he predicted, would not be decided through the struggles of the fighting man, but its resolution would lie in the grim and indifferent hands of famine and social upheaval.

In Bloch's dire vision the soldiers in the line would be more preoccupied with survival than with victory, driven to seek shelter in the belly of the cold earth from the storm of metal which would fill the air and accordingly, 'Everybody will be entrenched in the next war. It will be a war of entrenchments. The spade will be as indispensable to a soldier as his rifle,' with the unlooked-for consequence that the act of fighting would have little in common with the traditional, straightforward contest over open ground in which the soldiers would measure their skill, their physical and moral superiority against each other in the time-honoured way.

Completed sixteen years before the Great War, Bloch's book now

1 I. S. Bloch, *Modern Weapons and Modern War, being an abridgement of The War of The Future In Its Technical, Economic and Political Relations*, London, 1900.

appears extraordinary in its foresight. None of the General Staffs, for all their professional expertise and close concentration on the technical aspects of their profession, could discern the character of the coming cataclysm, with the exception of a few seers like Kitchener and Haig, crying in the wilderness. Wars between great powers are only won quickly when there is a significant disparity between the opposing powers in society, weaponry, technique or, more rarely, commanding genius. In 1870-1 the decisive disparities lay in the facts that Prussia possessed a mass conscript army, a speedy mobilization and a modern General Staff, and Napoleon III did not. By 1914 everybody had taken urgent steps to ensure that they, too, possessed these attributes, and everybody was on a more or less equal footing.

Bloch's words go to the very heart of the matter here too. The object of the fight between armies is the 'overthrow' or defeat of one of them. By what means is an army overthrown? Is the overthrow really accomplished just by reciprocal slaughter on the grand scale? And how can the chaos of the battlefield relate to the struggle between whole societies? The intention of any government in going to war is either to realize a political ambition or to prevent the enemy from realizing ambitions which would pose a serious threat to the survival and prosperity of the people for whom the government is responsible. It is a recourse to violence in order to force the hostile power to accept a political situation which would otherwise be anathema to it. Armies fight with the avowed objective of forcing one or the other of them to give up the fight by destroying the will to resist. 'Destroying the will to resist' is a bland, comfortable phrase which coldly covers something very complex and very human.

Few armies have ever been ruined – overthrown – by a simple process of slaughtering the men who compose them, so how is destruction of the will to resist achieved? The answer is a matter of common sense, for when the threat of death becomes too great for men to bear they run away or surrender. When they turn and run a vigorous pursuit should put the issue beyond all doubt – or so reads the traditional, classical script of warfare. Soldiers, whether conscripts or volunteers, march to the battlefield prepared to fight and kill and risk being killed themselves; but the prospect of flight is one which armies go to great lengths to deny them through the imposition of discipline backed by sanctions of varying degree, ranging from military punishment down to the pressure of peer groups, in this case the soldier's immediate comrades in his unit. These bindings really are psychological ones and are not loosed by the mere application of physical force, for armies which turn tail and run do so not because the men have been roughed up but because their nerve has gone and despite all the pressure of discipline and the threat of punishment they can no longer steel themselves to face the enemy. The decay of the bonds of discipline is the surest sign that an army has been ruined. In the First World War this became apparent in the Russian and French Armies in 1917 and the German Army in 1918. To bring this collapse of discipline about and thus enable soldiers to run away is the means by which battle achieves the overthrow of the enemy, which means in turn that battles are, in the end, moral conflicts directed against the minds and spirits of men rather than their hard-worn bodies. Total wars, wars where every member of a society is involved, are clashes of nerve and stamina, of staying-power, but between whole peoples rather than just their armed representatives; they operate over a long period of time but rarely through the direct and imminent danger of death. In making war a moral struggle not just between armies but between peoples, the morale of those millions of people is the real gauge of the rise and fall of Empires. The lesson is that the will of the people has to be worn away over a lengthy period of time before they can be induced to accept an unfavourable peace as a lesser evil than the awful continuation of war. Here, too, Intelligence has a considerable role to play. But this had not yet been recognized in 1914.

Once Kitchener was appointed, the General Staff departed hurriedly for France, going bag and baggage with the Expeditionary Force and leaving behind a vacuum in the higher direction of the war. This had perforce to be filled by a hastily assembled collection of retired officers genially known as 'Dugouts'. The Dugouts struggled with commendable valour to meet the responsibilities thrust upon them, but too often they were untrained and unfamiliar with their work. Having their hands full trying to meet the needs for food, clothing, equipment, training and billeting of the New Armies, whose eager and enthusiastic volunteers wanted for everything, they had little opportunity to master the intricacies of their new role, even if they fully understood them. Faced with co-ordinating and giving cohesion to a vast and unimaginably complex effort while trying to familiarize themselves with everything from matters of procedure to questions of grand strategy, these officers command our sympathy, especially since they had to work under such a secretive and jealous chief as Kitchener.

Their task was made no easier by the Cabinet, which, having abdicated responsibility, sought to reassert its proper authority by intervening from the sidelines with what, to its members, were brilliant and apparently foolproof schemes for winning the war by a single bold stroke. In their innocence these now appear as fatuous as the erratic brainwaves of Kenneth Grahame's Mr Toad and when acted upon produced, for example, the costly and near-ruinous Gallipoli campaign.

The Liberal Government and its successors urgently needed expert advice in the absence of any specialized knowledge of their own, and in this we can recognize one of the most awkward features of modern government. All too often such advice is distrusted since it removes decision-making from the hands of the politicians and may perchance cut diametrically across some favoured ideal upon which party hearts are set. Sometimes, too, the costs and consequences contingent upon accepting expert advice are daunting and fraught with danger, and that aspect was to haunt British civil/military relations throughout the First World War, in the shape of the struggle between the 'brass hats' and 'frock-coats'.

The Intelligence section of the Army crossed the Channel with the Expeditionary Force. It was a small section, a fact which tells us something about the Army's attitude to Intelligence but not nearly so much as does the fact that Intelligence was subordinated to the Directorate of Military Operations. It soon became apparent that the Operations and Intelligence sections of the General Staff co-existed in an atmosphere of mutual distrust and rivalry bordering at times on open enmity, an atmosphere vividly portrayed by Sir Edward Spears:

> Operations said – 'What can be the use of Intelligence knowing our plans? Their sole duty is to watch the enemy and report his movements and numbers.'
>
> 'That's all very well,' Intelligence would argue, 'but we have to divine the enemy's intentions. These are based largely on what he can guess of ours. He forms his conclusions on what he can see and hear of the movements of our troops, and how can we enter into his mind and read his thoughts if we know nothing of our own Army?'
>
> The Intelligence officers were right, but for a long time they had to work in the dark, much to the general hurt. Of course every possible means of preventing leakage of information had to be employed, but the absurd handicap of blinkers imposed on your own people should never again be allowed to increase the very great difficulties of the

> Intelligence in obtaining information as to the enemy's intentions and movements, without which the Commander-in-Chief is like a man groping in the dark.[1]

The need to take Intelligence seriously, instead of regarding it as a nuisance or as a convenient backwater repository for officers of peculiar abilities who did not readily fit in elsewhere, only came to be recognized through the searing experiences of the war, a war whose nature demanded more and ever more of the Intelligence services. A turning point came in October 1914 in an acrimonious exchange between the quiet, capable General Macdonogh, then head of Intelligence, and his vainglorious and mercurial chief, Field-Marshal Sir John French. French was marching his small force of exquisitely trained 'contemptibles' on the left of the Allied line in the confident anticipation of skirting the main body of the German Army and falling on their exposed flank, a heroic role which appealed to French's vanity and self-esteem. Macdonogh made his customary report to his chief: his tracing showed the disposition and movements of the Germans, who were now bolstered by three brand new Reserve Corps rushing headlong towards the BEF and threatening to swamp it. French, seeing the appearance of this unlooked-for threat on the Intelligence map, flew into a rage and exclaimed heatedly, 'How do you expect me to carry out my plans if you will bring up these bloody divisions!'[2]

The meeting ended therewith. French persisted with his now fantastic plan and marched Haig's I Corps straight into overwhelming German forces, there to fight desperately for very survival in what has gone down in the history books as the First Battle of Ypres, a battle which effectively killed the old regular Army where it stood and came very close to losing the Allies the war.

The status of Intelligence as a single strand in Operations' harp remained unchanged until the appointment of Lieutenant-General Sir William Robertson as Chief of the Imperial General Staff (CIGS) in November 1915. Robertson had started his military career as an illiterate cavalry trooper in 1877 and in the teeth of opposition from his working-class family. He taught himself to read and write and applied himself to the study of martial life with a thoroughness and dedication which were to be the trademark of his life in the Army. His

1 Major-General Sir Edward Spears, *Liaison 1914*, London, 1968, p. 27.
2 Obituary of Lieutenant-General Sir G. M. W. Macdonogh, *Royal Engineers' Journal*, September 1942, p. 251.

hard work and earthy common sense earned him steady though not meteoric rewards and he was commissioned as a Second-Lieutenant in the 3rd Dragoon Guards in June 1888. The same thoroughgoing approach was continued as an officer, and this at a time when it was almost indecent for an officer to take his profession seriously. Coupled with his lack of private means, his outlook made a career in a line regiment impossible, so Robertson found himself drawn willy-nilly into the distinctly unglamorous and tedious life of a pen-pusher. Here he deservedly established a sound reputation for efficiency, shrewdness and hard work which went far to redeem his *parvenu* background, and which also served him handsomely after the Boer War, when study of the profession of arms became a prerequisite for advancement. By 1915 his solid capabilities, steely demeanour and severely practical outlook had brought him promotion to Chief of Staff of the BEF in France, and with this experience safely under his belt, he donned the mantle of CIGS, the government's adviser on strategy as it affected the Army.

Being only too familiar with the functional shortcomings of the old General Staff, Robertson set in train a far-reaching reorganization of the War Office which, while it still enthroned the GSM as the apogee of strategic wisdom, went far towards opening up many provinces that had hitherto been regarded as outside the responsibility of the General Staff. For our purposes, the act which mattered was the division of the Directorate of Military Operations into the Directorate of Military Operations and a new Directorate of Military Intelligence. Officers with experience in both areas were recalled from France to lead and man the two Directorates, Brigadier-General Frederick Maurice assuming responsibility for Operations and George Macdonogh for Intelligence. The new structure at the War Office mirrored Robertson's decisions in France: after the near-disaster in the autumn and winter of 1914, the Staff there had been reorganized to put Intelligence on the same footing as Operations, a fully fledged branch of the Staff in its own right, no longer ignored or considered something akin to the Germans. The activities of the two branches were correlated and supervised by the Chief of Staff, which in London was the CIGS himself, who was responsible for forwarding the combined effort to the Commander-in-Chief. Impressed by the efficiency of the new structure in contrast to the chaotic squabbling which had reigned before, Robertson brought the lesson home to London and forthwith imposed it in place of the 'Dugout' regime.

Unity was still further enhanced by the interchange of personnel between both the Directorates and their different sections; thus we find Richard Meinertzhagen masterminding Intelligence for the Egyptian Expeditionary Force under Allenby in the field, but then transferring to Operations at the War Office to head MO2 before reverting to Intelligence again, this time on the Western front as the officer responsible for security and camouflage. The co-ordination of the two Directorates was further deepened by specifically charging one Operations section, MO3, with responsibility for liaising between the two and, in conjunction with Intelligence, considering special operational questions affecting both. Minor and immediate Intelligence matters fell to the lot of Operations in order that field activities would not be held up through having to consult another unit. So that an overall picture could be retained by the multitude of sections within the Directorates, weekly lectures by and for the heads of section were introduced, thereby ensuring that the activities of all were co-ordinated in pursuit of the common aim.

Robertson's restructuring of the War Office and General Staff was a masterpiece, permitting both Directorates the necessary freedom of action in their own special fields while reducing the friction and rivalry that had hitherto sullied relations. In a war effort which invaded so many diverse areas, a degree of specialization was a constant and necessary attendant in each. Robertson had perceived a danger of sections becoming so specialized that their work would grow apart from the general effort; his reorganized General Staff side-stepped this trap and gently pushed the different specialists into a cohesive force, in the best traditions of team work.

Flaws there may have been at the highest level of policy-making at the beginning of the war, but the same cannot be said of Intelligence at lower levels, for the simple reason that in the Army of 1914 there were no lower levels responsible for Intelligence. There was no unit whatever charged with gathering information at the sharp end, and for this there was no excuse. After the bitter experiences of the Boer War, Lieutenant-Colonel David Henderson, who had been Director of Military Intelligence (DMI) in Pretoria for the last two years of that war, wrote a pamphlet called 'Field Intelligence, Its Principles And Practice', published in 1904. In it he strongly recommended the creation of a standing Field Intelligence Corps so that the calamitous errors of the South African War would not be repeated, and laid down sound principles for its operation and administration. Nothing was done and Henderson's pamphlet was duly pigeon-holed. There was nothing new in this, for the history of the British Army repeatedly shows that Field Intelligence formations were raised for every major and nearly every minor war, only to be disbanded with ill-considered regularity upon the cessation of hostilities, with the inevitable consequences the next time around. Predictable peacetime economies contributed to the decision to disband the Intelligence unit after the Boer War, but there is nowhere to be found any suggestion that had financial circumstances been any different the Army would have chosen differently; nor was there any request for money to be voted so that the Army could form such a Corps. Army thinking, as we have seen, ran a very narrow course.

Intelligence is a specialized business and sudden attempts to create Field Intelligence units from men who lack both training and experience cannot realistically be expected to produce reports of any useful standard. The 1912 mobilization plans stated that 'an intelligence element' was to accompany the BEF, but this vague reference gave no clue as to how the element was to be manned or how it would operate. When the chips were down in 1914 and firm action was needed to replace hazy thinking, the creation of a Field Intelligence service was, unsurprisingly, casual; so casual in fact that nobody even thought of designating an officer to command it. This oversight was only rectified by the entirely fortuitous appearance of Major James Torrie from the Indian Army. Torrie, who happened to be on leave in England when war was declared, was as eager as his contemporaries to join the fray. Motivated chiefly by a fear that he would 'miss the war', he set out hot-foot for the War Office in an anxious bid to offer his services. To the General Staff at the War Office he must have seemed the answer to a desperate prayer: a trained and experienced professional officer with the necessary seniority to command a non-regular formation. They could be rid of both an embarrassing problem and yet another ardent volunteer eager for employment thus found himself in charge of the Intelligence Corps, a body which nobody had heard of and nobody appeared to know what to do with. Torrie's position, however, was merely the fruit of expediency and after just six weeks he gladly exchanged it for the first available regimental posting. He was succeeded in the job nobody wanted by a certain Captain Archibald Wavell, later Field-Marshal Lord Wavell, Commander-in-Chief in the Middle East in 1940-1 and later Viceroy of India.

Neither of these early commanders of the Intelligence Corps had much to work with. In 1913 Macdonogh had compiled a register of men drawn from all sorts of backgrounds who, due to linguistic or other qualifications, could be considered suitable for Field Intelligence duties, and these men in due course became the Intelligence Corps. Upon its formation the Corps consisted of a Headquarters Wing; a Mounted Section who rode off to war on horses requisitioned from the Grafton Hunt; a Dismounted Section; a Motor-Cycle Section; and a Security Duties Section staffed by Scotland Yard detectives. The only qualifications required of members of the new Corps were a knowledge of French or German, the ability to drive a motor-cycle or motor-car and the ability to remain on horseback for an undefined 'reasonable length of time' – qualifications any or all of which most of the recruits solemnly assured the recruiting officer they possessed, quite irrespective of whether they did or not. According to Marshall-Cornwall,[1] who was one of the regular officers called to join this motley crew, none of them had had any training in Intelligence nor were they told very much about what they were supposed to be doing. From the beleaguered recruiting offices around the kingdom came other recruits, straight from civilian life and disqualified from more active service because of minor health problems. Naturally, all passed as 'qualified'.

When it embarked from Southampton the fledgling Corps had a strength of 13 regular or reserve officers (1 major, 4 captains, 7 lieutenants and 1 temporary second-lieutenant) and 42 so-called 'scout officers', a very mixed collection of policemen and volunteers. Their duties in the first exhilarating months of mobile warfare ranged from interpreting for the cavalry, interrogating German prisoners, organizing civilian work parties, obtaining food for retiring infantry, translating claims for damages from French and Flemish peasants and, on one occasion at least, supervising a party of Royal Engineers seeking to blow up a bridge after their own officers had been killed or wounded.

One of the early volunteers who went to France with this polyglot unit was Sigismund Payne Best, rejected by the regular Army because of poor eyesight:

> You can not imagine how primitive everything was. When I came it was not long before I was stationed at GHQ and I can assure you that

1 Papers of General Sir James Marshall-Cornwall [hereinafter Marshall-Cornwall Papers], Intelligence Corps Museum, Ashford [hereinafter ICMA].

> the whole organization was based on ideas that had been evolved during the South African War. No one had any idea of what it was going to be like to fight a modern army. They had no maps of France to use. By chance I had taken with me a Michelin Guide to France and that became the bible of GHQ. It was the only clear map they had.[1]

Perhaps not surprisingly the new Corps was mistrusted by the officers of the regular Army, the vast majority of whom had never heard of it and had neither instructions nor precedent to govern their reactions. They had no idea, any more than the Corps, what Intelligence should achieve. Direction is the key to successful Intelligence work, and there simply was none.

Intelligence must be directed in accordance with the commander's strategy if it is to bring home the information he needs to make his plans. Instead of asking 'Where is the enemy?' the question should be 'Are the enemy at that place and if so in what strength?' As one Intelligence officer serving with the Military Attaché in the Netherlands wrote:

> My experience with Oppenheim taught me that the most difficult task in intelligence is not to obtain information, but to determine exactly what information one wants to get.[2]

A great haphazard stew of information is more of a hindrance than a help; it has to be painstakingly and tediously sorted through, prospecting for those few priceless nuggets which will reveal to the general what the enemy is doing or intending to do, and what progress his own forces are likely to make in following existing plans. No such direction was ever vouchsafed to the Intelligence Corps in 1914. And although the enthusiasm and multifarious skills of the scout officers could go some way to remedy their lack of training, they could rarely deliver the goods because they had never been told which goods were wanted. Nevertheless, the apparent uselessness of the Corps only served to reinforce old prejudices about the way to wage war. Intelligence reports were all too often irrelevant to the needs of commanders and so they were treated with contempt or simply disregarded; there was no thought of utilizing Intelligence to supply a perceived change in needs.

The clinically dispassionate approach of a General Staff is some-

1 Papers of Sigismund Payne Best [hereinafter Best Papers], 'The Origin Of The Intelligence Corps, BEF 1914', IWM.
2 Sir Ivone Kirkpatrick, *The Inner Circle*, London, 1959, p. 17.

thing fundamental for a modern army fighting a modern war; so far only the Staff has enabled massive conscript armies to move together, to be fed, armed, clothed and to fight according to a common strategic and tactical doctrine, and it remains the only agency by which a Commander-in-Chief can direct his numerous forces in a cohesive fashion. The story of how Intelligence came to play a crucial role during the First World War is a story which runs the full gamut of trial and error, disaster, stupidity and humiliation as well as triumph, glory and masterly insight; a story whose chief characters were some of the most remarkable men ever to have served Britain and whose actions gave a sharp twist to the spiral of Europe's destiny. Military Intelligence, like every sphere of human activity, is only as good as the men involved, those gathering Intelligence and those using it, and it would be too much to expect them to have got it right every time.

Nevertheless, some of these men were the hidden giants of their time, men whose decisions were made behind closed doors, decisions that exerted an influence over the lives of millions of people, not necessarily their own. An examination of what drove these men to take the decisions they did is vital to our understanding of their time and of the way they influence our own.

TWO

I Spy

WHEN the lumbering mass armies of continental Europe pounded down the roads to the fronts, the commanders needed, above all else, to know where their enemies were, what they were doing, in what strength they might be met and whether their own men would stay the course. For answers to the first three questions they were forced to rely on eyesight, chiefly the eyes of the light cavalrymen who ventured ahead of the main forces for the specific purpose of discovering this information. Surveillance in this context amounted to far more than the mere 'spotting' of hostile troop movements, for scouts had traditionally preceded the advance of armies from the first days of the employment of the horse in war. The commanders of 1914 were all familiar with Napoleon's habit of sending his mounted scouts deep into the theatre of operations not merely to locate his enemies, but to report on the bridges and roads along which an army could move, even to seize newspapers and letters in post offices for whatever information could be gleaned.

The pretty theory that is sometimes heard, which argues that the armies on the Western front should have stayed tamely in their trenches, is bogus. It is as if a soccer team decided to pack its penalty area and never attempted those sudden breakaway attacks which often lead to goals. In short, advantage in war can only be gained by an offensive, by going forward. But, as the First World War showed with stark and painful clarity, the offensive became ever more costly. The range and rapid fire of modern weapons can unleash a welter of lethal flying metal in an instant, making frontal assaults undertaken without minute preparation patently suicidal. As everyone knows, in the First World War the trusting, long-suffering, eager young manhood of Europe paid the price time after time. When attacking they were wholly exposed to this horrific firepower but at least when defending there was a measure of protection, however inadequate it might seem, from their earthen ramparts. Often when they did move forward, they found further progress firmly barred by uncut barbed wire which either brought them to a full stop, or worse, herded them along a chosen route to a specially designated killing ground dominated by cunningly veiled guns. While we may sympathize with the generals faced by this frightening prospect, it does not stand to their credit that they were so slow in understanding the true nature of the problem. Before the war was a year old, many of them would be desperately experimenting with new weapons, new techniques and new tactics designed to overcome or circumvent the dilemma, but though many tried to broaden their thinking, it still took time for them, and the Staffs who were willing, to familiarize themselves with new techniques and gadgetry; time, too, for the troops to master new tactics and weapons.

Despite more sophisticated weaponry, the Constant Tactical Problem (CTP), had altered not a jot: how to advance successfully into a hail of death. Today, this has been seen nowhere more clearly than in the vicious war between Iran and Iraq (1980–8), one of the few genuinely total wars of recent times. Both armies relied on entrenchments. Casualties were numbered in hundreds of thousands and they were accepted by both sides in exchange for short expanses of blasted sand; a veritable space-age Verdun.

During the First World War, tactics and weapons were assiduously developed to the limits of technology and human capacity, to try to redress the balance and reduce casualties. In the meantime, however, the search for an unequivocally decisive victory in the field went on, and it went on much as Bloch had said it would. It is all very well drawing large arrows on maps showing where armies – huge numbers of trained and organized men, often tired, cold and chiefly interested in food, rest and shelter – should march. But for these men to move as smoothly as the coloured arrows is quite another thing, for first they have to kill, capture or put to flight their opposite numbers on the bloody, chaotic and narrow confines of the battlefield, something that generally means closing with them *corps-à-corps*. Visibility was the key to the tactical deadlock. For the soldier needed to see his target before he could use his awesome array of weaponry with effect. In the great battles of 1918 we can recognize a factor common to all of the great breakthroughs. In each of these battles the assailants were able to come to close quarters with the defenders and penetrate their positions because a combination of fog, gas and smoke rendered the defenders blind, unable to see to fire effectively. Whether we are talking about the great German Spring Offensive, the British victory at Amiens on 8 August, or the magnificent storming of the Hindenburg Line on 29

September, the one factor which enabled the all-important early successes to be carried off was the fact that the defenders were deprived of vision. This fact exerted an enormous influence on the course of events and was far more influential than the employment of tanks – indeed, the Germans had very few tanks in their Spring Offensive and the 46th (North Midland) Division owed nothing to tanks when they broke the Hindenburg Line.

If one answer to the CTP lies in the matter of vision, another stems from the spirit of men. The difference in the end-results of the German and Allied offensives of 1918 can be summed up in one word: morale. Both scored early and impressive tactical successes, but once the sun rose on the advancing Germans and the mist was dispelled, Allied troops shot with accuracy and inflicted enormous losses on the dense-packed ranks of *feldgrau*. By the time of the Allied advance, the morale of the German soldiers had crumbled to dust; they had had enough.

The choice of specific objectives for a Field Intelligence unit rests with equal weight on the way the Army intends to fight and on the nature of the war being fought; it naturally presupposes full consultation and co-operation between Army and Intelligence. Intelligence gathering during the open fighting of August and September 1914 could remain limited to the location and disposition of enemy troops, but the baneful and irresistible growth of trench warfare meant that a shift was needed in direction. Ultimately, the strategy of attrition dictated that morale and manpower, and plenty of both, would decide the outcome of the war. So while knowledge of the enemy's whereabouts would remain important, it would have to be considered within a broader context.

Consequently, the direction of Intelligence in the field, or Operational Intelligence, I(a) as it is better known, came in time to concentrate on the enemy's Order of Battle. This means essentially the make-up of an army or navy, unit by unit, and how these units are grouped to fight under different sub-commands. In Napoleon's day a single regiment might still swing a battle, but since 1870 the basic tactical brick in the mass armies had been the division, a force of some 10–18,000 men (depending on the army and the period under consideration). By 1914, the division was a formidable tactical unit complete with infantry, artillery, signals, Staff and frequently a cavalry force and was thus not only formidable but versatile, reasonably mobile and capable of a high degree of self-sufficiency and resilience.

In the German Army, divisions were responsible for administration and a host of minor details which had hitherto been the province of the regiment. Once a regiment was assigned to a division it usually remained with that division, whereas divisions were switched at need between larger, more amorphous, formations like corps and army. Therefore, since the German Army was built around its divisions, the location and identification of those divisions by British Military Intelligence was fundamental to building up the picture of the Order of Battle. General Sir Walter Kirke, who served with Intelligence at GHQ in France as a major, described the Order of Battle as the 'bed-rock of all intelligence work'[1]:

> The basis of intelligence is the building up of the enemy's order of battle, for when this has been done the identification of one unit is *prima facie* evidence of the presence of the division to which it belongs, and possibly also of the corps or even army.[2]

In the conditions of the First World War it was not enough to know that some vague hostile entity casually referred to as 'the enemy' was 'over there', across perhaps 50 yards of miry shell-holes and thickets of wire: the commander and his Staff needed to know precisely *which* enemy it was. If the division holding the trenches opposite was new to the line, might it not indicate an offensive on the part of the enemy? Or did the arrival of a new division represent simply a relief in the line? But if so, what had happened to the division it had relieved? Was the new division there on its own or were there others? In short, the establishment of the German Order of Battle by Intelligence would permit the enemy's movements and deployment to be observed and explained, so shedding a chink of much-needed light on to his intentions. On any active section of the front this knowledge was especially vital since the casualty rate could rapidly wither a division – and new, fresh units arriving on the scene would materially affect the fighting, calling for a rapid re-adjustment of existing plans and intentions.

Beyond this, important as it was, lay a still deeper significance. As the war ground on through the hideous, bloody year of 1916, each of the combatant states had to recognize a growing crisis in manpower. The

1 Papers of General Sir Walter Kirke [hereinafter Kirke Papers], 'Reminiscences on Lieutenant-General George Macdonogh', 1947, ICMA.
2 Ibid.

problem faced Germany in the starkest terms of all, for not only was she the mainstay of the Central Powers, fielding an enormous army, but she was also the industrial powerhouse of that alliance. By the turn of the year, German industry and the German Army were competitors in a struggle over a dwindling reserve of able-bodied men, a struggle which neither could afford to lose. In a last desperate surge the German General Staff extended the call-up, conscripting many young men one and even two years ahead of their prescribed call-up dates with the object of building up a sufficient reserve of trained men to enable Germany to win the war in one terrific burst. The study of the German Order of Battle therefore attained an added importance, for the examination of the commitment of new reserves was a vital gauge to measure German military stamina, and the exhaustion or corruption of those reserves would indicate that Germany's war effort was spent at last.

In order to appreciate fully the radical changes in approach and technique for Intelligence work that evolved during the First World War, one must understand the methods previously employed. The first of these was patrolling and reconnaissance.

The mobile forces which clattered ahead of the BEF in August 1914 were there to find the enemy. It sounds exceedingly simple. Yet this was one of the most hazardous of all military activities, since for the men charged with this responsibility it meant advancing far beyond all help in case of trouble: the small parties involved were entirely at the mercy of any stronger hostile body they might meet, able to rely only on their own speed, alertness and resourcefulness to evade death, wounds or capture. Such circumstances are likely to appeal only to those brisk souls who enjoy a challenge which gives them the chance to meet the unexpected, aided only by their own instincts and ingenuity. There are indeed those who do actively seek the exhilaration of a few madcap moments when life and death are in the balance but, such rare spirits apart, what patrolling meant for most of those engaged on strategic reconnaissance was advancing nearer to mortal danger with every hoof-beat or, less frequently, with every revolution of the motor-engine. The most frequent notice a scout would have that he was in the presence of the enemy was the fact that he had 'drawn fire', in the deliberately neutral jargon practised in the services. If, after that, the scout was fortunate enough to survive and gallop out of range or at least out of sight, he could then report back that he had indeed located the enemy.

There was also a very real risk of encountering enemy scouts in a landscape which concealed overburdened, nervous infantrymen, their fingers tightening around their triggers as the scouts approached. Traditionally, clashes between opposing patrols had been an invariable ritual at the opening of every military campaign since armies first employed cavalry, but by 1914 German tactical doctrine demanded that their cavalry formations were accompanied by Jaeger detachments – units of highly trained, élite, rifle-armed light infantry. British cavalry seeking to sneak a view of what might be coming down the road towards the BEF found this combination an impossible one to beat; the sharp, ferocious but short-lived patrol clashes of former years became a thing of the past when the German cavalry retired behind their attendant riflemen who could soon put paid to any undue aggression by a British unit.

Not that scouts were sent out with the object of fighting – their numbers were too small for that – but there was always the risk that sudden clashes would occur when two parties of scouts met unawares. To cope with this contingency the *Field Service Pocket Book, 1914* recommended that 'the assumption of a resolute offensive may be the best course of action'.[1] Getting one's blow in first is a military maxim as old as time itself, and for sheer effrontery there can be no better example than that of Second-Lieutenant Marshall-Cornwall, a Gunner subaltern attached to the embryonic Intelligence Corps temporarily assigned to the Divisional Cavalry 'A' Squadron of the 15th Hussars. In the days following the German retreat from the Marne, the BEF was pressing hard on the heels of the Germans; and 'A' Squadron, under its keen young officer, was well to the fore. In later years Marshall-Cornwall was to recall:

> As the country seemed deserted, I was riding along some hundreds of yards ahead of my squadron, accompanied only by my trumpeter. On turning the corner of a village street, I ran into a patrol of four Uhlans, not 30 yards away. Drawing my sword, I shouted 'Troop, charge!' and then turned about quickly and fled at a gallop. The enemy patrol also wheeled about and galloped in the opposite direction. It was the only time that I ever drew my sword in the presence of the enemy.[2]

Such episodes apart, the cavalry enjoyed little success in scouting in

1 *Field Service Pocket Book, 1914*, reprinted Newton Abbot, 1971, p. 74.

2 General Sir James Marshall-Cornwall, *A Memoir: Wars and Rumours of Wars*, London, 1984, p. 16.

that whirlwind summer and autumn of 1914 and even when they did succeed in snatching important intelligence it was not necessarily heeded. On the very eve of the Battle of Mons, 'C' Squadron of the 4th Dragoon Guards pushed out two patrols towards Soignies, one of which discovered a German picquet on the road while the other, commanded by Major Sir Tom Bridges, clashed with German cavalry moving along the road from Soignies to Mons. The Dragoon Guards had the better of the affray and the surviving Germans were sent packing. The effect the patrols' information had on the cavalry commanders and Intelligence was to reinforce their existing conviction that German infantry in great force was in close support of the German cavalry, and they reported their views to GHQ. There the dominant voice belonged to Major-General Sir Henry Wilson, ostensibly the Sub-Chief of the General Staff but in reality Sir John French's *éminence grise*. Francophile to a fault, Wilson had been largely responsible for the pre-war discussions that had arranged for the BEF to be appended to the left of the line of French armies, smack in the path of the German masses traversing Belgium and northern France as part of the Schlieffen Plan. Once Wilson had set his heart on a course he not so much embraced it as smothered it with passion, irrespective of whether or not this accorded with the practicalities of the situation. In 1914 the cavalry's discoveries were placed on the desk of this quick-witted but unstable man who summarily dismissed them with the message:

> The information which you have acquired and conveyed to the C-in-C appears to be somewhat exaggerated. It is probable that only mounted troops, perhaps supported by Jaeger battalions, are in your immediate neighbourhood.[1]

Less than 24 hours later the BEF was fighting for its life against the serried ranks and massed artillery of General von Kluck's German First Army.

Ignoring the reports of patrols was by no means confined to the Wilsons of the world, for cases of missed chances or dreadful casualties continued to occur even after the fighting was locked into the entrenched straitjacket for which the war is chiefly remembered. Conspicuous among these was surely the attack on the Dujaila Redoubt in Mesopotamia on 8 March 1916, one of many launched to

1 Edmonds, op. cit., 1914, Vol. I, London, 1923, Appendix 12, p. 456.

attempt the rescue of General Townshend and the sore-pressed defenders of Kut. All previous attacks had been directed against the strong Turkish positions on the left bank of the River Tigris and each had shared the fate common to nearly all frontal attacks in the First World War. On 8 March, however, the British were going to try to steal a march on the Turks by shifting their weight to the right bank of the river, thus outflanking the Turks across-stream by marching up the Dujaila Depression, guarded by a formidable redoubt. All seemed to be going well and fortune seemed ready to place certain victory in British hands after Major Gerard Leachman, disguised as an Arab, had sneaked into the redoubt by night to find the position manned by a mere 40 somnolent Turks. Returning with this priceless information to his immediate commander, Brigadier-General Kemball, Leachman was told that his report must be submitted to Kemball's commander, Lieutenant-General Aylmer, VC – who refused to permit any alteration in existing plans, which included a bombardment of the redoubt before the infantry assault. The artillery arrived late, the Turks were alerted to the danger, hurried reinforcements to the redoubt and the subsequent assault was repulsed with heavy British losses, nearly 3,500 men.

Whilst Aylmer can be censured for a lack of initiative, heavier censure must fall upon Kemball for missing such an opportunity. The contemporary *Field Service Regulations* stated:

> A departure from either the spirit or the letter of an order is justified if the subordinate who assumes the responsibility bases his decision on some fact which could not be known to the officer who issued the order, and if he is conscientiously satisfied that he is acting as his superior, if present, would order him to act.
>
> If a subordinate, in the absence of a superior, neglects to depart from the letter of his orders, when such a departure is clearly demanded by the circumstances, and failure ensues, he will be held responsible for such failure.

This failure, directly attributable to neglect of Leachman's report, left the survivors of the Tigris Corps depressed and lacking confidence in their commanders. As for the commanders themselves, Aylmer's spirit was broken by the disaster and within three days he was suspended and ordered home, never again to be entrusted with an active command. Kemball was more fortunate, being retained with the Tigris Corps; this proved to be a wise decision by the War Office, for he later won several outstanding victories.

However, the occasional neglect of a report should not be considered a yardstick by which to evaluate patrolling and reconnaissance. The situation was far more complicated when returning from a night patrol.

So far as the men in the trenches were concerned, patrolling was yet another cross they had to bear and an exceedingly nerve-racking one at that. Edmund Blunden, serving as an officer in the Royal Sussex Regiment, penned words that capture the tension and clammy fear of those nocturnal prowlings through the topography of nightmare, where the unseen horrors of no-man's-land could suddenly be thrown into stark relief by the livid light of a flare:

> Then, we stoop along his wire to a row of willows, crop-headed, nine in a row, pointing to the German line. We go along these. At the third we stop. This may have been a farm track – a waggon way. But the question for us is, what about the German ambush, or waiting patrol? Somewhere, just about here, officers were taken prisoner, or killed, a fortnight ago. There is no sound as we kneel. A German flare rises, but the moonlight will not be much enkindled. I have counted our steps from the first pollard. We come to the last. There are black, crouching forms, if our eyes do not lie, not far ahead; but, patience at last exhausted, we move on again. The forms are harmless shapes of earth or timber, though we still think someone beside ourselves has moved.[1]

It might be argued that the poetic Blunden was not representative of the ordinary British soldier, that his experiences are somehow untypical of allegedly more solid types who simply and manfully did their duty without falling prey to the nervous anticipation displayed in Blunden's account. Yet the fire-eating and rumbustious Charles Carrington's account of a patrol he took out betrays no difference in the character of the experience:

> To patrol here meant to belly-crawl every inch of the way moving one foot or one hand at a time, sliding over the mounds and pits of the shell-torn ground, either in the frost or in the mud, lying dead still for a quarter of an hour or more until you could hear your heart beating, advancing ten yards, twenty yards, until you were midway and could listen to the stealthy sounds of their sentries in front and your own sentries behind. Easy to lose your way in the dark among the shell-holes, unless under a clear sky you could navigate by the Pole star – east

1 Edmund Blunden, *Undertones of War*, London, 1978, p. 138.

for Germany and west for 'Blighty'. You have a loaded cocked revolver in one hand and a bomb in your pocket, but dare you use them, however inviting the target, when the explosion will instantly raise up a sheaf of rockets and bring down a storm of fire from both sides? Better lie low and get exactly the information called for, that you have heard a German sentry coughing or whispering at such and such a point on your enlarged map, that you have seen a shadowy figure passing their wire by such and such a gap. Better get home alive with your scrap of news, and hope that your trigger-happy sentry won't shoot you before you can whisper the password.[1]

To the men who had to go out on patrol the common sensation was one of isolation, of being naked upon the face of the earth and watched by malevolent eyes. As Blunden wrote:

We cannot avoid the feeling that we are being stalked, and we are equally amazed that in this moonlight we are not riddled with bullets. The enemy's parapet is scarcely out of bombing range. Far off we hear German wheels; but the trenches are silent. Probably we are being studied as a typical patrol.[2]

It would be reasonable to ask the purpose in exposing men to such terrors when the return – information about a sentry coughing – seems to make it hardly worth the candle, the more especially since the War Diaries of British units habitually report that German patrols were conspicuous by their comparative absence. Nevertheless, patrols still retained some value for Intelligence purposes, particularly in respect of collecting information of small-scale yet immediate value about enemy positions and routine, any change in which could mean that trouble would not be long in coming. Brigadier Basil Rackham, a former sub-lieutenant in the Royal Naval Division, explained that 'Patrols to gain information, either about their wire or their trench system, or the location of a machine gun, were very frequently carried out – but they were not fighting patrols.'[3] The value of any patrol was assessed in terms of the information acquired set against the number of casualties suffered. As Rackham stated, 'If you got the information from a patrol which you wanted, that was successful – again you don't expect too many casualties in a patrol.'[4]

1 Charles Carrington, *Soldier From the Wars Returning*, London, 1965, p. 137.
2 Blunden, op. cit., pp. 138-9.
3 Brigadier B. B. Rackham, Hawke Battalion, 63rd (Royal Naval) Division. Interview with author, 27 February 1982.
4 Ibid.

In the first two years of the war, patrols would steal across no-man's-land to the enemy's wire and there listen to any conversation which might be overheard in the trenches behind. On such missions it was necessary to take someone who understood German, and occasionally useful information might be gleaned. Marshall-Cornwall provides an example of this from the time he was on the Intelligence Staff of the 3rd Division, II Corps. After providing himself with a revolver and a pair of wire cutters, he crawled across to the German front line on the Messines-Wytschaete Ridge and 'I got near enough the German trench to hear the men talking, and could recognize by their accent that the Bavarians on our front had been relieved by Saxons. Another time I came across a dead German whose shoulder straps I removed.'[1]

In both of Marshall-Cornwall's exploits the information he collected was important in building up the enemy's Order of Battle and so, by the standards of 1914-18, it was very valuable indeed. But patrols also had the job of preventing the enemy gaining such information. The domination of no-man's-land became almost an end in itself, preventing as it did any sudden descent by the enemy on British trenches and shifting the purpose of patrols subtly to the acquisition of chiefly defensive intelligence.

The Germans may not have mounted so many patrols as the British but they, too, needed to know about wire, saps, sentries and whether or not there was anything untoward going on. So German patrols also ventured into the cratered expanse of dereliction that separated the armies. With patrols of both sides sneaking about, occasional clashes were unavoidable. Irrespective of whether patrols were sent out to fight or not, short bursts of fierce and bloody fighting did suddenly explode. Patrol clashes were no neater or tidier than any of the other fighting and were usually a good deal more confused and panicky:

> After long creeping about in the dark and the cold there would be sudden bomb-explosions and bursts of fire, with no means of knowing who was firing at what: scurrying; eddies of panic; and drawing off with your wounded if you could find them; the whole thing often rather unheroic.[2]

Such fierce clashes could, of course, pay useful dividends for Intelligence, for prisoners, documents or identifications could fall into British hands if the fight had gone well. In this and other respects

1 Marshall-Cornwall, op. cit., p. 19.
2 Carrington, op. cit., p. 19.

patrolling was also considered a very good form of training, keeping men alert and up to the mark by having them practise the tactics they had been taught in an arena no training base could hope to emulate.

Patrolling and reconnaissance proved themselves to be important elements of military intelligence in theatres other than the West. A fine example of what could happen when reconnaissance was wanting is to be found in the battle of Kut/Es Sinn in Mesopotamia in September 1915. The intention was to outflank the Turkish entrenchments at Es Sinn by marching a column around their left flank by night. However, the route to be followed by the column was unknown to the British and no reconnaissance of it was made, with the result that the men plodded through the night to find themselves on the wrong side of the Ataba Marsh and much too far away either to take the defenders from behind or to hinder their withdrawal (see map opposite[1]). The column could hardly escape notice in the desolation of the desert and the Turks had ample time to make good their escape. Had a proper reconnaissance been made the British could have won a considerable victory; possibly much of the trial and hardship suffered in Mesopotamia over the ensuing three years would have been avoided. As it was, the flanking column's march more resembled a game of blind man's buff than the masterly stroke it was supposed to represent and which it ought to have been.

In the Cameroons, too, the British relied heavily on patrols and reconnaissance to acquire information about the enemy. One soldier, No. 1397 Private Buba Maimadi of the 2nd Battalion, The Nigeria Regiment, made scouting his speciality, and was mentioned in despatches for having 'shown himself a daring and efficient scout and of great assistance in gaining information of the enemy's positions'[2] on several occasions.

East Africa was the only theatre of war where the small size of the German forces and the vast size of the war zone effectively prohibited trench warfare. Here scouts had the freedom to move and it was still possible to find the space to pass the flank of any hostile position. Such conditions should have given British forces there an enormous advantage, but none of the second-rate mediocrities sent to command

1 *See* Brigadier-General F. Moberley, *The Official History of the War: Mesopotamia Campaign*, Vol. I, London, 1923, Map No. 7 'To Illustrate The Battle of Kut', 28 September 1915.
2 'Copies of Papers on the Military Situation in the Cameroons and Nigeria'. Colonial Office to War Office, 'General Dobell to the Colonial Office', 22 February 1915, Public Record Office [hereinafter PRO] (WO 106/645B).

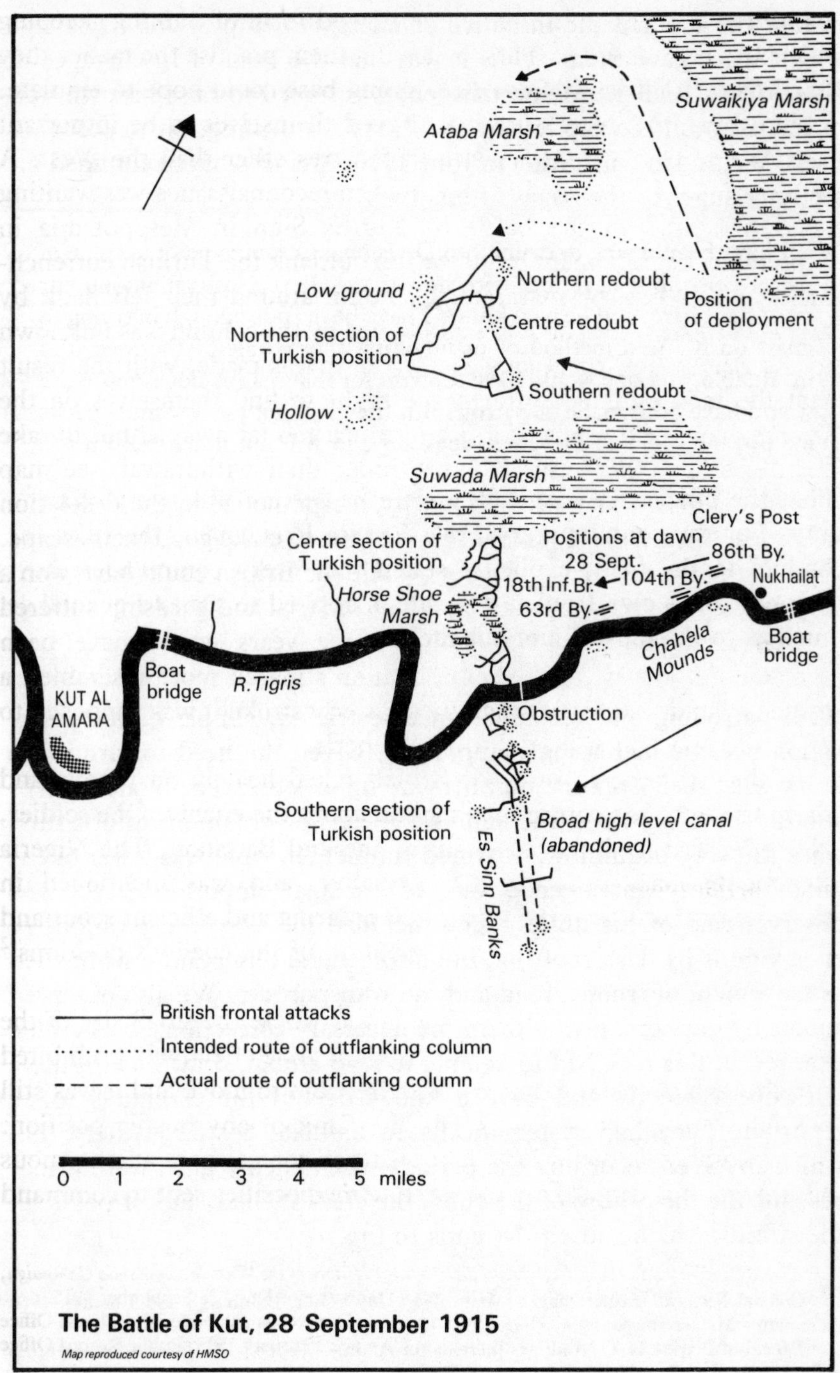

The Battle of Kut, 28 September 1915

Map reproduced courtesy of HMSO

in that theatre had the initiative or energy to employ the advantage which space gave them. Thus it was that the head of Intelligence in East Africa, Richard Meinertzhagen, was forced to raise his own unit of scouts to fill the gap left by the Army's unwillingness to scout for itself. Writing in frustration in June 1916, Meinertzhagen confided his seething anger to the pages of his diary:

> I have been trying to drum into Divisional Commanders the value of patrol work, but have met with no success. It is a lost art among our troops out here, and heaven knows I have been rude enough in trying to insist on it. As a method of maintaining the morale of the men it is invaluable, and one would have thought for that reason alone, more use would have been made of patrols. But they will not see it. Smuts backs me up, but old Van Deventer does not and will not understand it.[1]

What the officers in East Africa were neglecting was every officer's duty. For the contemporary *Field Service Regulations*, the rules for conduct in the field, explicitly stated that every commander must reconnoitre his own front, a rule which applied to a major-general as much as to the most junior subaltern.

With patrolling and reconnaissance restricted, simple direct observation became increasingly important. Given the need for armies to know what their opposite numbers are up to, observers in one form or another have provided the simplest means of obtaining information since the very beginnings of armed conflict. In what was a war of the guns, artillery intelligence was of cardinal importance. As one observer said of his duties, they included locating 'the positions of enemy guns by flash spotting, but also general observation work such as movement of troops, road and rail transport etc. We also observed shoots by gunners, giving them the necessary corrections.'[2] The men engaged in this task had to be able to read a map, draw a map, use a telescope correctly and have a knowledge of the essentials to be reported. They had systematically to tabulate hostile artillery fire, which involved recording the periods when enemy guns were firing, recognizing the calibre of the guns, the areas shelled, and, if possible, the stimuli which caused the guns to fire.

1 Colonel Richard Meinertzhagen, *Army Diary 1899-1926*, Edinburgh and London, 1960 [hereinafter Meinertzhagen *Army Diary*], p. 192.

2 Papers of Private G. C. Andrews [hereinafter Andrews Papers], 23 Observation Group, 4 Field Survey Battalion, Royal Engineers, IWM.

While patrols confined their activities to the night hours, observers were on call both day and night, trying to gauge the meaning of the bewildering variety of signal lights sent up by the enemy, nearly all of which would induce some unwelcome activity from his artillery:

> . . . but just as they were on the point of unravelling the multi-coloured skein, the code would change; for certain combinations, certain single colours they found a pragmatic significance, which stood all pragmatic tests: one sees now that some of those solutions were probably wrong, for one obviously interpreted the lights not by the instructions thereby signalled but by the accompaniment or immediate result.[1]

The location of enemy trench mortar and machine-gun positions was a vital necessity if the artillery was to knock them out in the event of an attack. Although most of the front would be quiet for the greater part of the time, those outside the all-knowing ranks of GHQ never knew when they might be called upon to go over the top, and the neutralization of those emplacements could not only mean the difference between success or failure but the difference between a casualty list numbered in hundreds instead of thousands. As Lance-Corporal F. Castle expressed it, 'we tried to identify bits of the line, any change, particularly where we were, on the St Quentin Canal area'.[2]

It was at battalion level that this form of surveillance had its greatest value, with the observers being responsible for watching the enemy opposite them and reporting every single thing that happened within their field of vision. The ridiculous extreme to which at times this was taken is colourfully illustrated by Private Frank Cunnington, who served in the new Intelligence Corps. Writing of his experiences in May 1917, Cunnington reported:

> One day we see a lone German near Ribecourt Station. He hangs up what appear to be blankets on a line. We call the Artillery Officer, as it is rare to see activity here. He sees the enemy for himself and gets quite excited. I go with him and hear him telephone the battery. 'I say Mr. so and so, the Dirty Old Hun has hung out some blankets at Ribecourt Station. Will you please remove them.' Shortly the battery fires a salvo. I return to see the result; half the building has been blown away.[3]

1 Eric Partridge, 'Frank Honywood, Private', in *Three Personal Records of the War* by R. H. Mottram, J. Easton and E. Partridge, London, 1929, p. 387.

2 Lance-Corporal F. S. Castle, Intelligence Police, 17 Lancers. Interview with author, 25 March 1982.

3 Papers of Private Frank Cunnington, ICMA.

The natural consequence of this was that there was precious little of real value for the observers to watch and report; by daylight the trenches would give the illusory appearance of being uninhabited except perhaps for the occasional wisp of smoke from a fire.

Once battle was joined, ground observation was further restricted by smoke and dust, gas and the general chaos. Of the battle of Neuve Chapelle in 1915, Woolrych says 'there was not much to be seen. The German parapet was certainly knocked about and their wire cut. In the open space some of our fellows were lying in the long grass.'[1]

When he was Allenby's head of Intelligence in Palestine, Richard Meinertzhagen, a trained Staff officer, seized an opportunity to observe the Turkish trenches near Ali Muntar from the front line, though not during battle. Even with the advantage of having the overall situation at his fingertips he could only note that, 'The Turkish line, some five or seven hundred yards away, showed little sign of life, an occasional head or a little dust from men digging, being the only indications of occupation.'[2] Battalions in the front line would, in accordance with the *Field Service Regulations*, provide their own observers, whose activities were described by Basil Rackham:

> We used to have people in the front line specially detailed to observe, as opposed to being on ordinary sentry duty, but of course the real Observation Posts were usually somewhere behind at a point of vantage where they could get a really good view, and with a good pair of glasses that was a much more effective way of observing than from the front line – although the front line got the immediate actions, you know, what was going on right up in the front, but the observer was usually looking a bit behind.[3]

In this case observation was a function of Operations rather than Intelligence. Generally, however, direct observation achieved little enough. Indeed, the humorous trench newspaper, *The Wipers Times*, was moved to mock its impotence on 10 April 1917 with a spoof report that is perhaps not too far removed from reality:

1 Papers of Lieutenant-Colonel S.H.C. Woolrych, OBE [hereinafter Woolrych Papers], ICMA. Woolrych was Intelligence Officer with the 7th Division, II Corps, rising to head I(b), Second Army.

2 Diaries of Colonel Richard Meinertzhagen [hereinafter Meinertzhagen Diaries], Vol. 19, 3 June 1917, p. 204, Rhodes House Library, Oxford.

3 Rackham interview, loc. cit.

7. – INTELLIGENCE
Our observers report:

3 p.m. A man wearing a shrapnel helmet, accompanied by a dog, was observed walking along the road between S5 a68 and S5 b96.
3.2 p.m. A stout man with red face and glass eye asleep by the side of road at S5 b94.
3.5 p.m. Dog (referred to above) seen to approach stout man asleep, and remain near him several seconds.
NOTE. – It is thought that possibly a relief was taking place.
3h 5m 6sec. Dog disappeared at S5 b95.
3.7 p.m. Man with shrapnel helmet observed wiping with a sandbag the head of the stout man with red face and glass eye who had been asleep, but was now evidently thoroughly awake, and showing unmistakeable signs of anger.
NOTE. – It is thought that possibly dogs have been trained to rouse sleeping sentries in case of alarm.
4 p.m. Smoke was observed at S10 b00.
NOTE. – It is considered that this is a clever ruse of the enemy to convey the idea that a fire had been ignited at this spot.

8. – REPORTS FROM OTHER SOURCES

2 p.m. Two men wearing spectacles were seen to disappear behind a hedge at K2 b57; our 60 Pounders searched this spot with H.E., the two men, previously seen, suddenly reappeared at K2 b59 and hastily took cover in a trench at K2 63. They appeared to be strangely hampered in their movements.
NOTE: – It is thought that this hedge conceals a strong point of considerable importance to the enemy.

MIDDLING OLD Lieut.,
Bde. Intelligence Officer,
–th Infantry Brigade.

Each level of command organized its own observers. As Rackham pointed out, the battalion usually observed from the front line, but further back would be concealed Observation Posts employed by higher formations. These observers, unlike the men at battalion level, were equipped for observation, utilizing either special telescopes or field glasses, and were usually connected by telephone to their respective headquarters. There might be a small stove for making tea or, in some of the more elaborate structures, spaces to sleep which were fitted and furnished by their occupants with whatever came to hand, whether it was issue or acquired by scrounging.

At army headquarters was an Observation Group, attached to the army's Field Survey Company, which was commanded by a captain with one or two junior officers under him. The rest of the personnel comprised telephonists, draughtsmen and linesmen from the Royal Engineers (Signals), a non-commissioned officer in charge of the plotting room, a quartermaster sergeant, Army Service Corps horse transport, a motor-cycle (later a car) for the use of the officers, with a driver. The Group contained three Observation Posts, each of which was supposed to have six or eight observer/telephonists trained in both duties, a cook, and a non-commissioned officer in charge. The latter carried a heavy burden of responsibility, for the nearest officer might be two or three miles away and, as telephone communications might well be cut in active operations, he often had to act on his own initiative and without overall knowledge of the situation.

Observation Posts were located wherever the ground or buildings would provide a commanding view, a factor which varied according to local conditions and the ground held. It is an unfortunate fact that for much of the war the Germans held the areas of high ground which gave the best observation, such as in Flanders, the Thiepval Ridge, Vimy Ridge, and the Chemin des Dames.

According to Captain Eric Partridge, permanent Observation Posts were uncommon and necessarily had to be very strong and well camouflaged:

> Often the post was simple and incapable of warding off anything more dangerous than a bullet, sometimes not even that: a mere cubby hole at the head of a short sap running off from a communication-sap, such a sap ensuring a certain amount of security by the avoidance of any considerable movement near the post; no one but an observer went along the offshoot, and no observer would be fool enough to disclose his whereabouts.[1]

Private Andrews experienced a number of posts:

> The most common was probably the one which was built into a trench on high ground, near the front. A sandbagged structure, built above ground, was sometimes used for observation from a ridge further back. I have also observed from the roof of a building, from an eighty foot tower specially built for the job, and also sixty-five feet up in a factory chimney. [Another post] was built with sandbags, entirely above ground, with walls two feet thick. The roof was of corrugated iron sheets and sandbags, supported by two steel girders. I noticed after

1 Partridge, op. cit., p. 388.

> a few days that we were right in the line of fire of a German battery, which regularly shelled a target 200 yards in front of us. This was a dangerous position to be in. A gun can fire very accurately for line but not so accurately for range. So if one dropped a bit beyond the target we were in just the right place to receive it. I told the sergeant the post needed reinforcing on the one side with a buttress of sandbags six feet thick. He was not very impressed and told me I had better get on with the job. The rest of the lads on the post agreed to help and the work was soon completed.[1]

Partridge also mentions observing from a captured German pill-box in the Flanders offensive of 1917, an occupation which entailed observing without overhead cover from a step made against the rearward wall of the pill-box over which they peered.[2]

By contrast Marshall-Cornwall observed from a ruined cottage a little distance behind the British front line facing the Messines-Wytschaete Ridge, a position which enabled him to look down the length of the German trench and, with the aid of a powerful telescope, read the regimental numbers on the Germans' shoulderstraps.[3] This had meant entering the cottage unobserved at night and remaining there the whole of the ensuing day; the post was eventually destroyed by shellfire.

The Battle of Loos in 1915 had shown both the ingenuity employed in creating Observation Posts and the advantages conferred by the better ones. Being a coalmining area, the battlefield contained a number of dumps or crassiers upon which loose shale, slag and waste from the mines was piled. Some crassiers were conical, others flat-topped, and they rose high above the surrounding plain: when tunnelled out they provided commanding and reasonably shell-proof Observation Posts. The British lines were dominated by the wheel-house and crassier of Fosse 8 within the enemy lines, which gave the Germans observation over the whole of the back area of the British lines so that 'from it every movement could be observed on the roads leading back to Béthune, and every battery brought to within 3,500 yards of the German front line could be located.'[4] The principal British Observation Posts were at Fosse 9 near Annequin and Fosse 5 east of Grenay; the field of vision of the latter was limited by part of the Cité St Laurent and the high ground known as Hill 70.

1 Andrews Papers, loc. cit.
2 Partridge, op. cit., pp. 384–5.
3 Marshall-Cornwall, op. cit., p. 18.
4 Edmonds, op. cit., 1915, Vol. IV, p. 146.

An even better example of the dominance which could be achieved by an Observation Post is to be found on the Salonika front, where the Bulgarian post known as 'The Devil's Eye' on the Grand Couronné Ridge permitted the Bulgarians to observe:

> . . . the arrival and departure of trains, the number of trucks reaching Kilindir Station, were noted on special comparative tables which gave a precise idea of the movements in the rear of the enemy. We could deduce where we must expect an attack and what, roughly, would be the timing of the operation.[1]

Occasionally observers might be in a position to spot the extraordinary, as in the Nieuport sector in 1917: 'To the back of Ostende, we used on occasions to see a revolving light. This was used to give the German airmen the bearings when raiding London. The operation of the light was immediately reported and was probably the first warning of a raid.'[2]

Position, however, was only one part of the problem. Whenever the front was active, be it a raid or a full-scale offensive, not much of use could be reported. Gas was a particular hazard, not simply because of its physical presence but because the gas mask was a cumbersome and uncomfortable piece of equipment which made breathing difficult, and the eyepieces were prone to mist up; the longer it was worn the worse these defects became. The observer had, at best, a blurred image of the view in front of him and the only significant observations could come from the rearward Observation Group. In fact, very little could be done on any scale in the front line without the observers being aware of it almost immediately, something which rendered their purpose sterile. It was the very closeness and accuracy of their watch that had driven the soldiers to take cover in the ground and under the cloak of darkness. In any case, it was behind the front that the moves which might bring victory or defeat were taking place – the movements of large reserves, the stockpiling of munitions and the comings and goings of railway traffic. To know what was happening *there* was what interested Intelligence officers, and the more stalwart among them campaigned vigorously for the use of a new means of information gathering – aerial reconnaissance, and photography.

Partly because of their novelty and partly because certain army

1 A Bulgarian officer cited by A. Palmer in *The Gardeners of Salonika*, New York, 1965, pp. 121-2.
2 Andrews Papers, loc. cit.

officers regarded aeroplanes as an irrelevance, even an unwarranted intrusion into the enemy's privacy, aerial reconnaissance was greeted with less than open arms. As the official historian commented: 'Observers in the early months of the war sometimes found it difficult to convince the military command that their reports were true.'[1] Even the future Lord Trenchard found himself forced to stalk the corridors of GHQ in a bid to ambush stray Staff officers, trying to persuade them to study the aerial photographs he carried stuffed into his pockets for the purpose.[2]

When Trenchard tried to give the reports of aerial observation to an artillery general during the battle of Neuve Chapelle in 1915, he was curtly told that the general was busy fighting a war, too busy to 'turn round and deal with your toys of the air'. Trenchard noted in his private papers that, 'After the battle I reported to Sir Douglas Haig and told him of the incident . . . He assembled all his Gunner Generals at once and told them he was not going to have any more "early Victorian" methods. He was going to use the air in this war, and they had to use it.'[3]

This was no isolated incident. Other generals continued to cling stubbornly to antiquated methods, seemingly indifferent to the price that would be exacted from their men. The attack of the 51st (Highland) Division under Major-General Harper at Cambrai shows that this attitude was still held as late as 1917 in some quarters, for here Harper refused to adopt the new tactics of co-operation between tanks and infantry, with the result that his division was the only one to be held up and suffer heavy losses during the famous attack on 20 November. Not all British commanders were as prescient as Haig. The tone of a letter from Lieutenant-General Sir William Pulteney (III Corps) really sums up the force of the tide of invention and change, and the bafflement which too often greeted it: 'What a science this war is becoming.'[4]

The first big breakthrough for aerial reconnaissance had come in the Marne campaign of 1914, when von Schlieffen's design appeared to be carrying all before it. The German armies had swept through Belgium, brushing aside the BEF at Mons and Le Cateau and driving

1 W. Raleigh, *The Official History of the War: The War in the Air*, Vol. 1, Oxford, 1922, p. 247.
2 Lord Brabazon of Tara, *The Brabazon Story*, London, 1956, p. 94. Reprinted by permission of the Peters, Fraser & Dunlop Group Ltd.
3 Trenchard Papers, loc. cit.
4 Letters of Lieutenant-General Sir William Pulteney to Lady Desborough [hereinafter Grenfell Papers], 16 September 1914, D/ERv C2130/18, Hertfordshire County Record Office .

the might of the French Army headlong before them in what has become known as the Battle of the Frontiers; it seemed that nothing could stay their advance on Paris. Yet in spite of their apparent success, all was not well within the German camp. The army on the extreme right was the German First Army commanded by the proud and impatient von Kluck. To his eyes the road before him seemed clear. The British had been sent packing and the only French troops which might be met would be the hotch-potch of units drawn from widely different commands now forming as the French Sixth Army under General de Maunoury. Von Kluck felt confident that his army could deal with this mongrel and envelop Paris from the west: the capture of Paris would surely bring victory to German arms and make von Kluck a national hero.

At this point the fledgling Royal Flying Corps (RFC) intervened, an intervention which was the beginning of a sequence of events that were to change the course of the war and the course of history. On the afternoon of 31 August, Captain E. W. Furse was flying on routine patrol. He had no particular expectation of meeting any enemy. Indeed, no one at GHQ actually knew the precise whereabouts of von Kluck's forces. What Furse saw on his reconnaissance must have sent the blood racing through his veins; for below him, trekking towards the west, swarmed von der Marwitz's cavalry corps, the spearhead of von Kluck's masses. Disbelief was the order of the day. A further reconnaissance was sent out by the doubtful British, an aeroplane from No. 4 Squadron manned by Captain D. Le G. Pitcher and Lieutenant (temporary Captain) A. H. L. Soames, and they confirmed the news brought back by Furse. The report was sped along the telephone wires to GHQ, to General Lanrezac commanding the French Fifth Army and to General de Maunoury with the Sixth, now in some peril.

In moving to the west, von Kluck was drawing away from the German Second Army on his immediate left commanded by General von Bülow. A gap was thus being created between the two German armies on the right of the German line and if the Allies had the ability to penetrate that gap they could fall on the open and undefended flanks of either army. This the Allies were not in a position to do, and it was Lanrezac, facing von Bülow, who inflicted a sharp check on the German Second Army at Guise. Von Moltke, the German Chief of the General Staff ostensibly directing operations in the west, was already concerned about the gap which was unmistakably growing between his First and Second Armies and, faced with von Bülow's call for help, agreed to von Kluck's design for an inward wheel which would bring his legions eastwards across the front of Paris and to von Bülow's aid. Von Kluck had decided to forego the chance of a triumphal entry into Paris less because of any liking for von Bülow, of whom he had no high opinion, but because German Staff doctrine demanded the crushing of the enemy's armies in the field before all else. Lanrezac's troops had continued to retreat after their success at Guise and, deluded by reports that they were retreating in disorder, von Kluck felt he had little left to do, and turned away from Paris.

Such a march could only take von Kluck's footweary soldiers across the Allied front, exposing in the process a weakly guarded right flank to de Maunoury's swelling ranks – but for de Maunoury or anybody else to take advantage of that, they needed to know that von Kluck had made the fatal turn. The crucial discovery was again made by the RFC during a reconnaissance on 3 September. Macdonogh described their work in glowing terms: 'A magnificent air report was received disclosing the movements of all the Corps of the 1st. German Army diagonally South East across the map towards the Marne.'[1] High praise indeed, for the reticent Macdonogh did not use words like 'magnificent' readily. De Maunoury attacked, forcing von Kluck to retrace his steps to parry the French thrust. Once von Kluck's army was embroiled with de Maunoury's, the BEF at last pressed into the gap between the German armies, forcing both into hasty retirement and bringing about the collapse of Germany's attempt to win the war in the west.

Aerial reconnaissance had in fact done precisely what the cavalry of old had been wont to do and after the experience of the 1914 campaign the new air arm underwent considerable expansion. Where there had been a mere 48 aeroplanes in 4 squadrons with fewer than 250 officers in the RFC when the battle of Mons was fought, the new Royal Air Force (RAF) could boast a strength of 22,171 aeroplanes in 200 squadrons with 291,748 officers and men by the time of the armistice.[2]

In a war of position, which the First World War became, no significant attempt could be made to go forward without amassing enormous numbers of men and shells, digging new gun positions,

1 Kirke Papers, loc. cit., letter of 2 November 1925.

2 Raleigh, op. cit., pp. 5-6, and John Terraine, *White Heat: The New Warfare 1914-18*, London, 1982, pp. 31-2.

cable trenches and jumping-off trenches. In effect, armies wrote their intentions on the ground for the aerial observer to see and it was from attempts to deny the enemy this facility that aerial combat sprang, along with an obvious need for more aeroplanes. Aerial supremacy was one of the key elements in conducting successful aerial reconnaissance without interference from the hostile airforce. As with infantry or cavalry patrols, the foremost aim was not to fight but, as with infantry or cavalry patrols, it was sometimes necessary to fight to get the information and to get it back, or prevent the enemy from doing likewise.

This is borne out in a letter from GHQ to the War Office in March 1916, which contains the following statement: 'Information can no longer be obtained by despatching single machines on reconnaissance duties. The information has now to be fought for, and it is necessary for reconnaissance to consist of at least five machines flying in formation.'[1]

At the height of the 'Fokker Peril' of 1915-16, the new German Fokker monoplane, armed with a machine gun which could fire forwards through the propeller, effectively dominated the skies above France. The Somme offensive of 1916 saw the situation reversed, with the British holding mastery of the skies, an advantage which they fully exploited to the terror of the German infantrymen, who knew that the appearance of a British spotter aeroplane would swiftly be followed by a nerve- and body-shattering barrage of frighteningly accurate shell-fire. By the time of 'Bloody April' in 1917, new-found German aerial superiority meant that the great majority of RFC long-range reconnaissances failed, attended by a heavy loss of life.

The wide variety of tasks upon which the young men of the RFC were engaged at the time of the Somme offensive is well illustrated by the work of a Corps Wing employed in the battle; the Corps Wing being two squadrons grouped under the direction of an Army Corps for employment as required. III (Corps) Wing of the IV Brigade of the RFC, serving with the Fourth Army, had 68 aeroplanes available. 30 were engaged upon counter-battery work, 16 on close observation and artillery direction against the enemy's entrenchments, 13 on contact patrols, and 9 on special missions including photography and attacking enemy observation balloons.[2]

1 Raleigh, op. cit., pp. 446-7.

2 Peter Mead, *The Eye In The Air: History of Air Observation and Reconnaissance for the Army 1785-1945*, London, 1983, p. 78.

Both sides soon grasped the value of aeroplanes for probing the enemy's vitals and steps were rapidly taken to deprive the questing spotters of their prey. Since aeroplanes had no night-flying or observers any night-vision capabilities, major troop movements were conducted by rail during the night. Kirke, who acknowledged Intelligence's dependence on the RFC on the Somme, also acknowledged the limitation inflicted on aerial reconnaissance by night movement, grumbling in his diary that 'trench warfare gives the RFC no such opportunities now as all moves are carried out by train or by night'.[1]

Even during daylight, entrenchment presented insurmountable problems. Concealment and protection from enemy guns became the two prime objects of both sides in the war, second only to the effort to destroy enemy positions; and while aerial observation and photography could locate surface works like trenches and redoubts, they could not disclose the depths of dug-outs or the condition of the occupants. Great efforts at camouflage were made by all combatants and the resulting spectacle left to the aviator was one of endless stretches of monotonous mud over which no one would risk discovery while hostile aircraft were within sight or hearing.

Then there was the weather. Weather conditions dictated the frequency and success of aerial patrols. Very early in the war, bouts of bad weather and low visibility prevented anything but the most scanty reconnaissances between 22 August and 2 September 1914; low cloud and rain on 11 and 12 September confined the RFC's work to two reconnaissance flights on the 11th and 'very few' on the 12th.[2]

Even if the weather was not bad enough to ground the aeroplanes, it could still seriously interfere with observation. British troops used to joke that the Germans could make it rain whenever they wanted it to, which was usually when the British were going to attack. The worst summer of the war was that of 1917, when torrential rain turned the chosen ground for Haig's offensive in Flanders into an infamous bog, destroying all hope of the RFC aiding the army's attack, a factor which went far to account for the survival of so many German pill-boxes after days of incessant shellfire. Haig's typically dry comments on the proceedings are worth noting:

> The unfavourable state of the atmosphere now began to make itself

1 Kirke Papers, loc. cit., 'Lectures on Intelligence', 1924.
2 Edmonds, op. cit., 1914, Vol. I, pp. 311-15.

> felt. Observation from the air was entirely impossible owing to the low clouds, and direction of artillery fire by aeroplane against special targets, for which most careful arrangements had been made, could not be carried out.[1]

In July 1917 No. 63 Squadron arrived in Mesopotamia from France. Many of the men went down with heatstroke and the wooden frames of the aircraft shrank. Many of the machines had to be rebuilt but despite this a number of them still succeeded in defying all attempts to make them airworthy, disintegrating in flight.

Such potentially crippling obstacles might have assumed proportions sufficient to fly aerial reconnaissance into the dustbin of history, were it not for the fact that in good conditions aerial observation covered a large area and conferred the ability to see quite literally what was concealed on the reverse slopes of hills and deeper areas of the enemy's position. Apart from verbal reports, aerial observers were soon bringing back another source of information – photographs.

Initially, photographs were principally used in mapping the ground to be attacked, with mixed success at Neuve Chapelle, Festubert, Aubers Ridge and Loos. Aerial mapping at Neuve Chapelle was on an unprecedented scale, the battle zone being photographed to a depth of some 1500 yards; and for the first time maps composed from aerial photographs were available showing the outline of the German trenches. They lacked the detail achieved later in the war when it was possible to recognize even small piles of shells, but the first efficient aerial cameras were not available until February 1915, a month before the battle. Nevertheless, 'a great advance in aerial reconnaissance had been made. The trenches were reproduced on skeleton maps (1 in 5,000), and 1,500 copies sent to each Corps.'[2]

However, the early efforts were by no means an unqualified success. A new issue of maps was made prior to the attack on Festubert which proved to be both inaccurate and confusing. Identical symbols were used to represent hedges, ditches and tracks, and the maps were printed upside down, with the south to the top and the east to the left, reversing the co-ordinate numbers from the normal practice. In an effort to correct this, small areas were mapped again from existing aerial photographs but the result of this was that details did not fit and

1 Field-Marshal Sir Douglas Haig, 'Report on the Battle of 31 July 1917, and its results', 4 August 1917, PRO (WO 106/1514).

2 Edmonds, op. cit., 1915, Vol. III, p. 27.

some features were duplicated. As aerial photography became more sophisticated, the whole area was photographed again and new maps produced.[1]

Aerial mapping perhaps exerted its greatest influence in Mesopotamia, an area where the army was desperately in need of guidance, for the country was generally flat and there were few accurate pre-war maps. Regrettably, very few aircraft were assigned to Mesopotamia, which was regarded as a sideshow by the War Office when it took over conduct of that campaign from the Indian Government in 1916, and therefore came near the bottom of the list for both men and equipment. The first maps were improvisations drawn by observers sketching from the air, but no one could pretend that these were an adequate substitute. An additional complication lay in the fact that there were two entirely separate departments responsible for supplying maps to the army in Mesopotamia, one working under the over-bureaucratized Survey of India and the other under field Intelligence. Such help as might have been forthcoming from the air arm was hindered by the fact that no flying officer had ever been detailed to co-ordinate and supervise the task. The work of the Survey of India was considered good, but there were some unfortunate gaps in it, notably between Ali Gharbi and Kut, which severely hampered field Intelligence, working from enlargements of existing maps with details added from aerial photographs. In any case, there was no good local printing apparatus and anything sent to India took six months to be returned.

The first step in changing this situation was taken in 1916, when both mapping and survey work were placed under the same officer, who was made responsible to field Intelligence. The train of disasters that had overtaken the army in Mesopotamia had at last forced upon the War Office the need to supply new and up-to-date equipment and an attempt to revitalize the dispirited and exhausted Expeditionary Force. With the reorganization of the higher direction of the war there, a new surge of activity swept along the development of mapping from the air. In August 1917 new aerial cameras at last made it possible to produce accurate maps from techniques tried and proven on the Western front. In the words of one observer, this was 'perhaps the greatest blessing that the RFC could bestow'.[2] By the end of the war the mapping service in Mesopotamia was arguably the most

1 Major S. R. Elliot, *Scarlet To Green*, Toronto, 1981, p. 27.
2 A. J. Barker, *The Neglected War: Mesopotamia 1914-18*, London, 1967, p. 317.

advanced in the world, inspiring Sir Arnold Wilson, the assistant to the Chief Political Officer, to remark that:

> Aerial photography began and was developed on a large scale with invaluable results. The maps prepared by the Survey sections in collaboration with the experts of the RFC were sometimes distributed by air to units only a few hours before the battle. The casualties amongst airmen were heavy, but were far outweighed by their value both practical and moral to the troops on the ground and in particular to the Artillery.[1]

The importance now attached to aerial photography can be gauged from the fact that over half a million aerial photographs were taken during the war,[2] a figure which startles the imagination when it is remembered that in August 1914 there was no aerial photography at all, and that the possibilities of it had not even been thought of, let alone investigated.

The first known attempt at securing information by photography was made on 15 September 1914, when Lieutenant G. F. Pretyman snapped five shots of enemy dispositions with a privately owned hand-held camera. The fruits of his efforts would have been a crushing disappointment to anybody expecting them to herald the dawn of a new age, for the photographs were nowhere near as clear as the Army needed. Photographs taken with an ordinary camera from high altitudes are swamped with material, but material so devoid of detail that useful interpretation is next to impossible. There were, of course, no official funds allocated to the development of the science and all the early work was done with cameras which officers had bought themselves and which were, naturally enough, totally unsuited to taking photographs from a moving platform hundreds of feet – perhaps over a thousand – up in the air.

What aerial photography needed was a dedicated advocate of its own and by good fortune the right man was in the right place at the right time, in the person of John Theodore Cuthbert Moore-Brabazon. Born on 8 February 1884, Brabazon was the son of an army officer of old Anglo-Irish stock. The family was comfortably established rather than wealthy; after a childhood spent in County Meath, Brabazon went on to Harrow and Trinity College, Cambridge,

1 Sir Arnold Wilson, *Loyalties (Mesopotamia 1914-17): A Personal and Historical Record*, London, 1930, pp. 252-3.
2 Raleigh, op. cit., p. 6.

following the pattern expected for young men of good family in those days.

The time spent at Trinity did not incline the young Brabazon to a sedentary career, and his studies had to compete with an increasing love of motoring which, once his Cambridge days were behind him, fast displaced any family notion of an orthodox career. Instead he threw himself into motor-racing, a passion which remained with him for the rest of his life, and was often to be found in the company of the Hon. C. S. Rolls, who became a firm friend. Brabazon's racing career was not without distinction, for in 1907, at the wheel of a Minerva, he won the Circuit des Ardennes against stiff competition. Even during those halcyon days Brabazon felt the lure of aviation and threw himself into the embryonic sport with all his typical vigour and industry. His early aeronautical exploits included the building of two aeroplanes, charitably described as 'not very effective', but in 1909 he won the *Daily Mail* prize of £1,000 for flying the first circular mile in an all-English aircraft. In 1910 he was issued the first-ever pilot's certificate by the Royal Aero Club, whose chairman he was to become in the 1920s. Hazard seemed natural to the man and in the 1920s he also became a champion performer with the bobsleigh on the deadly Cresta Run, winning the Curzon Cup in 1920, 1922 and 1927 and remaining amongst the top twelve in the sport even after his fiftieth birthday. He also acquired the dubious distinction of being known as 'the best bad golfer in England', a fact that deterred him not at all. His zest for life and adventure remained constant to the end of his life in 1964; for, after a distinguished parliamentary career, he celebrated his seventieth year by taking a bobsleigh down his beloved Cresta Run and at 79 drove a Mercedes sports car at 115 mph over Salisbury Plain. Most people at that age might find a bus journey daunting.

This was the dynamo who was to transform aerial photography from a few indistinct and haphazard snaps into a formidable tool of Intelligence and, in the process, revolutionize aerial observation. Brabazon had gone to France with the RFC, serving with No. 9 Squadron at St Omer, a squadron which did not fly and had no aeroplanes but was concerned with improving and maintaining those already in service. Ever to the forefront in ideas, Brabazon was fascinated by aerial photography, and the problems it faced fired his original mind to attempt a solution. It was a situation which might have been tailor-made for a pioneer like him. Like most crusaders, Brabazon found his advocacy tolerated rather than welcomed. His chance came, however, when Sir John French, the Field-Marshal commanding the BEF, was given some aerial photographs by the French Army. Not wanting to reveal his own ignorance and not really knowing what to do with his Gallic gifts, French took the easy way out and passed them over to General D. Henderson, commanding officer of the RFC in France. After all, since these wretched things came from aeroplanes, surely the people responsible for the British Army's aeroplanes would know what to do with them? Even if they didn't, they could at least find a pigeon-hole for them until they were either forgotten or a use for them invented.

Henderson was in a quandary. Nobody, so far as he knew, had the first idea about aerial photography so he in his turn handed the pictures to his chief of staff, Colonel Frederick Sykes. Sykes it was who had been badgered and harried by Brabazon over this very same business; so, one suspects with a feeling of relief if not one of mild malice, he unloaded the photographs onto Brabazon and charged him to interpret them for the Commander-in-Chief.

Brabazon was delighted, but found that he faced three problems rather than one. It was not only a technique to interpret aerial photographs that was needed. A suitable camera had to be designed to replace the awkward bellows camera then in use, with a lens that had to be pulled forward – hardly a convenient or easy thing to do in an open cockpit while being peppered by machine-gun fire. Then, of course, the new camera should not be hand-held but mounted to fit it into the aeroplane. With no experience to draw on and precious little help from his own service, Brabazon went with his French photographs to the only repository of knowledge in this field in the Allied armies, the French *Section Technique*, who were not so much the leading lights as the only ones. In company with a protégé of General Trenchard, Major W. G. J. Salmond, later Air-Marshal of the RAF, Brabazon proceeded to plunder French knowledge and experience, sometimes adapting, sometimes adding new ideas and at other times experimenting with the new tools and techniques they had borrowed or invented.

In the design of cameras Brabazon faced a serious problem in that, 'It was early recognized that, even if we could make the lenses, we did not possess the basic optical glass necessary for the advanced formulae that were the order of the day.'[1] The need was for an anastigmat lens

1 Brabazon, op. cit., p. 100.

which could focus both vertical and horizontal planes simultaneously. The manufacture of such a lens required a special type of glass, dense barium crown, which hitherto had been produced only by Zeiss of Jena which was, of course, a German firm. It took allied industry time to develop the capability to produce this glass; the first breakthrough was made by the French firm of Para Mantois who, however, could only produce it on a small scale. Eventually the firm of Woods of Derby solved the problem and their glass was used in the manufacture of the revolutionary new camera designed by Brabazon and C. D. M. Campbell in 1915. Not content with solving the lens problem, they had produced a camera that could develop the negatives while the aeroplane was still in the air and have them ready for printing when the machine landed.[1]

The camera mounting was a different problem altogether. The principal difficulty lay in the vibration common to all early biplanes. The nature of the vibrations in these aeroplanes caused the camera to move in no fewer than six different directions at once. Three of these directions were transitional, which meant that the movements went across the same plane, and three were angular, and it was here that the real difficulty lay. Angular vibrations caused the image on the plate to slide and blur, giving an effect similar to that achieved by someone using a simple Brownie to photograph Olympic athletes or galloping horses. The solution Brabazon reached tackled this problem by designing a mounting which kept the camera's centre of gravity firmly anchored in the plane of support, so that while the camera might shake a little in the transitional planes it was impossible to tilt it at all. The improvement was immediate and obvious; the central obstacles to actually taking aerial photographs were conquered. Only the question of interpretation remained.

Successful interpretation depended heavily upon the development of binary or stereoscopic vision, endowing the photographs with a three-dimensional effect; this would throw up buildings and other objects in relief and thus enable observers to recognize the object and its shadow. Eventually a stereoscope was devised, a flat piece of metal mounted on legs with two separate lenses inserted into the metal rather like a set of glasses. But whereas a normal pair of glasses co-ordinates vision so that one picture appears on the retina of the eye, the stereoscope separated the vision of each eye so that the resulting

1 Ibid., p. 102.

picture acquired a three-dimensional effect, disclosing shadows, heights and angles not revealed by normal eyesight. At last it was possible to distinguish between a dump, a battery position, barbed wire, long grass, a trench, a stream or a ditch.

Those inclined to think it either obvious or easy to distinguish these points of detail from the air or from aerial photographs would do well to heed the experiences of the newly formed No. 6 Squadron of the RFC, whose untrained observers succeeded in mistaking long patches of tar on macadamized roads for troops on the move, and on one occasion even reported the shadows cast by the gravestones in a churchyard for a military bivouac.[1] Objects on the ground have a different appearance when seen from the air. Men had to be trained to see in a new way and to acquire an understanding of the effects of light and shade on colour, a knowledge of camouflage techniques and an ability readily to adjust the focus of the eyes to variations in altitude and views from unusual angles. It was an enlightened move to employ the portrait painter, Sir Oswald Birley, to instruct aerial observers. His artist's eye was wholly attuned to subtle differences of colour and shade and, in common with all good portraitists, he could detect character and substance beneath the outer show. His instruction was instrumental in raising the standard of photographic interpretation for a generation of Intelligence officers and provided part of the foundation of experience upon which their eventual printed guide to the interpretation of aerial photographs was based. This guide won praise from the man who had started it all, for in his autobiography Brabazon wrote, 'I must give them credit – they produced during the war one of the finest works on the interpretation of aerial photographs I have ever seen.'[2]

Although the infantry may not have known it, the benefits of the improvements in aerial observation and photography contributed to saving many lives and gave the BEF tactical advantages on a number of occasions. Every German battery located and destroyed and every target spotted reduced casualties and made a useful and important contribution to winning and preserving dominance for the Royal Artillery. Occasionally the rewards could be of considerable importance in unbalancing the enemy, as was the case in 1917 when the fighting in Flanders was at its muddy worst. Haig recorded in his diary that:

1 Raleigh, op. cit., p. 304.
2 Brabazon, op. cit., p. 304.

> Trenchard reported on the work of the Flying Corps. Our photographs now show distinctly the 'shell-holes' which the enemy has formed into 'strong points'. The paths made by men walking in the rear of those occupied first got our attention. After a more careful examination of the photo, it was seen that the system of defence was exactly on the lines directed in General Sixt von Arnim's pamphlet on 'The Construction of Defensive Positions.'[1]

The action which followed this discovery switched the weight of British barrages onto the shell-craters and strong points, a change which dramatically increased German casualties and upset the new defensive system, causing a hiatus within the German command on the Western front. British losses may have remained heavy but they were undoubtedly at a lower level than they would otherwise have been.

With this new sophisticated equipment permitting aerial reconnaissance at what were, for the time, considerable heights, an explanation of the heavy losses among airmen already mentioned is called for. Visibility from the front line was at best sketchy and communications with the front so appallingly bad that the generals had little ability to influence the course of a battle. Generals did not command from *châteaux* miles behind the line because they were seeking a safe, comfortable life but to co-ordinate control over the men under their command. Two-way radios did not exist and the generals were bereft of any sure means of knowing where their men were or what sort of opposition they were facing. Hence the extraordinarily detailed plans which the staffs spent weeks over in exhaustive preparation prior to each attack, and which were rigidly adhered to. Innumerable experiments were made to give the generals some extra degree of control, and aerial observation was brought in to help through what was known as the 'contact patrol'. Pilots were required to undertake low-flying patrols in the very thick of the fighting, in an atmosphere full of flying metal and often severely limited visibility. 'Hazardous' hardly conveys the perils of this operation. Casualties were inevitably high and the wonder is that they weren't higher still.

The first such mission, although it was not then called a contact patrol, was flown by Captain L. E. O. Charlton of No. 4 Squadron at

1 Diaries of Field-Marshal Lord Haig [hereinafter Haig Dairies], 28 August 1917, National Library of Scotland [hereinafter NLS].

Le Cateau in August 1914, when he assessed the situation on both flanks for Smith-Dorrien, commanding the embattled II Corps.[1] These low-flying patrols soon became the norm, since it did not take the generals long to appreciate the value of their contribution. The most graphic account of a successful, indeed, vitally important contact patrol comes from Captain D. M. K. Marendaz, who was flying an Armstrong-Whitworth to spot for the cavalry at Cambrai in 1917. This was the first massed tank assault of the war and the Cavalry Corps, penned in behind the trenches over the preceding three years, were eager to seize their chance and ride through the gap created by the tanks as heralds of the long-sought breakthrough. Donald Marendaz could muster a mere 20 hours flying training when he took off on that dull November morning, only one hour of which had been spent in the cockpit of the machine he was flying. In his own words:

> Couldn't see a thing from up high, so came down to 150 feet. Bit close with all that rifle fire, but only way to get under the fog. Then I saw a British tank trying to creep over the bridge across the Canal at Masnières which the cavalry were to use. The bridge simply *bent* beneath its weight. Useless. I wound down my signal wire, and sent a message in Morse to tell them to stop ... go back.
>
> Just after that, my 'plane had all the air taken from its wings by a salvo of shells from the huge 12 inch guns they had brought up for the assault. Felt it go past. Plane started to side-slip down into the canal – about seventy feet wide and just as deep, as I recall. No water – just a sort of huge concrete trench. We had practically stopped dead and were just falling out of the air.
>
> Didn't fight the slip ... instead I *increased* it into a vertical bank. Then using the rudder, I climbed straight up out of the canal ... round and round like a corkscrew.[2]

In case the all-important message had not reached the cavalry, Marendaz touched down on a patch of flat ground near a field station and despatched his message again, finding, in the meantime, that his observer had fainted during the hair-raising slip into the canal.

The failure to exploit the initial success at Cambrai has been attributed to many reasons, two of which have achieved undeserved prominence. It has been claimed that Sir Douglas Haig was misled by his Intelligence Branch and the attack encountered stiffer opposition

1 Mead, op. cit., p. 54.

2 'A plane man's guide to the horse', Captain D.M.K. Marendaz talking to Brian James, *The Times*, Saturday, 6 December 1986, p. 7. © Times Newspapers Ltd, 1986.

than anticipated, and also that the cavalry took unnecessarily long to move up and so threw away a fine chance. Yet the fact that the tank had broken the bridge and so ruined the cavalry's chance is confirmed in a letter from Lieutenant-General Sir William Pulteney, who commanded III Corps in the battle: 'My crew did A.1. and but for an unfortunate incident of a Tank going through the Canal Bridge should have done still bigger things.'[1]

In fact there had been no failure by either Intelligence or the Cavalry, and had contact patrols only ever achieved this one success they would have amply earned their keep. As it was, contact patrols continued to prove their worth in the more fluid fighting of 1918. With the German offensive in the spring of 1918, the established communications systems used by the BEF had to be abandoned as the Fifth Army reeled back before the enemy assault. In the ensuing confusion commanders simply did not know where their troops were, let alone where the enemy was, so contact patrols were frequently their sole means of retaining some grasp on the situation and mounting any sort of coherent defence. In the words of the only modern historian of aerial observation, Peter Mead:

> In the confusion and fluidity of a hurried withdrawal the need for information is at its greatest but the means of obtaining it are at their least; the eyes of the aircraft pilots are then the most regular and reliable source of information, whether those of the tactical reconnaissance pilots or the contact sortie pilots over the battlefield.[2]

German tactics acted as midwife to the birth of the next major contribution of aerial reconnaissance to the Intelligence role. Since 1915 the Germans had been evolving a defensive system where the front line was lightly held by machine-gunners, snipers and artillery observers, snugly concealed from the sight of the Allies but supported by successive layers of reserves who were to deliver increasingly heavy counter-attacks on Allied troops who succeeded in occupying the outlying positions. The Germans had developed this form of defence into a skilled art and many were the occasions when Allied troops had fought their bloody passage into the German front lines only to be caught by sharply delivered blows whilst still disorganized and

1 Grenfell Papers, loc. cit., letter to Lady Desborough, 21 November 1917, D/ERv C2130/56.
2 Mead, op. cit., p. 133.

confused. It was not until 1917 that the counter-attack patrol was evolved. The idea originated in the Second Army for the assault on Messines Ridge in June that year, and required spotter aeroplanes equipped with wireless to patrol ahead of the assaulting troops and watch specifically for Germans forming up to deliver the counter-attack dictated by their tactical doctrine. Once spotted, these forces were treated to a concentration of Allied artillery fire directed from the air. This worked so well that it was decided to continue and extend the ploy but in the early stages of the subsequent Flanders offensive too few aircraft were allotted to the task, and consequently the achievement was less than anticipated. However, for the attacks of 20 August and 26 August 1917, preparation was much improved and again the German counter-attacking units simply became helpless targets for the Allied guns. Throughout the remainder of 1917, counter-attack after counter-attack was smashed before they got under way – much to the alarm of the German experts who had devised these tactics.

Aerial reconnaissance clearly went a long way towards redressing the lack of Intelligence created by trench warfare, to a great extent restoring the range and mobility lost to the cavalry and the depth of vision denied to observers. But the very fact that the armies had gone to earth limited what the airmen could see, despite new techniques and the development of aerial photography; which is why decisive successes occurred only at the beginning and end of the war when the armies were on the move in the open. Though there were instances when surveillance succeeded in acquiring raw information of the highest calibre and even, on rare occasions, material which deserves the appellation 'vital', the old reliance on frequent and consistently useful reporting had gone. No longer was it consistently possible to find a position from which to see and recognize the enemy, though for long the old surveillance techniques were applied with the same dogged, unyielding perseverance used in the conduct of the great offensives on the Western front.

The information that mattered more than anything else in this war of attrition, perhaps even more than news of the enemy's Order of Battle and his manpower reserves, was information about the morale of enemy soldiers – would they fight, or turn tail and run, or surrender? And what about the morale of the enemy's civilian population? Would they continue to give what was demanded of them again and again in ever-increasing quantities? Or would they suffer it no more and try to escape the crushing burden through revolution?

Could the enemy's industries continue to produce at the rate necessary to maintain the war effort? In these respects existing surveillance techniques could achieve very little.

THREE

Contact

THERE was nothing new about gaining intelligence from direct contact with the enemy. What was new in the First World War was the urgency which attended it. Deprived of the benefits of surveillance, the British Army had to lean ever more heavily on contact as the chief means of getting up-to-the-minute information about who, or what, was in front of it, rather like a blind man relying on a stick to tell him what was in his path. In the unavoidably rigid conditions imposed by trench warfare and the strategy of attrition, study of the enemy's Order of Battle was elevated to the very pinnacle of military Intelligence and staffs cried out for information on enemy units and their whereabouts in a bid to evolve a response to the baffling new warfare.

The scene was set, almost theatrically, for man to pit himself against man in order to secure the identification of his opponent, adding a bitter new poignancy to the responsibility that every unit had for establishing what was in front of it, since the knowledge would now be more dearly bought than it had ever been before. To go and get first-hand information of this nature meant crossing the wastes of no-man's-land and actually penetrating the enemy's entrenchments, demanding a highly organized effort, planned to the minutest detail and, increasingly, supported by artillery and trench mortars. 'Going and getting' was far more easily said than done, for the men in the trenches across the way would not become prisoners willingly nor were documents waiting for the plucking like apples on trees.

The soldiers themselves were not the only people in contact with the German armies. Armies do not operate in a vacuum, in conveniently sited areas of wasteland specifically set aside for their rough sports. War is a political struggle with the nature and direction of people's lives at the very heart of every conflict: governments use armies to impose their will on an enemy. Hence, civilian populations are drawn willy-nilly into the struggle, whether as victims when their homes are occupied by an invader, or as guerrillas who assist 'their' army in the field by harassing an invader. Sometimes, of course, the boundary between victim and guerrilla is hopelessly blurred; indeed, the ability of the guerrilla to merge into the civilian population is his greatest advantage and one which is never surrendered readily. But guerrillas exerted little influence on the course of the fighting in the First World War and less on its outcome. The first category of civilian, the victim, had far more bearing on events – in terms of friendly civilians, who had seen the enemy's forces and who could provide information about their location, strength and identity.

The Germans were well aware of the problems this could create for them when they marched into Belgium and France in the heady August of 1914 and they had prepared an answer to cow the civil population thoroughly. The policy of *Schrecklichkeit*, (lit. 'frightfulness'), was calculated to crush the people's spirit by deliberate acts of terror, intimidating the civilians by making them feel the heavy hand of war straightaway. To this end, hostages were taken in the towns on the line of advance and warnings issued that attempts to interfere with the progress of German arms would lead to their execution. In their bid to follow the dictum attributed to the dying von Schlieffen, to 'make the right wing strong', the Germans had stripped the forces available for occupying Belgium and France to the bone. *Schrecklichkeit* was supposed to take the place of an army of occupation by substituting in its stead a passivity founded on terror. This was perfectly in keeping with German philosophy and the GSM as expressed by Carl von Clausewitz: he held that terror was a perfectly legitimate method to shorten a war, considering that, 'We must place him [the enemy] in a situation in which continuing the war is more oppressive than surrender,' a view not all that far removed from that expressed by that other Prussian warrior, Frederick the Great: 'The soldier must fear his officers more than he fears the enemy.' The policy of using fear as a tool to force weaker people to do one's bidding is as old as mankind; ultimately it is the reason why wars are fought at all. The Germans overplayed this card, extending their war of terror to whole communities in their effort to subdue the conquered peoples, and perpetrating atrocities like the sacking of Louvain and mass executions at Dinant.

Like so many other would-be conquerors, the Germans understood neither the reactions of their victims nor the strength of the tide of nationalism they stirred against themselves. General von Hausen, commanding the Third German Army, was both angry and bewildered by the reaction he encountered when his headquarters imposed itself upon the Comte d'Egremont, occupying his *château* and dining at his table. Hausen was perplexed to find that the Count was invariably late for dinner whilst his two sons did not even deign to dine with their august visitor. Equally irritating was the count's refusal to utter one word to Hausen, as was his obvious dislike of the man and his habit of going around 'with his fists clenched in his pockets'.[1] How different from the peacetime manoeuvres where civilians had barely entered the calculations of the Staff and the only problems they presented were claims for damaged crops or property. *Schrecklichkeit* was counter-productive, engendering deep-seated resentment and an implacable, simmering hostility, ready to explode at the first opportunity.

Consequently, in the open fighting of 1914 as the armies traversed well-populated countryside, the BEF found no shortage of civilians eager and ready to pass on every scrap of information they had to help drive back the hated invader, as the commander of the Cavalry Division of the BEF, Major-General E. H. H. Allenby, later Field-Marshal Lord Allenby and conqueror of Palestine, discovered. His Intelligence officer, George Barrow, spent the whole day of 21 August sitting in the railway station at Mons telephoning every town and village where he thought he might get news of the Germans. He got so much information from the Belgians he rang that he was able to warn his commander of the danger of the British being outflanked on their left; unhappily GHQ, with its fixed ideas, declined to believe the reports. (The same thing was done in the Falklands War of 1982 with a happier outcome.) Such possibilities vanished in the horrors of the new mass-industrialized holocaust. In the world of the trenches, civilians who had had recent contact with the forces on the other side of the devastation were rare animals indeed, and Intelligence soon found that help from this source was restricted to refugees. They, however, were forced to follow a roundabout route through the neutral countries and, before they could reach the safety of neutral territory, were subjected to close checks by both sides who feared, with good reason, that numbers of these refugees might be spies. After that, refugees had to face the prospect of six weeks in an internment camp, the object of which was to render information borne by any spy who had evaded the scrutiny of counter-Intelligence obsolete before hostile Intelligence could get their hands on it.

1 B.W. Tuchman, *August 1914*, London, 1962, p. 248, citing Hausen's biography.

Nevertheless, to begin with, amongst the hordes who had taken refuge behind the Allied armies, there were numerous individuals who did have information of value to Intelligence. Rather than knowledge about the enemy, these people could provide useful information about the terrain within and behind enemy lines, terrain over which the Allied leadership were always expecting their soldiers to forge a victorious path and about the peculiarities of which they therefore had to know. Hence Lieutenant-Colonel Woolrych, who spent much of his time as a subaltern in Intelligence watching the Germans from an Observation Post, could write, 'I spent more time in tracking down farmers and villagers from areas in front of us now enemy-occupied, and from them I gained quite a lot of useful topographical details.'[1] Some of the refugees would have photographs and picture postcards of their neighbourhood, which Woolrych vaguely described as 'almost invaluable'. Such people were eagerly sought and questioned in depth 'whenever they showed up', the subject of the questions being 'nearly all about the kind of country we had to cross. One was examining them on what sort of impediments there were.'[2]

However, not once was small-scale information of this nature able to give the BEF the extra weight it was seeking to tip the balance and win a decisive victory, the victory which would destroy the German Army and force the Germans to make a peace on Allied terms. What this sort of information could do was to save lives and enable attacking troops to wring some slight advantage from the terrain in order to capture single objectives. The sort of success it could contribute to was the sort won at Courcellette on the Somme in September 1916, when the Canadian Corps had to storm the town, the approaches to which were covered by the strongly fortified ruins of a sugar factory. Refugees from Courcellette were sought, one of whom was a former nightwatchman at the factory who knew all about the buildings and even had picture postcards of the factory and village. His information was instrumental in helping the Canadians to secure the factory, a splendid achievement which enabled them to capture 145 prisoners – for once, more than the attacking troops actually lost in casualties.

In theatres where movement was still possible, civilians could and often did provide information of a far more useful kind. However, by mid-1915 the only theatre where movement was still possible was East

1 Woolrych Papers, loc. cit.
2 Woolrych. Interview with author, 19 March 1982 [hereinafter Woolrych interview].

Africa, where the railways reigned supreme as the only way to supply and reinforce the army. Long stretches of track straggling over hundreds of miles of bush, sometimes over a thousand, presented an attractive target to an enemy with any initiative; and one thing the German commander, the enterprising von Lettow-Vorbeck, had no lack of was initiative. Here he could disrupt British communications, harry the British commanders and tie down large numbers of British troops by employing only a small number of men. The incompetents who commanded the forces in British East Africa were shaken to their roots by von Lettow's raids and it took the brilliant head of Intelligence in East Africa to devise a method to put a stop to the Germans' success. Richard Meinertzhagen made the inhabitants responsible for reporting the movement of hostile raiders through their neighbourhood and, in Meinertzhagen's opinion, failure to report their presence was tantamount to treason. Raiding parties could not traverse strange country without the natives being aware of it and several were successfully ambushed, which speedily curtailed the German desire for this form of warfare. As Meinertzhagen expressed it: 'I have adopted this principle in the Chyulu Hills and from the day it came into force not one single enemy patrol has passed that way.'[1] He used the same method with equal success in Palestine in 1917 against the Turks, who sent raiding parties to cut the telegraph wires around Hebron. Each village in the vicinity was made responsible for the wires in its neighbourhood and each had to provide picquets and patrols to safeguard them.

Beyond information about raiding parties, civilians also passed information to the British which actively assisted the conduct of operations. In the Cameroons the natives became important enough as an intelligence source to cause the British to include their protection in operational plans, as in April 1915 when a limited withdrawal was contemplated by one column. The retirement was expressly forbidden on the grounds that, 'To withdraw from Ikom would have disastrous results as [the] natives would not trust us again. They are giving information of movements of enemy and in my opinion are withholding from [the] enemy our movements of troops.'[2]

The attitude of the native population of the Cameroons

1 Meinertzhagen *Army Diary*, op. cit., p. 142.

2 Governor General to Colonial Office, 'Operations in the Cameroons', 10 April 1915, PRO (WO 106/646).

was damaging to the morale of Germans serving there, dismayed to find their plans and dispositions betrayed by people they regarded as their own subjects:

> With few exceptions all the movements of our troops were betrayed. Honest fighting against the enemy was rendered practically impossible – there was treachery everywhere.[1]

Another grumbled:

> The English were helped by the natives in every possible way. The natives would tell any lies that were required and would feel themselves highly honoured if they were praised by English white men.[2]

There is much more in the same frustrated vein. Even allowing for the possibility that the Germans were covering their defeat by blaming it on native 'treachery', the fact that so many accounts refer to this, often at length, and receive confirmation from British sources, suggests that there is more to it than simply seeking a scapegoat for defeat or sour grapes at having been outfought. Nevertheless, what is again surprising is the blinkered German view: they treated the natives of their colony harshly, frequently humiliating them and permitting their troops to do just as they pleased in the villages, the natives having no means of redress through official German channels.[3] This differing form of *Schrecklichkeit* inspired hatred in native breasts, and the brutal reprisals meted out to those believed to have assisted the British only provoked 'revenge' assistance.

Of course, there were occasions when the boot was on the other foot, when the British experience mirrored the trials and tribulations to which the Germans were subjected. While the majority of the inhabitants of the Cameroons loathed their colonial overlords and would go far to assist the British, there were still those who remained loyal to the Germans and who used the activities of their compatriots and the trust they inspired in British breasts to sow false information which led to the undoing of British detachments more then once. One force, ardently pursuing the Germans covering the town of Fumban, had to hew its way through 50 miles of jungle before discovering that

1 NCO Bode, 'Intercepted reports on operations in the Cameroons by German prisoners released from S.S. "Appam" by the German auxiliary cruiser "Möwe" ' PRO (WO 106/656).
2 Ibid., Oberjaeger Adler.
3 'Copies of Papers on the Military Situation in the Cameroons and Nigeria', Colonial Office to War Office, 'Report by Lt.-Col. G. T. Mair, DSO, OC Cross River Columnal Commandant, The Nigeria Regiment', 4 February 1915, PRO (WO 106/645B).

the information they were relying on was completely bogus. More costly was the ambush of a party of Mounted Infantry at Tepe on 25 August 1914, led into it by native guides who had systematically and deliberately lied about the enemy's strength and position in the region.[1] In East Africa, where the population was considerably more faithful to the Germans, information was hard to come by and it took even the exceptional Meinertzhagen many months to organize an effective service. In the meantime the official view of the natives in East Africa was encapsulated in a gloomy report sent home in November 1914: 'Our sources of information are very meagre and depend chiefly on native reports which are not at all reliable.'[2]

The attitude of the civilians in the war zone, so often ignored or discounted in the standard military histories which focus almost exclusively on the operations of armies or on the conduct of individuals, depended on a combination of self-interest and the attitude of the warring powers towards them. This is reflected in Meinertzhagen's experience in the Middle East where, as head of Intelligence to Allenby, he found that:

> The Jew, or rather the Zionist, regards us frankly as the instrument sent by God to fulfill the Promise and restore the Holy Land to Israel. As such we are everywhere welcomed, and a very sincere relief is felt throughout all Jewish Colonies at the final removal of the Turkish yoke, which to them spelt oppression, massacre, a hopeless future and an effective check to peaceful development, whether industrial or agricultural.'[3]

In such cases the fact that there was – or appeared to be – something to be gained from British victory was the decisive influence. Having, often enough, little reason to side with either party, many inhabitants would assist whichever of the parties supported their best interests and offered them security and gain. What has since become known as the 'battle for hearts and minds' would in large measure turn in favour of whoever appeared most likely to serve the perceived aspirations of the inhabitants.

Certain conditions need to be present for civilians to help armies with information, close and recent contact with the enemy being one,

1 Ibid., Governor General to Colonial Office, 23 September 1914, and 'Report of Lt.-Col. P. Maclear', 27 August 1914, PRO (WO 106/645B).

2 'Memorandum. Précis of Situation of BEA and Uganda. Appendix I', 20 November 1914, PRO (WO 106/575).

3 Meinertzhagen Diaries, op. cit., Vol. 20, 2 December 1917, p. 76.

and the ability to contact those the civilian is trying to help another. On the Western front both these cardinal requirements were denied to Intelligence, with the inevitable consequence that nothing truly decisive could ever reach their hands. The unpleasant alternative was that the soldiers had to adopt more direct methods of getting the information they needed. It meant, in fact, that somebody had to go out and get prisoners.

In the halcyon days of August and September 1914, before the deadly trench lines embraced the armies and war still bore some resemblance to what the commanders had expected, prisoners could be taken without much of a fight. This unwary scout or that blundering patrol which ventured into the maw of the enemy could expect to see the war out behind the barbed wire of a prison camp. Large numbers of prisoners could also be taken from an army in flight, as happened during the German retreat from the Marne, when, footsore and utterly exhausted by their heroic, almost superhuman efforts to reach Paris, men fell by the wayside in droves, physically incapable of taking one step more. Marshall-Cornwall, leading 'A' Squadron of the 15th Hussars, had a field day and recounted how:

> We came across dozens of them lying worn out and often asleep in barns and ditches, so that I had the chance of examining prisoners of many different units. From their statements, and from the billeting and requisition notes left behind in the *mairie* of every French village, I was able to reconstruct and report back the complete order of battle of General von der Marwitz's II Cavalry Corps, which formed the German rearguard on our front.[1]

All this changed dramatically once the armies had gone to ground. Carefully organized and well-supported operations were then needed to come into contact with the enemy. Prisoners could be captured in battle, but full-scale battles were not in progress for more than a few months of a year, nor were they ever in progress over the whole front. Smaller operations were thus spawned to take the prisoners required and inflict the maximum amount of death and destruction on the enemy in the shortest possible time, but without the intention of capturing ground. These were the trench raids, which remain a thorny question whenever the conduct of operations in the First World War is discussed. Taking prisoners was not their only purpose, nor even a

1 Marshall-Cornwall, op. cit., p. 16.

stated one. Raiding was a matter of policy. In 1915 the BEF simply was not in a position to undertake major offensives on the scale the French Army did – it just did not have the munitions or the trained men for that. A GHQ order of 5 February instigated the policy of raiding in order to maintain some form of offensive stance, to foster an offensive spirit in the troops, to harass the enemy and gain local advantages. Nowhere is there any mention of taking prisoners or anything which suggests that raiding had any Intelligence connotation. The order is reproduced in Appendix II.

The British high command felt constantly embarrassed by French insinuations that the BEF was not pulling its weight and was leaving the dirty work – and all the heavy casualties – to the French. The order of February 1915 required the Army to be more aggressive and eighteen ad hoc raids were carried out in that year on the initiative of local officers. With Sir Douglas Haig's accession to the supreme command of the British armies in France, the picture changed dramatically and very quickly indeed. As well as being highly sensitive to French criticism, Haig was fully committed to the strategy of attrition, a strategy which demanded the continual wearing out of the enemy, both in terms of manpower and of morale. When no major fighting was taking place, what better way to achieve this than to launch many small raids all along the British front? With luck, casualties would not be too high. Hand-in-hand with the idea of ceaseless attrition went the aim of pinning down a considerable part of the German Army by forcing them to hold miles of trenches to guard against these sudden blows, thus denying the German command the ability to employ those troops against the major offensives that Haig had in mind. Altogether, it added up to a sensible policy from the GHQ viewpoint and as a result raiding was fiercely stepped up during Haig's tenure of office, increasing from the very few raids in 1915 to an astonishing 494 in 1916.[1]

Nevertheless, despite the stated motives for raiding, the raiding parties were always, without exception, ordered to take prisoners for Intelligence, as the following conversation shows:

> Joseph Murray: 'The idea is to get hold of a prisoner, or several prisoners . . .'
>
> Question: 'You were told specifically to get hold of a prisoner?'

1 All figures for trench raids are taken from the Army War Diaries in the PRO, Kew, in class WO 95.

Joseph Murray: 'Oh yes. The idea of the raid was to define who was in front of you.'[1]

Furthermore, in the specific apportionment of tasks given to raiders from the Second Army, men were detailed to 'take prisoners' and 'to look for identifications if unable to bring in prisoners'. The same document advocated that, 'If it can be arranged, an Intelligence Officer should accompany the party to assist in the identification of the enemy,'[2] all of which was designed to build up the picture of the enemy's Order of Battle, all-important to those charged with conduct of the war.

To many of the troops, however, the raids were an irrelevant and unnecessary danger which risked their lives for no apparent purpose. One soldier had no doubt about the true origin of raids when he wrote:

> After a time these raids became unpopular with regimental officers and the rank and file, for there grew up a feeling that sometimes these expeditions to the enemy trenches owed their origin to rivalry between organizations higher than battalions.[3]

In many respects this is typical of the First World War in microcosm: the staff and higher commands displaying their clinical, unemotional bent for sticking to dry, theoretical calculations from which victory would flow as a matter of course; and men in the muck and slime of the trenches facing death and wounds for no convincing reason. Raiding undoubtedly did inflict losses on the Germans and it did enable Intelligence to keep tabs on the movement of German divisions and locate possible danger points where the enemy might be building up his strength to inflict some new embarrassment on the Allies, but the men in the line knew nothing of these grand calculations.

The view of some front-line soldiers raises an argument about trench raids sometimes prosecuted as fiercely as the raids themselves, and that concerns their true value. Writers with a sociological bent are fond of arguing that raids were hated by the troops who regarded all of them as a futile waste of lives:

> . . . the basic idea behind the raid was wrong. In a territorial war the very existence of no-man's-land showed that a war was going on, for if

1 Murray interview, loc. cit.

2 Second Army War Diary, 'Lessons Drawn From The Various Minor Operations Carried Out By The Second Army Up To The 9th February, 1916', p. 7, PRO (WO 95/273).

3 Cited by John Ellis, *Eye Deep In Hell: The Western Front 1914-1918*, London, 1976, p. 79. Ellis does not give his source.

> ascendancy had been achieved then either a war of movement would have resulted, or the war would have been over. No-man's-land stood for a balance between two forces, an area into which either side was committed to apply maximum force if threatened – and a raid from one side could only be the application of a very slender force.[1]

The same author considers that raids had little Intelligence value for 'there were easier ways of finding out this information'.[2]

What the front-line soldiers thought about raiding is one way of assessing the value and impact of the strategy. One example frequently cited is Edmund Blunden's statement that 'The word "raid" may be defined as the one in the whole vocabulary of the war which most instantly caused a sinking feeling in the stomach of ordinary mortals,'[3] a view forcefully supported in Joseph Murray's blunter words: 'I don't think we liked them, you know, to be honest. And only on one occasion did I take part in a raid and I didn't like it at all.'[4] Yet most of the veterans interviewed for this book shared the view of Basil Rackham, then a subaltern in the same division as Murray: 'Well, I think they were essential. We always reckoned that wherever we were, we were going to dominate no-man's-land, and of course identification was very, very important, and so sometimes we thought they were unnecessary, but by and large we accepted them as essential.'[5] Sergeant Zealley stated:

> They [the troops] took them as part of the warfare, that was all, it, the whole outfit was perilous, you could die from so many ways, that to go over the top in comparative darkness, you see, and on the particular occasion when I went on snowy ground, we were clad in white overalls so we would not be really visible.[6]

Lance-Corporal Castle regarded raiding as,'Oh, a job to be done. We enjoyed it sometimes,'[7] and Colonel Woolrych stated all ranks 'thought they were necessary'.[8]

Opinions about raiding are clearly subjective and depend to a considerable extent on the perspective of the individual soldier and his

1 D. Winter, *Death's Men*, London, 1978, p. 94.
2 Ibid., p. 92.
3 Blunden, op. cit., p. 45.
4 Murray interview, loc. cit.
5 Rackham interview, loc. cit.
6 Sergeant P. R. Zealley, 10th Royal Fusiliers. Interview with author, 10 August 1981.
7 Castle interview, loc. cit.
8 Woolrych interview, loc. cit.

own experience in raiding, whether or not he had been on a successful raid with few casualties and returned a hero, or whether he had seen half of his platoon shot down and had a miraculous escape from the jaws of death. Yet it may well be asked whether the troops 'like' or 'dislike' of raiding was of any real consequence in the broad history of the war: going over the top in a major offensive, coming under artillery fire, living in filth, mud and water while surrounded by the dead and flies, Army food and the Sergeant-Major were all thoroughly disliked. As long as the 'dislike' did not grow into dereliction of duty or mutiny, it did not matter very much. Raiding was not instituted solely to show that there was a war on, or to enhance a staff officer's reputation. Undoubtedly, however, some commanders pressed the policy far more vigorously than it needed to be pressed and that for dubious reasons. To that extent one cannot disagree with General McNamara when he wrote:

> They [raids] are only justifiable as a definite military operation for a specific purpose conducing to the success of a commander's plan. They have no place in the conduct of war when carried out merely as a sort of competition between formations with no specific military object. When needlessly ordered they impair the confidence of the troops in their leaders and lower their morale.[1]

Raiding increased once the BEF was in a position to mount a serious offensive and the success of any particular raid was decided by whether or not it had captured prisoners or otherwise achieved its objectives. The alternative sources of Operational Intelligence simply could not deliver this kind of information. As one Intelligence officer at the very heart of the problem wrote, 'Under these conditions, actual attack seems the best method, as aeroplanes have ceased to be of any use for Intelligence.'[2] In terms of results, the *Official History* contains a representative breakdown of raids but since, for reasons of space, it does not cover all raids undertaken, it cannot reflect the true picture. Better, in this respect, are the Army War Diaries held in the Public Record Office at Kew, with their brief and very neutral weekly accounts of all the events on each army's front. They reveal that over the period between January 1915 and November 1918 the BEF carried out no fewer than 1,525 raids, in the course of which 4,711 Germans were taken prisoner, approximately three prisoners per raid.

1 Kirke Papers, loc. cit., 'Lessons Of The Great War Committee. Covering Report' – Part II.
2 Diaries of General Sir Walter Kirke [hereinafter Kirke Dairies], 8 December 1914, IWM.

There were wide variations in the number of prisoners taken, from none at all to the 4 officers and 160 men taken by the 3rd and 4th Canadian Divisions and the 46th (North Midland) Division on both sides of the Souchez river on the night of 9-10 June 1917.[1] No reliable figures for casualties sustained or inflicted exist. British casualty figures were not always given for every raid or were sometimes simply dubbed 'slight', 'light', 'heavy', 'a good many' or even 'rather heavy'.[2] Such figures as do exist for these raids show that the British armies lost 6,834 men killed, wounded, missing and prisoners as against 3,941 Germans killed alone, but they do not include the estimated or approximate losses referred to, so it would probably be correct to assume double these figures in both cases. Nevertheless, incomplete as they are, these figures represent the best contemporary statistical record that we have. What the available records do show is that, if viewed solely through the blinkers of attrition, and if notional German casualties for wounded and missing are included, raiding was achieving exactly what Haig wanted it to do, for German losses were substantially greater than the British.

The officers keeping the War Diaries judged 493 of the 1,525 raids to be successful, success being determined by a number of factors – whether or not the raiders managed to enter the enemy trenches, whether prisoners or identifications were secured, whether other valuable information was obtained – all, of course, being set against the number of casualties suffered. If the cost of establishing the enemy's Order of Battle was disproportionate to the achievement, then the raid could not be deemed a success. Raids might be launched with some specific objective in mind, as when the Second Army was ordered to mount a raid to discover why a man in civilian clothes had tried to cross no-man's-land and get into the German trenches. The man was shot dead and his body dragged into the German lines after dark and the only practical means of establishing 'the reason why' was to go over and find out the hard way. On this occasion the plan misfired in the face of German readiness. Other raids received a dubious accolade of 'success' simply because the raiders managed to enter the enemy lines and inflict some degree of loss or damage on the occupants: during 1916 the new, untried ranks of Kitchener's Army consistently found themselves caught out by the tactics of the better-

1 *See* PRO (WO 95/171).
2 For examples *see* PRO (WO 95/164, 171, 176 and 520).

trained German soldiers, a fact which only the destruction of the old German Army in the course of that year was to alter. 1916 also saw a steady alteration in the tactics of raiding as the facts of GHQ control and dearly bought experience began to pay dividends. Now the amateurish, haphazard air which had been the chief characteristic of the early raids, as if they were some deadly sport for overgrown schoolboys, was gradually displaced by a more professional approach. The number of raids made by stealth began to show a rapid decline: by mid-1916 it was increasingly common for a raid to be preceded by weeks of painstaking planning and, when the raiding party went over, the way was prepared for them by a sudden blizzard of shells and trench mortar bombs intended to wreck the German wire, send the defenders scrambling into their dugouts and isolate the target area within a box barrage. The number of daylight raids also declined, to avoid the unwelcome attention of enemy machine-gunners and Forward Observation Officers. The sudden tumult of night-time raids would, however, frequently catch the enemy by surprise and dislocate his defence badly for, in the darkness, even nearby German soldiers could rarely be sure exactly where the hostile raiders were.

Set against this is the fact that 223 raids were classed as unsuccessful, though 'unsuccessful' does not necessarily mean a bloody repulse was the only result. If we take the First Army as a case study, the table below will show that 10 out of 41 unsuccessful raids suffered no casualties at all.

Losses suffered by the First Army in unsuccessful raids
(Figures from the First Army War Diary)

Number of Raids	*Losses Suffered*
10	None
11	1 – 10
10	11 – 20
3	21 – 30
2	31 – 40
1	41 – 50
2	91 – 100
2	Over 100

The average loss per raid, and the distribution of losses, indicate that the raiding policy, while by no means cheap, was achieving its aims at less than prohibitive cost. Casualty figures exist for 423 raids overall, showing an average of 16 casualties (killed, wounded or missing) per raid.

A further 809 raids were not classified at all by the Army Staffs. A full picture of the raids carried out by the BEF appears opposite revealing how the raiding policy was staged to ensure that raids were at their most intense before and during the great offensives, in order to keep Intelligence aware of the German Order of Battle from day to day all along the front, and thus keep track of fresh and exhausted German divisions as they were variously committed to or withdrawn from the fighting. The graph also reflects the difference between the numbers of successful and unsuccessful raids, clearly showing that 1916 was the British Army's worst year of the war and tracking the remorseless but gradual decline of Germany's fighting power through 1917 and 1918.

Marshall-Cornwall states unequivocally that 'The best information we got was from captured documents, next best information was from interrogating prisoners,' and again, 'I think documents, captured documents, were the best evidence we got.'[1] The supreme importance attached to documents stemmed not only from the information they provided but from the fact that they did not lie and could not go back on what they said. They were hard evidence of the best sort and they still represent a commodity eagerly sought by Intelligence services even in the modern world of computers and electronics. The sort of documents which came into the hands of the Army's Intelligence staff might give details of hostile trenches, the condition of trenches and dugouts, the intended tactics of the enemy, the morale of his soldiers and civilians, and, of course, the ubiquitous Order of Battle.

The prize catch would be a document which revealed the enemy's plans in their entirety. This happened only once for the Allies and then good luck smiled on the French rather than the British. In the mobile warfare of 1914 a German motor-car was ambushed by a French patrol and in the wreckage they found the body of a German cavalry officer who was acting as a liaison officer with von Kluck's First Army. More important than the dead officer was his bag, which was hurried off to the Intelligence staff of the French Fifth Army. To the amazement and delight of the new owners, it was found to contain documents and a map,

1 Marshall-Cornwall. Interview with author, 10 September 1980 [hereinafter Marshall-Cornwall interview].

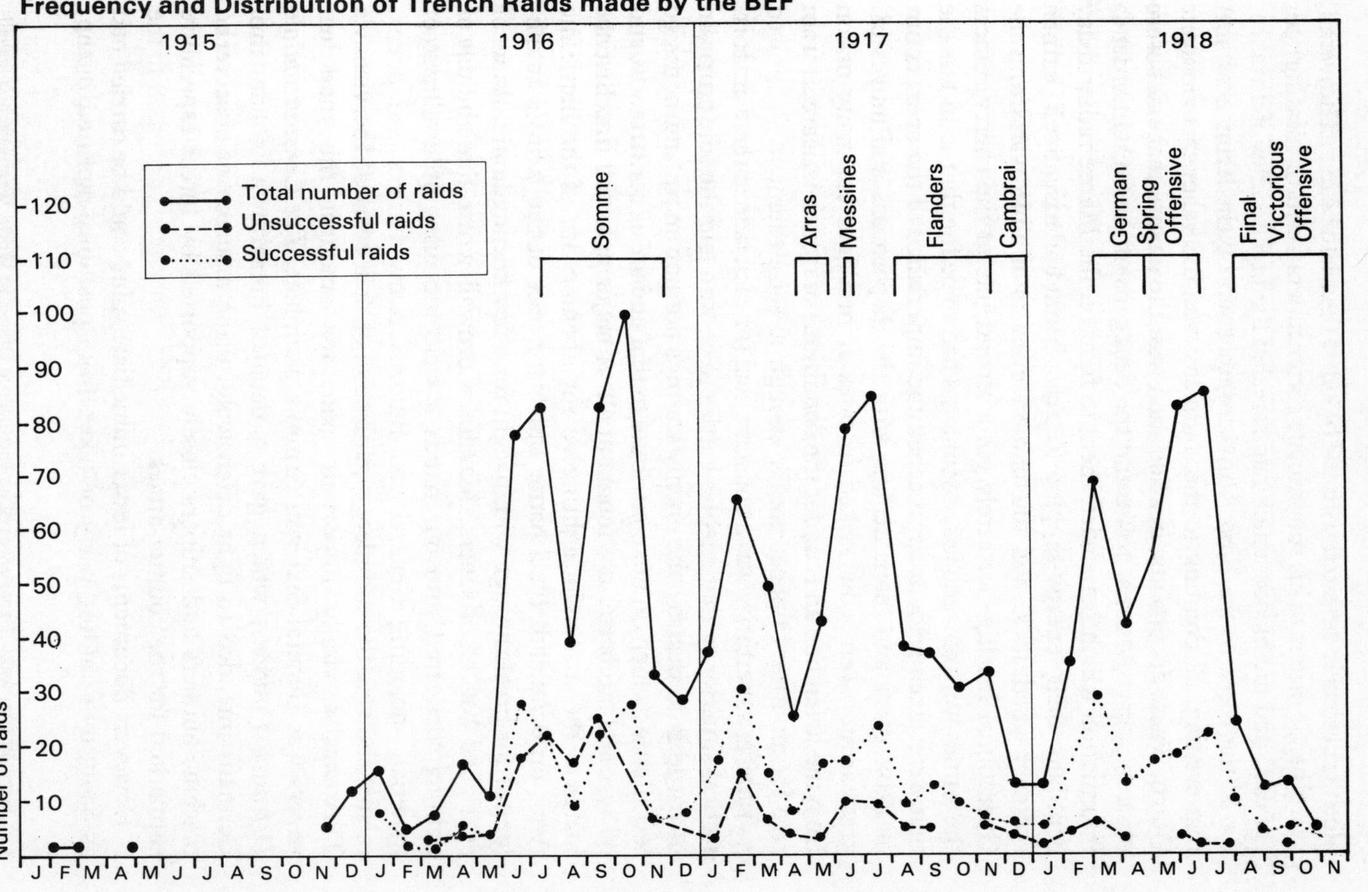

Frequency and Distribution of Trench Raids made by the BEF
1915
1916
1917
1918
Total number of raids
Unsuccessful raids
Successful raids
Somme
Arras
Messines
Flanders
Cambrai
German Spring Offensive
Final Victorious Offensive
Number of raids
120
110
100
90
80
70
60
50
40
30
20
10
J F M A M J J A S O N D J F M A M J J A S O N D J F M A M J J A S O N D J F M A M J J A S O N

albeit gruesomely smeared with the blood of their late bearer. They were von Kluck's orders to his subordinate commanders for the critical turn to the east, and the bloodstained map revealed the precise lines of advance for all the corps of the First Army, together with their destinations for that evening, all pointing to the south-east and the valley of the River Ourcq. These documents, in association with the reports of the airborne observers, gave Marshal Joffre and the demigods of the GQG the vital information which persuaded them to fight on the Marne rather than continue their energy-sapping retreat behind Paris. Such extraordinary good luck was uncommon even in mobile warfare, and Operational Intelligence rarely got a second bite of the cherry. Once the armies were entrenched, documents had to be fought for and those that were taken seldom approached the importance of the great coup of 1914: plans and maps dealing with the dispositions and moves of great armies were now locked in safes at headquarters many miles from the firing line and, under the conditions of trench warfare, it was rare for an army to penetrate far enough to seize them.

Tactical superiority was a constant goal for each side in the war. It is tactical superiority that enables battles to be won and the sole purpose of battle is to destroy the enemy's army: nothing more and nothing less. Battles which do not contribute to that end are a monstrous waste of lives and are better not fought at all. A major prize fell into British hands in the successful fighting on the opening day of the Battle of Arras on 9 April 1917, a battle which for once actually brought the longed-for breakthrough within sight for a few fleeting hours. As well as a good bag of prisoners, Marshall-Cornwall wrote that the day's fighting 'delivered into our hands a welcome mass of Intelligence material, including General von Bülow's Army Orders and documents, showing the complete organization of their rearward services'.[1] This was a vitally important gain, for amongst the mass of papers was General Sixt von Arnim's pamphlet, *The Construction of Defensive Positions*, which gave a detailed breakdown of how the Germans intended to fight defensively, using a screen of observers, machine-gunners and snipers closely supported by forces especially earmarked for the counter-attack.

However, documents of lesser immediate value could be carried off as booty by a raiding party or taken from positions captured in the

1 Marshall-Cornwall, 'Experiences of an Intelligence Officer in World Wars One and Two'. Extracts from the (unpublished) Memoirs of General Sir James Marshall-Cornwall, ICMA.

great offensives. Besides these official papers, a whole mass of revealing private papers were taken from prisoners or picked up from the bodies of dead Germans by parties specially detailed for this unsavoury and unpopular task. The private papers of enemy soldiers could corroborate much of the information that was found in official documents, with the added advantage that they revealed the state of enemy morale. According to Elliot,

> German soldiers had an almost universal habit of keeping personal diaries filled with details of places they had visited, of friends in other regiments, of where, when and how long they had stayed in rest billets. Letters often gave valuable information about their units. NCOs often carried battalion orders and, on at least one occasion, a man carried an order stating that his regiment was to be relieved by another at a stated time and by a specific route. Collecting and checking these papers was obviously vitally important and this accounts for the disapproval of the actions of souvenir-hunters.[1]

Equally important and just as frequently found was the paybook carried by each German soldier. These slim booklets, about the size and thickness of a small notebook or engagement diary, contained all the details of its owner's military service, including two details of paramount importance in a war of attrition. One was the conscription class to which the man belonged. Every German male was a possible candidate for conscription when he reached his twentieth birthday and the young men reaching that age in any particular year constituted the conscription class of that year; thus all men reaching the age of twenty in the fateful year of 1914 would be the class of 1914. By grading prisoners and casualties according to their annual class, Allied Intelligence was given a powerful insight into the state of German units, their fighting condition and the scale of their losses. This ran hand-in-hand with the study of the German Order of Battle, for the call-up of a new class would indicate either an increase in the size of the German Army or that more men were needed to maintain that Army at its existing strength, thus reflecting the losses it had suffered.

The second important detail was the company roll number each young man was given when he joined his unit. If he was killed, seriously wounded, taken prisoner or otherwise released from the service, his replacement would be allotted the succeeding number in the company list, a system which, with typical Prussian thoroughness, would reveal

1 Elliot, op. cit., p. 39.

the losses suffered by the company. Thus it followed that if paybooks from all the companies in a battalion, regiment or division could be taken, then the losses of that unit could be established with reasonable precision, as would be the wastage of German manpower through the study of the conscription classes. When large numbers of paybooks fell into British hands after a major action, either by being taken from prisoners or rifled from the pockets of the dead and wounded, it was possible to calculate the composition of German units by classes, to arrive at a reasonably accurate figure for overall German casualties, to observe the fluctuations in German manpower and to project the strength of the German Army's future prowess. Perhaps most importantly of all, these calculations would be derived from German sources.

The paybooks were examined at GHQ by Captain A. P. Scotland, who closely correlated information with the French via three Englishwomen who worked for GHQ Intelligence at the *Deuxième Bureau* in Paris, the Misses C. E. Bosworth, S. M. Bosworth, and L. Brooking. They worked for Captain D. d'Almeida who

> . . . showed us how to extract very important information from German soldiers' paybooks, taken from German prisoners captured by the French. Delivered in sacks at the French War Office after important battles, they were first classified by Captain d'Almeida and then passed on to us, to forward to Intelligence GHQ.[1]

The tables on pp. 91 and 92 were compiled from 849 paybooks belonging to men of the 14th German Division captured on 23 October 1917 at Laffaux-Allemant. They provide an accurate representation of the composition of that division when compared with the composition of the same division in 1916, and also reveal the losses suffered by the division. The accompanying graph on p. 93 shows the staggering wastage by classes in the 10th Company of the 202nd Reserve Infanterie Regiment, showing that as early as April 1917 the lads of the 1918 class were being put into the line over a year early and that by September the only members of earlier classes remaining with the Company were returned sick and wounded.[2] In human terms they make shocking reading: these cold figures mean that the hundreds of thousands of young men aged twenty in 1917 had mostly

1 Papers of Mrs C. E. Fisher (née Bosworth) [hereinafter Bosworth Papers], ICMA.
2 Ibid.

Information obtained from 849 paybooks of the 14th Division captured 23 October 1917 at Laffaux-Allemant

	Classes	*Captured December 1916 %*	*Captured October 1917 %*
Active	1918	–	29.87
	1917	12.37	12.38
	1916	7.30	6.73
	1915	12.77	8.53
	1914	9.32	5.52
	1913	8.92	2.21
	1912	2.83	1.95
	Reserve	5.38	2.95
	Landwehr I	3.85	3.69
	Landwehr II	1.82	1.80
	Ersatz Reserve	7.99	4.86
Landsturm I	1890-1895	7.09	6.96
	1885-1889	7.80	5.80
	1880-1884	6.89	3.40
	1876-1879	3.04	0.87
Landsturm II	1869-1875	–	–
	Kriegsfreiwillige (War Volunteers)	2.63	2.48
		100.0%	100.0%
Totals based on:		480 Pay-Books	849 Pay-Books

been slaughtered, maimed or imprisoned and that the men of 1918 were undergoing the same fate. They should provide a stock answer to those who glory in the persistent argument that German losses were nearly always far lighter than the British.

Paybooks therefore gave the Allies an accurate means of estimating the wastage of German manpower and also provided a guide to the casualties suffered by German forces in the field, for by subtracting the roll-numbers of the class already known to be serving from the roll-numbers of the new recruits, one was left with the total number of draftees required to bring the unit up to strength. Furthermore, study of the roll-numbers also revealed what proportion of any German unit was composed of new draftees. Thus the tables for the 14th Division

Losses sustained between May and August 1917 by 11 companies of the 14th Division (these being the only companies having dates) captured 23 October 1917 at Laffaux-Allemant.

Regiment	*Company*	*Lowest / Highest*	*Roll Numbers*	*Date of Joining Company*	*Minimum Loss*
16th Infantry Regiment	6th	1119	....	19.5.17	187 men
		1305	....	31.8.17	
	11th	1323	....	20.5.17	57 men
		1379	....	26.8.17	
	12th	1303	....	20.5.17	70 men
		1372	....	22.8.17	
56th Infantry Regiment	3rd	1582	....	10.5.17	97 men
		1678	....	25.8.17	
	4th	1412	....	10.5.17	137 men
		1548	....	25.8.17	
	6th	1272	....	19.5.17	107 men
		1378	....	22.8.17	
	8th	1298	....	19.5.17	80 men
		1377	....	24.8.17	
	9th	1708	....	20.5.17	53 men
		1760	....	15.8.17	
	12th	1292	....	19.5.17	99 men
		1390	....	25.8.17	
57th Infantry Regiment	9th	1460	....	6.6.17	121 men
		1580	....	25.8.17	
	12th	1350	....	23.6.17	117 men
		1466	....	18.9.17	

Total loss for 11 companies = 1125 men
Average loss per company during average period of 3 months (May-August) = 102 men

show that of the 849 pay-books tabulated, 517, or 60.89 per cent, belonged to new draftees.

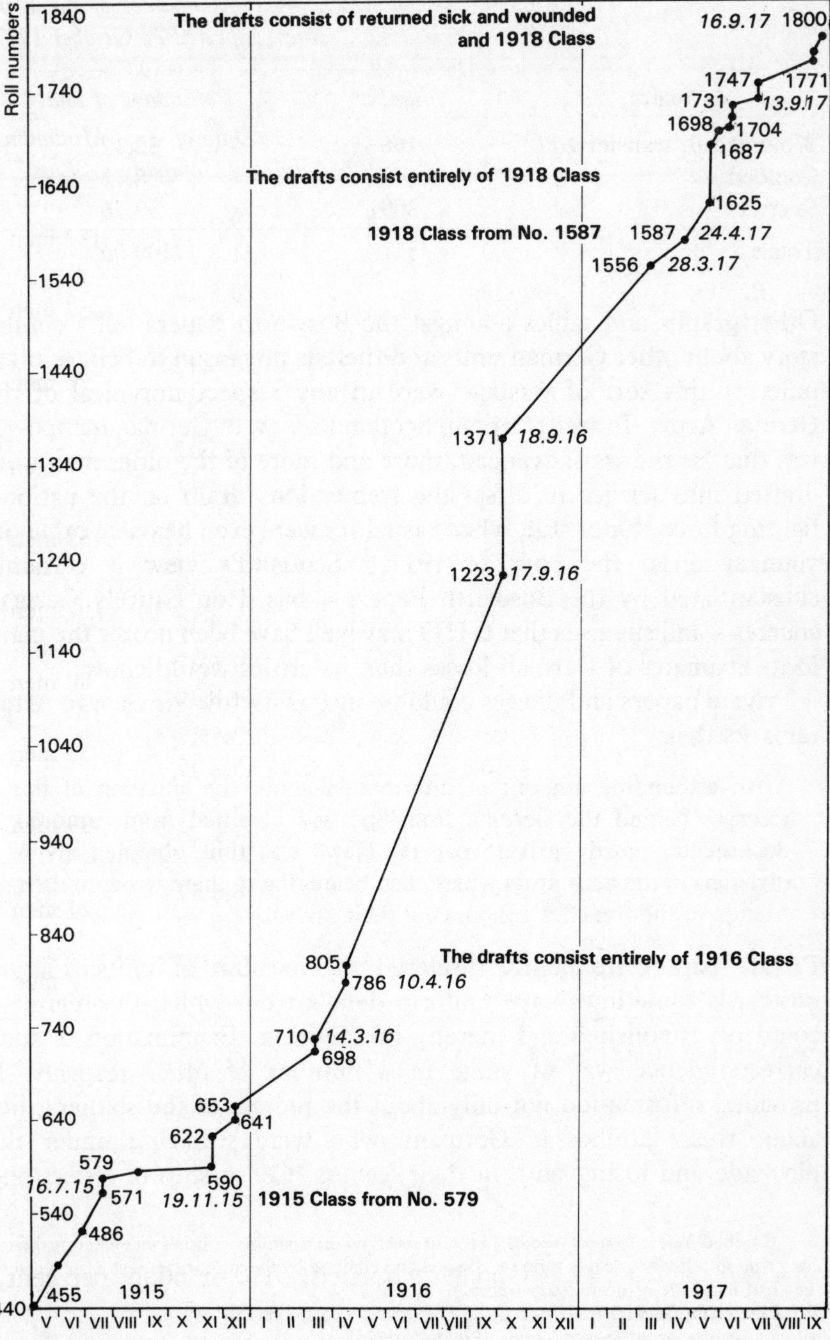
10th Company, 202nd Reserve Infanterie Regiment
Roll numbers
1840
1740
1640
1540
1440
1340
1240
1140
1040
940
840
740
640
540
440
The drafts consist of returned sick and wounded and 1918 Class
The drafts consist entirely of 1918 Class
1918 Class from No. 1587
The drafts consist entirely of 1916 Class
1915 Class from No. 579
16.9.17 1800
1747
1771
1731
13.9.17
1698
1704
1687
1625
1587 24.4.17
1556 28.3.17
1371 18.9.16
1223 17.9.16
805
786 10.4.16
710 14.3.16
698
653
641
622
579
16.7.15
571
590
19.11.15
486
455
1915
1916
1917
V VI VII VIII IX X XI XII I II III IV V VI VII VIII IX X XI XII I II III IV V VI VII VIII IX

The drafts were composed as follows:[1]

Source	*Number*	*Percentage of total*
Wounded or transferred	166	32.12
Combed[1]	42	8.12
Recruits	309	59.76
Totals	517	100.00

Other graphs and tables amongst the Bosworth Papers tell a similar story about other German units and there is no reason to believe these units or this sort of wastage were in any respect untypical of the German Army. Indeed, Captain Scotland's view of German manpower was that 'as the war advanced, more and more of the older men were drafted into service to offset the tremendous drain on the nation's fighting force. Later still, when casualties were even heavier, came the younger ones, the boys of 1917.'[2] Scotland's view is certainly substantiated by the Bosworth Papers – based on entirely German sources – and suggests that GHQ may well have been nearer the mark in its estimates of German losses than its critics would allow.

Private papers and diaries could be just as useful. Sir George Aston remarks that:

> An astounding amount of information about the situation of the reserves behind the German front-line was obtained from captured documents, mostly private papers. News was thus obtained about divisions in the back areas where men belonging to them wrote to their friends in the trenches announcing their arrival.[3]

Private papers frequently disclosed the location of units. Picture postcards sometimes gave uniform details from which the regiment could be established and thereby the division. Examination of such correspondence was of value in a number of other respects. It provided information not only about the morale of the soldiers, but about their families in Germany who were suffering under the blockade and losing faith in their leaders. Censorship of letters and

1 'Combed' refers to men who had been in reserved occupations or otherwise exempted from conscription but whose cases were re-assessed and combed by the authorities. Like the recruits, they had had little or no military training.

2 Lieutenant-Colonel A. P. Scotland, *The London Cage*, London, p. 38.

3 Sir George Aston, *Secret Service*, London, p. 255.

postcards from home seems to have been unaccountably lax on the German side.

As well as letters, the diaries of German soldiers were eagerly sought not only for the details they recorded but because, according to Major-General Thwaites: 'The German soldier always wrote down the names of his leaders in his diary, especially the names of his corps and divisional commanders.'[1] Once these names were known it was a simple step to recognize which division he served in, which was a contribution to the build-up of the Order of Battle. Maintaining a diary seems to have been a universal habit amongst German soldiers, and the damage resulting from these falling into Allied hands was serious enough for the German command to try and break it. Kirke recorded in his own diary that the 'Germans have prohibited diaries owing to the amount of information given to the enemy by them.'[2]

Items of enemy uniform and equipment were also of use in building up the picture of the enemy's Order of Battle: distinctive German shoulder straps, or field caps with a man's name and regiment inside were keenly sought by Intelligence as a means of identifying enemy units. The men who had to retrieve these articles were not always so keen. Personal papers and items of uniform could be taken from the bodies of enemy dead, but even this was not as easy as it sounds. It usually involved going over the top and thereby being exposed to the enemy's fire and it is unsurprising to find this task was not always performed as conscientiously as might have been desired.

A common experience was that of Leading Seaman Murray during the Battle of the Ancre in November 1916. Murray was in charge of a section of Lewis guns in advance of the main body of the infantry, and which destroyed a German counter-attack. Murray was instructed to take a small party forward to secure identifications from the dead Germans. Describing the haste with which this was accomplished, Murray recounts:

> You'd pick, because you were in the open, and in a minute you expected to be fired on, so what you did was to grab hold of anything, you know, you grabbed hold of his cap if you could find it . . . that would have been something, you see. This haste was fully justified since this was done in broad daylight! Broad daylight! So there, you see, we

1 Kirke Papers, loc. cit., Major-General Sir William Thwaites, 'The Roll (sic) of forward troops in the Collection of Intelligence in the Field'.
2 Kirke Diaries, op. cit., 10 May 1916.

> were walking about in the open and we weren't very pleased about it, you know.[1]

As Rackham explains: 'We were always told to get anything of value, get hold of it and send it back.'[2] Despite the risks, soldiers would often hunt for souvenirs, pocketing items of enemy uniform and equipment to sell to non-combatant soldiers in the rear areas, like the Army Service Corps or Royal Army Medical Corps, or to bear them home as trophies to their families. Consequently, Intelligence never had the opportunity to assess such findings. Apart from the Order of Battle, much of what was found was of little value to Intelligence, but it had to be collected nonetheless, for amongst the dross there might be one or two nuggets of gold, the pieces of information that justified the time, the effort and the risks, as was the case in February 1918 when the discovery of a new-issue gas mask helped Intelligence to determine the date and location of the German spring offensive. Such a coup was, however, a rare event. Most of the Intelligence gained thereby could do nothing to help the men in the line overcome their immediate problems. The documents, diaries, letters *et al* had to be taken back to Intelligence HQ and accurately translated, a time-consuming process which effectively ruled out any attempt to capitalize on the information in the short term.

Lieutenant-Colonel Richard Meinertzhagen, DSO, developed an unusual system of field Intelligence when he was in charge of the military Intelligence in East Africa and Palestine, known by its initials – DPM. Meinertzhagen perversely kept their true meaning to himself and even today's Intelligence Corps do not know what DPM was or how it worked, dearly though they would like to find out. Meinertzhagen gave a tantalizingly brief description of his brainchild in his published *Army Diary*, where he also explains why he kept it such a secret:

> My best agents who came and went into German East Africa were intelligent Swahilis, many with Arab blood in them. My method was easy, reliable and inexpensive. It was known as DPM and so far as I know has never been used by anyone else nor do I intend to disclose a system which might easily be used against us. I also found that the contents of German officers' latrines were a constant source of filthy though accurate information as odd pieces of paper containing mes-

1 Murray interview, loc. cit.
2 Rackham interview, loc. cit.

> sages, notes on enciphering and decoding, and private letters were often used where lavatory paper did not exist. I continued to use DPM in the Sinai campaign and for many years after I left the Army I used it in connection with my 'other work' not only in this country but abroad. So simple, so cheap and so accurate.[1]

Meinertzhagen comes across as a straightforward and honourable individual who had no time for fools and was additionally blessed with an uncanny streak of cunning which he employed to splendid effect in his career as an Intelligence officer. He balanced an inclination for derring-do with a fine and accurate judgement which was repeatedly proved right throughout his life, much to the consternation of his enemies and critics. Tall and athletically built, Meinertzhagen might have stepped straight from the pages of the *Boy's Own Paper* as a role model for British youth. He was at once one of the most colourful and brilliant soldiers in the King's service and a man of shrewdness and insight with the reputation of being an Intelligence officer of exceptional ability and above average ingenuity and foresight. A confidential report by the head of Intelligence on the Western front in late 1918, Brigadier-General G. S. Clive, said of him:

> This officer has only served with me for three months, but three weeks would have more than sufficed to have formed an opinion of his capabilities which are most exceptional. Wide experience and far-sightedness, good organizing talent and rapidity of grasp, with an exceptional instinct for any special Intelligence work, are his characteristics. I should have no hesitation in giving him charge of the widest Intelligence Organization in the Army.

Meinertzhagen's commander-in-chief in Palestine, Field-Marshal Allenby, paid handsome tribute, too, writing in his confidential report on Meinertzhagen that, 'This officer has been largely responsible for my successes in Palestine.' Nevertheless Meinertzhagen's criticism of his chief's policies cost him his job as Chief Political Officer in Palestine after the war, when he dared to condemn Lord Allenby's conduct of the post-war administration of the conquered territories. Field-Marshal Lord Wavell who, as a staff officer was a party to the proceedings, left his own account of Meinertzhagen's dismissal, relating how Meinertzhagen showed the letter he had written to the Foreign Office to a friend who advised him that Allenby would never

1 Meinertzhagen *Army Diary*, op. cit., p. 127.

permit such criticism by one of his staff. Meinertzhagen, Wavell tells us, agreed,

> . . . but persisted in what he held to be his duty. His dismissal was even swifter than the friend had prophesied, and followed immediately on Allenby seeing the letter. But Meinertzhagen had no fear of Allenby and always met him on equal terms. 'I suppose you realize that you would have had to give your housemaid longer notice,' was his only comment. Allenby laughed, and they parted friends.[1]

An honest and exceptionally capable extrovert, who was both able and willing to accept formidable responsibilities which would have crushed lesser men, Meinertzhagen proved the ideal choice for some singularly delicate missions. In February and March 1910 he was charged with the mission of discovering details of a new fort being built at Sebastopol. Despite being closely watched by the Russian counter-espionage service he successfully penetrated the fort and extracted the required information; his report was of such high calibre that he was in demand to undertake further missions of this nature, demands which he resisted, as he felt his memory was not good enough to make him a successful secret agent.

Meinertzhagen refers to DPM several times in his *Army Diary* without disclosing too many details and his unpublished diary, kept under restricted access in Oxford, sheds no further light on it. Apparently DPM worked best when the opposing armies were in close proximity and employed both scouts and agents:

> Now that we are in close contact with the enemy, my DPM service produces rapid and accurate results, so much so that I am often in receipt of information and enemy orders before German officers receive them.[2]

Given that DPM produced such good results when in close touch with the enemy, and remembering Meinertzhagen's statement cited earlier referring to documents used as lavatory paper, it may be that his only biographer to date, John Lord, was correct in guessing that the initials stood for 'Dirty Paper Method'.[3] On the other hand, this argument contains a significant weakness in that Meinertzhagen's own description stated that 'I *also* found that the contents of German

1 Field-Marshal Lord Wavell, *Allenby in Egypt*, London, 1943, (Vol. II of *Allenby: A Study in Greatness*), p. 33.

2 Meinertzhagen *Army Diary*, op cit., p. 188.

3 *See* John Lord, *Duty, Honour, Empire: Life And Times Of Colonel Richard Meinertzhagen*, London, 1971.

officers' latrines . . .', the word 'also' indicating quite plainly that 'dirty paper' was only part of the story. Meinertzhagen keeps us guessing just as much as he kept the Germans guessing.

And what of the value of information from prisoners? Was it merely restricted to the building up of the enemy's Orders of Battle or could they influence the struggle more directly? Tactical information not available from any other source *was* disclosed by prisoners, varying from such minor details as the position of shelters for the garrison of the Railway Triangle strongpoint on the Western front in 1915, to the revelation that the Bulgarians were expecting General Milne's offensive on the Doiran front at Salonika in April 1917. Regrettably, this offensive was not postponed; it was decided that preparations were too far advanced to permit any alteration in the timetable and the offensive was in any case tied to the French Army's larger attack. The artillery barrage, however, was altered to catch the Bulgarians as they clambered from their dugouts to man their battered trenches, but that was not enough to prevent the great assault being turned into still another bloody shambles where ridiculously small gains were made in return for a horrifyingly high number of casualties.

The timing and location of many major enemy offensives were also disclosed by prisoners and deserters, but the information gained was not always acted upon; frequently it was regarded as doubtful. Based on information obtained from interrogation, the British were able to give warning to the French of the impending German attack on Verdun in February 1916, but the French, complacent senior partners in the alliance, discounted the news. The initial German assault came dangerously near to breaking through their lines, which only held because of the magnificent heroism of the French infantry who, though hopelessly outnumbered, threw themselves at the Germans in costly counter-attacks and forced the German leaders to halt the advance; a case of the fighting man's valour redeeming the sins of his leaders. The German gas attack at Ypres in 1915 was also revealed by prisoners, but nobody had any conception of gas warfare and the warnings meant nothing to the commanders. In Italy the Central Powers' grand offensive at Caporetto was warned of in advance by Austrian prisoners, but the Italian command placed too much confidence in the staying power of their battle-weary troops, whose morale collapsed irrespective of Intelligence in the face of assault by well-trained and hardened German troops.

The Germans indisputably took the danger of prisoners revealing too much about their intentions seriously, even to the extent of solemnly warning their soldiers that the Allies brutally maltreated prisoners and even killed them, whether they gave information or not. In fact this lie backfired badly on the German command, since captured Germans were so surprised and disarmed by finding themselves well treated that many of them said more than they would otherwise. The Germans resorted to different methods to safeguard the secrecy of their great offensive in the spring of 1918, ensuring that British raiding parties could capture no prisoners of any value during the build-up by holding their front line with poor quality units whose men would not go over the top when the day came and whose personnel were kept in calculated ignorance of all the moves behind the lines which heralded Germany's last great effort. Then again, in a deliberate bid to foil raiders, new and unusual tactics were adopted, for 'The German policy seems to have been to scuttle to the rear as soon as a British raiding party was detected and leave the front line empty.'[1] In general, however, as Marshall-Cornwall summed up the situation in his typically tight and accurate language:

> The German private soldier knew remarkably little about anything except his own unit in the front line and they rarely had any information about any reserve troops in their rear so it was all very localized information we got from captured prisoners.[2]

Of more immediate value even than the Order of Battle, which was essentially the province of the Staffs and the high command, would be information about the timing and route of a relief, details about the movement of ration parties, or about the trench lines on the other side of no-man's-land. This could be extremely detailed, revealing the locations of hitherto unknown machine-gun posts, trench mortars, dugouts and Observation Posts, all of which would be prime targets for the artillery in the event of an offensive. On occasions a prisoner might yield such a crop of valuable information that he would be subjected to a further, more searching interrogation by officers from GHQ. John Charteris, Haig's head of Intelligence, tells us that:

> Most of the information which the prisoner has is information in detail regarding the enemy defensive works on his immediate front. To

1 Martin Middlebrook, *The Kaiser's Battle*, London, 1978, p. 188.
2 Marshall-Cornwall interview, loc cit.

extract this information from him requires time. It is sometimes necessary to take the prisoner back in the front line trenches, or to Observation Posts and almost always necessary to examine him with the assistance of aeroplane photographs.[1]

A great variety of other potentially valuable information could be derived from prisoners but much of it, again, was of greater value to the Staff with its broad outlook and its concentration fixed rather on the grand sweep of events than on the men trapped in the mire of the trenches. A prisoner could be a valuable yardstick to assess the morale of his own particular unit, and prisoners from numerous parts of the front would mirror the general state of feeling in the ranks of an army, together with some indication of the temperature of opinion on the home front. Broadly speaking, a prisoner's morale can be said to be low if he parts readily with information, but if he clams up and renders nothing more than his name, rank and number, then he is still prepared to do his duty and if so his morale is sound. Prisoners prepared to do their duty were the men Intelligence had to reduce, for the object of interrogation is to persuade a prisoner to talk about the subjects of the interrogator's choice. A prisoner of war is entirely at the mercy of his captors and enjoys nothing like the same protection under law as, for instance, a police suspect or witness. The British Army employed several methods of breaking a prisoner's resistance, ranging from threats of violence to what was in effect seduction. Meinertzhagen says of this latter:

> When [the prisoner was] brought in front of me I would dismiss the escort, offer the man a chair and then give him a cigarette and drink of either tea, coffee or beer. Only on one occasion did a German officer not only refuse to sit down but refused refreshments, glaring at me with hatred in his eyes, standing to attention the whole time. But he was an exception. I would then start asking them about their home, when they joined up, their families and their home life, slowly drifting into their Army life, what actions they had fought, what they thought of our Army, finally touching on the beastliness of war. By then the man was usually talkative and friendly. If you want to get the truth out of a man, the important thing is to start him talking. Do not start shooting a lot of leading questions; let him do the talking. Do not attempt to take notes and if he says something of importance do not at once jot it down; remember it as though it was of no importance.

1 Papers of Brigadier-General J. A. Charteris [hereinafter Charteris Papers], 'Lecture On Intelligence', 4 February 1916, ICMA.

> I have seen many interrogations of prisoners carried out in a rough, bullying manner. It does not pay. It might do so with an Arab or Egyptian, but not with a German.[1]

This seductive method was common throughout the Army by the later stages of the First World War, but it was not adopted until a whole range of other techniques had been employed with little success. The greatest problem in 1914 was that nobody had any training in the study and practice of interrogation techniques, since there was no standing Intelligence Corps in the Army to concern itself with them; a state of affairs which lingered until the establishment between 1916 and 1917 of the Intelligence Corps' schools at Harrow and Belgravia. Until then interrogation techniques, if they could be called such, remained at the whim or fancy of the officer conducting the interrogation.

Thus, according to Captain Tuohy, the method in 1915 was to sit opposite the prisoner with a sheaf of papers and try to undermine his confidence by pretending that the prisoner was of no account, studying the papers as if he was not there, then proceeding to question him as a solicitor would question a man on trial. Of course, this automatically put the prisoner on his guard with the result that nothing useful was obtained. Bullying tactics were the next weapon in the Intelligence armoury:

> There was the examining officer who favoured terrorism. This gentleman would come into the torture chamber, clamp down a couple of revolvers on the table, swill off a whisky and soda, scowl at his victim, and then start barking. This system rapidly fell into disuse.[2]

A prisoner's natural uncertainty was put to good use by the officers of British Intelligence, and by mid-1916 the manner advocated by Meinertzhagen was developing. Marshall-Cornwall, who interrogated hundreds of Germans in his career, tells how a prisoner's guard was undermined:

> Of course they always expected, prisoners when they were captured, to be badly treated, but our Intelligence officers were trained to treat them very pleasantly, gave them a cigarette to smoke and so on, and gradually drew them out and got very good information from them, and

1 Meinertzhagen *Army Diary*, op. cit., p. 226.

2 Captain F. Tuohy, *The Secret Corps, A Tale of 'Intelligence' On All Fronts*, London, 1920, p. 258.

> of course our best information came from Alsatian deserters, but on the whole, when the German prisoners found they were being well treated they would give away the information very freely as far as they knew it.[1]

Nevertheless, although the new broom swept the interrogation chamber nicely, there were still some cobwebs and pockets of dirt lurking in nooks and crannies. These usually came to light at the front line, where immediate information was needed urgently to save lives and where there was neither the time nor the inclination to fall back upon the sort of finesse that could be used at headquarters. One German who fell into British hands in 1918 was interrogated by a British major within minutes of being captured. The major was anxious to locate a German artillery battery, but his prisoner had not seen the guns and so could not furnish the information. The major then adopted different tactics and, drawing his revolver, said: 'Now I'm going to count to three and if you don't tell me by the time I get to three, I'm going to shoot you. That's all – I must know.'

The prisoner remained dumb as the major started counting. 'One . . . two . . .' and lifted his revolver: 'Now tell me before I come to three.'

The prisoner, a rifleman called Dan, was, in his own words 'frightened to death', wondering whether the major would adhere to the code or kill him. The major, getting no response, put his revolver back and closed the interrogation with the words. 'Oh, he's a good soldier. Take him away.'[2]

Lest it be thought that this was an isolated case, or exaggerated, the diary of D. H. Doe records that:

> Last night a German walked into our lines with a sack of rations and thought he had reached his *own* front line. He was one of a ration party, is about 5ft nothing high and won't say a single word so no information from him until – ! (We have a certain way!)[3]

Between the extremes of bullying and seduction lay another method, one in which the prisoner was asked short simple questions requiring short simple answers, often answers which the prisoner was aware were already known to his interrogators. It is difficult to dissemble in

1 Marshall-Cornwall interview, loc. cit.
2 Conversation as reported to Horace Barks by a German friend captured by the British in 1918.
3 Diary of D. H. Doe, Royal Engineers (Signals), 30 July 1917, IWM.

the face of such questioning, for the awareness that much of the information is already known sharply undercuts the inclination to remain dumb. Each answer given by the prisoner gradually restricts his further options for deceit since, having given answers to some questions, he can hardly backtrack without revealing himself as a liar. He has to abide by the earlier answers given and each answer, even if monosyllabic, builds up a momentum which is difficult to resist. A framework is thus established which controls subsequent answers and reveals weaknesses in the prisoner's resistance which can then be pressed.

Examples of this form of interrogation are provided by both Tuohy and Marshall-Cornwall. Tuohy states that the interrogators would concentrate on questions like: 'To what regiment do you belong?' 'What line does your regiment hold?' 'What are the regiments on the left and right of your regiment?' 'What troops are in support?' 'What troops are in reserve?'[1] Marshall-Cornwall says: 'Those captured in trench raids were questioned as to what unit they belonged to, what was its strength and morale, how long they served in the front line before being relieved, what their rations were like, and what units were on their flanks.'[2] In this process the first question was always about identity. The question: 'Who are you?' could not easily be ignored by the prisoner, since he was aware that his identity was already known from his documents and identity tag. Once this question was answered the prisoner could be nobody but himself – his range of options was narrowed and the process had begun. In addition, the prisoner was interrogated in isolation, which placed him at a psychological disadvantage. Then: 'Let them suppose that a great deal more is known by the questioner about the enemy than possibly is the case, and that questions are being put merely with a view to seeing whether they are speaking the truth or not, the answer being known.'[3]

The utility of this tactic was confirmed by Major-General Hotblack, then a captain in Intelligence: 'The efficiency of intelligence personnel, in all roles, but particularly in the examination of prisoners, depends directly upon the knowledge that Intelligence personnel already possesses', and, 'At whatever stage prisoners were examined,

1 Tuohy, op. cit., p. 254.
2 Marshall-Cornwall interview, loc. cit.
3 *Field Service Pocket Book, 1914*, op. cit., p. 14.

success always depended upon the amount of information that the Intelligence Corps' officer already possessed.'[1] In this context it is worth noting that today's Intelligence Corps uses a Hotblack motto: 'The more you know . . . the more you will find out.' If a prisoner lied, an officer with accurate information could immediately trap him, which was invariably demoralizing for the captive.

The value of interrogating prisoners as soon as possible after capture was soon discovered. Apart from the prospect of wringing information of immediate value from men brought in fresh from the fight, the knowledge that prisoners would still be shaken and disorientated from the experience of battle and fearful of their treatment as prisoners meant that there was a discernible advantage in questioning them before they could regain their composure. The state of shock and fear that all save a few hardy souls underwent on a major battlefield was quite enough to unhinge all but the most steel-willed, and British Military Intelligence utilized this fact to the full.

Richard Meinertzhagen was anxious to impress the policy of immediate interrogation on all his subordinates, explaining that:

> When in East Africa I soon learned the importance of questioning prisoners immediately they are captured. When a prisoner is captured he is frightened, he does not know what is going to happen to him, what sort of treatment he may get, in fact the German African soldiers and the Turks expected physical ill-treatment if not death. They would be most anxious to please and answer questions which after twenty-four hours' captivity, a good meal and a night's sleep they would refuse to answer. I impressed this method on all Intelligence officers and the results were striking. Most German officers refused to talk at all, very few did. Most Turkish officers would talk within a few hours of capture, but once they had recovered from shock they would become obstinately silent or would excel themselves by lying.[2]

So eager were Intelligence to take advantage of this state of shock that, according to the Official Historian of the Canadian Intelligence Corps, on one occasion an interrogation was even carried out over the telephone.[3] Generally, where large numbers of prisoners were taken in major battles, battalion Intelligence officers would ask each of them a few quick questions about immediate tactical matters, then pass the

1 Papers of Major-General. F. E. Hotblack, ICMA.
2 Meinertzhagen *Army Diary*, op. cit., pp. 220-21.
3 Elliot, op. cit., p. 40.

prisoners back through divisional and corps headquarters for further interrogation.

The emotions of the prisoner had usually been affected to such an extent by the sights and sounds of battle followed by captivity rather than death or injury, that he was vulnerable despite his will to stand firm. His circumstances had suddenly and dramatically altered, he was in a frightening and abnormal environment where he was completely at the mercy of the enemy. Not only was he emotionally battered but he was alone and without the support he normally enjoyed from his group and its hierarchy, a factor which contributed substantially to his impaired resistance. Interrogators who exploit the emotions as opposed to the intellect, and who use the often unwitting compliance of the person being interrogated, are those who achieve the best results.

Occasionally a prisoner's nationality provided additional leverage, and given the national divisions within the Central Empires, there were many opportunities. Thus Jews and Arabs captured from the Turks were usually willing to co-operate, as were many of the Slavs in the Austro-Hungarian Army. As for the Germans, 'there were still a good many prejudices within the German Army, which could be exploited in conversation: Prussians despised all the others: Bavarians didn't think much of Württembergers or Saxons.'[1] The subject races of the German Empire were usually prepared to co-operate, Alsatians, Lorrainers and Poles in particular. Woolrych observed that:

> Some prisoners were patriotically dumb, some just dumb, while others of subject races – e.g. Poles and Alsatians – almost glad to give information. On the strength of a Pole interrogated at the Indian HQ in August 1915 we published a report of 3 closely printed pages on his information, together with 5 appendices containing 4 maps and 2 diagrams.[2]

Beyond exploiting the national or political divisions within the enemy states, individual reactions to interrogation were still a subjective matter, albeit one which might be influenced by variable factors such as physical debilitation due to food shortage or strain from recent fighting. Meinertzhagen showed how impossible it was to generalize about the response of prisoners in this game of cat and mouse, for each

1 Woolrych Papers, loc. cit.
2 Ibid.

prisoner was still an individual in his own right irrespective of the uniform he was wearing, and as such he still remained unique:

> German soldiers varied; some sullen and unbending, other bursting into tears when persuaded to talk about their homes, others desperately anxious to please – but they seldom knew very much outside their unit, its morale, discipline, relation with officers, etc. German officers were a very different proposition unless very young. Some said: 'I fear I cannot enter into any conversation with you.' Others remained perfectly silent; but a few would open out and talk.[1]

German officers were the hardest nuts of all to crack. Bound by principles of honour and loyalty inspired by their oath, their background and the knowledge of what was expected of them, they habitually clammed up when face to face with the interrogators. As Woolrych ruefully admitted, 'officers were practically no good. You wouldn't stand much chance of getting much out of an officer.'[2]

More subtle techniques could be employed if direct methods of interrogation failed. For sheer cynical manipulation of a prisoner's sense of security, a ruse practised by Captain A. P. Scotland would be difficult to better. Scotland was surprised to find an Oberleutnant Kastel from Gibeon in German South West Africa (today's Namibia) amongst a batch of prisoners. As it happened, Scotland himself had lived in the Protectorate before the war and had actually inveigled his way into the German Army there and done a little discreet spying for the British. Far more importantly, he knew Gibeon and was distantly acquainted with Kastel's parents. It was an easy job to disarm Kastel by arranging for a hut with a glowing stove, tea, toast and jam to be set aside for a friendly conversation. The chat opened by turning on the prisoner's home and family and soon the relaxed and cheerful Kastel was talking freely about all manner of things, unaware that Scotland was surreptitiously guiding the conversation and that four men with notebooks and pencils were hidden around the hut noting down all that was said.[3]

A more usual ruse was the employment of a stool-pigeon, either a Briton in enemy uniform or, more usually, a renegade German, planted amongst the prisoners to direct their conversation – to forthcoming operations, losses, rations, morale or politics – which

1 Meinertzhagen *Army Diary*, op. cit., p. 227.
2 Woolrych interview, loc. cit.
3 Scotland, op. cit., pp. 46-8.

would then be picked up by concealed microphones. The 'pigeon' would appear to be a sympathetic listener in whom the prisoners could confide and for this reason they were most successful when used before the shock of battle had worn off and the men were less on their guard. It was essential that the 'pigeon' was conversant with German dialects and army routine, and for these reasons renegade Germans were the best stool-pigeons. Meinertzhagen used such a renegade, a German naval lieutenant who deserted to the British in 1914 and was disguised 'with a red beard and dark glasses and he gladly lived in the prisoner of war camp near Nairobi where he was most useful in extracting information from fellow prisoners'. The renegade was Baron von Maydell, whom Meinertzhagen deemed 'an utter worm' – dealings with him were 'most unsavoury'.[1] Maydell continued to render his new masters sterling service until the Germans discovered what was going on and warned their troops to have nothing to do with him if they were captured. The British rewarded Maydell by giving him a false identity and allowing him to emigrate to the United States.

Wounded men were also interrogated if no unwounded ones were available. Marshall-Cornwall said of this:

> We used to catch them when they were in the casualty clearing stations, and after a big raid and if there were wounded in the casualty clearing station the divisional or corps' Intelligence Officer would be sent to the casualty clearing station to interrogate them, and the prisoners being well treated as they were, they generally were quite forthcoming with what information they could give us.

However, it was not standard practice to interrogate the wounded:

> I think the information we got from wounded was comparatively little, as we generally brought back from these raids only walking people who were unwounded, and so we concentrated on them rather than on the wounded ones.[2]

Deserters, naturally enough, proved to be amongst the most valuable prisoners. This was especially so before any major enemy attack – part of the intelligence the British acquired about the German spring

1 Meinertzhagen *Army Diary*, op. cit., p. 187, and Diaries op. cit., Vol. 17, 12 May 1916, p. 36.
2 Marshall-Cornwall interview, loc. cit.

offensive of 1918 was betrayed to them by deserters. As Kirke says, 'It is a fact that most of the big attacks were given away by deserters.'[1]

The War Diaries of the First Army[2] reveal that 66 deserters came over to that Army in the course of the war; of these one was from Lorraine, two were Polish and eight were Alsatian. The Diaries do not give the deserters' nationality in every case, so it might be reasonable to assume that other deserters were also from the subject races. Even on the basis of the quoted figures, one-sixth, or over 16 per cent, were from the subject races, a figure far in excess of the proportion of troops from these races serving in the German Army.

Few accounts of the interrogations of prisoners and deserters have survived the attention of the weeders who examine all documents before they are passed to the Public Record Office. Few official documents dealing with Intelligence have escaped them and come into the public sphere but occasionally documents do pass their guard. Among the War Diaries of the Second Army appears the examination of a German deserter, Paul Sacksteder of the 4th Bavarian Infantry Regiment, reproduced in full in Appendix I.[3] It covers in detail all the elements seen to matter in interrogation: the Order of Battle, morale and defensive works and a useful miscellany of minor information which might or might not have proved valuable, depending on circumstances. The name of the interrogating officer was Captain James Marshall-Cornwall.

Contact Intelligence showed itself to be superior to surveillance techniques not only in respect of the information acquired, but in terms of the frequency and consistency with which it delivered the goods. What it could not do, of course, was to deliver the marvellous victory at a single stroke that statesmen and soldiers alike were seeking. Contact Intelligence did not provide a means to win the war, least of all in one blow; it could only chart the decline of German fighting power and follow the movements of German troops. What it could not do was to disarm those troops or force them to throw in the towel. Thus it was a reactive rather than an initiatory form of Intelligence: it followed the course of the war rather than led it, and so it was a long-drawn-out, costly business, like the war itself.

1 Kirke Papers, loc. cit., 'Lecture on Secret Service', 27 November 1925.
2 First Army War Diary, PRO (WO 95/154-184).
3 Second Army War Diary, PRO (WO 95/278).

FOUR

Oh, What a Specialized War

WHEN people are confronted by some unexpected development they are faced with a choice over the way they deal with it: generally they either grouse but accept it with a bad grace or they regard it as a challenge, an opportunity, and look to see how they can make the best of it. A smaller number may even try to ignore it. In the new industrialized warfare with which the British Army was now confronted, a bewildering array of scientific developments was hastily pressed onto a suitably bewildered General Staff which had to decide not only whether or not to use them but also how to gain the maximum benefit from any measure they did adopt. All too often these decisions had to be made without experience and the new measures employed without trained men. The Intelligence service was as raw as any other in this regard and it seems surprising that its initial forays have rarely been surveyed by historians of the First World War, and only occasionally signposted as they pass in search of the big game of decisions reached or disasters borne on the battlefields.

Macdonogh compared Intelligence to a man groping in the dark, a blind man trying to feel his way by a stick in contact Intelligence. But blind men do not just rely on their sticks to tell them of obstacles or dangers – they also have their ears, and often the hearing of a blind man will sharpen astonishingly to compensate in some small way for his loss of sight. So too did the Intelligence branch of the British Army try to use their ears to help find a way forward and compensate for their restricted vision. Wireless interception, codes, ciphers and listening sets became (for a time) as vital as maps and the Order of Battle in the fight to gain advantage over the enemy.

That is not, of course, the whole story. There was a more active part to play, in wrong-footing the enemy by confusing his own eyes and ears so that he would fall flat on his face. The fertile province of deception and press surveillance fell into the purview of Intelligence and more than ever revealed a need for special training and for men out of a different mould.

Specialized fields need specialists to cultivate them if they are to yield a profit. By their very nature specialists are not common and this is nowhere more clearly demonstrated than in a modern mass war. During the First World War men had to be trained as specialists in technology that was sometimes subject to change in a matter of months. Men were drawn into this unstable world by a form of lucky dip, sometimes from an appropriate civilian background but more often than not plucked from fighting units with little attention paid to their fitness for the task ahead of them, chiefly because so little was known about that task.

The first two years of the war, characterized by the brutal and unforeseen birth of trench warfare and the British Army's first faltering attempts to find its feet in the world of prolonged slaughter, saw adventurous spirits crawl across the scarred and blasted expanse of no-man's-land and, from the edge of the enemy's wire, listen to what the men in his trenches might be saying. It was all in the best traditions of public school, a daring prank to be played on the neighbouring dorm – but a prank where machine guns and starshells supplanted house-masters and prefects in grim earnest. Little was gained by these nocturnal escapades since the usual booty would consist of no more than a German NCO bellowing at some hapless working party, or German soldiers chatting about their families. Marshall-Cornwall's success in reaching the enemy's trench on the Messines Ridge was qualified by the admission that 'on one occasion' he got near enough to hear the enemy talking, which suggests that this was an event so rare that it warranted inclusion in a memoir full of far more important incidents.[1] Perhaps even more significant was the fact that Marshall-Cornwall could distinguish which part of Germany the speakers came from by their dialect, something which only a linguist with exceptional ability could achieve. Marshall-Cornwall was qualified as a first-class interpreter in German, French, Norwegian, Swedish, Dutch and Italian. There simply were not enough men of this calibre to make such hazardous eavesdropping either frequent or profitable.

Wireless was in its infancy in 1914, as was the encoding of wireless messages. Marshall-Cornwall explained with his habitual precision that, 'Wireless information was not much use, it was rather in its infancy and we got very little information through intercepted radio messages either in clear or in code.'[2]

1 Marshall-Cornwall, op. cit., p. 19.
2 Marshall-Cornwall interview, loc. cit.

The disastrous Russian attack on East Prussia in 1914 was not only characterized by confusion, bad blood between the commanders of the Russian First and Second Armies, and the general inefficiency and backwardness of the Tsarist Empire, but by the appalling fact that the Russians transmitted all their wireless messages in clear, which enabled the Germans to read and use this unexpected bonus to engineer the catastrophic defeat of the Second Army at Tannenberg. Less well-known is the fact that the Germans were also sending wireless messages without code, which the Allies were just as delighted to read. Wireless intercepts materially affected the course and outcome of the fighting on the Eastern front and thereby the story of humanity ever since. While Intelligence derived from aerial observation and captured documents did admittedly play a major role in the defeat of Germany's bid for early victory in the west, that was by no means the whole story, part of which still lies hidden amongst the most secret recesses of French Intelligence archives. The tight-lipped Marshal Joffre once made the revealing remark that, 'German wireless stations were one of our most precious sources of information',[1] a statement which, coming from a man notoriously chary of disclosing his sources of information, speaks volumes about the decision to redeploy the French Army for the Battle of the Marne.

The BEF might not have discovered anything as important from wireless intercepts, but useful information was so secured and on one occasion it saved the BEF from disaster. While the decision was being reached on the Marne, GHQ were receiving the content of wireless messages between the German cavalry divisions of von der Marwitz and von Richthofen, all sent in clear and completely oblivious of the fact that they were being read by the enemy. At this stage, with the Germans beginning the retreat which was to herald four years of trench-bound slaughter, the messages were both revealing and highly encouraging. The Official Historian commented that:

> According to a wireless message intercepted on the 11th September, the German 2nd and 9th Cavalry Divisions were south west and south east of Soissons, on the night of the 10th/11th, their horses exhausted and their movement blocked by transport. The French XVIII Corps reported that the German retreat in front of it was nearly a rout; otherwise there was no definite information.[2]

1 Terraine, op. cit., p. 103, citing Joffre's *Memoirs*, Vol. 1, p. 289.
2 Edmonds, op. cit., 1914, Vol. 1, p. 315.

Far more vital proved to be the messages intercepted during the First Battle of Ypres, the grave of the 'Old Contemptibles'. The BEF had advanced into Flanders expecting to find a clear road by which it could fall on the German flank. Having ignored the Intelligence reports delivered by the painstaking and extremely precise Macdonogh, GHQ marched the men headlong into what seemed numberless hordes of Germans who, like the British, had been expecting to find an open flank through which they could march to triumph. The resulting battle wore out the old BEF, lasting over a month during which the outnumbered and outgunned line of khaki was only held by putting dismounted cavalrymen into the line to fight as infantry and even, on occasion, by scraping together all sorts of oddments from the rear of the Army – cooks, clerks, transport drivers and signallers, men who would not normally be expected to come within rifle-shot of the enemy. With such slender reserves the BEF had reason on more than one occasion to be thankful for its wireless intercepts. On the cold, grey morning of 29 October the German XXVII Reserve Corps rose from their jumping-off places at 5.30 a.m., their leaders confident of the knock-out blow which would finally dispose of the interfering British. German military Intelligence had indicated the British line between Kruiseecke and Gheluvelt as an ideal target, being thinly held and lacking reserves. So it had been the day before, but the Germans had made the mistake of transmitting their orders to the XXVII Reserve Corps by wireless. The message had been picked up by the British who were just able to scramble troops from other parts of the line to the threatened point. Of less direct but equal importance was the fact that intercepts gave GHQ the priceless gift of knowing the condition of the German forces facing them: knowledge of the exhaustion of the new Reserve Corps the Germans had pitched into the battle at the very beginning enabled the British to reduce their own troops and send the men to parts of the line where they were really needed.[1]

These life-saving successes at Ypres were won by the Army's first-ever Interception Station, established in September, a bare month before the battle which was to bring it close to the heart of military Intelligence; an improved version, the Compass Wireless Station, was introduced in October, manned and operated by the Signals Branch of the Royal Engineers rather than the Intelligence section. A line of

1 Ibid., Vol II, p. 387.

these stations was established behind the battlefront and bearings were taken on enemy transmitting stations, the point where two or more bearings intersected giving the enemy location. Each enemy station had an association call-sign with the formation it was serving. Reading the call-signs disclosed the location of the formation, a means of monitoring changes of disposition and therefore the enemy's Order of Battle.

The success of these stations proved to be their swan-song, both sides realizing the dangers of uncoded wireless transmissions and call signs. Signals were no longer sent *en clair* and strict discipline was enforced to ensure that progressively fewer signals were made. By early 1917 the British had succeeded in breaking the German wireless code (*see* Chapter 6), but this apparently fruitful breakthrough was rendered nearly useless since the German transmitters retaliated by remaining silent except in emergency, when there was never enough time for the men opposing them to capitalize on the information. By the time the message had been decoded, translated, then passed to Intelligence who then passed it to GHQ and the Staff of the Army at the centre of the action, who then had to relay it to forward units by runner, German reserves were already on the spot. The great German retreat to the Hindenburg Line in the spring of 1917 demonstrated the benefit of imposing silence on wireless communication: no message was ever picked up prior to the German withdrawal and the Allied Staffs were caught unprepared. The only wireless intercept I have succeeded in discovering is a brief message dated 17 March 1917, when Fifth Army's Intelligence intercepted a signal to the commander of the German rearguard, which only said: 'Brigade Sector M has been evacuated.'[1] Intelligence could not even be sure what the Germans meant by Brigade Sector M, since a footnote to this brief message reads: 'Sector M apparently [grid reference] N.22.d central to N.29.a.0.1.'

The picture was very different among the dust, stones and heat of Palestine. Here the British were confronting a more backward foe than the Germans, a foe who neither understood the intricacies of encoding nor appreciated the need for wireless silence. The British Intercepting Station, conveniently situated atop the Great Pyramid in Egypt, tuned in to Turkish transmissions and the officer in charge of coding and decoding, the scrupulously dedicated and ingenious

1 Fifth Army War Diary, PRO WO 95/519.

'Cipher' Williams, was able to provide Intelligence with a constant stream of up-to-date information. This paid handsome dividends on a number of occasions but perhaps most importantly in the *annus mirabilis* of 1917, when the men of the Egyptian Expeditionary Force (EEF), following up their great victory in the Third Battle of Gaza, were threatened by a counter-attack devised by the Turks' German commander, the one-time Chief of Germany's Great General Staff, Erich von Falkenhayn. According to Richard Meinertzhagen, then head of the EEF's Intelligence:

> Last night we got Falkenhayn's order for a counter-attack. It was sent out in cipher by wireless from Jerusalem. Von Kress received it but had to have it repeated as he said it was badly mutilated. We deciphered the first message and by this means our troops got the enemy's orders and were able to act on them before the enemy commander himself knew what was expected of him. This must be almost unparalleled in war.[1]

The EEF was able to turn the tables on Falkenhayn and Kress and change their counter-attack from a bright deliverance into a crushing rebuff. There was an interesting sequel to these events when the Turks broadcast their final message from Jerusalem on the eve of its capture, barely a fortnight later. This was also picked up and deciphered by Williams and makes a fitting epitaph to the ruin of Falkenhayn's hopes:

> To Damascus. Important and secret.
>
> Oh Friends. Let us repudiate all our debts. The enemy is in front of us only half an hour from here. Guns are firing and roaring all round us; our ears can hear nothing else. For three and four days fighting has been going on day and night without cessation. This is our last resistance. There is no lack of British aeroplanes over the city. Adieu from Jerusalem.[2]

The supremacy won by the British in wireless interception in Egypt ensured the failure of one of the more unusual exploits of the war. The story begins in 1917 with the German forces in East Africa, fighting a lonely war of raids, ambuscades and long marches through difficult territory. British command of the seas had left the German forces there under von Lettow-Vorbeck in a state of isolation, deprived of

1 Meinertzhagen *Army Diary*, op. cit., p. 225.
2 Ibid.

supplies of every kind; deprivation the Germans overcame only by dint of heroic improvisation and great courage. Imperial Germany hoped to make von Lettow-Vorbeck and his dedicated *askaris* a sharper thorn in the flesh of the British and score a major propaganda coup by sending a Zeppelin laden with supplies on an unprecedented trip from Germany to East Africa. The Zeppelin duly took off with her precious cargo and laboured southwards, actually reaching Africa, but there the ship suddenly turned about and made for home. The usual excuse served up to explain this *volte-face* is that the vessel suffered from engine trouble and had to abandon her daring mission but it is an excuse which lacks conviction, since engine trouble which prevented her from reaching East Africa would surely have prevented her from returning to a safe harbour in Europe.

The true reason for the failure of this audacious mission has long been bound in the secret files of British Intelligence, as Joffre's wireless intercepts were buried in those of French Intelligence: it was the British Intercepting Station on its lofty perch in Egypt which flummoxed the airborne Germans. Meinertzhagen, who was at the centre of these events, takes up the story in his record of a conversation he had with von Lettow-Vorbeck at Bremen in 1926:

> Von Lettow knew nothing at all of the airship which attempted to reach East Africa from Asia Minor via the Sudan. The history of this air ship is interesting. When I was Intelligence Officer to Allenby in Palestine, we got a wire from the War Office saying an airship had left for East Africa. We knew the ship was in wireless communication with Europe and picked up many messages both to and from the ship. Knowing the code we deciphered them. I wired to East Africa warning them, and sent a message out in German code recalling the ship. She returned. She was sighted by us near Sollum both on her way south and on her return trip. It was a very fine effort on the part of the Germans.'[1]

This fascinating information, along with much else, never appeared in any of Meinertzhagen's books – some things remained too secret to be told, since such methods might be used again. But even Meinertzhagen's suberterfuge was not original, for precisely the same thing had been done in 1914 by Naval Intelligence: they sent Admiral von Spee's German East Asia Squadron at Valparaiso a message ordering them to attack the Falkland Islands, whereupon the Germans sailed into the

1 Meinertzhagen Dairies, op. cit., Vol. 27, 1 June 1926, p. 118.

waiting guns of Admiral Sturdee's battlecruisers. To give orders to enemy forces which lead to either their destruction or to the foiling of their designs is to pull the strings with a vengeance. The value of wireless interception was appreciated by Meinertzhagen at an early stage, for when head of Intelligence in East Africa in early 1915, he had protested vehemently against the proposed attack on the German wireless station at Bukoba because he found its emissions so valuable for Intelligence. Alas, he was ignored and a strong raiding party destroyed the station, an act which says much about the myopia of British leaders in East Africa, for while they were desperate to record some sort of success to restore their own faltering reputations, they habitually disregarded Meinertzhagen's original thinking and masterly reports.

Nevertheless, despite a number of important successes, wireless interception never lived up to its early promise. German wariness after 1914 frustrated most British attempts to gain information of real value on the Western front, the front that really mattered.

Listening Posts, of course, studded the front of every army like lamp posts on a street, frequently consisting of one frightened, lonely man marooned in a shell hole with instructions to report on anything he could hear, an experience contrasting dismally with the derring-do of the Marshall-Cornwall breed. Horace Barks, a private in the 1/5th North Staffordshire Regiment, who later became Lord Mayor of Stoke-on-Trent, said of his sojourn in the wastes of no-man's-land: 'They put me out on a listening post that night, and I didn't have a fine lot of instruction, just, if there was anything untoward, if I saw any folks coming, just fire, and then get back ... it was only a bit of a hole in the ground when I was there, and I must have been there most of the night.'[1]

Horace Barks's hole in the ground, however, was quite adequate for the Western front of 1915 when there was an appreciable distance between the wire-bound lines, but not when the lines were so close it was possible to throw a bomb across the intervening space. In the ancient, sun-baked battleground of the Gallipoli Peninsula the Army had to adapt its tactics so that to all intents and purposes listening posts became short extensions of the front line, used at night, 'usually saps which struck out from the main trench, and you would post

1 Conversation with Private Horace Barks, 1/5th North Staffordshire Regiment, 46th (North Midlands) Division, 30 October 1981.

special people, usually a sniper squad, specially trained in rifle shooting and listening.'[1] The sniper squad was the Intelligence Section attached to each battalion, men hand-picked by the Battalion Scout Officer and marked by some outstanding ability. Such sections had been part of every battalion since the post-Boer War reforms. The men received negligible training and had no connection with the Intelligence Corps or Intelligence beyond the most immediate level. Until they underwent special training and were officered, as began to happen in the First World War, their usefulness had been minimal. Rackham's Scout Officer was A. P. Herbert. 'He used to train these chaps, firstly in rifle shooting . . . and then in listening and differentiating ... interpreting the noise, as it were . . . and he was very adept at laying these things on as practice, you know, in training rather than in action, and it was extraordinary how much they did develop.'[2]

It was nevertheless rare for listening posts to detect signs of impending attack, though on two occasions during the Battle of Neuve Chapelle in 1915, an unremarkable encounter amounting to little more than a gesture when set beside the great French offensives of that year, they did stop German counter-attacks in their tracks. The men in one post, near the Port Arthur Salient, heard more than the usual level of noise and movement in the German trenches and were able to warn the troops they were protecting that an attack was in the offing: the 1/39th Gharwal Rifles and 1st Seaforth Highlanders stood-up and the ensuing attack did not even reach the British trenches. Similarly, another German attack directed against the centre and south of Neuve Chapelle village was discovered by a listening post and proved equally unsuccessful. Such events became even less common as the Germans realized what was happening; attacking troops were not moved into the front line until shortly before the attack, and efforts were made to reduce noise. Quite apart from the risk of detection, sudden tactical surprise attacks were rapidly going out of fashion as it became harder to press them home against uncut barbed wire and alert defenders. Attacks would now be preceded by hefty bombardments, just as with trench raids. Sometimes these lasted for days, rendering listening posts obsolete since the enemy's intention was obvious. The steady decline in the value of listening posts,

1 Rackham interview, loc. cit.
2 Ibid.

however, had even more to do with the development and increasing use of listening sets. Officers creeping stealthily up to the enemy's wire or a soldier isolated in a god-forsaken shell crater just might pick up something of value if they were lucky, but that could not compare to listening in to a military conversation when the speakers thought they had complete privacy.

Field telephones were the ideal means of transferring information secretly and rapidly from a static battlefront. Tapping a telephone wire is now an established practice amongst Intelligence services the world over, but between 1914 and 1918 the military Intelligence services needed to be able to listen in without touching the enemy's wire, distanced from them by the trenches. In fact, this very distance, which appeared to pose such difficulties, provided instead a means of access, a means which the Germans, with splendid insight, exploited to the full. The conditions at the front necessitated miles of telephone wire to be laid well forward. In the explosive chaos of the trenches, they were frequently only hastily buried and necessarily lacked any proper earthing. Consequently, conversations held over these wires could be carried some distance by rivers or by barbed wire or by the very ground itself, all vulnerable to any suitably placed listening device.

The Germans were first off the mark with their 'Moritz' listening set. Not only were they able to pick up orders sent to Allied units in the front line, often before the soldiers who had to carry out those orders received them, but they were as a result able to chart the movements of Allied units moving in and out of the line and so build up the Order of Battle, detecting any concentration of troops without risking the dangers of raiding. Many a memoir tells of British units arriving in the front line to be disconcerted by the Germans opposite yelling a welcome: one Highland regiment was angered to see a banner hoisted over the enemy trenches bearing the greeting, 'Hello Scottish bastards'. At first the British suspected the unfortunate and almost entirely loyal civilian population of betraying their positions, but conditions at the front very largely proved that an impossibility. Before long they understood the means at German disposal – the improved 'Moritz II' gave even better results – but lamentably poor telephone discipline at the front did nothing to deprive the Germans of their advantage. Indeed, Colonel Kirke, in charge of the section responsible for defeating 'Moritz', later warned Staff College students that until the middle of 1916 this apparatus had given the Germans more information than every other source put together[1], a statement borne out in the figures supplied by Major-General Thwaites, showing that of 24 unit identifications obtained by the Germans from January to 5 March 1916, 6 had come from prisoners, 1 from interrogation, 3 from dead bodies, 2 from captured equipment, and no fewer than 12 from 'Moritz'.[2] Indeed, the success of 'Moritz' handed the Germans the all-important information they needed about the Allies' main effort on the Somme in 1916 – the date when the troops would go over the top. A great part of the carnage on that disastrous first day of the campaign stemmed directly from bad telephone discipline. One harassed Staff officer of the 34th Division, opposite La Boiselle, feared that the Order of the Day would not reach the infantry in the trenches in time. He decided to take a chance and relay the message by field telephone. It was a disastrous gamble and one taken in defiance of orders forbidding the use of telephones for important messages. The Germans heard the message, with results that are still mourned on every Remembrance Sunday.

This was the culmination of a whole chapter of German successes. As early as February 1916 British Military Intelligence saw the need to emulate 'Moritz', a process begun by adapting sets used experimentally by the French Army. The new sets promised well, picking up telephone conversations at a range of 500, even up to 1000 yards. Messages sent by morse buzzer were audible for several miles. In addition, telephone discipline was more strictly enforced, and the Fullerphone was introduced, which effectively scrambled telephone messages for all except their intended recipient. The difference was shown in practical terms, too, for urgent British counter-measures in the summer of 1916 led to a sharp increase in German raiding. Now German troops were again forced to take precisely the same risks as their British opposite numbers and suffer the losses that raiding inevitably entailed. Kirke made the point to his budding staff officers: 'In 1915 he hardly ever tried to raid, it was unnecessary. The fact that he is constantly trying to do so on this corps front is the best possible proof that our precautions are having effect.'[3]

However, it was not until early May 1916 that British listening sets had become fully operational in the battlezone and even then they

1 Kirke Papers, loc. cit., 'Lectures on Intelligence', 1924.

2 Kirke Papers, loc. cit., Thwaites, 'The Roll (sic) of Forward Troops in the Collection of Intelligence in the Field.' Major-General Thwaites became DMI in 1918.

3 Kirke Papers, loc. cit., 'Lectures on Intelligence', 1924.

became victims of poor staffing. Naturally battalion commanders preferred to retain their best officers and men, and therefore pushed the less good to work on listening sets. Nor were the personnel as yet adequately trained for their new role and reports of their work were damning: 'Dug out bad, sap heads blown in and wires not re-established, accumulators uncharged, no officer been there for 7 weeks. So quite useless, not supervised at all.'[1]

At last GHQ recognized the need for skills and training and as a first step in the process appointed Captain Rathbone as Inspector of Listening Sets in July 1916. Relieved of all other duties, this officer was able to give the listening sets and their problems his full attention but GHQ were forced to admit that one man on his own was not going to be able to wave some sort of magic wand and cause the gremlins to disappear. To give Rathbone the support he needed, his inspectorate was transferred from I(b) to the section responsible for Special Intelligence, I(e), who did have specialist staff and knew who else to consult if they faced a difficult problem. Another belatedly sensible move was to make listening sets subject to the Director of Army Signals, who also had a team of experts to draw on and helped to ensure that men suited to the task by inclination, background and training were henceforth assigned to the sets. Finally, in August, a training school was established at Compagne precisely to meet the section needs.

Towards the end of 1916 the improvement had been good enough for Kirke to note in his diary that results were now 'very encouraging' and to record with glee that '6 sets [are] getting German and one is listening to the Bosche installing a set on our front'.[2] Success, however, proved shortlived. The British reaction had come too late to be of real assistance, for the Germans soon became aware of what was happening. A new code was promptly introduced to replace the simple substitution code they had been using and strict telephone discipline became the watchword in forward areas. Thus, at the end of October when hopes at GHQ were beginning to rise, a note of caution was sounded by one officer as Kirke, his expectations on the verge of dwindling, recorded in his diary: 'Dillon of V Corps thinks [the] time [has] gone when we could get good results from Listening Sets.'[3] By 1918, on the eve of their great spring offensive, the Germans had forbidden

1 Kirke Diaries, op. cit., 6 July 1916.
2 Ibid., 29 October 1916.
3 Ibid.

the use of telephones within seven miles of the front line. Long before then, however, the very success of the British listening sets proved to be their undoing and, by 1918, the Intelligence Summaries in the Army War Diaries had virtually ceased to mention them at all as a source of intelligence.

Deception was potentially the most powerful weapon in the special intelligence arsenal, and on the Western front this weapon was placed in the hands of I(b) who were responsible for the secret intelligence and counter-espionage facets of the intelligence jewel. Warfare is as much the province of deception as it is of fighting. The goal of all strategy, tactics, logistics, Intelligence, special techniques and the hundred and one different but interlocking activities which enable an army to take the field with any prospect of success, is to fight successfully on one's own terms, and to put the enemy at a disadvantage. In a war, each side is on the alert for deception and tends to regard much of the Intelligence they gather with suspicion. But deception of armies in war is anything but easy. It generally means deceiving the opposite Intelligence service rather than the enemy commander and consequently any misinformation has to be not simply plausible but very convincing. The deceptions that worked in the First World War set a fine example, veiled by a sufficient number of unimportant items of genuine information to lend credence to the intended hoax. For instance, bogus documents or wireless signals had to be supported by the appearance at least of troops in the area to which the enemy's reserves needed to be drawn, in compliance with the old military maxim that 'troops draw troops'.

The most successful deception in the West, however, happened entirely by accident, being the product of the imagination of the people of Britain rather than a masterly piece of wizardry hatched by the General Staff, and worked directly on the sensibilities of a top commander. In the wild, exuberant atmosphere of the first months of the war, rumour was rife but one rumour in particular was to exert more than a little influence on the campaign in the West. In the crisis of 1914, when the Allied armies were being driven back helter-skelter from the frontiers of France and Belgium, great hopes were pinned on the Russian Army, an army depicted as 'the Russian steamroller', a great, slow-moving mass which, once set in motion, would be irresistible and impossible to turn aside, rolling steadily and remorselessly forward to crush everything in its path. There was an anxious period of waiting for this saviour to rumble into action on the Eastern front. This hope disappointed, it sprouted with renewed vigour – or new desperation – in a different soil: if the Russian steamroller was not carrying all before it on the other side of Europe, then it stood to reason that it must be doing so elsewhere. Of course. It was *en route* to help its allies in the West. Russian troops were seen travelling by train from Scotland to the Channel ports, stamping the snows of the steppes from their boots at northern railway stations.

The rumours spread like wildfire. Soon reports were to hand from people who had actually seen these marvels and could give graphic descriptions – though all the descriptions characterized typical Russian cossacks of the nineteenth century, even down to the fact that many of them were armed with bows and arrows. For the most part this was the early twentieth-century Briton's standard picture of the fighting Russian: never having come into contact with any real Russians, he thought of them as depicted in caricatures and picture books or in the violently anti-Russian newspapers of the nineteenth century. Soon stories were circulating about hordes of Russians, speaking a strange tongue, arriving at London termini and being marched by dead of night to other stations where they boarded trains for the south coast. People would spend the whole night looking out of their windows in the hope of catching a glimpse of these secret saviours and the country was agog waiting for news of their arrival in France. It was a favourite topic of conversation, with each reported sighting being eagerly capped by listeners who should have known better.

This extraordinary groundswell of public belief and expectation reached such a pitch that on 15 September, *The Times* formally denied that huge numbers of Russians were traversing Britain on their way to help the French, but by then the rumours had achieved a success probably beyond the scope of the most carefully contrived deception. The German armies, pounding the *chaussées* into the heart of France, were leaving an ever-lengthening and ever more vulnerable line of communication behind them. This the timorous von Moltke, his nerves already rocky from the weight of the responsibility thrust on his shoulders and from the Kaiser's uncontrollable impulse to change meticulously detailed plans at the drop of a hat, found a source of continual worry. Now that the British were in the war, might they not use their mastery of the seas to land an Army in the German rear to strike at these all-too-weakly guarded communications? A small-scale incursion of Royal Marines under Sir George Aston at Zeebrugge and the unheralded appearance of the Royal Naval Division at Antwerp fuelled his fears. Then the stories of Russians in Britain reached von Moltke. If a powerful Russian Army was at that moment in Britain, where would it go next? With the British stabs on the coast fresh in his mind, von Moltke saw the prospect of a major Russian descent on his long and relatively unprotected communications: if the Russians were to fight on the Western front, they could hardly find a more propitious target.

It is usual for people to study war as if it were some great game of chess in which moves can be made in a relaxed and comfortable environment according to the dictates of common sense, with plenty of time to consider options. Nothing could be further from the truth. War is a game of chance and generals rarely enjoy the luxuries of calm and time to make decisions. In headquarters, where the officers may be fighting their first major war as commanders of great masses of men, knowing that the fate of their country rests on their decisions, the picture is very different. The situation is always and inevitably unclear – conflicting reports come in, subordinates fail to carry out their orders, or the enemy does something quite unexpected. In these circumstances a sense of urgency, of fear, if not of panic, prevails, something which the GSM had been designed to keep within bounds.

In the mind of von Moltke the unwelcome news of Russian troops barely twenty miles away across the English Channel generated a new bout of wobbliness. The German leaders began to cast worried looks over their shoulders towards the Belgian coast. They took half-measures that helped to deprive Germany of the quick victory in the West she needed. The fictitious Russians even helped to precipitate the withdrawal from the Marne, for they were one among a number of weighty factors which persuaded the nervous von Moltke to send Colonel Hentsch of the General Staff to the headquarters of von Kluck and von Bülow, after which the exasperated von Kluck finally issued the orders which sent his First Army streaming back in retreat.

On the Western front the British had one inestimable advantage where the possibility of deception was concerned, and that was their command of the sea. The possibility that they might play this trump card and land an army behind the trenchwork door barring the way to Germany was realistic enough to haunt the Germans to the extent that they fortified the coast of occupied Belgium and tied up a proportion of their manpower to garrison it against the threat. Haig's plans for the summer of 1917 did indeed envisage an amphibious landing on the Belgian coast to combine with his great offensive in Flanders; it remained for I(b), the section responsible for deception, to make a possibility, already plausible enough to be taken seriously by both armies, into a convincing certainty.

I(b) had first become enmeshed in deception early in 1915 when, at Macdonogh's bidding, Kirke began to investigate means of drawing German troops away from the Neuve Chapelle area, the chosen locality for the BEF's small part in the Allied offensive in the West. Kirke arranged for misinformation to be leaked through wireless transmissions, by planting bogus information on refugees returning to their homes in the occupied territories and by persuading Belgian refugees, writing to friends and relatives living under the German heel, to include further humbug in their letters – letters which would be censored by the Germans as a matter of course. The degree of success achieved by any deception can only be measured by the enemy's response to it, seen chiefly through the disposition of his reserves. True, the Germans had very few reserves to meet the British attack at Neuve Chapelle but it is debatable to what extent that was due to British deceptive measures: the Germans were concurrently facing a much larger French offensive which imposed a far more severe drain on their reserves than any of I(b)'s conjuring tricks were likely to do.

For the next round on the Western front, the Battle of Loos in September, two competing ideas for deception held the stage. The Intelligence section of the Directorate of Military Operations at the War Office, under Major-General Callwell, suggested covering the attack by spreading false information about an amphibious landing on the German North Sea coast, in Schleswig-Holstein. The General Staff in France countered this with a project designed to bluff the enemy into thinking there was instead to be a new offensive in the Dardanelles with a heavily reinforced army. It is difficult to understand the reasoning behind this. Given the maxim that movements, or the threat of troop movements, usually draw troops from the enemy to face them, the threat must be perceived as aimed at a point of importance to the enemy, so that he will feel obliged to move reserves to counter it. It is hard to believe that any British threat on the Gallipoli Peninsula would have persuaded the Germans to withdraw any substantial number of reserves from the Western front: the Turks already held Gallipoli safely and it suited German strategy far better for the Allies to dissipate their strength in secondary theatres. In the event, this design was shelved and plans reverted to what was to become the stand-by for the next two years, the threat of a landing on the Belgian coast. To make such a threat appear realistic required time and time was short due to the wrangling over the Schleswig-Holstein and Dardanelles ideas. Nevertheless, the first scheme went ahead and the Royal Navy duly bombarded Knocke, Blankenberghe, Westende, Middelkerke and Raversyde on 25 and 26 September, suffering some losses in the process. The Germans responded by moving some troops towards Ostend to cover the coast, but not enough to influence the battle further south. The deception plan fell short of complete success because it had not been selected and thought out well in advance: it had failed to gain reality when it should have loomed ever-larger and more dangerous in the mind of the enemy through an accumulation of misinformation from several sources. Intelligence were determined to avoid making the same mistake in the following year.

The year 1916 was the year when Allied hopes soared. The meticulously prepared offensive on the Somme was, so they thought, going to be the battle which would drive the Germans out of France in disorder. The German stroke at Verdun in February had thrown all the carefully laid plans out of gear and the main burden of the Somme offensive devolved onto British shoulders as more and more of the French Army was drawn into the fighting on the Meuse. To cover their great effort, the British Army adopted the Flanders bluff again, only on this occasion they made sure that time was on their side. Leave was stopped early in June and the important railway centre of Amiens was declared off-limits except to authorized personnel in order to suggest that important movements were taking place by rail. A false advanced headquarters was formed at Cassel to distract attention from the headquarters at Beauquesne and Lieutenant Burton Alexander was detailed to concentrate on the spreading of false information. This plan entailed deceiving friends as well as foes: since the gossip of the moment was likely to be related to the Germans by their secret service, it was arranged for a bogus question to be asked in the House of Commons in late June. On the 25th Kirke noted that 'Our false information scheme has gone v. well in Paris and is fully believed in the best circles.'[1]

Again, however, I(b) scored only a partial success. The Germans

1 Kirke Diaries, op. cit., 25 June 1916.

were bogged down in the slaughter-house they had created at Verdun and did not deploy more troops than usual in Flanders, especially with a week's unprecedentedly heavy bombardment to guide them and the information they got from 'Moritz' to act as a tip-off. The only deception that fooled the Germans on that tragic first day of the Somme was one which they had fixed in their own minds. Anxious to believe that the French Army had been worn away at Verdun, they convinced themselves that there would be no French attack in Picardy and that the French artillery preparation on the Somme was a bid to hoodwink them. Consequently, when the great attack went in, the German reserves were all behind the front facing the British and the southernmost quarter of their line was only weakly supported. It was there that the only lasting gains of the first day's fighting were made, gains which might have led to the elusive Allied victory in the West had General Rawlinson, commanding the Fourth Army, only known what lay within his grasp. As the chance of victory in the south dwindled away through inaction, the monstrous tragedy on the rest of the front went unredeemed, to stand as a monument to the futility of war – and in some measure to the failure of British deception plans.

When the Fourth Army launched its relatively successful night attack on 14 July, a further attempt was made to deceive the enemy, but following the attack instead of preceding it. Again, ignoring the need to fool the enemy's Intelligence, the plan was intended to destabilize the German command and create panic in the German headquarters leading to hasty, ill-considered orders, orders which might even command the Germans to retreat. Once they were retreating, opportunities could present themselves to send the cavalry through and turn the withdrawal into a rout. To this end, a British observation aeroplane was especially detailed to fly over the confused battlefield at 1 p.m. and transmit a wireless message which, if all went well, would be picked up by the Germans and create the desired havoc in their headquarters. The message read:

> 'B.7. Enemy second line of defence has been captured on a front of six thousand yards. British Cavalry is now passing through in pursuit of the demoralized enemy.[1]

German headquarters had indeed been shaken by a daring night attack but they had by no means lost their nerve. Reinforcements were rushed in to shore up the threatened sector and it was as if the wireless

1 Fourth Army, *Battle of the Somme, Summary of Events*, PRO WO 158/328.

message had never been sent. There is not the slightest scrap of evidence that the Germans ever picked it up and if they did, their reaction shows that they were not at all influenced by it. There was no hurried withdrawal and the front ground to a halt on a new line when the British advance petered out. It had been an imaginative and even promising attempt to shake the German will to fight; its failure owes more to plain bad luck than to any want of planning.

In October 1916, as the last real chance of winning any recognizable victory was on the point of expiring, I(b) returned to the Belgian scheme again with a ploy scheduled for mid-November. On this occasion the dummy was well and truly sold to the Germans, who responded by rushing troops to the coast. But the consequences were rather different from those anticipated by the red-tabbed warriors of I(b), for the greatest effect was felt in London rather than Brussels, still less by the hard-pressed infantry at the front. The British Government had not been made privy to the plot, and the sudden and unheralded appearance of German troops on the Flanders coast sent ripples of panic through Whitehall, where a descent on the English coast was now hourly expected. Urgent demands flew to France for Haig to release some of his battle-weary divisions immediately to defend the homeland. Embarrassed explanations were given and ruffled government feathers were smoothed.

When the British did open a genuine offensive in Flanders in 1917, the old chestnut of threatening a landing on that coast had to be replaced with a fresh idea. The Canadian Corps had earned itself a deserved reputation as one of the hardest fighting formations in the war. The Germans held them in great respect and could safely calculate that wherever the Canadians appeared some new form of mischief would follow, as surely as night follows day. In that grisly summer of 1917 GHQ ordered the Canadians to mount a limited operation in the neighbourhood of Lens, well away from the expected point of decision in Flanders. The move paid splendid dividends, drawing more and more German troops to the Canadian front. In a series of remarkable minor attacks, lamentably forgotten by later generations, the indomitable spirit of the magnificent men from the Dominion met and broke that of two or even three times their number of Germans. As a deception it was arguably the most successful on the Western front and inclines one's thought towards the possibility of what might have been achieved had the Canadians been given more support, for division after division of the German Army was thrown into their path, only to reel away much depleted after a severe mauling. Though no great victory was achieved in the more hideous battle in Flanders, British troops engaged there had good reason to thank the Canadians for the fact that the opposition they encountered was not even stronger.

It was the Canadians, too, who spearheaded the breakthrough at Amiens in August 1918, in the battle which finally pushed the German Army towards defeat. This time GHQ played the Canadian card by keeping the move of the Canadian Corps to Amiens a closely guarded secret and misleading the Germans over its true whereabouts by a series of ruses. The Canadians had been in Flanders before their move south and, to give the Germans the impression that they remained fixed there, a Canadian wireless section remained behind, transmitting just as if the whole Corps was present, whereas in fact only three battalions stayed in the line to deceive raiding parties and patrols. The Germans did eventually realize the Canadians had moved, but by then the morale of the German soldiers and people was fading and when the attack went home it did so against an enemy for the most part no longer prepared to fight.

Deception on the Western front never succeeded in drawing away sufficient numbers of German troops to enable the Allied armies to exploit such initial successes as they won. This was partly due to the fact that German Military Intelligence was usually good enough to see through the deception attempts, but equal weight must be placed on the fact that GHQ rarely had sufficient troops to spare to make their threats appear really convincing. That said, it must be admitted that rarely does any general have troops to spare for punching at air and he must always beware that the number of men he commits to a feint is not greater than the number of enemy soldiers he attracts to counter it. The key to any deception is that the threat the commander wishes to convey must be made against a point peculiarly sensitive to the enemy, one that he must guard no matter what. On the Western front there were all too few such points. It was not so in Palestine.

There, under the aegis of the brilliant Colonel Richard Meinertzhagen, the most dramatic and spectacularly successful deception of the war was engineered. By 1917 the war in Palestine had ground to a halt in front of the Turkish line running from Gaza to Beersheba, in much the same way that the war in the West had stuck fast. Conventional means to break the Gaza-Beersheba line had been tried and failed utterly; two major attacks had been made on Gaza, at the right of the

Turkish line, and both had been repulsed, the second ignominiously. A new commander, Sir Edmund Allenby, resolved in the summer of 1917 to throw the Turks out of their entrenchments by attacking the left extremity of their line at Beersheba. Easily said, but something more was needed to pin Turkish attention to their citadel on the right, and that something was the brainchild of Meinertzhagen. The method he chose was to drop a notebook near the Turkish lines which supposedly belonged to a GHQ officer on reconnaissance towards Beersheba. The notebook would contain details of British offensive plans centred on Gaza, together with personal papers, vital documents it was hoped the Turks would presume an officer would not wish to lose if he could help it. The assignment was a risky one for the officer concerned but on 12 September 1917 Captain A. C. B. Neale duly dropped the notebook – and, alas, the Turks failed to pick it up. A second attempt was made on 1 October; this time an Australian officer dropped a dummy notebook but again the Turks failed to pursue him and the opportunity went a-begging.

There is an old saying that if you want a job done properly you do it yourself. On 10 October Meinertzhagen rode out into the desert towards Sheria, carrying a haversack containing the notebook with its bogus dispositions and strengths, together with some spurious maps. To add credence to these documents, Meinertzhagen added £20 in used notes, a letter purporting to come from his wife announcing the birth of a son (which would naturally be held by the Turks to be of tremendous sentimental value to a husband and father; in fact the letter was writen by Meinertzhagen's sister Mary, who had never been a mother). There was also another private letter relating the postponement of the offensive against Gaza, a copy of an agenda for a GHQ conference which confirmed said postponement, a copy of GHQ instructions showing completely false preparations for an eventual attack on Gaza, and two telegrams, one showing that a GHQ Staff Officer was going on patrol to El Gerheir and the other that British Intelligence considered topographical obstacles around Beersheba too severe to allow any enveloping movement. Finally there were some notes on an old cipher which would enable the enemy to read any messages sent in that cipher.

Meinertzhagen's story can best be related in his own words:

> I was well mounted and near Girheir I found a Turkish patrol who at once gave chase. I galloped away for a mile or so and then they pulled

> up, so I stopped, dismounted and had a shot at them at about 600 yards. That was too much for them and they at once resumed the chase, blazing away harmlessly all the time. Now was my chance, and in my effort to mount I loosened my haversack, field-glasses, water-bottle, dropped my rifle, previously stained with some fresh blood from my horse, and in fact did everything to make them believe I was hit and that my flight was disorderly.'[1]

The pursuing Turks picked up the items jettisoned by Meinertzhagen, who rode hard for home and soon gave his adversaries the slip. To reinforce the bluff he rode to the headquarters of the Desert Mounted Corps, who themselves were in ignorance of his devious game, and reported the loss to them as if it were genuine, pleading with them to send out a patrol to recover the 'lost' haversack. Not only did the Corps send out a patrol but they played into Meinertzhagen's hands by sending an angry message by wireless to Allenby not to employ 'such inexperienced young officers on reconnaissance'[2] and saying that Meinertzhagen had done untold harm by his negligence and stupidity. Matters were not allowed to rest there. Wireless messages were sent out in the cipher which the Turks could now break, thanks to the material in the haversack and a notice was put in the Desert Mounted Corps' orders on 11 October stating that a notebook had been lost by an officer on patrol and the finder was to return it to GHQ. A copy of this order was placed into Turkish hands by a method similar to Meinertzhagen's, when a specially briefed officer wrapped his lunch in it and threw it away when on patrol near the enemy. To further enhance the deception, troop movements were made which indicated an obvious intention to attack Gaza once again.

The digging of defences round Beersheba declined drastically and was stepped up to a furious pace round Gaza. Misled as well over the actual date of the attack, which they believed would not be until mid-November, the Turks moved troops towards Gaza at a casual pace but did concentrate their central reserve of two divisions there, leaving Beersheba naked to the storm which was shortly to engulf it. They even sent 50 new aeroplanes in crates by rail to Gaza, all of which the EEF would eventually burn or capture in their packing cases.

The depth to which the Turks were hoodwinked is shown nowhere more clearly than in one of their orders captured when Gaza itself finally fell to the victorious British on 8 November. The order read:

1 Meinertzhagen, op. cit., p. 222.
2 Ibid.

1. On 10 October 1917, one of our NCO patrols sent out to Abu Sahiban Tepe came back with some very important maps and documents left by a high-rank General Staff Officer of the British Army and thus have rendered our Army important service. The NCO has been handsomely rewarded.
2. These maps and documents are no doubt as important and valuable to the enemy as they are to us, and we may be sure the loss of these documents has greatly annoyed the enemy.
3. I am instructed to inform you that the information contained in these documents is of such great value to us that we have been able to ascertain the date of the enemy's offensive and it will enable us to forestall him in that all our reinforcements will now be near Gaza in time for us to crush the arrogant English.
4. I therefore particularly request Divisional and Regimental Commanders to see that extreme caution is observed by officers who are sent out for purposes of reconnoitering and observation, etc., and that they absolutely abstain from carrying on their persons such papers as would tell the enemy about our strength and positions, disposition of our forces and our plans, etc..

Col. Ali Fuad
O.C. 20th Army Corps.[1]

The whole story of the Gaza-Beersheba deception bears the stamp of a master. It was properly timed, well thought-out and presented cumulative evidence from different sources. Equally important was the fact that the apparent threat to Gaza was directed against a vital point in the Turkish defences, one which they had to guard as its loss would spell ruin for the Turkish forces in Palestine. Moreover, a British attack there could reasonably be anticipated, for had not the British assailed its defences on two previous occasions, and was it not the only place where a large British force intent on taking the offensive could find a ready supply of the water so necessary for fighting in Palestine? Was not Gaza, too, the only one of the two sectors where the 'arrogant English' could exploit their much-vaunted naval superiority? Meinertzhagen's success underlines the fact that deception depends on far more than spreading false information. Those who served in the Second World War might think there were echoes of the Gaza-Beersheba deception in Operation Mincemeat, when a body dressed in a British officer's uniform, and bearing misleading docu-

1 Ibid., p. 285. The full story of this amazing coup can be found in the *Army Diary*, pp. 222–3 and 283–6.

ments in a waterproof bag, was released off the coast of Spain by a British submarine. As expected, the corpse was found by the Axis powers who fell for the trick, much to the hurt of their forces.

Even after Meinertzhagen's departure from Palestine for the more august sphere of the War Office, Intelligence still scored successes. The final great victory at Megiddo in 1918, arguably the most brilliant cavalry success of the war, owed as much to deception as it did to the fighting quality of the British soldier, and was largely due to M. V. Nugent (head of Intelligence, EEF) and to Wavell. On this occasion the British needed to inspire the belief that they would be attacking the Turks on the left of their line, while in reality the knock-out blow was to be struck on the right, along the coast. No forged documents were used this time. Instead large camps were constructed in the area where the British wished to make the Turks believe their troops were concentrating, camps in which numerous bivouac-fires were lit every night, and where canvas dummies populated the horse lines. Troops were marched openly into the camps by daylight only to be secretly transported north by lorries at night. Next day the same troops would march into the camps, giving the appearance of additional troops arriving. A wireless section was stationed in these make-believe camps, emitting a steady stream of transmissions commensurate with the headquarters of an Army Corps.

In the meantime, the British strike-force lay hidden amidst the conveniently sited orange and olive groves in the coastal sector, shielded from the prying eyes of enemy airmen both by the leaves and by a very solid British aerial superiority. The numerous irrigation channels which ran throughout this cultivated region supplied man and beast with all the water they required, though the water was invariably drawn by night to fox watchful eyes. Then, on the very eve of the offensive, the whole plan was placed in jeopardy when an Indian non-commissioned officer deserted to the Turks and told them all he knew. But the Turks, anxious to avoid a replay of the Beersheba deception, treated the deserter's revelations with contempt, in no wise prepared to believe the word of a single deserter who had arrived too fortuitously to be anything other than a plant. The Turks remained in ignorance until the British struck them a blow which utterly destroyed the Turkish Army in Palestine and played no small part in breaking up the Ottoman Empire, forcing the Turks to sue for peace.

The success of deception in Palestine and its lack of impact in France needs explaining. The fact that GHQ France did not have a

Meinertzhagen on its books is only part of the reason; a more general application is to be found in the scope that mounted troops had in Palestine, a scope denied them along the Western front. The Turkish seizure of Meinertzhagen's haversack was precisely the type of event that cavalry would expect in open warfare but it was an event of a nature that had become quite impractical in France, where Staff Officers could not and did not ride around in no-man's-land without being immediately shot down by a multitude of different weapons. Allowance must be made, too, for the fact that German Military Intelligence was superior to that of the Turks. It was technically far more advanced, much better disciplined and considerably less gullible than its Ottoman counterpart, though one wonders why the possibilities of passing misinformation by telephone remained so neglected, given the known excellence of Germany's 'Moritz'. Even so, the chief deterrent on the Western front was the continuous and unbreakable barrier presented by the garrisoned trenches, denying GHQ the opportunity to steal a march on the enemy through deception, which there remained just an interesting sideline.

Since so much of the General Staff's understanding of war stemmed from the Franco-Prussian War of 1870-1, it is unsurprising to find that the Intelligence Sections of the armies of the First World War were fully sensible of the source of information which had enabled von Moltke to win his greatest victory. The bulk of the French field army had been imprisoned in the fortress town of Metz, lying idle with Marshal Bazaine at its head. A relief army, scraped together from odd detachments supported by a conglomeration of National Guards, set out from Paris to the rescue under the command of Marshal Macmahon. Macmahon's force was the last body of trained French troops of any account that could take the field against the all-conquering Prussians with any reasonable hope of success, and von Moltke knew only too well that if he could destroy that army then the end of the war should be in sight. The London *Times* was covering the war and from its informative pages von Moltke was able to glean information about the route and progress of Macmahon's force and its standard of discipline and training, information which he turned to good account in bringing Macmahon to battle at Sedan and destroying France's last hope.

In 1914 every army assiduously scrutinized foreign newspapers in the expectation of aping the Prussians, but since every army knew the risks so every army took stern measures to ensure that the journalists who dogged their tracks could report nothing which would be of value to an enemy. Rigorous field censorship was enforced which smothered newspapers as a source of information, though the General Staffs still maintained a careful watch in case something significant but apparently worthless should escape the censor's eye. The British Army was no exception to this rule and small sections, one at the War Office in London and one at Le Havre for GHQ, were detailed to study the foreign press.

For the most part, information gained in this way was of slight importance but once, when it really mattered, the press scrutiny paid off. In 1918 it was known that the Germans were going to launch a final great offensive in the West intended to destroy France, sweep the British into the sea and bring the war to a victorious conclusion. It was already known that new German offensive tactics had been developed, tried and tested on the Eastern front in 1917 where they had easily opened up the Russian front. These tactics were the brainchild of General von Hutier, who invariably commanded the troops putting his theories into practice.

At the beginning of 1918 the location of the German attack still remained a mystery to the General Staff and it continued to be a mystery until a British censor, working for the War Office in Switzerland, read a local newspaper from Baden, dated 5 January 1918. His eye fell upon a letter from the mother of a German aviator killed while flying over the British lines at the beginning of the month. The grieving mother quoted a letter she had received from von Hutier, commanding the Army Group in which her son had served. The airman had been killed in the British Fifth Army area and if von Hutier was in command opposite that Army then it was a natural deduction that the German offensive would fall on that front. This conclusion was supported by another letter, signed by von Hutier, seen in another German newspaper shortly afterwards, commiserating with the family of a senior officer known to have been killed on the Fifth Army front. Eventually discounting the possibility that the letters were hoaxes, Sir George Aston relates the deduction drawn from them: 'The main German attack may be expected against the Third and Fifth British Armies, with Amiens for its objective.'[1]

1 Aston, op. cit., p. 205.

However, uncertainty prevailed for some time until the location of the offensive was discerned from other sources.

Nearly all the successes gained by various strategems belonged to defensive Intelligence. Few could do what was really needed, which was to break open the lines of trenches and deliver a major victory in the open field. Wireless had shown the most promise for offensive Intelligence, having been found useful in interception and deception but, as Marshall-Cornwall said, it was still in its infancy and its scope was further narrowed by the strict wireless discipline enforced by the Germans. Without computers, the codes used were generally safe until the Secret Service helped the codebreakers to overcome German ingenuity. If wireless showed the most promise, deception still achieved most in real terms for offensive Intelligence when used in relatively open warfare in Palestine. On the Western front deception attempts tended to be repetitive and myopic and the fact that G H Q France had put deception under a mere lieutenant argues a lack of confidence in it. Under these conditions there was little realistic hope that deception could sow the seeds of victory, especially when the Commander-in-Chief, Sir Douglas Haig, preferred straightforward bludgeoning to beat the enemy down. His concept of the war (*see* Chapters 10 and 11) and the nature of the road to victory forced deception to confine its best efforts to the tactical sphere, where subordinate commanders were left very much to their own devices.

Technical problems bedevilled both wireless and listening sets from the beginning to the end of the war, problems which were exacerbated by the shortage of suitable, trained personnel. Every branch of the Army suffered alike in this respect. Faced with a war of masses, the Staff had an enormous amount of work to do and, so far as the strength of units was concerned, they held that their job was done if they provided the required number of men, an attitude entirely inappropriate for a war which cried out for more and more specialization at all levels, even amongst infantry platoons where specialist bombers, bayonet men, rifle grenadiers and Lewis gunners placed unheard-of strains on the structure of the old army. Special Intelligence may have differed from the more usual sphere of Operational Intelligence in so far as it rarely required men to risk their lives face to face with the enemy, but it had this in common with I(a): although there were occasions when great achievements came from it, these were too sporadic and inconsistent to show the Army the road to a quick victory. It was not until the Second World War was well under way that the services adopted a policy of really selecting men for the jobs to which they were best fitted, allowing Intelligence to add to the country's fighting power in a way they did not in the war of 1914–18.

It is easy to be critical of the Army and of the level and usefulness of the Intelligence branches, so it is perhaps worth reviewing the difficulties imposed in the First World War by contemporary communications, difficulties which today are hard to comprehend.

Military formations need to be able to communicate and co-operate with each other and they have to be able to pass information back to their commanders who, in turn, need untrammelled channels to forward orders and information. Not only must units and commanders be able to communicate securely, but they must be able to do so rapidly, for time is the hinge upon which most things turn in war, where the race is nearly always to the swift. The means at the disposal of both staffs and soldiers in the Great War battlefields were neither swift nor sure, a fact which meant that not only Intelligence, but the whole Army was faced with an impossible task.

Communications were generally limited to semaphore, heliograph, telephone, morse buzzer, lamps, carrier pigeons, runners and, to a very limited extent, wireless. In most cases, 'Fullerphone and runner were about all we'd got, certainly up in front; on special occasions it was possible to use semaphore, but on very rare occasions.'[1] Yet these feeble means had to bear a heavy burden, a large proportion of which was devoted to Intelligence, according to D. H. Doe, who was handling incoming messages during the assault on Messines Ridge in 1917.[2] In a 1970s exercise, 70 per cent of signals traffic was devoted to Intelligence, and half the reports failed to reach the required standards of reliability and accuracy.[3]

Telephones provided the most rapid means of communication available, and the British Army went to war equipped with the D-III telephone. However, apart from the risk of enemy eavesdropping, the surface cables were also extremely vulnerable to shellfire, to wheeled vehicles and to what John Terraine described as the 'thieving propensities of unscrupulous soldiers' in his account of how a cavalry unit cut 100 yards of telephone cable for use as a picket line.[4] Burying

1 Rackham interview, loc. cit.
2 Doe Diary, op. cit., 7 June 1917.
3 *See* P. Watson, *War On the Mind*, London, 1978, p. 171.
4 Terraine, op. cit., p. 149.

the cable gave a degree of protection against shellfire for a time, but this required much time and effort. The wearied tone of an extract from a conference at Third Army Headquarters on 31 July 1916 refers to this persistent problem: 'The Army Commander again drew attention to the necessity of Corps paying more attention to the telephone lines which, except in case of active operations, should either be buried or poled.'[1]

'Active operations' meant when a battle was in progress and then, of course, the precious lines were cut time and again. But even with the lines intact, a general officer's ability to influence a battle was just about restricted to decisions of where and when to commit his reserves. In a desperate bid to keep these tenuous links with the front open extraordinary efforts were required from the men charged with their maintenance. Writing of his experiences at the Battle of Arras in 1917, fought by the men of the Third Army, Guy Buckridge recalled that, 'Our 'phone lines rarely lasted more than a quarter-of-an-hour and finally we became too tired and wet to make more effort than would keep one line working forward and one back.'[2] During the Somme another luckless Engineer, Private J.R. Parkman, wrote that damage occurred 'so often that we had to give up and revert to runners'.[3]

Once any army started to advance, however short the forward move, the entire telephone system was reduced to chaos simply because the lines had to be run over the face of no-man's-land in the first instance, usually still under fire. Matters could be even worse if an army had to give any substantial amount of ground. Writing of the dislocation caused by the German spring offensive of 1918, D.H. Doe commented, 'Throughout the whole battle we had hardly any lines working as the French had none to give us. Most of our work was done through Civil exchanges and urgent messages by D[espatch] R[ider].'[4]

Various alternatives were tried, but semaphore and heliograph were of limited use in the prevailing tactical conditions:

> It was difficult sometimes to find a suitable site for the chap doing semaphore up in front, and it didn't happen right in the front line, but

1 Third Army War Diary, PRO WO 95/360.
2 Papers of Guy Buckridge, IWM.
3 Cited by Martin Middlebrook in *The First Day on The Somme*, op. cit., p. 163.
4 Doe Diary, op. cit., 31 May 1918.

> you must remember that if the front was active, the telephone lines would be invariably cut and so you were down to bedrock with a runner.[1]

Neither could pigeons always provide an adequate substitute. They were used during the battle of the Marne and as soon as the front settled down into trench warfare measures were taken for their control and requisition. In April 1915 a small number of birds with men trained to use them were distributed to the cavalry for Intelligence purposes only, and in May 1915 it was proposed to use them when communications were broken. From these small beginnings the pigeon service grew rapidly and was formally authorized in August that year, comprising units of 80 birds, called a 'loft'. One pigeon was even awarded the Victoria Cross and its stuffed body ended up in the now defunct museum of the Royal United Services Institute for Defence Studies in London. By 1918 the Army had 20,000 of these feathered recruits in the care of 380 experts. Yet the pigeon service, too, had its drawbacks. Only the briefest messages could, as a rule, be written down under fire and carried by pigeon. The birds, in their baskets, were cumbersome to carry and understandably some soldiers regarded them as a tempting supplement to Army rations. They were no less vulnerable to the gas used in such quantities by both sides as well as falling casualty to bombardment. Nor were their numbers unlimited. In late 1917 there was a serious shortage of birds on the Western front; they were not there for the asking.

Superficially, wireless appears today to have been the ready-made answer. However, that is to neglect the fact that the wireless equipment of the day was hardly appropriate for the rough conditions at the front where it would be of greatest service. In the first place long-range wireless was heavy and bulky and required more space than was available in the battlezone:

> The W/T station is well laid out and consists of Engine Room, room for banks of condensers and spark gaps, Instrument room and several others for writing, sleeping accommodation etc. The aerials are most elaborate, three steel tower masts 320 feet high support an umbrella aerial. A shorter aerial twin 'L', is used for transmission (power 2½ KW). Large aerial used for reception on a Pack Panel and Mark III amplifier.[2]

1 Rackham interview, loc. cit.
2 Diary of A. E Thomson, Royal Engineers (Signals), 5 October 1918, IWM.

Such a monstrosity was clearly not a practical proposition for the front line. An attempt was made in the fighting at Hooge Château in August 1915 to establish communication by wireless between divisional and brigade headquarters with portable wireless sets, but it proved unsuccessful. Quite apart from bulk, problems were also encountered with power supplies, jamming, weather and unsuitable terrain. Undeterred, the Army tried to employ wireless in the front line again during the Somme campaign in 1916, with the First Australian Wireless Company attempting to maintain communications during the ANZAC attack on Pozières. Two wireless stations were ready for transmission on 28 July — or so they thought. In fact, one station, once in place, found it was impossible to erect its aerial because of the intensity of the shelling, and the other only came into action at 1.30 p.m. Its first message to the Receiving Post on Tara Hill read: 'Everything okay', meaning to initiates that the station was at last in working order. But the words sent a thrill of exhilaration through its recipients at Divisional Headquarters, where it was interpreted as meaning that the Australians had taken their objectives — which they had not. The resulting confusion put wireless back in the dog house so far as its employment in the front line was concerned and henceforth it was restricted to the rear — where, of course, it remained out of touch with the up-to-the-minute situation.

Nowadays, familiar as we are with instantaneous satellite relay beaming words and pictures straight into our homes, it is perhaps difficult to grasp that wireless was still very much a novelty in 1916 — Marconi had only made his famous first broadcast fifteen years before. Things could not be done at the flick of a switch or the twist of a dial. Radio-telephony, which came to replace wireless telegraphy, did not appear until 1918 and then it was a generation growing before it became commonplace in the armed services. Had technology been even a decade in advance, one could say with justice that the history of the First World War would read very differently, as would the story of the lives of Europe's peoples in the remainder of the century.

When all else failed, runners had to fill the gap; battlefield communications that would have been familiar to John, Duke of Marlborough, who had commanded the British Army in France and Flanders in the opening years of the eighteenth century. When the front was quiet, runners experienced little difficulty, but on an active front, particularly when the BEF advanced, they were in great danger and the losses, in men and messages, were considerable: 'in fluid battle, fifty per cent, something of that sort'.[1] A runner had to run and in any advance this meant leaving cover to cross no-man's-land to return to a point where he could deliver his message, with considerable risk that neither runner nor message would get through. It was also a slow means of communication: runners could take half-an-hour or more to deliver a message, depending on circumstances, which meant that the situation had almost certainly altered, making the message inapplicable. Runners were therefore only an adequate means of communication when things were quiet.

Individually, the tools of Operational Intelligence — prisoners, captured documents, aerial observation, wireless interception and the rest — all had serious shortcomings, but all were also mutually dependent, a point illustrated by Marshall-Cornwall: 'I think we tried to rely as far as possible on captured documents, prisoners' statements and the interpretation of air photographs and we liked direct information from as many sources as possible.'[2] Information from all these sources was gathered, checked and collated back at the different divisional, corps and army headquarters, until a distilled version of the whole ended up on the desks of the GHQ Intelligence section. Each level of command had its own need for Intelligence, each level requiring a broader and more complex picture than the last. One quite different problem raised its head in this process and that was the unforgiveable tendency of particular commands to keep some choice bit of information to themselves in the expectation of being able to use it and pick up the glory of any success. This conduct prevailed even in East Africa, where Meinertzhagen complained:

> I am experiencing the greatest difficulty in making divisions send back information to GHQ. Each commander thinks he is a law unto himself and that his division is a watertight little compartment. There is even jealousy among commanders and they are too prone to keep valuable information to themselves from this motive alone. Even Smuts is kept in the dark for fear he passes on the piece of news to some competitor.[3]

However, even when information from all sources was taken in conjunction, there were still significant gaps: the information presented was known to be both partial and unreliable. Certainly the

1 Rackham interview, loc. cit.
2 Marshall-Cornwall interview, loc. cit.
3 Meinertzhagen, op. cit., p. 192.

Army seems to have conceded the latter point, for in September 1915 the Second Army produced a summary about the forces opposed to it which began with the preamble: 'N.B. The following information has been derived from various sources, i.e. prisoners, documents, etc., and must be treated with a certain amount of reserve.'[1]

It seemed there was no source available which could furnish close and immediate information about the enemy which did not involve some form of attack. Contact was critically important, for ultimately the best information comes from the enemy himself. Neither surveillance nor special intelligence could provide the information required with the same immediacy and consistency. However, not even contact could achieve the penetration necessary to discover what the Germans intended to do with their floating reserve of some 15 to 30 divisions, a question of the greatest significance to the Allied commanders. The only means which Operational Intelligence had to hand to observe this reserve was aerial reconnaissance, which was itself restricted by a number of factors.

It is true, as Sir Walker Kirke states, that 'Generally speaking every unit is responsible for knowing what is on its own front,'[2] but much depends on the tactical environment and what the troops understand about what is required of them. Yet in the 1914–18 war, the troops were usually not informed:

> We weren't supposed to know anything, and even not supposed to understand anything, and honestly, we were never told anything about what we had to do or what to expect, or what to shoot at. Oh no, we simply had to obey orders. All we were told was how to form fours, how to lie down in the mud and get up again. We were *never* told anything about tactical strategy at all. Nothing at all. I suppose they thought we were so dumb that we couldn't understand it.[3]

It all amounted to the virtual emasculation of Operational Intelligence and increased dependence on studying the German Order of Battle as the best possible gauge of the enemy's ability to maintain his effort. Study of the Order of Battle also gave indications of the enemy's intentions and fluctuations in that it could betray a change of plan as well as provide a token of the weakening of his staying power. The

1 Second Army War Diary, 'Notes on The German Forces Opposite The Second Army', 15 September 1915, PRO WO 95/272.
2 Kirke Papers, loc. cit., 'Lectures on Intelligence', 1924..
3 Murray interview, loc. cit.

study of the enemy's Order of Battle was absolutely vital to a prolonged war of attrition, the type of war into which the Army had been drawn willy-nilly. It was the one field where I(a) could provide the required information. The trouble with the focus on the Order of Battle was that it was something which was important to the General Staff only, not to the men in the trenches. There was no easy way out. Victory in the field was a hopeless will-o'-the-wisp in the context of the First World War. The strategy of attrition had not been adopted gratuitously, but it was a strategy that appealed to a mind cast in the frame of the GSM; it was beautifully correct in theory and theory was a prime mover in the General Staff ethos. Nevertheless, with fighting reduced to a long-term grapple that would end only when one or other of the contestants collapsed, the nature of the war dictated that the nature of the collapse, in the case of every one of the defeated nations, would be as much social and moral as military. The social aspect of the war was barely touched in the concern with the Order of Battle. Only one agency could bring all the necessary Intelligence elements together, and that agency was the Secret Service.

FIVE

The Hidden Hand

BEFORE looking closely at the work of Secret Service personnel in the field, it is necessary first to consider the organization of secret Intelligence. Two sources of difficulty immediately become apparent, in the existence of several parallel Secret Services and the conflicts engendered between them by the differing views and personalities of the various service heads.

At the beginning of the twentieth century, a spate of spy novels by the novelist and adventurer William Tufnell Le Queux alleged that Britain was in deadly danger from numerous German spies, whose menacing designs were only foiled by the intervention of individuals with all the right traits of British pluck and sportsmanship. Other fictions fed British fears about the dark underworld of spying, such as Erskine Childers's *The Riddle Of The Sands* and John Buchan's *The Thirty-Nine Steps*, serialized in the popular *Blackwood's Magazine*, just as the story of the Russian hordes landing in Scotland for transportation to France would catch the national imagination in 1914.

Until 1 June 1887 there had not even been a Director of Military Intelligence at the War Office, such procurement of spies and guides as existed being left to the commanders of forces in the field. Until the Boer War the DMI had been helped by the Assistant Adjutant General, who handled administration and miscellaneous subjects and who also 'controlled the small amount of secret service money that was doled out by the Foreign Office to pay persons who offered information, as there were no regular agents in DMI's employ'.[1] The Boer War transformed the situation, with demand for Intelligence hopelessly outpacing the DMI's ability to provide. To help cope with the burden Major James Edmonds of the Royal Engineers was directed to take the recently formed Secret Service section, Section H, under his wing and found himself in charge of a handful of staff and a

1 Edmonds Papers, loc. cit., VII/3, 'The Origin of MI5'.

munificent allocation of £200 per annum with which to claw secret Intelligence from the four corners of the world. The escalation of the Boer War and the threatened intervention of European powers on the Boers' behalf proved a drastic demonstration that Britain's 'splendid isolation' was a grave drawback in Intelligence terms. By the end of the war Edmonds's position had been somewhat improved. He wrote, one suspects with his tongue in his cheek, that 'affairs improved slightly after 1902. I think we had sometimes as much as £2,000 a year — little enough to conduct enquiries over nearly the whole globe.'[1] A salutary lesson had been taught the British Army — that lack of preparation is an expensive business — and a variety of commissions and committees were appointed to repair the errors of the late nineteenth century.

One of the most influential reforms to stem from this sudden flurry of activity was the reorganization of the General Staff, with the Staff now being modelled on German lines. In the new scheme of things Intelligence was lashed firmly to the Directorate of Military Operations, representing the sum total of Britain's military Intelligence organization. There was as yet no formation responsible for acquiring Intelligence by covert means, a deficiency which was only remedied by government reaction to public opinion in the wake of literary spy-fever.

Certain officials rode this wave of popular feeling and turned it to good account. The first witness at a sub-committee of the Committee of Imperial Defence, meeting in secret session at Whitehall Gardens in March 1909 to consider hostile espionage in Britain, was Major James Edmonds, naturally enough hankering after more money and influence for his small section. His audience, primed by the spy scare, were ready and willing listeners. The sub-committee's deliberations lasted over four months, at the end of which it reported that organizations were needed to safeguard Britain against espionage and acts of sabotage, and to carry out espionage for Britain abroad.

Sir Vernon Kell headed the counter-espionage organization (today's MI5) and continued to do so until 1940. During the inter-war years it was publicly announced that he had retired, but it seems probable that this was an exercise in concealment, for he certainly served as head of MO5 from his appointment until he was succeeded by Sir David Petrie.

1 Ibid., IV/11, 'Engineer Intelligence'.

The new service for espionage abroad owed a triple allegiance — to the Foreign Office, the Admiralty, and the War Office — with the government deliberately taking great care to avoid acknowledging its existence in order, with some degree of justice, to plead ignorance if any of the service's agents were caught by a foreign power. Yet for practical and administrative purposes, such as finance and official address, some form of overall management was necessary, so the embarrassing baby was fostered out to the Intelligence Section of the Directorate of Military Operations where it became section MO5(j) and later, after the reorganization of the winter of 1915–16, MI1(c), responsible for what were euphemistically termed 'special operations'. The military side of the new Secret Service's work was both directed and financed as one part of a larger scheme and in real terms the connection with military Intelligence became increasingly tenuous as time went on. Although more money was made available there were inevitably competing demands for it and the Intelligence section at the War Office were dissatisfied. Sir Walter Kirke, who was close to these events, grumbled after the war that 'As our allotment for all purposes, Foreign Office, Navy and Army, before the war was only £40,000 we could not do very much.'[1] Kirke's figure was confirmed by his chief, General Macdonogh, who pencilled a distressed note in the margin of Kirke's paper: '£40,000 was the total Foreign Office grant but is it wise to say so?'[2] — a comment which reveals much about the degree of secrecy with which this area of Intelligence was regarded.

In time of war the triple harness worn by the Secret Service raised particular problems since it meant that the DMI was not in sole charge of its operations. The head of the Secret Service therefore had a considerable degree of latitude in both collecting and evaluating information for his various employers. Relations between the Army and the Secret Service were set off on the wrong foot from the very start because of this. Traditionally the duty of the War Office, which received its secret Intelligence from the Secret Service, was to provide information to the Army relative to the higher conduct of the war — that is, it dealt with the enemy's policy, resources and grand strategy. By contrast the Army in the field was always left to organize its own Intelligence regarding enemy operations in the immediate theatre of war. In both the Peninsula War and the Waterloo campaign, for

1 Kirke Papers, loc. cit., 'Lecture on Intelligence', 1924.
2 Ibid.

instance, the Duke of Wellington had been well served by a secret service under the direction of Lieutenant-Colonel Colquhoun Grant of the 11th Foot (the Devonshire Regiment), and the habit of forming local networks of agents directed by the Army in the field was of long standing. Accordingly, the BEF of 1914 kept in step with existing practice when its Intelligence Section formed its own Secret Service from the motley collection of men who made up its Intelligence Corps, a process repeated in all theatres in which the Army was engaged.

In East Africa Richard Meinertzhagen found secret Intelligence for the Army virtually non-existent. He raised an Intelligence Unit which, under his expert direction, delivered excellent material to the hands of the British commanders there, who proceeded to ignore it. In the Cameroons, General Dobell's force lacked any Intelligence Officer at all if the list of GHQ personnel and Army headquarters troops is to be relied upon.[1] The Intelligence burden devolved onto the capable shoulders of Lieutenant D. McCallum, who spent a considerable amount of his time producing badly needed plans of the towns of Duala and Viktoria, together with maps of the numerous creeks around Duala. Once again a Secret Service was created but in this case, in view of the vast distances to be covered, the agents were made responsible to the commanders of the various columns.

In Egypt the Intelligence component of the EEF was a victim of divided responsibilities, with Brigadier-General Gilbert Clayton being responsible for both military and civil Intelligence. As a result Operational Intelligence got lost between the competing demands of higher strategy and the security of Egypt, and when Meinertzhagen took charge of Intelligence for Allenby in July 1917 he complained that, 'On arrival here I found a good system of agents based on Cairo and operating in Central Palestine, but there was no "front line" intelligence. At advanced headquarters security arrangements were nil and not one single agent was employed.'[2]

True to form, Meinertzhagen took urgent steps to repair this deficiency and brought the EEF into line with all the other British forces, complete with its own Secret Service. And so it went on in every theatre of war, the Intelligence Section of each Expeditionary Force speedily erecting its own secret Intelligence services: each major

1 'Copies of Papers on the Military Situation in the Cameroons and Nigeria', PRO WO 106/6458.
2 Meinertzhagen, op. cit., p. 216.

command — Salonika, Mesopotamia, East Africa and even Russia, wherever British Forces served — created its own secret networks. This aspect has been emphasized with a purpose, for the number and diversity of all these spy rings had a profound impact on that form of Intelligence during the war.

For the first months of the First World War the dual arrangement between War Office and Army operated smoothly enough, for warfare was still open and the fighting bore some resemblance to traditional classic warfare. But once the opposing forces were helplessly locked in the misery of the trenches the Army in the field was deprived of information from its usual sources.

In the west, with the official Secret Service already at work, together with its French and Belgian counterparts and the various Army field Intelligence Units, the opportunities for chaos were unlimited.

As the war got ever more deeply bogged down in the dire morass of entrenchments, it became clear that GHQ's Secret Service would have to channel its information through neutral countries just as did MO5(j) and in an attempt to head off confusion in this sphere a conference was held at Furnes near Veurne in Belgium on 22 November 1914 to consider forming an Intelligence service common to the Allied Armies in the field, one which could deal with their specific needs without upsetting the arrangements of any Allied official Secret Service. Colonel George Kynaston Cockerill, later the Director of Special Intelligence in the Directorate of Military Intelligence, proposed that a central bureau of Allied military services be established at Folkestone, since agents could conveniently meet and report there by virtue of the fact that so many shipping lines operated from that port. It would be easier for the responsible officers to co-ordinate and direct their activities, and to sort and check their information without the necessity of agents making a time-consuming journey to their respective headquarters. There was the added bonus that a large number of French and Belgian refugees arrived in Folkestone and might well be recruited to serve as agents.

Cockerill's proposal was accepted and each of the Allied military Intelligence sections appointed one officer to represent them there, the idea being that they should meet at least once every day to form a pool of information common to all and construct a single bulletin from it for transmission by telegraph to their respective GHQs. Each officer, though, would have a free hand in running his own service network and would be able to direct it in accordance with the needs of his own GHQ.

The British representative to the Folkestone Bureau was Major (then Captain) Cecil Aylmer Cameron, Royal Artillery.[1] Born in 1883, he had been commissioned in 1901 and, until 1912, enjoyed an unspectacular career. Then disaster struck — apparently. According to the official line, Cameron's wife faked the robbery of a pearl necklace in order to claim the sum insured of £6,500; she was tried and convicted by the High Court in Edinburgh in December 1912. Cameron had had nothing to do with the crime but had allegedly tried to cover his wife's misdeed, for which he was sentenced to three years' imprisonment. Three years seems a severe sentence for Cameron's alleged part in the business, but more extraordinary still is the fact that Captain Cameron suddenly reappeared in 1914, over a year before his sentence was due to expire, to take up the reins of Secret Service work in Folkestone like an old hand. Such positions are not filled by what the Americans call 'greenhorns' and it seems probable that Cameron's 'sentence' was in fact a 'cover' to enable him to vanish from his regiment and enter the new Secret Service without anybody being inclined to enquire further. As Colonel Richard Drake, a later head of GHQ secret Intelligence wrote, 'Actual experience of secret service work is the only real guide to the attainment of the ideal system to be adopted.'[2]

The success of Cameron's cover, as it appears to be, is upheld by an entry in the diary kept by Major Walter Kirke, the head of the GHQ Secret Service in France from 1914 to 1917. In his observations on one of the interminable conferences to put Secret Service operations on a sounder footing, he made the revealing remark that 'C's objections to draft of conference are that it put him under his old subordinate Cameron, and that he did not see why he should not do what he liked in Belgium.'[3] The key words are 'his old subordinate', words indicating that Cameron had in fact already been transferred to the *Special Duties List* in order to serve under Commander (later Captain Sir) Mansfield George Smith-Cumming RN, who headed the official

1 Cameron's substantive rank in 1914 was captain but he was made a brevet major (with the power, responsibility and nearly the same pay as a major), which rank would be surrendered at the end of the war unless previously confirmed. In fact, his promotion to major was made substantive in 1915.

2 Colonel R. J. Drake, *History of Intelligence (B), British Expeditionary Force, France. From January 1917 to April 1919*, PRO WO 106/45 and ICMA.

3 Kirke Diaries, op. cit., 13 December 1915.

Secret Service responsible to the Foreign Office and both Army and Navy, recruiting from both the latter. Officers on the *Special Duties List* were selected men with some special talent who could be useful in various fields. Not all of them were chosen for Intelligence purposes, but a certain number were and it was from amongst them that the Army drew its Intelligence personnel, often in conjunction with work for the official Secret Service.

Whatever the circumstances of Cameron's posting, he showed himself to be a proud and prickly individual who frequently adopted high-handed methods and did not get on well with his colleagues, particularly those in other services. Kirke, his commanding officer, remarked, 'If Cameron does a little giving as well as taking I think that the show should run. If not we must take over the whole root & branch and cut out the WO [War Office] altogether,'[1] a comment which not only sheds light on Cameron's attitude but shows that GHQ's response to any awkwardness occasioned by his behaviour was not to curb him, but to put his rivals out of court, a solution that would have been completely unacceptable to the War Office. Cameron was certainly a difficult man to get on with, as the history of his continual clashes with Major Edmund Wallinger, head of GHQ's other service, initiated in April 1915, illustrates. When it became necessary to engineer closer co-operation between the official Secret Service and the operations of the GHQ services, Cameron went to the Netherlands on 15 December 1916 and provoked a regular caterwaul of protest from the British officials there and the Military Attaché at the Hague, Lieutenant-Colonel Laurence Oppenheim. Oppenheim's protest, smoothed over by the Directorate of Military Intelligence's in-house historians (MI2(e)) is reported:

> Finally he commented on the unfortunate result of Major Cameron being in any way connected with the proposal; this fact prejudiced the other three against it, and Major Cameron in addition had shown little or no tact, especially in hinting at 'Direct orders' for the Legation's compliance with the proposal. As the plan now stood, it seemed to involve a constant stream of instructions between Major Cameron and a member of the Legation; this position was frankly impossible.[2]

1 Ibid., 9 September 1915.

2 *The History of the British Secret Service In Holland*, Part II, p. 13 [hereinafter *The History, MI2(e)*]. This document was written under the aegis of MI2(e) and is held in the Papers of Lieutenant M.R.K. Burge [hereinafter Burge Papers], ICMA.

Colonel Drake, Kirke's successor after 1917, had no liking for Cameron either, writing to Sigismund Payne Best, one of the original members of the Intelligence Corps and later one of the most excellent British agents in the Netherlands, that:

> I know from my experience the lengths to which people will go in vilification. *Nothing*, literally *nothing* was too bad for old pegleg Wallinger to say about me because he imagined that I favoured Cameron. I can tell you now that I had no favour for Cameron: *I* would never have employed him. I inherited him from Kirke who shared with Macdonogh [Kirke's chief] a weird belief in Cam's innocence in the Pearl Necklace business. This I did not share and Cameron's presence in a job with command of vast sums of money and a wife with her record caused me vast uneasiness. So much so that I was infinitely relieved when he resigned! This is for you and you only.[1]

Apart from the rancour revealed here, it is obvious that Drake knew less than he thought about Cameron's past. The 'need to know' system stalks the corridors of Intelligence just as it does any other branch of officialdom: if facts were not necessary to your work, you were not — and are not — told of them. Drake had previously been employed in Sir Vernon Kell's counter-espionage service and had no way of knowing of what I presume to be Cameron's innocence or the subterfuge employed to disguise his real activities.

Cameron, for all his faults, had the ability to see to the heart of a question. The mass armies of the First World War could only be easily transported by Europe's railway system. Cameron was the first man to realize that spies watching those railway lines could report any significant movement of troops along them and thus open the eyes of the generals to any change in the enemy's deployment and make them aware of any hostile reorganization or concentration. His idea was speedily seized upon by all Allied Intelligence services in every theatre of war, and through his ability to organize and to develop this new idea he made a tremendous contribution to the eventual success of the Allies on the battlefield. Even Drake was moved to pay tribute: '. . . great credit is therefore due to him for the success which his own, and other services, achieved in this field'.[2]

With Cameron's GHQ service forced to operate through neutral

1 Best Papers, loc. cit., Drake to Best, 29 July 1947.
2 Drake, op. cit., p. 10.

countries, hitherto the exclusive province of C's official Secret Service (Cumming was known as 'C' from the way in which he initialled his reports, always written and signed in green ink), potential battlelines were drawn between the Intelligence Services and the powerful, sometimes abrasive, personalities at their head. Cumming's service was neither designed nor intended to discover and convey the sort of detailed information GHQ needed and could not, therefore, be an effective substitute for GHQ's own service. S. P. Best worked for Wallinger's service and had close, if not always friendly, contact with Tinsley's service in the Netherlands. He wrote in 1914 of the rival MI1(c):

> My service was started simply because the BEF could not fight the war in France without accurate information and this they could not obtain from official sources. 'C's' official secret service, the War Office, the Foreign Office and the Admiralty, all published Intelligence summaries daily. (For private circulation only, of course.) And their system was to include every rumour that was going and every tall story retailed to them without further examination. Eventually some story would turn out to be true, but at the time no-one could possibly weed out the grains of truth from the vast mass of falsehood![1]

Since GHQ was directing the operations of Britain's main force, on whose success or failure the future of the Empire depended, it was obviously nonsense to expect them to rely on such a service. On GHQ's pressing need for information regarding the enemy in its theatre of war Kirke trenchantly observed:

> It would be no excuse for us to say 'The War Office or the Foreign Office are not sending us any.'
>
> This implied no criticism of 'C' in any way, because it would be impossible for any man to supply information to all our various expeditions which would satisfy their detailed requirements. Each Army alone knows what it wants and is responsible for getting it.[2]

Awkward as the problems of organization were, they were not insoluble given common sense and goodwill from all concerned. Alas, it was not to be and if Cameron had a hand in the ensuing difficulties

1 Best Papers, loc. cit., 'The Origin of the Intelligence Corps BEF 1914'.
2 Kirke Diaries, op. cit., 30 November 1915.

he was by no means alone: Cumming, too, must share some of the responsibility.

Cumming was a short, stockily built, white-haired naval officer, 55 years old when the war began, with a round, jovial face, sporting a gold-rimmed monocle. He was generally respected by all who served with him and was devoted to his work, which he regarded as a great game. His public persona was that of an old English eccentric, an eccentric who enjoyed driving his Rolls-Royce at high speeds through London, to the irritation of the police who were powerless to stop him.

Compton Mackenzie, working for Intelligence in the Middle East and Greece, related the story of what was very nearly C's last drive in his *Greek Memories*, a tale which did the rounds amongst Intelligence officers and certainly went far towards adding to Cumming's mystique:

> In the autumn of 1914 his son, a subaltern in the Seaforths, had been driving him in a fast car on some urgent Intelligence mission in the area of operations. The car going at full speed had crashed into a tree and overturned, pinning Captain Cumming by the leg and flinging his son out on his head. The boy was fatally injured, and his father, hearing him moan something about the cold, tried to extricate himself from the wreck of the car to put a coat over him; but struggle as he might he could not free his smashed leg. Thereupon he had taken out a penknife and hacked away at his smashed leg until he had cut it off, after which he had crawled over to his son and spread a coat over him, being found later lying unconscious by the dead body.[1]

It was all a myth. Cumming ('Captain Spencer', as he was usually known in an effort to conceal his identity) had been taken to hospital and his leg was amputated there; he nearly lost the other leg, too. The accident apparently did nothing to dent his buoyant spirit, which was soon employed in brightening his fellow patients' lives and later led to more irregular behaviour, such as the habit of driving a penknife into his wooden leg to emphasize points made in conversation, and the purchase of a child's scooter on which he used to plant his wooden leg and propel himself around the corridors of the War Office.

1 Compton Mackenzie, *Greek Memories*, Maryland, 1987, pp. 90–91. This is a reprint of the original 1932 first edition which was suppressed by the British Government under the Official Secrets Act. Mackenzie was fined, but permitted to publish his book later, only after sensitive details had been edited out. Copies of the first edition are now few and far between — and very expensive. This unabridged edition from the United States is therefore to be welcomed.

Mackenzie met C in London at the end of 1916:

After about ten minutes of this embarrassed waiting a young man came in and announced that the Chief wished to see Captain Mackenzie immediately. I followed him into C's private room, tucked away under the roof, crowded with filing cupboards and shelves, and with the rest of the space almost entirely filled by C's big table. The dormer windows looked out across the plane-trees of the Embankment Gardens to the Thames, over which twilight was creeping. I saw on the other side of the table a pale clean-shaven man, the most striking features of whose face was a Punch-like chin, a small and beautifully fine bow of a mouth, and a pair of very bright eyes. He was dressed in the uniform of a naval captain.

C paid no attention when I came in, but remained bent over the table, perusing through a pair of dark horn-rimmed spectacles some document. I stood watching the blue dusk and the tarnished silver of the Thames until presently C took off the glasses, leant back in his chair, and stared hard at me for a long minute without speaking.

'Well?' he said finally.

'Mackenzie, sir,' I replied. 'Reporting to you from Athens.'

'And what have you to say for yourself?' he asked, putting in an eyeglass and staring at me harder than ever.

Somehow I suppose I must have embarked on my tale in such a way as to win his attention, for after a few minutes he murmured in those faintly-slurred, immensely attractive accents of his:

'There's no need to tell me all this standing up. There's a chair beside you.'

So I sat down and went on talking until about a quarter to seven, when a pink-faced secretary with a bundle of papers put her head round the door. She conveyed an impression that she had been deputed as the least likely person to have her head bitten off if she was interrupting a conversation. C held out his hand for the papers and signed his name on them one after another in the bright green ink he always used. Presently we were left alone again.

At half-past seven he said:

'Well, you'd better stop and have some dinner with us.'

'Thank you very much, sir,' I said. 'Would you mind if I went downstairs and sent away my taxi?'

'Have you been keeping a taxi waiting two hours?'

'Yes, sir, I thought you would probably be finished with me in a few minutes.'

'My god,' C exclaimed. 'No wonder you're always asking for another thousand pounds every month!'

I went down to pay off the taxi, and when I came back the offices were empty. C took me into the dining-room where I was introduced to Mrs Cumming as the man who had given him more trouble than anybody else in his service.

After dinner C showed me various books he had been buying. They were mostly sets in bright leather bindings.

'These ought to be in your line,' he said. 'You're a writing fellow, aren't you?'

Those books and the large oil-painting of a young officer in the uniform of the Seaforth Highlanders were the chief features of the room. I remembered the tale of how C had cut off his leg with a penknife in order to reach his dying son and put an overcoat over him, and the little room filled with that large portrait expressed how large a place the original must have held in his heart.

It must have been after eleven o'clock when I got up to leave.[1]

GHQ maintained the philosophy that a number of Secret Services was a vital requirement: one system would be able to pick up information missed or overlooked by another — in short, the systems were to be complementary and the more there were the more information would be obtained and shared. It was also thought that if any system was penetrated and broken by the Germans, the other systems could continue work unhindered. Here GHQ were worshipping a false god, as will become apparent.

Major Wallinger, another officer with a wooden leg, ran GHQ's second Secret Service, parallel to Cameron, reporting to Kirke and later to Drake. Part of his brief was to monitor the ferry service from the Netherlands to Tilbury. It was generally felt that Cameron at Folkestone already had his hands full and could not cover Tilbury with the attention it deserved as a means of cardinal importance for passing agents and reports between Britain and the Netherlands.

Wallinger's service had originally been intended to concern itself solely with Belgium but, as was always the case with so many systems in existence, artificial demarcations were found to be wholly impractical, as in their eagerness to acquire information of value to GHQ the various different services inevitably found themselves poaching on each other's preserves. Although Kirke's view was that 'the more independent systems we had the better',[2] he was soon to comment ruefully in his diary:

1 Ibid., pp. 394–96.
2 Kirke Diaries, op. cit., 22 March 1915.

> Wallinger and he [Cameron] seem to be running the same show only separately. This was not the original idea, as Cam was to send all written compiled reports, whilst Wallinger & Delporte were to get telegraphic information of *movements* of troops only in a certain restricted area close to our front.[1]

Proof of the strength of GHQ's belief in a plurality of Intelligence services lies in the fact that Wallinger's unit was set up after an important meeting of British representatives in the Netherlands on 24 January 1915 about close co-operation. Sir Alan Johnstone, British Ambassador at the Hague, forwarded and supported a joint memorandum from Ernest Maxse, the Consul-General at Rotterdam and Laurence Oppenheim, Military Attaché at the Hague, proposing that the Allied Military Attachés in the Netherlands should work in conjunction with each other, along the lines of the Military Intelligence Bureau at Folkestone, to pool, collate and forward their information. Maxse at Rotterdam would also direct selected agents of Oppenheim's who had been sent into Germany and pay them from a special fund of £300 set up for the purpose.

The intervention of the diplomatic community in the Netherlands is of special importance, for it had long been an established fact of British diplomatic life that the Foreign Office and its employees did not engage in acts of espionage in any shape or form, a ruling flouted with increasing frequency as the war ground on. The proffered excuse in the case of the Netherlands was that 'in time of war there could be no objection to secret service being undertaken by the Consul General or by the Military Attaché so long as their espionage was not directed against the country to whose Government they were accredited'.[2]

Sir Alan's proposals were not greeted with open arms at the War Office, where Colonel French, whose duty it was to collate all the different Intelligence activities, had enough to handle without more being thrust onto his plate by well-meaning amateurs such as Maxse. Since French, in common with the rest of the Intelligence staff at the War Office, was opposed anyway to the GHQ idea of complementary services, the argument of dual control was raised against the proposals as was the fact that the plan attempted no possible co-operation with the existing services. French did, however, place a compromise

1 Ibid., 1 April 1915.
2 Burge Papers, loc. cit. *The History, MI2(e)*, p. 3.

solution on the table to placate the eager beavers at the Hague, recommending that a head agent should be installed at the Hague as the executive controller of all Intelligence work who would take his directions from Oppenheim and Maxse. This head agent would pass all the information he collected to Oppenheim, who could then expertly edit his reports before sending the distilled versions to the War Office in London. French was quite happy to agree to the extra money requested by Maxse to be made available, though it was made perfectly clear that the object of the exercise was to improve military Intelligence and that in no circumstances were either Maxse or Oppenheim to impinge on Naval interests.

Although the War Office went along with Colonel French's views, the Foreign Office were very much taken aback and in March 1915 they decided that their officials would have no connection whatsoever with espionage, on the grounds that if they were to complain to neutral governments about German activities in this field then they themselves had to have clean hands. Instead it was arranged that Oppenheim should lend his experience to the editing of the military aspects of the reports gathered by C's agents through his chief of operations in the Netherlands, Captain Richard Bolton Tinsley RNVR. Maxse nevertheless went ahead in spite of the Foreign Office's ruling.

In the meantime events were taking place in France that were to force the pace and upset all arrangements, whether existing or proposed. There the overall head of Intelligence at GHQ, Brigadier-General George Macdonogh, was heartily dissatisfied with the way that secret Intelligence reached him, arriving as it did piecemeal, often contradictory and even obsolete by the time it had been subjected to review by the War Office. Thus, in May 1915, he urgently requested that the originals of all reports, whether from GHQ services or not, should be sent to GHQ without delay. He was under the impression that Oppenheim was running a service in Belgium and felt that as Belgium was the theatre of operations for the BEF, GHQ should be the sole channel for the direction of the Secret Service there, even if that meant placing Oppenheim under his authority. That idea was, of course, anathema to the War Office.

Colonel French pointed out to Macdonogh that Oppenheim controlled no agents but merely edited the reports of C's agents, though admittedly he wrote as if they were operating under his authority. Nevertheless he agreed to forward the official

Secret Service's reports to GHQ at once, although he made the point that GHQ had raised no objections to the January agreement.

Colonel French took the sensible step of informing Oppenheim of what had transpired and defined the latter's duties with more precision in order to eliminate the undesirable delays which were arousing anger at GHQ. Oppenheim was instructed that he would now have to decide which reports he would send back himself and which reports Tinsley would send direct to C. This meant that he would now have to sift all the reports himself and make difficult decisions in borderline cases, but in practice the arrangement successfully eradicated delays and was more in keeping with the original idea accepted by the Foreign Office, who now further accepted that Oppenheim would telegraph 'all important military information' through C.[1]

The arrangement promised well, but as early as July a problem shook the superficial harmony, demonstrating that in reality none of the services knew what the others were doing, that they were operating without regard to the safety and efficiency of their *confrères* and that they simply had no trust in each other.

Cameron's system was employing a Belgian, M. Georges Gabain, a close lieutenant of Cameron whom the latter sent to the Netherlands in June 1915 to expand the all-important train-watching service. Gabain's activities were brought to Oppenheim's attention by a Dutch informant, M. Reyntiens, who portrayed Gabain's activities as an effort to create an entirely new train-watching service. Oppenheim had heard nothing about any new train-watching network and his wrath was fed by complaints from Tinsley, also incensed about a 'new' system. Two stiff letters, of 4 and 7 July, winged their way from Oppenheim to French, complaining roundly about the conduct of Gabain in the first instance and, in the second, denouncing the idea of parallel but separate systems.

Swift enquiries by Colonel French elicited the information that Cameron's lieutenant had only been trying to recruit good train-watchers for existing systems. Oppenheim had been seriously misled by Reyntiens, a fact which served to illustrate how far those directing operations were in the hands of their agents and how apparently trivial rivalries could be blown up out of all proportion. As Drake was to

1 Ibid., p. 10.

observe, 'competition and bitterness were the natural outcome of the system then in force, and of the vital necessity, coupled with keenness, to obtain information for the Armies in the field.'[1] In this case Oppenheim was asked to placate Tinsley and reassert the idea that parallel organizations were part of a considered policy by GHQ.

Whatever faults Tinsley may have had, a disinclination to fight his corner was not one of them. He was a daunting figure. A member of the Royal Naval Volunteer Reserve, he had spent his life involved with ships and the sea, and when war broke out he was a director of the Uranium Steamship Company, in which capacity he had made very valuable contacts which were to serve him well as C's chief in the Netherlands. Kirke's description of him is a penetrating one, though coloured by the resentment felt at GHQ against him. On meeting him for the first time at a conference in November 1915, Kirke confided to his diary:

> He strikes me as being a smart fellow, but not a man for whom any really high class agent would work, such as Ramble. With him it is a matter of business and I doubt his imparting patriotic enthusiasm to agents. He therefore misses the best people, and I should never consider him capable of running our show in toto, without an officer in charge and always at his elbow.[2]

Tinsley, however, controlled an organization which was both nebulous and ubiquitous to which his businessman's methods were ideally suited. During the war he directed no fewer than three different services in Belgium which in turn managed no fewer than eighteen different spy systems. One service, run by a man called Amirauté, operated three different systems, those of Parenté, Lefèbvre and Desnoyettes; another was run by Brazil Frankignoul, controlling the services of Bordeaux and Legros. The most important of Tinsley's services from a military point of view was directed by Henry Landau, a captain on the Army's General List who ran no fewer than fourteen systems by 1918.[3] Many of the systems themselves ran subsidiary enterprises, all of which brought Tinsley's haul to 60 systems employing 300 agents, who in turn employed other sub-agents. This was only the Belgian section, and a section which dealt only with the German Army in that country. Tinsley also operated in

1 Drake, op. cit., p. 10.
2 Kirke Diaries, op. cit., 29 November 1915.
3 Papers of *La Dame Blanche*, IWM. *La Dame Blanche* was one of the principal British Secret Service systems in Belgium in 1918. *See* p. 187 et seqq.

Germany, and in the Netherlands from Rotterdam, and he maintained a valuable Naval section under Captain Powers RN, together with a counter-espionage service. The successful control of such an organization could only be managed by a man of character and dedication.

The problems aroused by Gabain's incursion into the Netherlands had managed to rattle cages at GHQ as well as the War Office, with the almost immediate result that Kirke prepared a memorandum addressing the problems faced by secret Intelligence in that country and identifying three key factors influencing any plan for a greater degree of centralization:

a) The quantity of information and the speed of its arrival.
b) The security of the systems.
c) The effect of any change in the position of the Army in the field, whether occasioned by victory or defeat.

He again propounded the ideal of parallel services, arguing again that if one organization broke down others would remain to carry on the good work. Equally, if one or other of the contending parties established a recognized supremacy in any field it would still be unable to cater for all the matters of detail which the others required. GHQ were not equipped to handle the more specialized functions of the War Office, such as supplies and contraband, and they had no experience of operating in Germany, where C was very active. On the other side of the coin, C could not hope to cover all GHQ's tactical and operational requirements which Kirke thought were better served by a spread of corroborative information from as many different sources as possible. The only concrete proposal for change suggested by Kirke was that GHQ should send an officer to the Netherlands to clamp down on the activities of pseudo or indiscreet agents and so prevent upsets like that occasioned by Gabain.

The War Office accepted the idea even if they did not take it to their hearts, and in August 1915 Captain Branston was sent to the Netherlands under the guise of an Aliens Officer. Obstacles were immediately placed in his path by Maxse, who seemed determined to obstruct GHQ at every turn. Initially Maxse objected to the use of diplomatic cover, as that would mean Branston could not legitimately have any direct contact with the agents who were to be his concern. When an alternative identity was offered in the shape of a supplier of clothing to Belgian refugees, Maxse argued that Branston did not 'look the part'. In the end GHQ had little alternative but to recall Branston and the idea was not revived.

While the heads of service were fighting like cats in a bag, some of their agents in Belgium were seeking to exploit the disarray in order to turn the situation to good account. In particular Kirke recorded a sorry tale in his diary in July 1915 about an agent named Putman. Not only had he become a danger, having been recognized by the Germans who were now pressing the Dutch authorities to expel him, but

> Cameron says PUTMAN very jealous of other agents, spends his time ferreting out other systems and tries to bribe them to give him their reports first and to delay forwarding them to their proper owners.[1]

Indeed, the Germans were pressing the Dutch Government heavily to clamp down on the ill-disciplined Allied agents inhabiting their country and were backing up their diplomatic pressure with a thinly veiled military threat which included massing troops near the Dutch frontier. This sent ripples of panic through all the Secret Services. Oppenheim and Tinsley made the GHQ services scapegoats for the situation, finding a useful target in the person of one Briggs, one of Cameron's men, guilty of the unpardonable crime of sending his reports through the open post. The practical difficulties and the escalating crisis in morale occasioned yet another memorandum from GHQ in a bid to defuse the situation. It received short shrift from the War Office, chiefly on the grounds that it advocated most of Tinsley's Belgian operations being subordinated to GHQ's control. On 7 September, the Director of Special Intelligence, Brigadier-General Cockerill, pointed out that if GHQ were determined to maintain parallel organizations, then friction between their units and C's was inevitable and that GHQ would just have to accept that. In his eyes there were two possible solutions: either all Secret Service in the Netherlands would be subordinated to the professionals working under C, or the GHQ memorandum could serve as a basis for further discussion — but discussion there would have to be. As things stood it was not just a case of the right hand not knowing what the left was doing, but each limb, each hand and each finger going different ways.

1 Kirke Diaries, op. cit., 19 July 1915.

Forced actually to speak to each other directly instead of going through the helpful medium of Colonel French at the War Office, Cockerill, French, Drake, Kirke and C met at the Hotel Crillon in Paris on 9 September. The meeting was, as might have been predicted, somewhat acerbic, since C objected to the draft conclusion of an earlier conference, held on the 3rd, between Kirke, Cameron, Wallinger and Oppenheim, that Tinsley's operation should be placed under GHQ control. Kirke's diary relates in reserved tones that 'French said that D.M.O. (& C) rather objected to our taking over C's show without paying for it and that C was sore at not being sufficiently recognised in the transfer, as the show was his and not Oppenheim [sic].'[1] GHQ had to abandon the agreement of the 3rd, and Macdonogh sent C a conciliatory letter thanking him for his valuable services in the previous few weeks. The GHQ memorandum was quietly swept under the carpet as being nothing more than an attempt to secure a closer degree of co-operation between Tinsley and Cameron through the good offices of Oppenheim but in practical terms, beyond discussing the formation of an International Intelligence Bureau, nothing was done to settle the disputes between the British services, which continued to rumble on.

On 24 November the ever-diplomatic Colonel French circulated a paper summarizing the situation and suggesting improvements to all the interested parties to be embodied in a new bureau to be known by its French initials, BCI. As regards the central issue of the number of competing services, he wished to combine two ideas generated by the War Office and GHQ on previous occasions. Some degree of necessary centralization was to be achieved by establishing Tinsley as overall head agent in the Netherlands, with all instructions and reports to flow to and from him through C. Tinsley had run so many diverse services of his own that he would be ideally suited to do the same work for all parties, in keeping with GHQ's preference for parallel systems. Then and only then would the GHQ proposal that Belgium be divided into areas be practical. The greatest need would be to convince Tinsley, who was becoming increasingly irked by what he regarded as the unwarranted and ill-considered activities of GHQ, especially of Cameron. The recipients of French's paper met to discuss it at the War Office on 29 November, a meeting hardly less acrimonious than its predecessor in Paris.

1 Ibid., 9 September 1915.

According to his own account of the conference, the only one that records the details of all that transpired and is open to public scrutiny, Kirke opened the proceedings by insisting that there were certain principles on which GHQ could not afford to compromise. These he listed as follows:

a) The Field Army must be responsible for all Intelligence on its front.
b) The British had no more than a partial responsibility in Belgium; the French and Belgians had even greater interests there.
c) A joint organization had already been appointed to ensure co-operation between the national military services at Folkestone and everything else should be subsidiary to that arrangement.
d) Subject to the above principles, he proposed that occupied Belgium should be divided into zones in accordance with his earlier views expressed in October. GHQ would be happy for the War Office to look after Eastern Belgium, so long as GHQ could deal with any difficulties that might arise with the French and Belgians.
e) Advanced areas could be reallocated as was proved necessary.[1]

Major R. Campbell of the War Office attempted — at C's instigation, according to Kirke — to obtain a free hand in Belgium for C, to which Kirke responded by pointing out that GHQ was just as anxious as the Foreign Office to avoid complications with neutral governments ' & no more injudicious than C's people and more careful than the French or Belgians'.[2] Kirke then painstakingly explained once again that GHQ had the primary interest in Belgium as it was there that the war was actually being fought: GHQ could not afford to subordinate that interest to anybody else. If Kirke's account is to be credited, Campbell 'saw the point, and it was quite evident that he was merely trying to get increased power for C over our organisations'. Discussion then turned to Switzerland, where the official Secret Service were paramount, with GHQ's systems being few and small in comparison. Here Kirke was perfectly willing to make concessions, which he hoped would be offset by concessions from C in the far more important Dutch sphere.

1 Ibid., 29 November 1915.
2 Ibid.

The conference accepted the GHQ proposal for the division of Belgium into zones, the dividing line being drawn north-south from Antwerp to Namur through Brussels, with GHQ controlling the western zone almost exclusively and C having exclusive domination to the east of the demarcation line. Air Service Intelligence, however, had to be drawn from all parts of Belgium, and Wallinger's service was not restricted in its activities, as it was small and confined to certain specific subjects. Moreover, neither Tinsley nor Oppenheim had any quarrel with him, only with Cameron. There was also a division of responsibility over relations with outside bodies. Thus GHQ were to be responsible for handling any difficulties with the Belgians and French, provided they observed the principle that the service responsible for any area where this prerogative was exercised should be left to decide the precise methods of practice to be employed there. In the meantime, C was to settle any difficulties with the foreign Military Attachés at the Hague through Oppenheim, and all the Intelligence targets peculiar to the War Office, such as trade and contraband, were to be confined solely to Tinsley's hands.

Nobody was really satisfied with the compromise, as the artificial division of Belgium greatly hampered the free flow of vital information and in itself presented grounds for new bouts of quarrelling. C thought his rightful preserves were being poached and complained long and loudly about it, while GHQ were aggrieved over the loss of posts at Liège, which prevented them from gaining information about whether German troops were coming to Belgium from the French sector of the Western front or from Russia, a fact that had an important bearing on the crisis in Intelligence of the summer of 1916, when the Somme offensive was raging and all information was desperately needed. The frustration felt at GHQ that summer pervades Kirke's diary: 'Our posts are not v. much use without other posts further East, as we cannot tell where movements have originated. But W.O. [War Office] will not allow us to start posts in their area so we are helpless in that matter.'[1]

In his history of secret Intelligence in the west, Colonel Drake condemned the artificial limit as fundamentally unsound, as not only did it

> . . . prevent, in many cases, the natural overflow of an existing sound system, operating on the border of the delimited territory, into

1 Ibid., 2 August 1916.

> the forbidden zone on the other side of the border, and so deprive forces in the field of useful information from a known and reliable source; but it prevents, in many cases, the acquisition of information from certain portions of the forbidden territory, owing to the fact that individuals who are capable of setting up systems in that territory are unwilling to work for the headmen and other chiefs to whom their territory has been allotted.[1]

For all its faults, the new organization did quell the disruptive, internecine warfare for a short period but the confidence placed in it on all sides was conditional at best and too many opportunities remained for unscrupulous individuals to traduce the terms of the agreement. One final attempt was made to iron out the problems. When the War Office was reorganized by the strong and efficient hand of General Sir William Robertson, the new CIGS, in the winter of 1915, one of the major changes was the creation of a new Directorate of Military Intelligence and George Macdonogh was recalled from France to head it.

With his experience of the unhappy state of secret Intelligence in the Netherlands, one of his first moves was to pen a memorandum with the object of re-establishing affairs on a sounder footing. The original division of responsibility between the War Office and GHQ for strategic and tactical intelligence was confirmed. The Folkestone Bureau was to be the only GHQ service to work through the Netherlands and its activities would be restricted first by having to send all its reports through the War Office and second by its operations being confined to an area west of the line Lierre-Wauvre-Tamines-Anginy inclusive. It was also required to send a list of its agents to the War Office together with a monthly chart of operations, so that the risk of disputes arising from overlapping systems could be reduced to a minimum. Finally, Wallinger's system in Belgium would now come under the wing of the War Office and work under Tinsley with the proviso that the War Office would not accept responsibility for obtaining tactical information, though they would try to obtain any special report required by GHQ. The memorandum promised a far more centralized organization that would have removed many of the causes of the trouble of the preceding twelve months, but GHQ continued to dispute its terms out of suspicion and self-interest and a

1 Drake, op. cit., p. 4.

disinclination to suffer any curtailment of their activities without a fight.

The personal bitterness between Cameron and Tinsley now became a serious threat. Many of the British systems had been penetrated and destroyed by the Germans, who had imposed such a harsh reign of terror in occupied Belgium that the services had been finding it difficult to recruit new agents in the autumn and winter of 1915. Another conference met at Folkestone on 19 April 1916, this time an inter-Allied one, in a new bid to put affairs in order. This time no attempts were made to introduce collaboration at the command level. Instead it was to be reform from the bottom up. To this end the delegates agreed to ensure that every *chef de service* in Belgium had detailed knowledge of his agents and their whereabouts and also a blacklist of agents who had been discharged from services for one reason or another. Everybody was to know of the information collected by C, who would pass copies of train-watching reports to Cameron for dissemination. Agents were to be forbidden to sell their work to more than one service, a practice which resulted in more than one network sending in identical information, which then took on the lustre of truth. Where there was any doubt about a report, Oppenheim was to send the original to Folkestone so that it could be compared with the material in Cameron's hands. Personal consultation between the various heads of service was advocated but not demanded.

The French and Belgian services were drawn into the scheme of artificial zones, though they were reluctant parties to it. This time the division ran east-west through Belgium, along the line Namur-Charleroi-Mons. The Belgians were to cover the area to the north of this line and the French to the south, a half-measure which, like all the others, was still-born because it failed even to approach the root of the problem, namely the number of different services operating in complete independence of each other and the bad personal relations between their quarrelsome heads.

1916 had already got under way in its usual style with the standard round of denunciations, bribes, buying-up and double employment amongst the agents, while their service heads fumed and glared at each other. Cameron had tried to send his second-in-command, Captain McEwen, to Rotterdam in a bid to resolve difficulties on the spot, but his presence there was resented by both Oppenheim and Tinsley and in the end McEwen had to flee ignominiously from the Dutch police who had got onto his trail. This escapade incurred the wrath of both C and the War Office, who

> . . . seem to think we are merely doing it to annoy them! C full of stories of our having started the BCI on purpose to stop him doing anything in Paris, whereas of course, we have handed over BCI entirely to the War Office and C can put in anyone they like to let him — rather to GHQ's disadvantage.[1]

Behind this lay personal annoyance over GHQ contacting MI1 directly about the move instead of going through C. In fact MI1 had not consulted C at all, though GHQ had expected them to. Kirke commented:

> There is an extraordinary difference between dealing with a p.s.c. man and others. If a Staff College man were in C's place, say French, we should never have had the slightest trouble, as he like ourselves, would be working for the common good, and not for self-aggrandisement.[2]

A few weeks later another row had erupted when the War Office and C accused Cameron of 'jumping', i.e. of taking over without consultation two of Tinsley's services, and hopelessly disrupting them. To make matters worse, the Dutch newspaper *Telegraaf* had publicized the fact that Tinsley was a British Intelligence agent and the Germans had seized the opportunity to denounce him to the Dutch government and demand his immediate expulsion. To fill Tinsley's cup of woe to the brim, the Germans had simultaneously arrested some of his agents. The blame for all this was laid squarely at Cameron's door and Kirke quickly sprang to his defence:

> None of the above can have any conceivable connection with Cameron, and the accusation is most unfair. I can not take action as it has not been made openly, but if it is we shall have to nail it down.[3]

A further disagreement even arose between Wallinger and Cameron, with Kirke recording that Wallinger

> . . . writes that Cam has pinched his Gand man. This is probably correct but one of Cam's men has done so unwittingly and McEwen is already investigating the case. Marcel [a smuggler on the Dutch/Belgian

1 Kirke Diaries, op. cit., 27 May 1916.
2 Ibid. 'p.s.c.' is an abbreviation for 'passed Staff College'.
3 Ibid., 28 July 1916.

> border who ran a spy ring for GHQ] is giving trouble and T [Tinsley] has been summoning Carlot [one of Cameron's headmen] to his assistance. This latter I do not mind personally, if they don't turn on him afterwards.[1]

The problems continued even after the April Folkestone conference. Kirke recorded that 'Difficulties arising between WL [Wallinger, London] and Cam; quite unnecessary distrust of Cam in London generally,'[2] while Tinsley was still using Carlot despite C's orders to the contrary and Tinsley's systems were still silent, with Tinsley's idea of restarting them being to employ Cameron's men without Cameron's knowledge or consent.[3]

Nor was this all: a long running dispute between Cameron and two of Tinsley's agents, José and Van Sands, further soured relations, a dispute which ran, incredibly, from May to November 1916 and involved the obstruction of Cameron's reports at Flushing and attempts to 'jump' his systems. Bitter wrangling and petty obstructionism were the characteristics marking inter-service relations in 1916 and each fresh blow directed at any one service automatically upped the stakes when that service made its response. This was more the fault of the personalities than the organization, for the situation would never have become so volatile had not two such vigorous and sharp characters as those of Tinsley and Cameron been on the scene.

More was at stake in 1916 than ever before, a fact that added both urgency and, from the observer's viewpoint, a considerable degree of exasperation to the struggle. The summer of 1916 was a summer of titanic effort by all the combatants, the summer when every government and every General Staff invested huge quantities of their best blood in an all-out bid to win the decisive victory. The British Army's efforts were concentrated into the uncompromisingly mechanical Battle of the Somme, a long-drawn-out agony which pitted the frail bone and pulpy flesh of men against a torrent of industrialized artillery fire. In a desperate bid to break out, the generals badgered their Intelligence staffs mercilessly for information which might swing the struggle their way and terminate the dreadful slogging match. With Operational Intelligence helpless, the pressures on secret Intelligence grew apace. The inter-section quarrelling and the successes of

1 Ibid.
2 Ibid., 17 August 1916.
3 Ibid.

German counter-espionage gave the Secret Service a hard time in 1916 but even worse was to come.

The Intelligence reports of the various Secret Services were normally shipped across the channel by the ferries plying between Britain and the Netherlands. In the case of the GHQ services, the reports were still in their original form, but Tinsley's military information for the War Office had been edited by Oppenheim. In February 1916 one of the ferries sailing from Flushing had been mined and the sailings of her sister vessel had been reduced to four journeys a week. On 28 February the bottleneck was increased when the Zeeland ferry was sunk by a mine and the Tilbury-Flushing service was discontinued, much to the dismay of all the Intelligence chiefs, who found their channels of communication reduced even further. It was not until July that the real disaster struck: German destroyers from Zeebrugge intercepted the ferry S.S. *Brussels* and forced her into Zeebrugge, seizing all passengers and mail aboard. Her master, Captain Fryatt, had attempted to ram a German U-boat in 1915 and to commemorate his bravery had been presented with an engraved gold cigarette case. This proved his undoing when the Germans discovered it: as he was a civilian, they court-martialled him as a *franc-tireur* and shot him. Far more serious to the war effort, though, had been the capture of the couriers and the Intelligence reports aboard his vessel, for, armed with these, the Germans were able to smash a considerable part of Tinsley's Belgian spy rings.

On the final day of July hard on the heels of the *Brussels* disaster, the ferry *Zeelandia* struck a mine shortly after leaving Flushing and sailings from there were halted for a time by the Dutch authorities. Tinsley, C and the War Office were thrown into consternation bordering on panic by this calamitous month and lashed out in a mixture of anger and frustration at the nearest target, the unfortunate Cameron. The disaster which had befallen Tinsley was directly responsible for his irresponsible actions of the summer of 1916 in trying to 'jump' Cameron's systems, actions which nearly spelled disaster for both of them. There can be little doubt that the cautious Tinsley had been badly rattled by these events and the German demands for his expulsion, as this sort of behaviour was quite out of character and can be explained in no other way.

The consequences of the capture of the *Brussels* had been visited chiefly on Tinsley's services and, whilst GHQ suffered, their losses were minor in comparison. The German seizure of the ferry actually passed an ironic bonus to GHQ, for the collapse of Tinsley's services meant that little Intelligence was coming from Eastern Belgium from secret sources. GHQ were known to be rather miffed by losing their posts at Liège and now the replacement posts had gone too. Under pressure from the head of Intelligence to the BEF, John Charteris, the War Office grudgingly agreed to permit GHQ to extend their services into its area of Belgium — doing, in fact, precisely what GHQ had always intended the philosophy of parallel services to do. Thus Cameron's service opened several posts in the War Office zone, whilst Wallinger took over Liège, but the agreement to do so was not secured until the end of August and produced little to help the Somme offensive.

The chapter of disasters continued throughout the autumn. On 23 September the ferry S.S. *Colchester* was seized and escorted to Zeebrugge, where once again the passengers and mailbags were taken by the Germans. The messenger from the British Embassy at the Hague had been carrying the reports edited by Oppenheim in a Foreign Office bag which he had the presence of mind to throw overboard. Those who had equipped him with this item of luggage had not, it seems, the same presence of mind as the messenger, as they had omitted to provide the bag with proper sinkers, so that instead of finishing up in Davy Jones's locker the bag floated, was retrieved by the Germans and completed its journey in the hold of a German warship. Again, the consequences were disastrous, for Tinsley's Belgian services were now reduced to tatters and the French Secret Service lost a complete system which smuggled German deserters and escaped French prisoners-of-war into the Netherlands.

On 10 November another ferry was hauled into Zeebrugge by the Germans and this time the ferries were withdrawn from service for a time. The GHQ services were badly hurt by this, two of their agents being arrested (though one managed to escape) and the whole of the system at Gand St Pierre destroyed by the Germans. It signalled the end of a disastrous year for all the Secret Services and the beginnings of a long overdue reformation.

The initiative was taken independently by the head of Intelligence at GHQ, Brigadier-General John Charteris. On 18 December he took a leaf from the War Office book and proposed that not one but two officers from the GHQ services should be sent to the Netherlands and do for the GHQ reports what Oppenheim had been doing for Tinsley's — to sift and collate the agents' reports, edit the results and telegraph them back to London. It was hoped that this would lead not only to more amicable relations between the services and their leaders, but would drastically reduce the risks from reports falling into German hands in the event of any further seizures of the ferry boats. Charteris recommended that the officers sent over should be the deputies to the GHQ service chiefs, S. P. Best to represent Wallinger's service and McEwen to represent Cameron's, the latter being installed with the British Legation at the Hague as Assistant Military Attaché.[1]

Charteris's idea was sound in every way and certainly would have had a favourable impact on inter-service relations. As such, it received warm support from Colonel French at the War Office, the only doubt being cast upon McEwen's suitability, as French expected that he would hardly be acceptable to Oppenheim and he was also known to, and wanted by, the Dutch police. C agreed to the proposal, though without enthusiasm[2], but after nearly two years of continuous quarrelling, two years in which the patience of individuals had not so much been worn thin but cut to the marrow, inspiring frustration, distrust and even spite, a predictable response was forthcoming from all parties concerned in the Netherlands. They rejected the proposal out of hand, even when it was suggested that Captain Verdon, who had upset nobody, should take McEwen's place. Indeed, Tinsley went so far as to say that the only practical solution would be for the reports for the GHQ services to be collected by himself and then passed to Oppenheim for editing, ignoring the facts that Oppenheim already had his hands full coping with Tinsley's service and that editing alone was not the answer — the quality of the reports was not being questioned, only the rivalry and squabbling between the services which could best be cured by establishing some sort of on-the-spot supervision. French now took the unusual step of hitting the ball back at Tinsley, Maxse and Oppenheim by urging, in a letter dated 20 December, that they should suggest some practical alternative. In the meantime, Major Cameron had made his ill-fated trip to the Netherlands to see Oppenheim and the other officials, and had once again aroused their ire.

It fell to Oppenheim to reply to French's letter and, after consulting Sir Alan Johnstone, the ambassador, he suggested that 'the least impossible solution' would be for an acceptable officer from GHQ to

1 Burge Papers, loc. cit., *The History, MI2(e)*, p. 4.
2 Ibid.

be sent out who would be entirely subordinate to himself, would keep him fully informed and act under his advice to edit and control the GHQ systems. This was going much further than the original proposal, Oppenheim adding the caveat that it was the best he could offer and even as it stood it went much further than anything to which the other officials in the Netherlands corner were likely to agree. In addition he voiced his objections to Cameron being in any way involved in the Netherlands.

French then resorted to the time-honoured ploy of the previous two years: he suggested a conference to resolve the issue. The tide was now flowing strongly in favour of some sort of compromise to create one centre to govern all Secret Service work in the Netherlands. Colonel Kirke at GHQ wrote to French and resigned GHQ's interests into his hands, thus removing one possible obstacle. French took Kirke at his word and told Oppenheim on 3 January 1917 that he fully accepted the notion of one head centre in the Netherlands and the conference would discuss the question on that basis.

The conference duly assembled in the War Office on 19 January 1917 and, after two days of discussion, formally rejected the idea of sending officers from the GHQ services to the Netherlands. The view was that officers without experience of the situation in that country could not but help jeopardize the security of every service by laying open the Legation and the Military Attaché to interference from the Dutch government which would have little choice in the matter when faced with German pressure, a pressure only too often backed by the threat of military force. The idea of central control was upheld, however, and the conference recommended that all British agents should in future come under Tinsley's wing and all reports should be sent through Oppenheim, who was to be assisted in his work by an assistant appointed on the recommendation of GHQ. This was not the end of the unhappy affair, however, for these arguments failed to sway John Charteris in France. On 3 February another meeting was held at the War Office between Macdonogh, Maxse and Charteris to try to thrash out a solution. Charteris had genuine misgivings about the new arrangements for the old reason that while the War Office could afford to take an Olympian view, such a view had little bearing on the immediate problems that GHQ had to face, problems like fighting the armies across the shell-blasted wasteland and through the barbed wire, and defeating a powerful enemy who was prepared to fight.

Yet the switches of argument made by Charteris at the meeting on 3 February indicate that both a competitive instinct and some degree of bloody-mindedness were at work as well. The tried and tested philosophy of GHQ of maintaining parallel systems was again trotted out, but Mr Maxse undermined this argument by pointing out the sensitivity of the situation in the Netherlands *vis-à-vis* the Dutch government. Moreover, Charteris's idea would have placed Tinsley in a subordinate position which he was not prepared to accept and anyway there was no officer in London with the ability to run two such complex services in tandem.

Charteris now had his back to the wall and, despite being the officer who had set the reorganization ball rolling, he now fought hard to retain what he saw as GHQ's independence in these matters, holding that if there was only one service then its breakdown would mean the end of all information from the Netherlands. As for Tinsley, he might not be prepared to accept a subordinate position but equally Cameron would not work under him. Two final arguments were advanced: that GHQ would have no control, which seems to have been the factor which really disturbed Charteris, and that the reports from C's service had been of little value in the last six months of 1916. These points were all convincingly answered. The argument of a breakdown of one service was countered by pointing out that there was an even greater danger of existing systems being compromised by the continual friction and, while there would be one centre for secret intelligence, the services would still be able to operate autonomously under its guidance. In Maxse's opinion there would be no difficulty in the subordination of Cameron's service to Tinsley. As regards the final points raised by Charteris, he was told that GHQ had never had any direct control save in matters of policy but now they would be in direct touch with Oppenheim and could therefore direct the services towards the points of importance to GHQ, a fact that would certainly be to GHQ's benefit in the all-important business of the acquisition of information. On the morning of the 3rd, Colonel Edgar Cox of MI3 had presented Macdonogh with a table comparing the results of Tinsley's service with those of GHQ. Whether this was fortuitous or done by design, it cut the ground from under Charteris's feet, since the table showed quite clearly that the reports from the GHQ services would have been incomplete without the corroborative evidence from the posts of MI1(c). The organization of the latter service was superior too and, with the advantage of having Oppenheim to edit them, the reports attained an excellence which those of the GHQ services could not approach. Armed with this report, the War Office party were able to cite concrete examples which conclusively proved the value of Tinsley's reports.

It was not in Charteris's nature to surrender either easily or willingly and he now bought time by saying that he would have to refer the question to his own chief, Sir Douglas Haig. This threatened the process of reorganization with failure, for Haig would be certain to base his opinion in such a matter on the views of his personally chosen head of Intelligence.[1]

When the meeting broke up, it must have seemed to all participants that all the labour and all the hopes of the last two months were on the point of being tossed out of the window. However, Charteris, in a move for which he has been given little credit, offered the hope of a solution. After pondering the conference questions deeply, on 8 February he suggested a compromise that promised the hope of greater centralization through establishing a 'clearing house' under Tinsley to which all reports, irrespective of their origin, should be sent, from where they should be passed to Oppenheim for his expert editing. He would telegraph the most important elements of the material he held to the War Office in London, which would then distribute them to the field commands. It was a compromise which did not meet all the War Office's requirements but it did promise a solution of sorts to a long-running and increasingly dangerous problem. Also, and importantly, it did not preclude the possibility of further reorganization based on that arrangement. Charteris had suggested attaching one of GHQ's Intelligence officers, Captain F.R.P. Verdon, to the Hague as Assistant Military Attaché, which would satisfy at least the basic needs of both the War Office and GHQ. On 9 February, at a further meeting between Charteris and Macdonogh, the latter accepted the compromise on a trial basis and finally a sounder, more centralized organization was successfully achieved, with Best also going to the Netherlands to represent Wallinger's service.

The new organization was soon able to prove itself in practice. The existing systems continued to function but all transcripts of the agents' reports were delivered to Oppenheim by the head men, those from the GHQ systems being accompanied by a summarized digest of the

1 Ibid., p. 23.

essential features of the reports in order to guide Oppenheim when drawing his conclusions. Oppenheim was also vested with the right to call for the originals of the reports so that he could satisfy himself about their accuracy or otherwise.[1]

Reports were now compiled and collated by one trained man who, by virtue of his right of access to the originals, could detect the sale of information between agents and the provision of information from the same source to more than one system. This failed to eliminate resentment and rivalry at one stroke for, as Drake, who had succeeded Kirke as head of I(b), says, 'It was impossible in some cases to forget the bitternesses of the past and personal feelings which these had left behind, especially amongst the subordinate personnel.'[2] However, it represented a considerable improvement. Oppenheim was also empowered to investigate and settle all disputes between members of different systems, becoming a court of first instance to deal with claims from both parties in dispute. If any officer felt unable to abide by the Attaché's decision, he could have the case referred to a higher court in London composed from the officers in charge of MI1, MI1(c) and I(b) GHQ, with subsequent reference to the DMI if necessary. The work of the 'court of first instance' soon proved its value as, in Drake's words, it

> . . . led to the discovery that consciously or unconsciously, certain organisations and individuals had undoubtedly been working for more than one British service, in some cases at the same time, in others intermittently or alternately.[3]

The myriad faults of the previous chaotic and haphazard growth were also starkly revealed and the lie given to that central tenet of GHQ's belief, that several services were a good safeguard against the collapse of any one service because the remaining networks could continue to operate and provide cover for any gap. That idea, while plausible in theory, had introduced such confusion into operations that it had proved to be an actual hazard:

> I am personally convinced that where one service showed a marked improvement which synchronised with the decline of another, and where such improvement, as was nearly always the case, was practically equivalent to the decline of the other, such improvement was probably

1 Drake, op. cit., pp. 4–5.
2 Ibid., p. 5.
3 Ibid., p. 6.

due to the fact that services and posts had been 'jumped' by the successful concern.[1]

Drake also records that:

> At GHQ there was no doubt whatever as to the beneficial results of the new system. The officer to whom had been allotted the task of reducing to graphic form on a map the movements of enemy divisions was able to report that it was considerably easier for him to arrive at a really coherent idea of these movements, that he no longer received so many confusing and contradictory reports or apparent confirmations of news which really originated from the same source.[2]

The improvement was general, extending a beneficial influence into every aspect of secret Intelligence. The process was continued into 1918, for in the January of that year Major Cameron resigned from the GHQ Secret Service. According to Drake, he applied to join the Army in the field because his systems were now in decline to the point where they were 'practically non-existent'[3] and his health was suffering after the strain of more than three years' continuous work in this field. His service was accordingly merged with Major Wallinger's. In this case Drake's statement is hopelessly inaccurate but in view of his ignorance of Cameron's career one hesitates to describe it as a deliberate lie. The *Army List* for July 1918[4] shows quite plainly that Cameron continued in the service of the Intelligence staff at GHQ before going to the War Office to serve with MI2(d), a section responsible for Intelligence relating to Russia, Persia and Afghanistan and information emanating from India.[5] This move was in order to familiarize himself with the background for his new job as head of British military secret Intelligence in Russia. This position can be established both from the *Army List* already cited, where, from 18 October 1918 to 20 March 1919 he is described as 'GSO3 Military Mission to East Russia', and confirmed in the Public Record Office, Kew, where he is listed (with his name rendered incorrectly) as a GSO3 Intelligence to General Knox, the head of the Military Mission.[6] Nevertheless, Intelligence cover-up notwithstanding, Camer-

1 Ibid., p. 7.
2 Ibid., pp. 5–6.
3 Ibid., p. 10
4 *The Army List, July 1918*, HMSO, London, p. 536.
5 *The War Office List, and Administrative Directory For The British Army, 1918*, HMSO, London, held in the Public Record Office.
6 *See* PRO WO106/318.

on's departure permitted an even greater degree of centralization that could only benefit the Army in the Field.

Although these improvements had stabilized the relations between the British services, unity could not be considered complete until it was extended to the whole of the Allied Secret Services. To this end another conference was held, but not until 31 August 1918, and Macdonogh presided over its deliberations. All the Allied services on the Western front were represented; the imagination boggles as to the effect a lucky bomb dropped from a German aeroplane would have had on the future of Allied Intelligence. Those present were:

General Boucabeille, French Military Attaché at the Hague.
Lieutenant-Colonel Wallner, 2ème Bureau, Ministère de la Guerre, Paris.
Commandant Smets, Belgian GQG.
Colonel R. van Deman, United States Army.
Captain Mansfield Smith-Cumming, MI1(c), War Office, London.
Colonel C. N. French, MI1, War Office, London.
Lieutenant-Colonel R. J. Drake, I(b), GHQ, France.

Drake claims that 'considerable progress'[1] was made towards the desired end after a luncheon given in honour of those attending.

Although the desired goal of one service was not fully achieved due to the

> . . . fact that agents who are working and have been working for some time past for one service, the chiefs of which are known and trusted by them, are unwilling to change over to the tutelage of another, in the personnel of which they may have no confidence,[2]

the goal was partially achieved with the establishment of an Inter-Allied Commission under General Boucabeille, though it really came too late to exert any decisive influence on the course of the war. This commission was to collate the reports of all the Allied services and had the power to call for the originals of the reports from the heads of any of the services. It was also empowered to act as the court of first instance in any inter-service dispute and to adjudicate the case. As

1 Drake, op. cit., p. 12.
2 Ibid.

Drake says, 'There is no question that this step formed a considerable advance in secret service organisation.'[1]

The new system also had the unexpected effect of leaving the field clear for the British Secret Services, the French and Belgian services not having sent in any useful reports since October 1917, at least in the opinion of Drake.[2]

Looking back over the sorry state of affairs during most of the war it is impossible not to sympathize with GHQ. In theory it sounds ideal to have one service supplying all information, but that is conditional upon that service being able and willing to do so. Mansfield Cumming's official Secret Service simply could not do that in 1914 and, as GHQ were directly responsible for the success or failure of the main force Britain put into the field, they needed timely and accurate information before anyone else did. If the War Office were slack in supplying this information then GHQ had to go and get it for themselves — they certainly could not afford to be without it. This had been fully recognized in the pre-war division of responsibilities, but the advent of trench warfare had forced GHQ to use the same routes as the official Secret Service. In itself that did not necessarily mean that in-fighting would ensue, given a reasonable degree of goodwill, some tact and an inclination to co-operate on all sides. Unfortunately it was precisely these attitudes that were lacking amongst the powerful, aggressive characters commanding the services.

At times it seemed as if knocking another service was more important than damaging the Germans. Even Drake had to concede the point here, writing of Tinsley and Cameron:

> This was particularly the case between the GHQ 'C.F.' Service and the War Office 'T' Service, between whom, both as services and as between individual officers in charge, it is necessary to record that the greatest competition and some bitterness had existed.[3]

A massive understatement if ever there was one.

The poison was still at work thirty years later, still dominating personal relations, still leading to mutual recrimination, a fact well-

1 Ibid.
2 Ibid.
3 Ibid., p. 7.

illustrated by a letter Drake wrote to Best about the proceedings at an I(b) reunion dinner in 1946:

> I was surprised by the bad feeling, animosity and active abuse by three people for whom I did much more than I did for anyone else, Wallinger, Wilkinson and Lamb. The two latter particularly spread it abroad that S.M. [Stewart Menzies, then Sir Stewart Menzies, the C of his day] did all the good and clever work and I rushed in and took the credit: they were just S.M. aficionados and worshipped him in a pansy and sickening way, as did Langley another pansy.[1]

Perhaps the general effect of this form of work on the characters of the men engaged in it had a hand in shaping such sentiments. It was work which Meinertzhagen, one of the more honest and able practitioners, described as 'dirty work'[2] and of which Best wrote, 'After all, none of us are innocent of unfriendly gossip about our friends and I do not think that S.S. [Secret Service] work breeds an altruistic spirit.'[3] Drake concurred:

> There is something fatal to most natures in S.S. work, especially to those whose first consideration is how it is to advance their own careers and enhance their reputations. Starting from that is only a small step to jealousy, suspicion and underhand doing, until one gets to putting the Almighty Double Cross on a pedestal to be bowed down to every day. Everything else is put away and trampled down – honour, duty, friendship and self-respect.[4]

These are not opinions voiced by nonentities with chips on their shoulders, but officers of influence and standing in the First World War whose work had done much to shape the events under review; their opinions must be accorded an appropriate weight. In a world where deception and subterfuge were the norm, it would need an exceptional man to distance himself from such an atmosphere in the other paths of his life. Nor were these influences restricted to the Western front. Compton Mackenzie's record of events in the Mediterranean mirrors the picture exactly. Different services competing against each other, personalities who displayed an unnerving tendency to get bogged down in personal quarrels that threatened to knock the bottom out of any achievement. Indeed, when commenting on the

1 Best Papers, loc. cit., Drake to Best, 20 November 1947.
2 Meinertzhagen Diaries, op. cit., 8 October and 2 December 1956, pp. 6 and 48.
3 Best Papers, loc. cit., Best to Drake, 8 September 1947.
4 Best Papers, loc. cit., Drake to Best, 11 September 1947.

types of people he met in Intelligence in that theatre, Mackenzie was moved to write on meeting Sir Eric Holt-Wilson:

> At last I had found a man who was capable of understanding at once all our difficulties. The shock of meeting somebody connected with Intelligence work who could understand immediately what was wanted, and why it was wanted, proved too much for my nerves.[1]

Of course there were incompetents and flawed characters as well as genii and honest men engaged in Intelligence just as there are in any activity. However, in the past the emphasis has always been placed on organizational faults to explain the problems faced by the Intelligence services of the First World War. That card has been over-played, for although the organization was everything short of ideal, it was not in itself responsible for the early trials and tribulations. Where the fault in organization really lay was in the scope it gave to strong, unyielding characters to indulge in harmful activities – it is with the Camerons, Tinsleys, Cummings and Maxses of the world that the error truly belongs. It is with that knowledge that we can turn to study the operations of their services in the field.

1 Mackenzie, op. cit., p. 115.

SIX

Standard and Special Operations

WHEN survival of the state, a way of life, is at stake, as it was between 1914 and 1918, anything which guarantees one's own survival at the expense of the enemy has some justification manufactured for it. If we are honest with ourselves we must recognize that mankind usually acts first on the basis of expediency and only afterwards finds moral justifications to explain the action. The morality of total war is brutally different from the morality of comfortable peacetime. Killing is regarded as the ultimate crime within a state at peace, but when war intervenes, killing receives the state's sanction, indeed its blessing, as does much else which is normally considered reprehensible. The problem is not a new one. Young Cyrus objected to his father's advice that a general needs to be an arch-plotter, cheat, robber and thief as the price of outwitting his opponent, the very antithesis of all he had been taught. His father, Xenophon, solemnly answered:

> Those lessons were for friends and fellow citizens, and for them they stand good; but for enemies – do you not remember that you were taught to do much harm?[1]

Total war engaged whole societies, citizens as well as soldiery, whether they liked it or not. As the briefest acquaintence with the history of siege warfare alone will demonstrate, it has ever been the aim to waken or subvert not only the fighting men but the populace too, to exploit every rift and weakness in the defence in order to undermine moral endurance and the will to fight. Going back to the Peloponnesian War (431– 404 BC), one finds innumerable attempts by the Spartans and their allies on the one hand and the Athenians and their allies on the other, directly to incite the populations of hostile cities to overthrow their rulers and throw in their lot with them. It was a common practice in medieval times too, but rulers from the end of the Thirty Years War forebore to use incitement because of the

1 Xenophon, *Cyropaedia*, Book I, Vol. VI, pp. 27–8.

unsettling consequences of putting the power to make war or peace into the hands of the common man. This hesitation held good until the American Civil War, when the Union deliberately waged a war of unmitigated terror against the population of the Confederacy in a bid to persuade them to renounce secession and Jefferson Davis. Sherman's march to Atlanta had no military aim in mind – it was a calculated attempt to force the population of the South into demanding peace at any price.

Before reviewing certain special operations activities during the First World War and the men who conducted them, we need to consider the attitudes of the neutral governments since it was very largely through their territories that the Secret Services operated and sent their reports. Did they remain strictly neutral and try to clamp down on all this activity? Did they turn a blind eye and remain idle bystanders? Did they favour one party more than another? The stance they took could not but affect the operations of Intelligence, since it would dictate whether services could operate openly or not, which in turn had a bearing on how efficient a service was.

Sir Vernon Kell provides a valuable assessment of the attitudes of the neutral powers, clearly illustrating the wide spectrum of their responses to these questions. He described Switzerland as a happy-hunting ground for the spies of all the world but the Swiss government and police were strictly neutral and took steps to guard that neutrality.[1] The Army, however, was reputed to be very pro-German and the Swiss police arrested an Army officer along with a number of German agents; in October 1915, 120 persons were arrested as German spies.[2] Macdonogh, too, noted that the Swiss were far stricter than the Dutch, and at one time 50 per cent of the German spies in Switzerland were reported to be locked up.

Switzerland was a vital part of MI1(c)'s operations against the German heartland and diplomatic cover was used extensively, the Foreign Office façade of being whiter than white notwithstanding. In 1917 it was suggested that Colonel S. H. C. Woolrych, an officer with GHQ Intelligence, should be sent to Switzerland as Assistant Military Attaché with the Embassy there, to aid the Military Attaché with the direction of Intelligence, and for this task he was duly briefed. When asked what part was played by Military Attachés in the gathering of

1 Kell Papers, loc. cit.
2 Ibid.

Intelligence he replied, 'Quite a lot because all the agents we had reported in person to the fellow in Berne.'[1]

Woolrych received special training for this position which 'was run by the War Office'[2] and he also stated that the penetration of Germany by spies 'was the job of the Foreign Office and the War Office and their Intelligence'[3], which was MI1(c). As it transpired, Colonel Woolrych never went to Berne in this capacity, due to what he describes as 'one of the periodic silly wrangles' between GHQ and the War Office[4], both of whom claimed Woolrych as their own subordinate. As the post was controlled by the War Office, that body solved the dilemma by appointing one of their own officers, whilst Woolrych became head of I(b) with the Second Army.

The Military Attaché was in a delicate position. Being in a neutral country which kept a close watch on foreign espionage activities, he could not afford to compromise the Foreign Office, to which he was officially attached. But the Foreign Office were kept in the dark about some, at least, of his activities in this field for during the discussions about reorganization in November 1916, involving a GHQ officer being attached to Oppenheim's staff at the Hague, the DMI had actually objected at first because he did not want the attention of the Foreign Office called 'to M.A.'s exact duties, as Foreign Office might veto them'.[5] On both counts the British had to tread warily in Switzerland.

Kell remarked that Denmark definitely favoured the Allies and that the Danish police did a great deal to check German espionage organizations whilst allowing the British a free hand. By contrast, Sweden was 'distinctly pro-German'[6], although this does not appear to have affected British activities unduly.

Norway was definitely pro-Ally[7], with the Norwegian police and Navy actively supporting the British to the extent of reporting the movements of German ships and submarines to the Norwegian Admiralty, who 'at once' passed the information to the British Naval Attaché.[8] The Netherlands from 1916 onwards clearly went beyond

1 Woolrych interview, loc. cit.
2 Ibid.
3 Ibid.
4 Woolrych Papers, loc. cit.
5 Kirke Diaries, op. cit., 30 November 1916.
6 Kell Papers, loc. cit.
7 Ibid.
8 Kirke Diaries, op. cit., 17 April 1916.

the bounds of their neutrality. Marshall-Cornwall tells us that the War Office 'had a very good system organized by our military attaché, Colonel Oppenheim, at the Hague, who worked in conjunction with the Dutch Military Intelligence, but of course they had to keep that very secret'.[1]

Fear of Germany inspired this collusion. That country had shown itself to be no respecter of neutrality and on several occasions moved troops to the Dutch border to reinforce diplomatic demands. This led the Dutch Secret Service to send Lieutenant Schuhmacher to the Belgian consul at Maastricht to ask him to request the British to give the Dutch Secret Service information about these movements. In return the Dutch would render 'every assistance' to British agents, giving them advance warning if German 'diplomatic' pressure was going to lead to searches by the Dutch police. The Dutch approach ended up on Kirke's desk, but GHQ were not in a position to handle an issue which so directly engaged the political relations between two countries. So Kirke 'came to the conclusion that the M.A. had better deal with this matter. He is already in touch with the Dutch Secret Service and probably they are trying to get in touch with the W.O. Secret Service. Their reason for not going to the M.A. seems hardly convincing -viz- that they don't want to do anything officially; and they think going to the M.A. would make it official.'[2]

Oppenheim was only too pleased to become the recipient of the Dutch initiative; under his hand co-operation between the Dutch and British Secret Services flourished, semi-official contact which repaid the British handsomely. Their own services were left unhindered and valuable Intelligence was gained on both the German Army and the German home front.

One of the most valuable methods by which the Dutch rendered assistance was to allow British agents covert access to German deserters in internment camps. There were many German deserters; a letter of April 1917 from the Netherlands stated: 'Holland is full of Boches, and there are now 90,000 Boche deserters.'[3] The number of deserters was released to the British by the Dutch from the bread ration cards issued to these men, and valuable information was gained about the German Army, particularly about its morale. Although

1 Marshall-Cornwall interview, loc. cit.
2 Kirke Diaries, op. cit., 8 February 1916.
3 G.G. Bruntz, *Allied Propaganda And The Collapse of the German Empire in 1918*, California, 1938, p. 79.

there were bouts of harassment of known British Intelligence by the Dutch as a response to German pressure, these appear to have been cases of merely going through the motions, for no British system was ever destroyed in the Netherlands, and Kirkpatrick relates that while some of Wallinger's agents were arrested on suspicion, 'not a single man or woman was convicted of espionage'.[1]

It is noticeable that those states that had done most to assist the British all fell victim to Nazi aggression in the Second World War. The possibility that British Intelligence activities in the First World War inspired these invasions of neutral countries is a question that demands further research. We do know that they served as a public excuse for the attack on the neutral Netherlands in 1940 because the Germans openly stated this as the reason for their attack, after they had kidnapped two British agents, including S. P. Best, at Venlo in 1939.

Undoubtedly the use of agents and spies among the civil population brought the fight directly and actively into the heart of a society whose support for either side had heretofore been less directly, more passively engaged.

By late 1918 the networks of British agents built up behind the German lines were so numerous and well-organized that it was planned to use them in the way resistance groups were to be employed in the Second World War. There was nothing new in this, for a general uprising led by the secret networks had been discussed as early as 1915. The idea belonged to Commandant Zopff of the French Deuxième Bureau, who proposed just such a plan to coincide with the Allied offensive of September 1915. The French and Belgian Secret Services had been smuggling explosives and equipment to their agents since the beginning of August and Zopff appealed to the British to join the plot.

Although in many respects it was ahead of its time, the idea proved to have serious practical shortcomings in September 1915, not least of which was the short notice given. Zopff only broached the subject at the beginning of September so the only possibility for the British to get arms and explosives to their spy rings in time would be to air-drop them, and here other difficulties intervened. In 1915 the range of the available aeroplanes was too short to offer any realistic hope of equipping more than a token percentage of the groups available. Then

1 Kirkpatrick, op. cit., p. 18.

there were difficulties in locating dropping zones and ensuring that the recipients would be on hand to collect the drop, remembering that all this had to be arranged without the benefit of radio communication. Inevitably this meant that all arrangements had to be made through the neutral Netherlands, a time-consuming process that effectively hamstrung the British effort. As if that was not enough, the Royal Flying Corps were fully committed to the coming offensive and simply could not spare either the aeroplanes or the aviators for such a dubious enterprise at such short notice. Consequently the plan fizzled out, but the idea did not die. As it was the Germans discovered a barge packed with explosives designed to destroy the railway bridge at Liège as late as November 1915.

When the idea to mobilize secret networks was revived in 1918 things were on a very different footing. By then the British Secret Service reigned supreme in Belgium and both agents and rings were far more numerous and much better organized than in 1915. Perhaps even more importantly, confidence was soaring as it became ever more clear that the German Armies were disintegrating. Preparations were certainly put in train and weapons and explosives were secreted into Belgium. Had the armistice not pre-empted them, concerted strikes against the weakening German lines of communication would have been made. The German rear areas were already in disorder and confusion, and such actions might very well have had considerable bearing on after-events. The scale of the planned operation can be gauged from the fact that the best Secret Service rings were actually formed into battalions and companies like a regular army.

By far the greater part of the secret systems run by the British services concentrated on train-watching and they had by far the closest bearing on the fortunes of the armies. Fortunately there is a collection of papers in the Imperial War Museum deposited by Hector Demarque, the Belgian historian who specialized in the study of Belgian resistance to German occupation. Among them is a breakdown of the various services run by the Belgians, the size and scope of which were breathtaking when one remembers that their country was occupied by a far stronger hostile power. The breakdown was prepared immediately after the war by the Commission des Archives des Services Patriotiques Etablis en Territoire Occupé au Front de l'Ouest under the patronage of the Belgian Ministère des Sciences et des Arts. Train-watching came under the wing of Les Services d'Observation, composed of no fewer than 200 systems, of which 130 were directed by British services, such as Tinsley's or Cameron's. In addition there were 40 French and 25 Belgian systems; the remaining 5 are not detailed. Between them the British services employed 4,350 agents as against 650 in the French and 500 in the Belgian services.[1] To set beside the immense train-watching enterprise there were 5 systems engaged in aerial intelligence – watching aerodromes, reporting on German aircraft and assisting Allied aviators to escape; 27 engaged in smuggling information across the Dutch-Belgian frontier; 1 only working in counter-espionage and assisting imprisoned agents; 3 involved in smuggling mail from Belgian soldiers to their families and friends and 7 in smuggling Allied propaganda and prohibited goods; and a further 3 small systems involved with Customs, historical records and clandestine payments.

Every train that ran on the railways of occupied Belgium was of interest to the British and the observation systems were accordingly directed to report on every train they saw[2]. However, some trains were of greater interest than others. The movement of leave trains, hospital trains, or trains carrying trench stores and munitions were obviously of much less importance than those which transported German troops. Since the division was the basic tactical brick of the Order of Battle, any significant change would occur through the movements of divisions. A division was moved by what Intelligence called a 'constituted unit' — 'constipated eunuch', in contemporary slang. Some 40 separate trains were required to transport a division and it was this long queue of rolling stock that comprised the constituted unit.[3] The 'Instructions For Posts' contained in the papers in the Imperial War Museum relate to *La Dame Blanche* (The White Lady), one of the single most important systems in occupied Belgium, belonging to Tinsley's service and controlled and directed by Captain Henry Landau. The system's name may have been chosen with malice aforethought: legend had it that the Hohenzollerns always saw the ghostly figure of a white lady immediately before they died.

The detailed instructions tell the system's observers exactly what to look for:

> To note that the value of the reports lies in the precise observation of constituted units (T.T.U.C. [sic] — trains d'unités constituées). These

1 Papers of *La Dame Blanche*, loc. cit.
2 Ibid.
3 Kirkpatrick, op. cit., p. 16.

> trains are recognizable in that they simultaneously transport officers, soldiers and war material.[1]

Each piece of rolling stock employed was to be specifically identified by the observers, who were told: 'To designate the type of transport, use the natural abbreviations, in general, the first 2 or 3 consonants of the word.' A lengthy list of abbreviations, 63 in all, then follows to enable observers to identify each part of the train in the minutest detail. A model report was included to demonstrate:

1735 1VOF/28WSL&CHV
4W=4CN/5W=12CAIS
1W=2CUIS/15W=20
CHR/band noir
épaulière jaune
No.15.[2]

When translated this reads:

5.35 p.m. One officer's carriage/28 wagons for soldiers & horses
Four wagons with four guns/5 wagons with 12 artillery caissons
One wagon with two field kitchens/15 wagons with 20 trucks
black capbands
yellow shoulder straps
Regiment No. 15.

This recorded the composition of each train and its cargo – whether human or material — down to the last item, which could be traced from the stations of origin right along the route to the destination. With this sort of detail, it was not just knowledge of the enemy's movements of troops that passed into British hands but the identification of those troops, and that played a vital role in building up the picture of the enemy's Order of Battle. Indeed, such was the standard of train-watching that by November 1918 GHQ knew the precise locations of all but two of the German divisions on the Western front. Drake's comments emphasize the value of these reports: 'This information was of vital importance in drawing up the enemy's Order

1 Papers of *La Dame Blanche,* loc. cit.
2 Ibid.

of Battle. It had a direct effect on the operations and movements of our own forces and became therefore the first objective of our secret service system.'[1]

Information of this depth could not be obtained without a high degree of organization so it will be helpful to dwell on *La Dame Blanche* in order to get some idea of how a good system operated and how it came to deliver such outstanding results. This system was created by Tinsley's service and its controller, Captain Henry Landau, was South African. He had studied Natural Sciences at Cambridge, gaining a First-Class Honours degree, but on the outbreak of war he enlisted in the Royal Field Artillery, and was badly wounded in France. Recovering, he was sent not back to the front but to the Army's General List for employment on special duty under the War Office, there to be recruited by Cumming and sent to the Netherlands to pick up the pieces after the disasters of 1916. Little else is known about Landau, except that he was head of the British Military Intelligence Commission in Belgium immediately after the war, responsible for winding up the systems of agents and rewarding those of outstanding ability. A letter from the Army Record Centre at Hayes in Middlesex dated January 1971 reveals that he was released from military service in 1920 and there are indications that he lived for a time in Berlin in 1923.[2] At a later date, in Hungary, his clothes were found on a river bank and, as no body was found, he was presumed to have drowned. He surfaced, in fact, in the United States, having absconded with the funds from his office in Budapest. From the safety of America he proceeded, to the horror of the War Office, to write and publish two books on his days with Intelligence. The system this elusive man created was almost certainly the best of the Allied systems in the occupied territories in the West.

La Dame Blanche operated on a tightly run and disciplined cell structure which made it impossible for the Germans to destroy the entire system even though they might eliminate certain of the cells. The papers of the organization reveal that its members held military ranks, were subject to military discipline and were closely directed by Landau, so that each member knew exactly what to look for, how to interpret it and how to communicate it. They used a simple but effective code that substituted numerals for words and then expressed

1 Drake, op. cit., PRO WO 106/45 and ICMA.

2 Papers of *La Dame Blanche*, loc. cit. Letter from L.W. Burnett, Army Records Centre, to the Defence Attaché, British Embassy, Brussels, 27 January 1971.

their meanings under a different guise. Thus the letters spelling out the capital of Belgium, BRUXELLES, would appear as 13, 22, 28, 34, 19, 53[LL], 190, 24. An artillery unit would be recognized by either the phrase 'merci de ta lettre' or 'bien reçue ta lettre'. There were detailed instructions on how to report aviation matters, details of German uniforms and helmets, and advice in case of arrest. This warned agents and sub-agents not to confess to anything, indeed to say as little as possible to interrogators and never to give up hope. A strong caution against the various ruses employed by the Germans against prisoners suspected of spying formed a central part of this advice.

Each member of the system had to swear an oath upon enlistment. The oath for those who joined as soldiers read:

> I declare that I will enlist as a soldier in the military observation service of the allies until the end of the war.
>
> I swear before God to respect this commitment, to carry out conscientiously:
>
> [1st formula:] the functions which will be entrusted to me.
>
> [2nd formula:] the functions of . . . for which I engage myself, and any which I may accept in the future. To obey the instructions which are given me by the appointed representatives of the direction, not to reveal to anyone without formal permission, anything of the organization of the service, even if this attitude should bring about the death of me or mine; not to join any similar group or to take on any role which might expose me to prosecution by the occupying authority.[1]

The oath for the civilian element began differently:

> I swear before God to carry out conscientiously, and until I withdraw, the functions of . . . for which I engage myself, and any other function of the same sort which I accept in the future. To obey [etc].[2]

In return the recruit was given a lead identity disc stamped with his or her name, number, place and date of birth. The discs were folded and then soldered, to be buried by recruits in a place of their own choosing: being captured by the Germans in possession of such a disc would certainly spell torture, even death. The disc was to remain buried until after the war.

1 Papers of *La Dame Blanche*, loc. cit.
2 Ibid.

La Dame Blanche was centred on Liège, a vital hub of the rail network in eastern Belgium and a crucial link for the transport of German troops across the country. In the words of *Le Bastion De Liège*, the journal of the Commission des Archives, the city represented: 'Essentially a strategic knot, Liège in fact dominates the great line for manoeuvre which the railway of la Vesdre, and from 1917 that of Vise, constituted for the Germans.'[1] The cells of *La Dame Blanche* extended outwards from Liège along the railway lines like the spokes of a wheel. Post 49 is a good example. Formed at the Château de Conneux in the spring of 1918 by the Baronne de Radigues et Chennevière, it seems to have attracted a substantial leavening of the Belgian aristrocracy to its ranks. The château was used as a rest-billet for German artillery officers and initially the cell consisted of just the Baronne and her daughters. However, their circle of friends and acquaintances included people whom they could trust implicitly and these were speedily recruited, beginning with the Comte and Comtesse de Villermont at Barcenal and M. André Eggermont at Leignon. Other reliable people were then approached including, through the good offices of the Comtesse de Villermont and her niece Anne de Boussu, the Baronne Clémie de l'Epine who was instrumental in extending the cell southwards. Each member of the cell knew other reliable people who could be prevailed upon to help in the good work. Even so, 'the number was not great, but that was unimportant in view of the quality of our brave soldiers; we would have had no use for cowards in post 49'.[2] Though the cell's personnel had a high proportion of aristocracy, there were also men like Walther Dewe, a telegraphic engineer living in Liège who became a director of *La Dame Blanche*. He continued his excellent work during the Second World War, and became a Belgian national hero.

As the cell grew stronger and more proficient, the leaders of the system invited its members to create new posts at Sedan, Givet, Fumay, Monterme and Charleville, so they were now extending their web into France. Clémie de l'Epine was chosen to spearhead the move on Charleville and in September 1918 she and Marie-Antoinette de Radigues travelled there armed only with the name of a priest who might be helpful. They returned having found a man to lead the new cell, M. Donnelier. With Madame Graffetiaux as deputy, he orga-

1 Ibid.
2 Ibid., 'Account of Post 49'.

nized a chain of posts from Charleville through Monterme, Charneuse and Gedinne. The feelings which inspired these brave people are best expressed in the words that they used to greet the Baronne and her companion: 'Why didn't you come sooner?'[1] Such sentiments and such efforts reproduced throughout the whole of *La Dame Blanche*, added up to a truly formidable network that in both its organization and its motivation was second to none, and that achieved remarkable results. Those results can be measured in a letter from C which Landau forwarded to the system's leaders in July 1918. In it he said:

> We very much wish to inform you of the appreciation felt for you at the Allied Council. Our War Office has informed us quite recently that the work of your organization represents 70% of all the information obtained by all the allied armies, not only via Holland, but also via the other neutral countries. This fact will make you realize the unique and marvellous role which you fill, and at the same time will give you some idea of the great responsibility which is yours . . .[2]

Even if we may doubt the attribution of 70 per cent of all information obtained by the Allies from all sources through secret Intelligence to *La Dame Blanche*, we must nevertheless concede the group's outstanding contribution to Allied victory.

Intelligence had been greatly frustrated in their attempts to establish an effective spy ring in the important rail centre of Luxembourg, straddling as it did the main railway line linking the German armies in Flanders and north-west France with the Fatherland. Along this route poured the reserves, reinforcements, munitions and supplies of all kinds which those armies needed. Every attempt made to observe these movements had been either ineffective or short-lived, due largely to Luxembourg's distance from Secret Service headquarters and the difficulty of establishing a reliable channel of communication. Luxembourg was of such importance, however, that in 1918 it was resolved to make yet another bid to establish a secret network there.

The task fell to the Secret Service section run by Captain A. Bruce (later Lord Balfour of Burleigh and Chairman of Lloyds Bank). When the Germans invaded Belgium and the Grand Duchy of Luxembourg in 1914, large numbers of the citizens of these countries had fled to France or to the neutral countries of Switzerland and the Netherlands.

1 Ibid.
2 Papers of *La Dame Blanche*, loc. cit.

Not all could sustain four years' exile, however, and many wished to return to their homes irrespective of the Germans. Those who wished to return were known by the French term, *repatriés*, and were much used by the Intelligence services of both sides. One of Bruce's contacts was a Madame Rischard, a very capable and intelligent lady who was eager both to return to her home in Luxembourg and to help the Allied cause and so liberate her homeland. It was arranged that she should return as a *repatriée* and use her local knowledge and contacts to recruit an Intelligence network for Bruce.

Mme Rischard's cover withstood German examination and she arrived in Luxembourg in the traumatic spring of 1918 when the Germans were once again threatening the gates of Paris. British Intelligence were chiefly interested in the military traffic passing through Luxembourg by rail. Mme Rischard's husband was a doctor with the Luxembourg State Railway and, like his wife, an ardent patriot. He was soon won over to the cause and between them he and his wife were able to persuade several of the principal railway officials to join them. In their turn, these engaged some of their subordinates whom they could trust. A tightly knit, well-informed, reliable and dedicated community of spies was established at the heart of one of the most sensitive points on the German-controlled rail network, superbly placed to observe all troop movements through Luxembourg. But this was only half the battle. Secure communications are just as important to the spy as the ability to acquire information and just as Mme Rischard's work in creating the spy ring was excellent, so her achievement in the field of communications was outstanding. One of her contacts was the editor of a local newspaper, the *Landwirt*; he and other personnel were won over to her network and the *Landwirt*, arousing little suspicion in German minds, became Mme Rischard's chosen channel to communicate the information her ring gathered to the British. The next step was to place a British agent in Luxembourg to control and direct the ring's activities. The officer selected was Lieutenant Baschwitz-Meau, bi-lingual in English and French and possessed of the deliberate cold-blooded courage so essential to this type of work.

He flew to his meeting with destiny in a free balloon launched from the shattered ruins of Verdun on the night of 18–19 June 1918, wafting unnoticed over the tangled skein of battered trenches alive with the activity of tens of thousands of men engaged on the usual nocturnal labours of repairing and improving their earthen defences and carrying stores and supplies up to the line. He sailed on to land just before dawn within half a mile of his objective.

Under Meau's direction, the Rischard ring flourished and was soon sending back valuable reports about German troop movements through Luxembourg. The Germans, meanwhile, suspected nothing and ignored the paper's exiled subscribers in Switzerland, blissfully unaware that its leading articles contained detailed encoded reports on German railway traffic. The code was the brainchild of Captain Campbell of GHQ Intelligence's cipher section and could be used in any letter or newspaper article on any subject. So successful did it prove that the mysteries of the code were unveiled to C so that it could be used by the official Secret Service. As each edition of the *Landwirt* was forwarded as soon as it was printed, the reports of the Rischard ring were received by GHQ in five days as opposed to a minimum of three weeks had they been sent through the usual Intelligence channels via the Netherlands. This most successful service was, in Drake's opinion, the best in the GHQ repertoire. He wrote that 'Lieutenant Meau was able to set up the best train-watching service as far as the reporting of results goes, which had up to that time been established, and this service operated successfully until the conclusion of hostilities, when Luxembourg was occupied by American troops.'[1]

The Luxembourg operation shows the British Secret Services at their best, a best fundamentally due to the choice of personnel. It would be hard to imagine two people better fitted for their tasks than Mme Rischard and Lieutenant Baschwitz-Meau, who both displayed the coolness, inspiration and depth of character so necessary to this type of operation. This is borne out by the dividends paid, dividends so handsome that Field-Marshal Haig was led to comment that his secret Intelligence was worth two army corps to him.

There were, of course, many other organizations which, while successful to a lesser degree, nevertheless ran the same risks and penalties. Drake tells us that the number of agents employed by the GHQ services alone was 'roughly 6,000', of whom 98 lost their lives – 91 executed, 4 dying in prison, 2 shot and 1 electrocuted when trying to cross the Dutch-Belgian frontier. A further 644 were imprisoned for sentences totalling 700 years (the time actually served amounted to 175 years), and 10 were deported.[2] Major Wallinger, however, told

1 Drake, op. cit., p. 20.
2 Drake, op. cit., p. 33.

Colonel Kirke that the total number of GHQ agents in the occupied territories was 5,500 of whom 1,200 were imprisoned, serving an average of 14 months, and 200 were shot or died in prison (though in a later letter he gave the total shot or dying in prison as 120).[1] The reason for the disparity between the two men's figures almost certainly resides in a question of terminology, a question of what was precisely meant by the words 'agent' and 'spy'. An agent is an individual directly employed by an Intelligence Service and sent into a foreign country to obtain information. A spy is an individual who serves in the enemy's own ranks and, more often than not, is recruited by the agent. As with Cell 49, many sub-agents were recruited and numbers of these might themselves have employed others, so distinctions between agent and spy were (and doubtless still are) ambiguous at best, and open to different interpretations. Even so, the numbers of which Drake and Wallinger wrote referred to the two GHQ services alone; when the agents of Tinsley's service were included, the numbers employed both directly and indirectly by the British Intelligence Services was one that the Germans simply could not contain, much less control. Every sort of person was employed, ranging 'from abbés, high officials of the Gendarmerie, a Marchioness of some 60 years of age, big industrialists and prominent barristers, down to seamstresses, poachers, smugglers, bargemen and railway officials'.[2]

It might be imagined that so many secret systems covering the whole of the occupied territories would represent a prohibitive cost to any but the best-funded Secret Services. In fact it was not so. Costs were kept surprisingly low, given the scale of the enterprise and the dangers to which the participants were exposed. As the Commission des Archives said, 'The occupation of their country by the Germans during four long years of implacable war was the occasion for the Belgians to give the measure of their national conscience.'[3] Given that a single train-watching post meant the employment of at least 2 people on a 24-hour basis, the rate of pay was extremely low: late in 1915 the monthly bill for Tinsley's service was £5,000, of which only £2,000 was devoted to train-watching.[4]

The comprehensive nature of the train-watching services under the wing of GHQ is revealed by the map of its systems between 1914 and

1 Kirke Papers, loc. cit., Wallinger to Kirke, 31 December 1923 and 2 November 1925.
2 Drake, op. cit., p. 33.
3 Papers of *La Dame Blanche*, loc. cit.
4 Kirke Diaries, op. cit. 30 November 1915,.

1917 on pp. 198–9, from which it can be seen that all strategic rail junctions, notably Liège and Luxembourg, were covered by GHQ agents. This meant the Germans could not undertake any serious movement without the British being aware of it. Of course, the service run by Tinsley had systems covering the same area too, so the cover was more than adequate for the whole of the occupied territories.

Train-watching was extended to all theatres of war by Britain's spy-masters. To the Central Powers, quite unable to prevent it, the networks may have seemed like some creeping disease which they might stamp out in one or two areas only to see it flourish in others. Thus British agents were to be found watching the Anatolian railway as it passed the Gulf of Alexandretta, along which all Turkish reinforcements for the fronts in Palestine and Mesopotamia had to travel. In Palestine the train-watching service was nothing less than superlative thanks to the Jewish NILI organization. Following their destruction of Al Ahad, the society for Arab independence, the Turks had turned their attention to the Jewish population of Palestine. Under the leadership of Djemal Pasha, one of the Young Turks with aspirations of his own towards the Sultanate, they subjected the Jews to a merciless persecution. This included, amongst other 'pleasantries', a scorched earth policy directed chiefly against Jewish farmers in order to drive them into the desert, the rape of Jewish women in the streets by Turkish soldiers and, Djemal's own favourite piece of sadism, pushing captive Jews head-first into the fire boxes of locomotives – he liked to hear the victims' heads burst with a pop. This revolting policy was brought to a head at the beginning of 1917 when Djemal chose to order the removal of all civilians firstly from Jaffa and then from Jerusalem. With grim irony, he selected the Feast of the Passover for the evacuation of Jaffa, 9 April 1917, and 9000 Jews were herded aboard cattle trucks and most were never seen again; their Arab co-residents were simply driven into the desert to take their chances with the Bedu. Jerusalem escaped a similar fate only because of urgent intervention by the German generals who had been sent to ensure that the Turkish forces in Palestine remained a realistic threat to the British and the Suez Canal.

The Turkish atrocities not surprisingly brought about a determination to resist among numbers of the Jews. In particular, a young Jew, Aaron Aaronsohn, saw the salvation of his people not only in an Allied victory but in the work of freedom fighters. With close relatives and friends he formed a group calling themselves the Gideonites, to resist Ottoman oppression. Early attempts to assist the British had foundered on British apathy and mistrust, but the arrival of Richard Meinertzhagen at the Intelligence desk of the EEF transformed the picture. Meinertzhagen met Aaronsohn and was immediately impressed by his self-confidence, force of character and genius. He wrote of him years later: 'My best agent in the 1914–1918 war was a Jew – Aaron Aaronsohn, a man who feared nothing and had an immense intellect.'[1] Aaronsohn was an agricultural scientist of international repute and his proposals to form a secret Intelligence network from trusty Jews, based at his agricultural research station at Zichron Yakov, was gladly accepted by Meinertzhagen and the organization began to flourish. The NILI group took its name from an event in 1917 when British Intelligence had first begun to show a genuine, if rather slothful, interest in Aaronsohn. On 21 February 1917, several of his men were rowed ashore from the British vessel *Managam* at Athlit. As the boat was about to return to the *Managam* her captain, a New Zealander called Smith, asked what password Aaronsohn intended to use for his new system. The idea had never been mentioned before and had not even been considered. Aaronsohn turned to his friend and co-conspirator, Liova Schneersohn, and asked 'What shall it be?' Schneersohn was in the habit of carrying a copy of the Talmud, the Hebrew Bible, with him and, seeking inspiration, he opened it. The pages parted at 1 Samuel 15:29, whereon lay the striking words: 'Nezah Yisrael Lo Yeshakker' – the strength of Israel shall not lie. There and then the Hebrew initials were adopted as the name of the new system.

It is not intended to relate the history of NILI here – it is worthy of a book in itself. NILI has been touched on because it played the key part in the train-watching service in Palestine. This was in the hands of one of Aaronsohn's close friends, a German Jew who was chief medical oficer to the Turkish Army at Affulah in Syria. All Turkish troop movements in that theatre passed through Affulah's vital railway junction.[2] Dr Neumann, recruited in precisely the same way as agents in *La Dame Blanche*, was able to provide Aaronsohn with a complete breakdown of all Turkish forces in transit and their destinations. Coupled with the information C gleaned from his train-watchers in Syria and with the Intelligence the Army got from DPM,

1 Meinertzhagen Diaries, op. cit., Vol. 55, 19 June 1946, p. 72.
2 H.V.F. Winstone, *The Illicit Adventure: The Story of Political and Military Intelligence in the Middle East from 1898 to 1926*, London, 1982, p. 292.

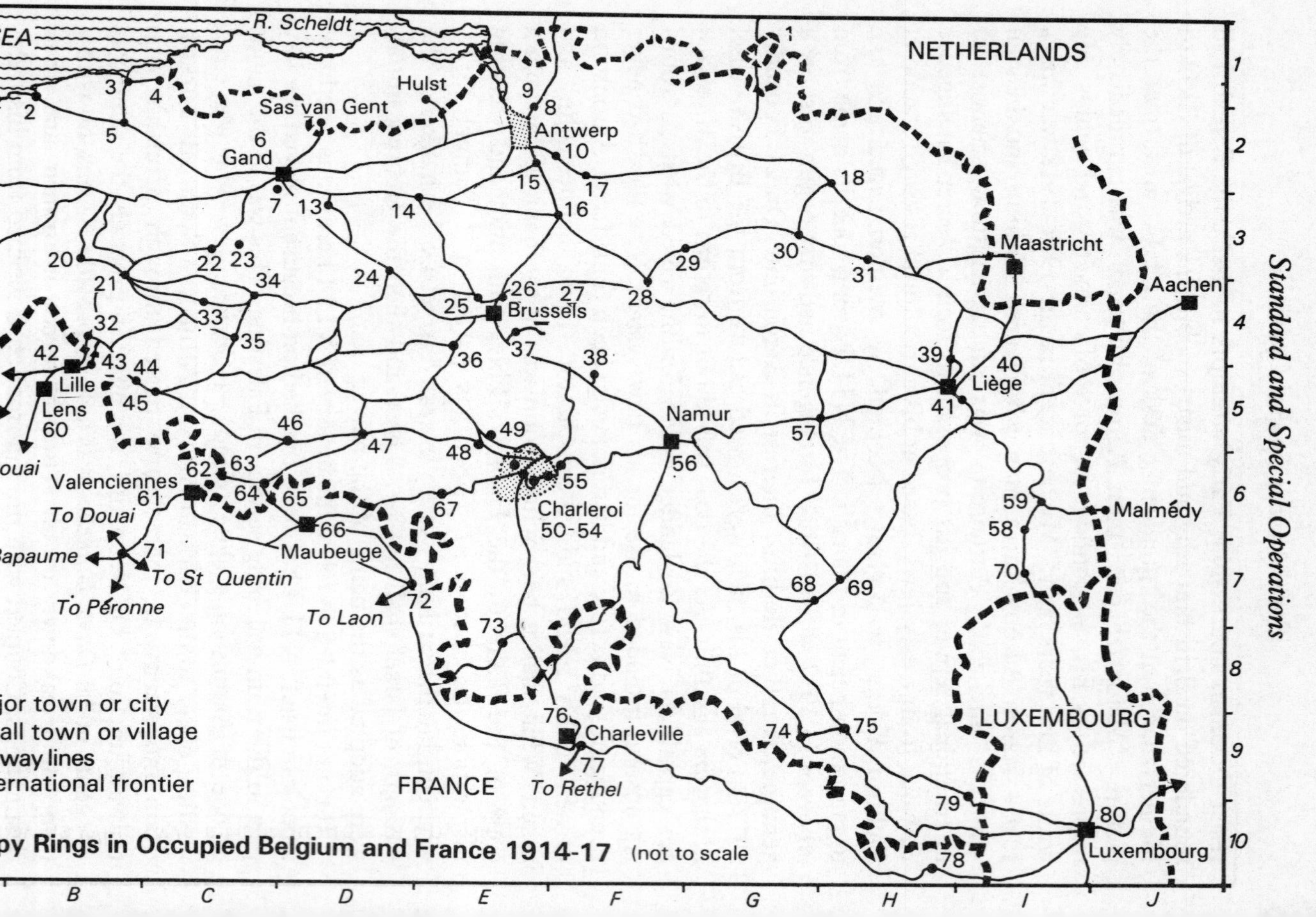

GHQ Spy Rings in Occupied Belgium and France 1914-17 (not to scale

Key to Towns Which Were Headquarters of Spy Rings

WL: Wallinger's service, London
CF: Cameron's service, Folkestone
?: service unidentified

Where none of the above symbols appears, no spy ring has been located.

1 Belgian enclave of Baar-le-Hertoge
2 Ostend
3 Zeebrugge
4 Knokke
5 Bruges
6 Gand/Ghent (CF & WL)
7 Gand St Pierre (CF)
8 Antwerp (CF & WL)
9 Dam (CF)
10 Boechout (CF)
11 Nieuport
12 Dixmude
13 Alost
14 Termonde (?)
15 Kontich (CF)
16 Malines (CF)
17 Liers (CF)
18 Beverloo (CF)
19 Ypres
20 Iseghem (CF)
21 Courtrai (CF & WL)
22 Waereghem (WL)
23 Cruyshautem (WL)
24 Denderleeuw (CF)
25 Laeken (CF)
26 Schaarbeek (CF)
27 Brussels (CF)
28 Louvain (CF)
29 Aarschot
30 Diest
31 Hasselt (?)
32 Mouscron (CF)
33 Avelgem
34 Oudenaarde
35 Renaix (?)
36 Hal (WL)
37 Auderghem (CF)
38 Louvain La Neuve
39 Liers
40 Liège (CF & WL)
41 Angleur (WL)
42 Lille (WL)
43 Wattrelos (?)
44 Froyennes (?)
45 Tournai (?)
46 St Ghislâin (CF)
47 Mons (CF & WL)
48 La Louvière (CF)
49 Manage (CF)
50 – 54 *All in Charleroi*
Marchienne au Pont (CF)
Marchienne Est (CF)
Charleroi Sud (CF & WL)
Châtelineau (CF)
55 Tamines (?)
56 Namur (CF)
57 Huy (CF)
58 Trois Points (CF)
59 Stavelot (CF)
60 Lens
61 Valenciennes (CF)
62 Marchipont (WL)
63 Blanc Misseron (CF)
64 Elouges (?)
65 Aulnois (CF)
66 Maubeuge (CF)
67 Lobbes (CF)
68 Jemelle (CF)
69 Marloie (CF)
70 Gouvy (CF)
71 Cambrai (WL)
72 Hirson (CF)
73 Chimay
74 Libramont (CF)
75 Bertrix (CF)
76 Charleville (CF)
77 Mézières (CF)
78 Montmedy (?)
79 Arlon (CF)
80 Luxembourg

the wireless intercepts and I(a), they provided Meinertzhagen with the whole Turkish Order of Battle, from which the enemy's intentions could be deduced without difficulty. British success in Palestine owed everything to this achievement and NILI was the crucial element in it: C's train-watchers could locate the Turks on their way to the front and I(a) methods could find them after they had arrived, but NILI provided the all-important link between the two, enabling the EEF to know which Turkish forces would go to which part of the front.

It was too good to last. The Turks captured a carrier pigeon bearing a NILI message and made deductions of their own. On 1 October they raided Zichron Yakov and discovered enough evidence to incriminate all whom they found there. Despite that, or perhaps hoping for information about other parts of the network, they repeatedly raped Aaronsohn's sister, Sarah, before proceeding to pull her teeth out one by one. To her eternal credit this marvellous woman uttered not a word about NILI. In the end the Turks killed her. It was the end of the line for arguably the most influential train-watching group of the war. In the process, though, they converted Meinertzhagen to the Zionist cause, of which he became a redoubtable champion in the ensuing decades.

All of this, whether in Belgium and France, Syria or Palestine, would have been absolutely impossible without willing co-operation from civilians. Money was certainly not the force that motivated them to undertake this hazardous service. Patriotism and, arguably, self-interest were prime movers but so also, at least in some cases, was a love of danger and excitement and the feeling that at last they were doing something really important and useful. As the historian of Cell 49 made clear, the armistice was not welcomed, for 'We remained at Liège, and received our dismissal for us and our post, like a jet of icy water.'[1] Knowledge of such motives '. . . is the best answer to the often heard opinion that the Belgians as a race are devoid of courage. My experience is that there are no risks which they are not ready to undertake, and that the remuneration for which they are prepared to undertake them is, in most cases, absurdly small.'[2]

In many respects the Secret Services were now fulfilling the role once played by cavalry scouts in obtaining information from friendly civilians who had had recent contact with the enemy. The information was now better organized, specifically directed and available in

1 Papers of *La Dame Blanche*, loc. cit., 'Account of Post 49'.
2 Drake, op. cit., p. 34.

copious quantities, and outshone by far anything the cavalry of old had been able to procure, but more importantly it concentrated on the most sensitive sections of the hostile armies, the vulnerable rear areas where their intentions could be divined and their stamina assessed. The use of civilians in this way by the Secret Services not only produced information which was most valuable and, on some occasions, decisive, but in one stroke it engaged the key to the whole war and the key to every total war – the people themselves, for it is *ultimately* their thoughts, feelings and actions that dictate the outcome of such wars in the modern world.

When the occupied population was either hostile or indifferent, then Intelligence had a different battle to fight. Fortunately such cases were rare; the only occasion where it presented a genuinely threatening scene was in Mesopotamia, where the inhabitants, a mixture of farmers, poverty-stricken Marsh Arabs and rapacious Bedu had no particular love for either the British or the Turks. The warring armies both sought their help and the Arabs not unnaturally exploited the situation to the full, alternately hunting with the hounds and running with the hare, depending on which side held the upper hand and which could profit them most. As British forces advanced deeper into Mesopotamia, the need to control the Arabs became ever more urgent. The greater part of the credit for the relative success in this undertaking belongs to Lieutenant-Colonel Gerard Leachman, who almost single-handed dominated the wild tribesmen by virtue of his charisma and standing, thereby depriving the Turks of information from them while winning much of value for the British.

His adventures, such as are known, appear almost incredible. Leachman sped from tribe to tribe on camel-back, enforcing his will either by wise words or by fierce beatings with stick or fist. Tall and very lean, Leachman was a dedicated professional soldier who had already travelled widely over some of the roughest country in the world and among some of its toughest peoples. He was very much a loner and his usual fare when in the desert – he rarely saw the inside of an office – was a handful of dates; yet when he was in contact with British soldiers his concern for their well-being was both genuine and touching. When one of his brother officers suggested that he ought to write an account of his exploits, he replied disarmingly that no one would be interested.

Leachman's outstanding ability to disguise himself as an Arab, together with his mastery of the language, enabled him to pass safely through the Turkish lines and haunt the towns and villages in the Turkish rear. Apart from the tribesmen he won over to the British cause, his main agents were Arab children, devoted to him because of his kindness and geniality and addicted to the sweets he always carried with him. Children had the incalculable advantage that they would be neither suspected nor taken seriously; under Leachman's direction, they proved themselves first-class spies. Corporal Wing, Leachman's driver in the final year of the war, recounted in his diary: 'Colonel Leachman was wonderfully well informed – no information was too trivial for him . . . He used to employ a lot of children to whom he paid a small fee.'[1]

Leachman's strength of purpose, strength of character and a body that seems to have been made of iron resulted in a career as full and successful as Meinertzhagen's. He was indispensable to the British in Mesopotamia, for not only did he provide the Army with an enormous amount of secret Intelligence but he kept the erstwhile Arab marauders in check, freeing the troops to get on with the job of beating the enemy. Without the influence Leachman wielded, the British would have been marooned amongst a viciously hostile people who, if left unhindered, would have made any form of military operation impossible. Such was this powerful man's sway over the Arabs that he became known to the British Army as 'OC Desert'. Pilots of the RFC used to carry a chit with an inscription to inform any Arab who found the pilot, were he to force-land in the desert, that if he returned the aviator whole to a British unit he would be rewarded by Leachman – but that any other course of action would lead to dire punishment from the same source. Rarely in the course of human conflict can so handsome a tribute have been paid to an enemy than the one which Conrad Preusser, Leachman's German opposite number, paid in his diary, captured with its owner in March 1918:

> Not all the blandishments of the Turks, nor all the gold they have distributed, nor any German effort can undermine the influence among the tribes of *one* man, Leachman.[2]

When Leachman went to see Preusser after his capture, the German sprang to his feet, saluted and asked if he might shake Leachman's hand, saying that although circumstances made them enemies he had long desired to meet the man for whom he had so great an admiration.[3]

1 Cited by H. V. F. Winstone, *Leachman: 'O.C. Desert'*, London, 1982, p. 210.
2 N. N. E. Bray, *A Paladin of Arabia*, London, 1936, p. 349.
3 Ibid. For more on Leachman *see* Winstone, op. cit., and G. D. Martineau, *History of the Royal Sussex Regiment 1701–1953*, Chichester, 1953.

The routes into the enemy's camp used by the Secret Service were diverse and one such route was provided by commerce, which could not be halted simply because of a state of war. As Colonel Nicolai, head of the German Secret Service expressed it: 'In her own interest, Germany had to keep up traffic with abroad. The enemy put no difficulties in the way of this in order not to block the path of his agents.'[1] It was certainly true that the British utilized this avenue, but not necessarily that they put no difficulties in its path. They could and did do so by virtue of their command of the sea, by which they rendered neutral businessmen dependent on British goodwill to continue their trade.

According to S. P. Best, who spent a year in the Secret Service in the Netherlands and was therefore in a position to know, a British diplomatic consortium there was engaged in what he termed an 'absolutely scandalous business'. Necessary parties to this affair were Oppenheim and Maxse, already deeply involved in secret Intelligence, and Sir Francis Oppenheimer, Commercial Attaché at the Hague. This triumvirate, with the aid of Tinsley's agents, ran what was virtually a system of blackmail known as 'The Black Book', listing firms which traded with Germany via the Netherlands. Their trade was profitable because a proportion of it was in contraband goods which would fetch a high price on the black market in Germany and they were thus extremely vulnerable to British pressure, both Naval and diplomatic. The firms listed were politely asked to help by having their representatives send back information for the British from Germany and even to pass selected British agents into Germany disguised as their representatives. Behind the polite request, as they knew only too well, hung the threat of ruin, but in return for active co-operation the passage of their goods was left unhindered. In most cases the pressure worked. In one case, at least, a salvage tug company, Smits, paid the triumvirate 100,000 guilders to be kept off the list and out of active compliance with British wishes.[2]

Even before the war the commercial world had been approached to assist in espionage. Edmonds relates his attempts to woo several British firms to this end, approaching the Union Castle Line, the Eastern Telegraph Company and Rothschilds. The only help he says he obtained came from the Union Castle Line, who went so far as to

1 Colonel W. Nicolai, *The German Secret Service*, (trans. G. Renwick), London, 1924, p. 198.
2 Best Papers, loc. cit., 'Pinnacle 90'.

tell him they had one British employee at Hamburg, a stevedore. Other than that, Edmonds gives no details except to say that enquiries were made at local police stations for Britons living on the north German coast, on the pretext that they were needed to witness legal documents.[1]

Nevertheless, agents were acquired within Germany either through subverting native Germans or by placing British agents. As Marshall-Cornwall said, 'I think they were a rather mixed lot . . . I think that most of them were British, but foreigners were in.'[2]

That agents did gain access to the German North Sea coast is beyond doubt, for a report by Agent R16 survives intact in the Public Record Office at Kew. British agents were numbered in accordance with the first letter of the city where they were based followed by their number on the list of agents employed at that base; thus the famous Sidney Reilly's number from 1918 to 1919 was 'ST1', meaning that he was the first agent on the list of the Stockholm service. The 'R' of Agent R16 signifies Rotterdam and from there this man sent in a report on 27 June 1916 on the condition of the High Seas Fleet after the Battle of Jutland. He was clearly able to travel without undue hindrance, for he journeyed by train to Bremen, Danzig, Kiel, Rostock, Geestemunde, Emden and Sande. Most of his information was acquired by speaking and listening to the seamen of the fleet and the dockers who worked on the vessels. He was able to send in a very full report on the losses the Germans had sustained, together with the damage to the surviving ships and the length of time required to repair them, and to identify the various ports to which the Germans had straggled back after the battle.[3] His information was of the highest calibre, enabling the Admiralty to put the results of the engagement into true perspective, and to know when and in what strength the Germans might put to sea again.

Businessmen and their representatives needed to be able to travel and that in itself was reason enough to employ them for Intelligence purposes. Sir Vernon Kell, head of MI5 explained, 'It is not easy to find good excuses for frequent travelling unless you have real business, and those who have real business are probably making too

1 Edmonds Papers, loc. cit., III/5/1 – IV/5/33, General Staff, War Office, MO5 and 3, 1906–1910.

2 Marshall-Cornwall interview, loc. cit.

3 Report of Agent R16, papers deposited by Lieutenant-General Sir George Macdonogh, PRO WO 106/510.

much money to risk their necks as spies'[1] – unless of course, the business was put at risk by the Black Book.

It can be safely assumed that an Intelligence service will exploit every rift and weakness in its enemy. The weaknesses and carnal flaws of humanity are convenient and ever-present levers which a good Intelligence service will seek to use, though at times such defects can have quite unlooked for consequences. One such weakness in the German Empire was resolutely turned to good account by one officer of the British Secret Service, who discovered the Teuton Achilles heel while serving in occupied Belgium.

Apart from alcoholism, the main addictive passion of the late nineteenth and early twentieth centuries was the smoking of opium, but in Germany at least there was also a considerable demand for morphia and cocaine. Homosexuality was also rife – even the Kaiser was implicated. The Secret Service was to employ this demand for drugs as a form of currency, better than gold, to bribe the narcotics-hungry German soldiery.

The officer who recognized the opportunity and was quick to catch it, was Sigismund Payne Best. He had been one of the first civilians to be recruited by the embryonic Intelligence Corps on the outbreak of war. His lack of any previous military experience proved no handicap – indeed, he seems to have regarded the more stultifying effects of military life with a well-founded contempt. On the Western front his energy, imagination, insight and swift grasp of the central issues ensured his speedy recognition with the result that in 1915 Smith-Cumming personally approached him with an invitation to join the Secret Service. He was a shy, sensitive man for whom music was the most important thing in life. Despite his diffident manner he was possessed of immense charm. Not only could he bend people, including generals, to his will but he could read character with uncanny insight. For that reason he was often deputed to select personnel for specific missions. Best regarded Intelligence primarily as a means to save lives and prevent suffering. He was adaptable and imaginative and could turn his hand to most things. After his return from the Netherlands in 1917 he became a kind of troubleshooter, sent to wherever any apparently intractable problem arose. Best was captured by the Nazis early in the Second World War and their assessment of him sheds valuable light on his character, not least in

1 Kell Papers, loc. cit., 'Security Intelligence in War, Lecture Notes', 1934.

respect of the way he kept his interrogators guessing how much he really knew:

> Unlike Stevens he is not a professional soldier. But he is superior to him as far as experience in intelligence service is concerned, and as a result his attitude is more penetrating; these qualities he combines with considerable character defects and a complete lack of scruples. He is not a British officer like Stevens. He is a civilian who loves to live well and be a successful businessman. He may therefore see things in a clearer light in spite of a pretended lack of significance, or he may say more than Stevens.[1]

Best's captors reveal themselves as both perplexed and nonplussed, unsure of precisely what to believe. To some extent the answer may lie in the carefully calculated response Best had prepared against the eventuality of capture: as a skilled interrogator himself, he was perfectly aware of the prisoner's weak position and with commendable foresight made sure that he remained in wilful ignorance of operational details and was adept at fudging difficult issues. He wrote of this:

> I had always followed the practice of knowing as little as possible about the people actually working for me and had worked on the familiar link system by which men knew only the men directly above and below them. After all, in my work it is too much knowledge that is the dangerous thing. It is the report and not the men that matters.[2]

He made the point even more explicitly in an undated letter, probably written towards the end of the 1940s, to Colonel Drake, his commanding officer in France from 1917 to 1918:

> You know, as well as I, that men caught under our circumstances have got to talk, either voluntarily or under extremest pressure. Looking upon my capture as a very possible risk, I had made my plans beforehand. I did not know my power of resistance to torture and chemical stimulants and therefore decided that it must be my policy to talk, to conceal essential facts behind much verbiage and, as far as possible to retain the initiative under interrogation.[3]

Between 1908 and 1913 Best had been living in Munich where he was studying both at the University and the Music Academy. During

1 *Der Britische Nachrichtendienst*, cited in Nigel West, *MI6 British Secret Intelligence Service Operations 1909–45*, London, 1983, p. 248.
2 Best Papers, loc. cit.
3 Ibid.

those five years he travelled widely in Western Europe and learned to speak perfect French and German. What was, perhaps, of even greater importance was the fact that he acquired a great wealth of understanding of both human frailties and human potential. Apart from his natural ingenuity and aplomb, Best was endowed with striking shrewdness, a quality which would greatly benefit him in his Intelligence career. And his career advanced rapidly. Arriving in France as a Second Lieutenant in August 1914 he brought in one of the first reports that the Germans had moved deep into Flanders and were bearing down on Haig's I Corps. After trench warfare had extended its unforgiving grasp, he established the Decauville railways, which were to prove so valuable in moving supplies and evacuating the wounded from the front. His early success earned him a mention in despatches from Field-Marshal Sir John French and in June 1915 he was promoted to full lieutenant. A year later he rose to captain and was recommended for the Military Cross, which was refused him, though the French showed their appreciation of his services in November 1916 when he was decorated with their highest award, the Légion d'Honneur, by Général Pétain in person. Best was again recommended for the Military Cross in January 1917 and the honour was again denied him, after which he departed from the Intelligence Corps to join the Special List. At the end of the war he was again mentioned in despatches and admitted to the Order of the British Empire as well as receiving the Croix de Guerre with palm leaves from the Belgians. At this time Drake paid tribute to his signal services by writing to him personally:

> I am glad to have this opportunity of thanking you for all the excellent work you have done during the two years we have been associated together. It has contributed very much to the success of Intelligence, and especially of Intelligence (b), and in this way to the general success of the Allied cause. I hope it will be possible to obtain for you the reward for which I recommended you in the last Gazette and also that you will receive some recognition from one or other of our Allies.[1]

It is uncommon for such fulsome praise to be accorded to someone in a semi-official letter and provides some measure of the man who was sent to the Netherlands to revitalize the shaken British spy rings and

1 Ibid.

inject new life into their operations. Best's understanding of humanity, with all its faults and foibles, equipped him with a key to the very heart of successful Intelligence work in the field, the ability to inspire men working alone against impossible odds. Such inspiration must needs come from close at hand; a bureaucrat sitting in an office a hundred miles away, be he ne'er so wise, cannot match this asset.

As soon as Best discovered the German craving for drugs, he was not slow to recognize the use to which this could be put if handled with discretion and dexterity:

> In those days the Germans were just as keen to get hold of morphia or cocaine as addicts are nowadays with heroin. I had a great deal of difficulty in getting permission to do this drug-pushing, in fact, I had to go to the Prime Minister, to Lloyd George, and get his authority to buy large quantities of morphia tablets and cocaine. With this I was able to suborn quite a number of people in the German Army.[1]

The lack of scruples referred to in the Reich Security Agency's summary stands out boldly and unequivocally here. Best had the soul to do and dare, though, and since he specifically states that the drugs were bought in large quantities, that would indicate exploitation on a grand scale. Indeed, according to his own account he 'even managed to get as far as the German General Headquarters where, as a result, I got most valuable documents'.[2] It goes without saying that the penetration of such inner sanctums was an achievement worth its weight in gold, providing the British with up-to-the-minute Intelligence of unsurpassed value. The value of Best's drug-pushing was not confined solely to trading drugs for information: he was able to overcome one of the greatest difficulties facing Intelligence, the passage of the Dutch-Belgian frontier.

Not being stupid, and having Intelligence Services of their own operating in the Netherlands, the Germans were fully awake to the dangers of permitting untrammelled access to Belgium, which by now had become a hotbed of Intelligence activity, and took extreme measures to close off the flat, sandy wastes of the Dutch-Belgian frontier. Guards, mines and dogs were all used, supported by a zone where civilians were forbidden either to reside or travel. They also erected two lines of electrified fencing. They had, so it seemed, taken everything into account – everything, that is, save the weaknesses of

1 Best Papers, loc. cit., 'Pinnacle 90'.
2 Ibid.

Major (later Brigadier-General Sir) James Edmonds, 1905. He became the war's official historian.

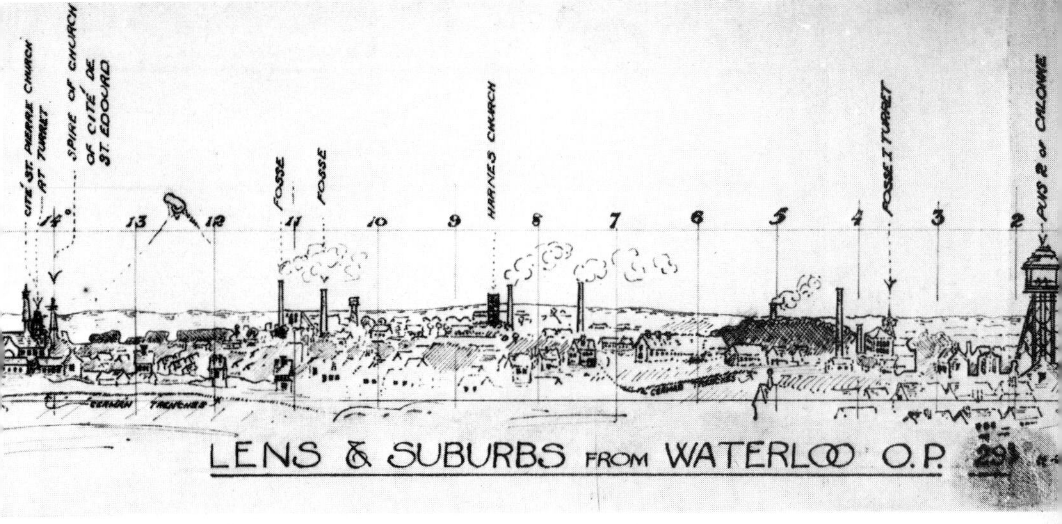

Panorama of Lens and suburbs sketched from Waterloo Observation Post near Loos.

Pilot's observation report, 22 August 1914, on the eve of the Battle of Mons.

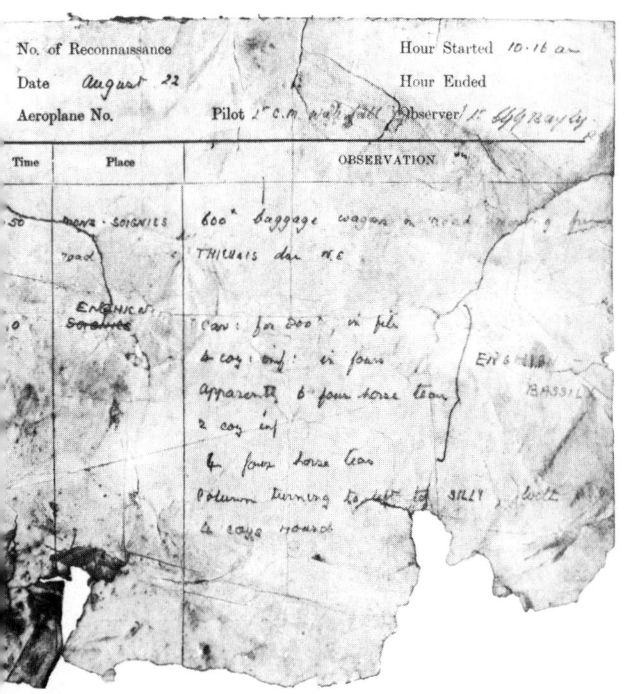

No. of Reconnaissance | Hour Started 10·16 am

Date August 22 | Hour Ended

Aeroplane No. | Pilot Lt C.M. Waterfall | Observer Lt G.W. Bayly

Time	Place	OBSERVATION
50	MONS - SOIGNIES road	600x baggage wagons on road moving from THIEUSIS dir N.E
0	ENGHIEN Soignies	Cav: for 800x, in file 4 coy: inf: in fours apparently 6 four horse teams 2 coy inf 4 four horse teams Column turning to left to SILLY ... 4 coys ...
		ENGHIEN BASSILY

'Perhaps the greatest blessing that the RFC could bestow' – a staff officer in Mesopotamia retrieves an air-dropped message, 1917–18.

ft) General Sir Walter Kirke.

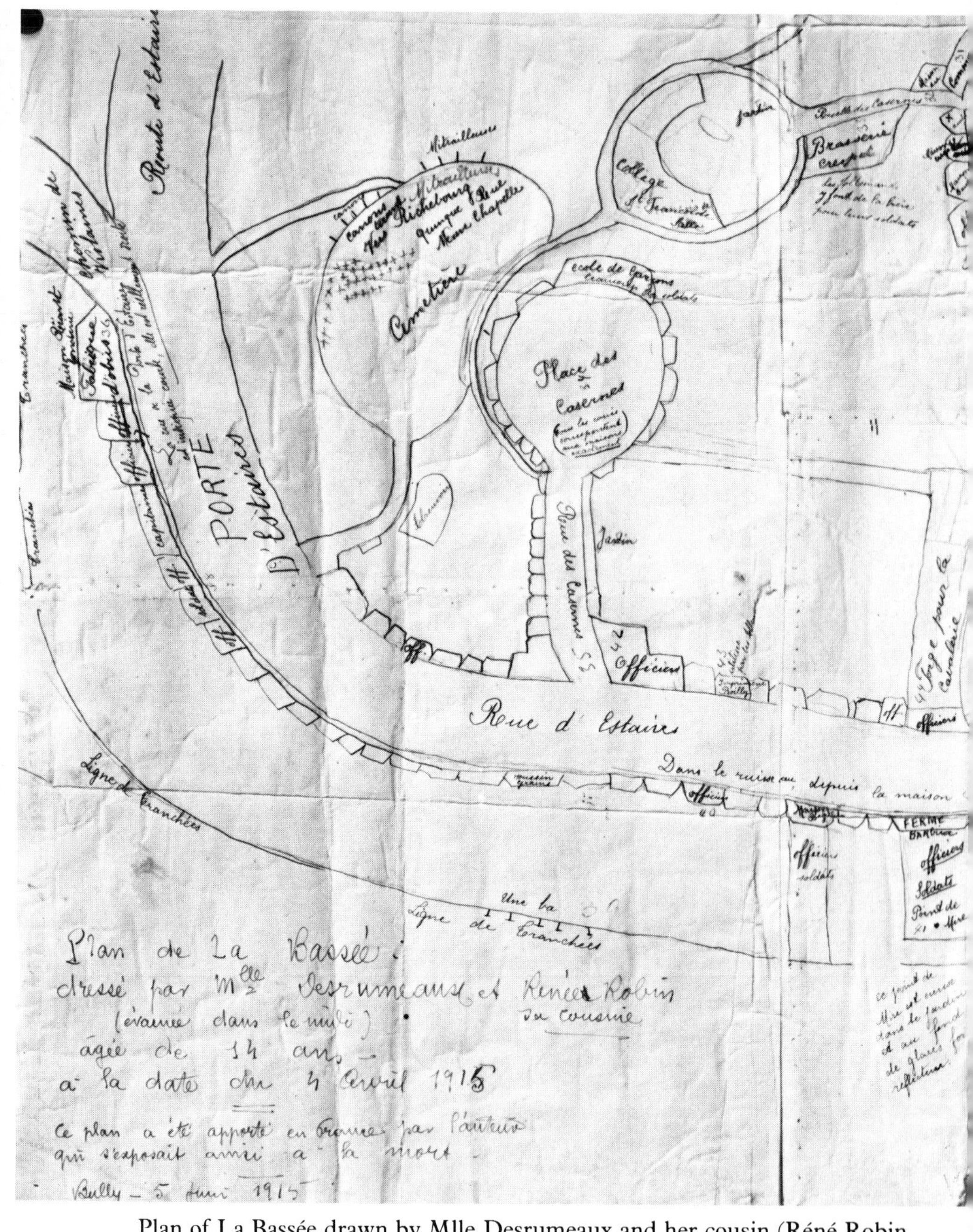

Plan of La Bassée drawn by Mlle Desrumeaux and her cousin (Réné Robin, age fourteen). This plan was brought into the Allied lines at the risk of Mlle Desrumeaux's life.

A British officer interrogating an Austrian prisoner in Italy: note the relaxed attitudes.

Leading Seaman Joseph Murray, Hood Battalion, Royal Naval Division, 1917.

General James Marshall-Cornwall, 1942 (as GOC Western Command, Second World War).

Sadlier Jackson (Siemens) listening apparatus.

The GHQ Intelligence Staff, Montreuil sur-Mer, 1916. *Standing, left to right*: Captain E. W. Shepherd; Major S. G. Menzies; Colonel G. R. Church; unknown; Major J. A. Dunnington-Jefferson; Major J. H. Marshall-Cornwall. *Sitting, left to right*: Lieutenant-Colonel E. M. Jack; Lieutenant-Colonel W. M. St. G. Kirke; Brigadier-General J. A. Charteris; Lieutenant-Colonel B. W. Bowdler; Lieutenant-Colonel H. Goldsmith.

Flag of the German cruiser *Königsberg*, captured as a result of Lieutenant-Colonel Richard Meinertzhagen's Intelligence work in East Africa. After the sinking of the cruiser, the crew fought on land and used the flag as their standard. Meinertzhagen set his heart on capturing the flag and his planning led to a raiding party, under the South African Major Pretorius, ambushing the colour party and capturing the flag. Flanked by Mr H. Halliday and Colonel F. G. Robson, respectively former assistant and former curator of the Intelligence Corps Museum, Ashford.

the low-grade troops they assigned to guard the sensitive border. Throughout 1916 these measures had presented the British with a formidable obstacle but Best's drugs provided a key to the door.

Best relates that he 'had a friend who had a big estate part of which was on the Belgian side of the Frontier and he made friends with the frontier guards. He gave them food and drink and so on and the bosses were giving [given?] morphia. We started passing huge quantities.'[1] The guards were supplied with drugs in return for which they turned a blind eye to the comings and goings across the frontier. Thus, 'if anyone wanted to come from Belgium to Holland, he came through our special door. He got into Holland without the slightest difficulty.'[2] Best's safe passage was also used later to smuggle propaganda into Belgium on a grand scale, and not just propaganda for German consumption. Belgian underground newspapers, like *La Libre Belgique*, were smuggled through in large quantities to boost Belgian morale and encourage their belief in the liberation. The tremendous scale of this operation can be judged from the fact that Best could quietly record that 'we used to send through about thirty or forty pounds at a time'.[3] Corruption takes as many forms as its encouragement, but occasionally Intelligence would be plain lucky and a useful prize fall into their waiting hands without undue pressure. Such a prize did indeed come their way when the German Army's Field Post Office Book was brought to the Netherlands. This document listed without exception all the units in the German Army, together with the higher formations, such as Armies or Corps, in which they served, and as such it represented the best possible source for the study of the German Order of Battle. The pre-1914 German Army had been expanded to the point where it was hardly recognizable; many new and specialized units had been created to meet the changing face of war and there had been several organizational changes. All this was but imperfectly understood by the Allies and new information was always eagerly sought.

There were few copies of the Field Post Office Book, only one at each of the head Post Offices of the Germany Army; because of their value to an enemy, these few copies were closely guarded. Each time a new edition of the book was issued the old ones were burnt in the presence of three senior witnesses who then had to sign an affidavit

1 Ibid.
2 Ibid.
3 Ibid.

stating they had seen their copy totally destroyed. The chances of obtaining one of these valuable books were slim indeed and British Intelligence had never yet succeeded in stealing a copy.

One summer's day in 1916 an unknown German walked into the Rotterdam office of Tinsley's service — its whereabouts was an open secret — with a parcel under his arm, which, he said, contained the copy of the Field Post Office Book that had just gone out of service. He produced a charred volume of which the first few pages were missing and permitted the astonished officers who had greeted him to have a brief look at this burnt offering in order to quash any doubts they had about it being the genuine article. He offered to part with what was now recognized as a glittering prize for a substantial amount of cash.

The German had been one of the senior witnesses at the German army's head Post Office in Cologne, gathered to watch the incineration of the previous volume. No doubt in complete trust of their colleague, the other two witnesses had signed the official statement as soon as the volume was thrust into the fire and then left. The remaining witness seized the book from the flames and smuggled it out of the building when he went home. His sole interest was to make money; he well knew the value of the book to the British and had no other motive. Biding his time and taking advantage of an official visit to the Netherlands, he made his offer to the British. Oppenheim took the risk of paying for the book and secured a valuable prize for Intelligence. Once assured of the book's worth, he indulged in a real extravagance and transmitted the whole text to London by telegraph for such a windfall demanded priority treatment.[1] His decision proved wise on both counts, since this unlikely purchase enabled the British to discover many new technical units of the German Army whose previous existence had been quite unknown to them. More important still, it enabled Intelligence to chart the course of a further expansion of the German Army in 1917 from which they were able to deduce that Germany would reach the maximum pitch of effort in that year, a fact which had grave implications for the British choice of strategy.

Such flaws of character as were displayed by the officer who sold the Field Post Office Book were eagerly exploited by Intelligence whenever possible. In late 1916, Wallinger was able to report to Kirke

1 Kirkpatrick, op. cit., pp. 20–1.

that his 'best transmission is by a Belgian who has a hold on a German officer in Brussels. The latter goes to Holland once a week for unnatural purposes, and our Belgian got to know of this, and threatens to denounce him.'[1] It is one of the most dangerous facets of Secret Service work that its practitioners so frequently employ methods contrary to accepted moral standards. Information gained thereby may be vital, it may save lives, but its acquisition may involve conduct of a nature that can explain the fog of official secrecy that shrouds Secret Service operations, even though those under discussion here are over seventy years old and cannot possibly prejudice the safety of the state.

In 1915 and 1916 Cumming's service penetrated Germany from Denmark by way of the cattle trade. Germany, labouring under the food shortages imposed by the British blockade, bought as much food as she could from her neutral neighbours and Commander Stagg RN, head of C's Scandinavian Section, was attempting to capitalize on this fact through his aide, Major Holmes of the Royal Artillery. Representatives of the Danish cattle exporters resident in Germany had been won over by Holmes and gave their Intelligence reports to the Danish drovers bringing the cattle across the border, who then carried them on to Denmark.[2] The Germans eventually caught on and put a stop to this by replacing the Danish drovers with Germans at the frontier.

The main advantage of commercial cover, of course, lay in its ability to enable agents and couriers to enter and leave enemy territory, but even this facility took second place to the need for people on the spot who had the capability both to acquire intelligence and to pass it on. In this respect it was difficult to rival the work of the Roman Catholic Church for British Intelligence.

When the Germans invaded predominantly Catholic Belgium, the head of the Church there, Cardinal Mercier, had called on his fellow Catholics to resist the invaders. Many of his flock heeded the call and presented a continuous front of quiet, implacable hostility to the Germans which, more often than not, led to their taking more active part in espionage. Belgian Catholics even formed their own spy systems. One of them, code-named BISCOPS, grew up in 1915 and numbered so many priests and nuns in its ranks that it was widely

1 Kirke Diaries, op. cit., 25 October 1916.
2 Ibid., 17 April 1916.

nicknamed the 'Sacré Coeur'. It was directed by Cameron's service and amply repaid the trust vested in it by providing exceedingly valuable information about German troop movements over the length and breadth of Belgium. BISCOPS remained one of the mainstays of Cameron's service until 1917 when the Germans finally succeeded in breaking it.

In connection with a minor civil misdemeanour, the Germans searched the property of a certain optician. Looking through his diary, they found an appointment with one 'W' was entered. Questions about the identity of W followed. The optician was a member of BISCOPS and the W in his diary referred to Marguerite Walraevens whose home in Brussels was the centre for receiving, collating and forwarding the system's reports. By September 1916, the Germans had discovered her identity and she was kept under close but discreet observation; all who called at her home were traced and their names recorded. Once they felt they had all the information they could get from this means, the Germans moved like lightning, swooping on all of Marguerite's contacts and breaking the back of the system. The scale of the disaster was marginally diminished through the fact that one of the members, Léon Deboucq, managed to escape the net and went to ground in Brussels, later emerging to rebuild the system once German attention had turned elsewhere.

Even *La Dame Blanche* had a heavy Catholic bias. Miscellaneous correspondence held amongst its papers in the Imperial War Museum reveals that it maintained close links with the Church and that once again a considerable proportion of its members were Catholic clergymen and women; even the small Cell 49 contained two parish priests and two Carmelite nuns. Walther Dewe himself was a devout Catholic and his views, expressed amongst the system's papers, suggest that he was very active in promoting the inherently religious character of the network. When Best wrote to Sir Stewart Menzies[1] in 1950, it was with both justice and experience to back him that he remarked, 'I am sure you know from our First War experience how valuable the church can be to Intelligence.'[2]

Best's experience was gained when he was Wallinger's representative in the Netherlands in 1917. There, the systems run by Wallinger communicated their reports by invisible ink which was in fact the acid

1 Chief of the Secret Service from 1940 to 1951.
2 Best Papers, loc. cit., Best to Menzies, 12 August 1950.

used to power the Leclanché batteries of the electric door bells used on the continent. Used on a piece of greasy paper such as a banknote the acid was a completely successful ink and accordingly Best 'arranged with the Catholic Church to have offertory boxes in every area of interest to us, and people used to put bank notes in there, usually German one mark notes. They were all taken to a central office in Antwerp, deciphered and we used to get beautifully tabulated replies.'[1] The Church was in many ways better placed and equipped for an Intelligence role than commerce, for it enjoyed a certain immunity through its religious status and received an additional bonus from its international scope backed by the diplomatic weight of the Vatican. It should come as no surprise to learn that information was frequently passed by word of mouth in a confessional, and that an abbé in Lille concealed a wireless in his house for use by Cameron's service in what must be one of the first, if not the very first, example of the use of wireless in espionage.

Technological limitations effectively excluded wireless communication in the occupied territories as they did in the battlezone. If it had been possible to use this medium then many of the difficulties facing the services would have been removed.

The need to transmit the bulk of information in writing placed great emphasis on the use of invisible ink, which had the value of permitting technical details to be sent in a lengthy message. Apart from battery acid, Best found one other substance to be worthwhile: saliva. Individual letters in an otherwise innocent missive were marked by touching them with a matchstick dipped in saliva. This was immune to all known development agencies such as heat, iodine, or chemicals and could only be developed by brushing the paper with blue-black ink and then washing it off under a tap, the letters marked with saliva then being revealed by an intensely black mark.[2]

C, however, considered semen to be the best invisible ink as it, too, was immune to iodine, charring, 'or to any test so far tried'.[3] Kirke wondered what agent *did* develop this unusual ink, the answer being that exposure to ultra-violet light did – though it gives pause for thought as to how C discovered this 'ink' and the nature of the experiments made to test it.

1 Best Papers, loc. cit., 'Pinnacle 90'.
2 Ibid.
3 Kirke Diaries, op. cit., 11 October 1915.

For most Secret Service systems, it was down to bedrock with the need to get reports to the Netherlands to be forwarded from there. The Germans knew this and took swift, firm steps to seal the frontier, beginning as early as September 1914 with simple wire fences. A constant battle of wits came to be waged between the Intelligence services and the occupying power, with the latter increasing the complexity of the frontier barrier ever and anon as the services trumped their latest tricks. The fences were patrolled by sentries assisted by flares, searchlights and dogs; there were few portals for legitimate entry and exit. By 1915 there were three rows of barbed wire — perhaps the symbol of the whole war — at 100-yard intervals. In May 1915 one of these was electrified, though not continuously, but it still represented a major new hazard. The next step was to clear the crops for a space of 100 yards on the Belgian side of the wire, leaving anybody trying to crawl up to the wire dangerously exposed. With trenches guarded by wire to the front and a wire-guarded frontier to the rear, Belgium seemed now like a dismal forerunner of Berlin and its iniquitous wall.

The trench lines were only formidable because they were manned. But Germany did not have enough soldiers to fight a war on two fronts and to keep the straggling miles of the Dutch border secure; agents and their reports continued to seep through. The Germans had to do something more, and their 'something more' was the creation of a five-mile frontier zone which nobody was permitted to live in without express permission or to cross without a special pass. In January 1916 they upped the stakes and increased the depth of the forbidden zone to ten miles. The couriers had to exercise considerable ingenuity in devising means to carry information through the frontier – a key the top of which unscrewed from a hollow bottom; a milk churn with a false bottom; and watches with hidden cavities which were sent to Switzerland for 'repair'. Trains, of course, were also used; the daily train from Brussels to the Belgian enclave of Baar-le-Hertoge in the Netherlands had messages concealed in the axle-box of a marked carriage, and Wallinger's services concealed reports from Germany with the driver of a train running from there to the Netherlands.[1]

Use had earlier been made of numbers of professional smugglers who knew every blade of grass in their areas. The smugglers bribed the German frontier guards with both food and money, the latter paid

1 Kirke Diaries, op. cit., 22 August 1915.

by the British. Where the guards were not so corrupt, the smugglers 'put a square insulated frame between the wires, forcing them aside and having room to get through'.[1] Barrels without tops and bottoms were used in a similar manner, or messages would be inserted into a beet which would be thrown over the wire; another system used a hinged, insulated ladder to climb over the wire.

If the Germans had to keep some routes, like the train services, running so that commercial life did not completely grind to a halt, they nevertheless shut the frontier whenever important, large-scale troop movements were in progress; then neither trains nor postal traffic could get through and the intensification of the watch on the frontiers made the smugglers' lives even more difficult. The frontier with the Netherlands was shut in this way in May and June 1915, and again in February 1916, seriously dislocating all systems. Attempts were made to float bottles containing messages down streams flowing into neutral territory, to carry messages in model aeroplanes powered by a rubber band, to shoot them over the wires by bow and arrow; yet none of these was reliable enough to solve the problem.

In default of effective information retrieval, minds in the Secret Services turned to other ways of achieving success, if not against Germans in the field then elsewhere. In 1915 the subject of biological warfare was broached. The British would attempt to destroy the German potato crop by infesting it with Colorado beetles. Not only could it be expected to ruin the potato harvest and so enhance the effect of the naval blockade, but it would cause alarm and despondency at home and perhaps force the Germans to switch troops from the battle-fronts and training depots to eradicate the menace. It was already known that a purely local appearance of the beetle at Stade on the Lower Elbe in July 1914 had caused farmers, landowners and public authorities to embark on a frantic programme to wipe out the beetles and destroy the damaged vegetables, even to the extent of calling in the Army to help: Colonel Kirke alluded to it in his diary for January 1916. Great hopes were invested in the British scheme and the operation swelled into a joint venture between War Office Intelligence and the French, the British end being directed by Colonel Leader with scientific backing provided by the entomologist, Professor Mitchell. The idea, like all the best military plans, was fundamentally simple,

1 Kirke Diaries, op. cit., 19 May 1916.

requiring only a few aeroplanes based at aerodromes in eastern France to fly into Germany and release their cargoes of insects. But, when preparations were gathering momentum nicely, the Germans opened their great offensive at Verdun on the surprisingly early date of 20 February.

The carefully calculated plans were thrown awry, for not unnaturally the aeroplanes and French airfields earmarked for the beetle project were hurriedly mobilized to meet the new threat. Without French co-operation the scheme was doomed. It fizzled out and no attempt appears to have been made to resuscitate it later in the war; there was no outbreak of Colorado beetle in Germany until 1939, and then it came without help from the British.[1] Nevertheless, it had been an undeniably ambitious and imaginative plot which might have had far-reaching consequences. Ironically, the fears it was hoped to instil by the real possibilities of such a stroke returned to haunt the British a generation later. In 1940 a research student, on completion of his degree in biochemistry was employed by the Welsh Plant Breeding Station at Aberystwyth in Wales. I learned from him that during the Second World War it was widely feared that the Germans would launch an identical attack against Britain's potato crops and an alert was issued to Britain's farmers to send all suspect insects to Aberystwyth for examination. The farmers took the threat very seriously and innundated the laboratory with thousands of beetles of all shapes, sizes and descriptions down to the humble cockroach, none of which ever proved to be Colorado beetles.[2] The 1916 plan had indeed been a serious proposition and it was still enough of a threat to be taken seriously 25 years later by its originators.

In the early days of total war it was quite quickly grasped by some that there was no longer any strict and finite division between soldier and civilian, for the one was as essential to the state's ability to wage war as the other. The opposing powers were quite prepared to countenance the starvation of civilians as a legitimate act of war when it was enforced by more conventional means, the British through the naval blockade and the Germans through U-boat warfare. As with the

1 Kirke Diaries, op. cit., 26 February 1916. Information on the spread of Colorado beetles in Germany was supplied by the Ministry of Agriculture, Fisheries and Food, Harpenden, Hertfordshire, and the Biologische Bundesanstalt Für Land-Und Forstwirtschaft, Brunswick, Federal Republic of Germany.

2 Conversation with the late Dr R. Evans, recently retired Reader in Biochemistry at the University of Keele, Staffordshire.

sack of besieged cities in the past, so too did the commanders in the First World War first sanction direct attacks on civilian targets by aerial bombardment. The consequences of defeat in total war would be so cataclysmic that any government is forced to do all in its power to avoid them. Had the Colorado beetle operation been successful and starved the Germans into surrender in 1916 there would be few who would reasonably criticize it when it would have avoided the monstrous blood-letting which so characterized this war. Then the success of the strategem would be taken as having entirely vindicated its progenitors.

Nevertheless, before the establishment of effective spy rings, the Secret Services were up against it and constantly aware of the need to perform satisfactorily. Something had to be done, and done urgently. The only remedy anyone could think of was a body which came to be called 'The Suicide Club'. The idea was to establish a unit of trained agents variously mounted on horses, motorcycles and motor cars, who would pass through the expected breach in the German trench lines and send back information from the areas immediately ahead of the advancing army. The major source on the work of the Suicide Club is Colonel R. J. Drake's *History of Intelligence (B), British Expeditionary Force, France*, written by the officer in charge of the Secret Service on the Western front from February 1917 to December 1918. Drake stated that the club was formed from 'time to time during 1917', but it seems he was possibly unaware of his predecessor's work in this field, for the idea sprang directly from the frustrations of 1916 and received powerful backing from John Charteris, the new head of Intelligence at GHQ, who dearly loved a scoop and was ardently searching for a dazzling success with which to impress the Commander-in-Chief.

There proved, however, to be a great many practical difficulties, the most obvious being that agents, however mounted, could no more penetrate the matted tangle of the entrenched front than could cavalry or any other mobile force. Until the trench lines were completely breached any hope of passing agents through the front was unrealistic. Had such a breach been made then the cavalry could get the information just as rapidly and probably far more effectively – they were, after all, the traditional arm for scouting and reconnaissance and had the benefit of full military training. There was certainly no prospect in the summer of 1916. As Kirke ruefully observed after watching yet another costly assault on the German bastion of Thiepval: 'From what I saw today I have no doubt that any question of putting an agent through the line is out of the question until the front is broken and the cavalry can get through.'[1] Whoever got through would still have the problem of getting information back to base. The only means with any prospect of achieving the necessary range and mobility were carrier pigeons and wireless. During the First World War the latter was bulky and cumbersome and had so far failed hopelessly on the occasions when it was attempted to employ it at the front. It shared another problem with the basket of pigeons, which was that both were immediately recognizable and impossible to conceal. Anybody found by the Germans wandering about the forbidden zone with such things would have a better chance of being shot out of hand than relaying any worthwhile information.

So keen was John Charteris that other ideas had to be found. Air-dropping carrier pigeons from aeroplanes or dirigibles was given deep consideration but rejected on the grounds that it would be impossible to locate the agent accurately and would have to depend on good weather to permit an aircraft to fly. Enemy troops in the vicinity could also be counted as a certainty and that meant the agent would be running an absurd risk in trying to retrieve the pigeons after they had been dropped. It was a forlorn hope to expect anything to be achieved in the conditions imposed by trench warfare. Despite all this, the idea of the Suicide Club stuck and throughout all the major offensives of 1917 it waited in the wings. Men familiar with the area in which they would have to operate were few and far between and the ten-mile restriction effectively deprived any agent of his most valuable asset – the ability to merge with the local population.

Opportunities did occur, as on the first day of the Battle of Arras and the tank assault at Cambrai, when British troops did penetrate the trench lines, but these were cast to the winds by excessive secrecy. In one of his laconic understatements, Drake commented that the task was made even more difficult by the Operations Division of the General Staff 'whose policy of secrecy towards even those sections of Intelligence charged with the duties of secret service was perhaps on conservative lines'.[2] Admittedly, secrecy is essential to the success of any military operation, but conduct such as this smacks more of petty rivalry than reasonable security. So the Suicide Club continued to wait

1 Kirke Diaries, op. cit., 3 September 1916.
2 Drake, op. cit., p. 31.

in depressing frustration, until the entrenched stalemate was broken in August 1918, and the Germans began to retreat and open fighting resumed. From 21 August onwards several successful attempts were made to use the Club as the Germans fell back into areas with sizeable civilian populations and they did succeed in returning some information 'of a useful though not perhaps highly important nature'.[1]

In the face of these early setbacks, the Secret Services found another chance to redeem their faltering reputation through the medium of a special operation closely tied to a plan which might revolutionize the strategic scenario. One of Field-Marshal Haig's pet projects was for a powerful British offensive in Flanders coupled with an amphibious landing on the coast. One of the conditions upon which Haig had insisted, when the plans for the joint Anglo-French assault on the Somme were laid, was that should the great offensive fail the weight of the British effort could be switched northwards. A landing on the Flanders coast was hardly a task to be undertaken lightly. The Germans were all too aware of the dangers of a sudden seaborne descent upon their coastal flank and bent their efforts towards insuring against one. Solid fortifications, constructed according to the latest and best engineering techniques, and bristling with powerful armaments covered by a formidable garrison, protected this sensitive spot against any British foray. Equally well guarded were the ports of Ostend and Zeebrugge which harboured the flotillas of cruisers and destroyers the Germans employed to wreak havoc amongst British Channel traffic.

The elementary conditions for such a daringly ambitious campaign were not only having the men and ships necessary, but also sure and reliable Intelligence about the fortifications, the nature of the beaches, the topography of the surrounding countryside and the humdrum details of wind and tide. Alas, neither Naval Intelligence nor C's Secret Service could supply the required information since the focus of attention for their pre-war efforts had been Germany herself; so far as coastal reports were concerned, interest had been restricted to Germany's North Sea and Baltic shorelines. Now, fostered alike by the Army's new interest in the Flanders coast and the pressing need to strike at the German flotillas, great efforts were made to supply the necessary facts. Since the GHQ Secret Services were paramount in

1 Ibid.

Belgium they were promptly presented with this unenviable task. Since the Army in 1916 was locked in battle on the Somme, this was their first priority; little time and few resources could be siphoned off for chasing a new and possibly theoretical hare. What was more, the rings of agents run by GHQ were operating in the interior of Belgium, pursuing their real task of tracing the movements and deployment of the German Army. Confronted with this new burden, I(b) shouldered it reluctantly and though they earnestly sought to infiltrate their men into this fresh field of endeavour, the results did not justify the effort. Much of the information demanded of the agents was beyond their ken – what did they know of tides, reinforced concrete or harbours and docks? Their lack of specialized knowledge proved an impossible handicap and in spite of valiant and determined exertions, the venture foundered. The Dover Patrol, the naval command responsible for both Channel security and the naval side of the amphibious project, had no hesitation in damning the reports on the Zeebrugge area unequivocally as 'useless' though they grudgingly conceded that the coastal reports *might* be of some value.[1]

By the autumn of 1916 all hope of the plan becoming reality that year had evaporated and the reports were pigeon-holed until 1917, when this time Naval Intelligence assumed responsibility for the coastal areas. It is worth noting that part of the plan for the 1917 landings called for tanks to be landed with the first wave of the attack. Once ashore they were to be harnessed to specially designed rafts crowded with infantry, artillery, engineering stores and all the heavy equipment the invaders might need, and would then tow the rafts ashore. An officer with a more than passing interest in tanks, the great theorist of armoured warfare, Major-General J. F. C. 'Boney' Fuller, visited the proposed landing beaches in the 1920s and poured scorn on the idea in his memoirs. He found the low-lying Belgian countryside defended by a substantial seawall, smothered with slime and seaweed upon which his precious tanks could not have gained a necessary footing. The intelligence reports had failed completely to mention this.

Special Operations, like so much else in war, depend heavily on having the right man in the right place at the right time. Wireless, as has been seen, was still very much a novelty during the First World

1 Kirke Diaries, op. cit., 13 October 1916.

War. Still more rare were wireless experts who were understandably in great demand. So great was the need of them that their expertise even outweighed the strictest questions of nationality. Thus it was that Alexander Szek, a wireless enthusiast born of an Austrian father and British mother living in Croydon was more or less press-ganged into working for the German Army's wireless office in Brussels.

The Secret Service was tipped off about Szek by Sidney Reilly, reputedly Britain's 'ace of spies'. C then notified Colonel (later Sir) Vernon Kell as head of MO5 (later MI5), the counter-espionage service responsible for monitoring enemy aliens living in Britain. Mrs Szek was traced without great difficulty and her son's anti-German sentiments were made known to the British. Almost immediately messages were sent through her to Alexander in an attempt to persuade him to steal the German wireless cipher. Naval Intelligence took a hand in the case, since they were directly concerned – the Admiralty's Room 40 carried responsibility for breaking foreign codes and ciphers – and in any case, C himself was a naval officer. He was obliged to obey the orders of his superiors in the Senior service; even more to the point, Naval Intelligence was at that time not only the senior but the largest Intelligence service and better able to devote resources to the task in hand.

Captain Reginald 'Blinker' Hall, Director of Naval Intelligence and in charge of the Szek case, was not imbued with the same 'gung-ho' spirit as Smith-Cumming. An altogether more serious character, he pushed his work on with singleminded dedication and whereas C regarded it all as great sport, Hall viewed the job coldly; his general attitude towards Intelligence work could reasonably be described as severe, and he expected the same dedication and unbending resolution from his subordinates. In his hands, what had begun as the persuasion of Mrs Szek and her son soon turned into pressure. Mrs Szek was told in no uncertain terms that unless Alexander complied with the demands made on him, she and her other children would be seized and interned as enemy aliens. The Szeks were a close-knit family, and Hall must have counted on the threat being relayed to Alexander. Unsurprisingly, Szek fell in with Hall's plan but he was careful enough to make one stipulation. If his life were ever in danger because the Germans discovered their cipher had been broken, the British were to smuggle him out of Belgium and back to Croydon. Hall had considerable misgivings about this condition but reluctantly accepted it in order to conclude the operation. The Szek case was now passed back to the Secret Service since they had agents in Brussels and routes by which Szek's information could be filtered back to Britain.

Because of tight German security Szek had to work on the theft of the cipher over several months, copying a few words at a time on to tiny slips of paper when unobserved. These he had to conceal until he needed to relieve himself and in the privacy of the latrine could insert them into his rectum. This means of concealment had been taught him by the British; it had long been an established practice on the grounds that nobody would think of looking there; continentals did not, in C's words, 'associate arse with paper'. Over the course of several nerve-racking months, a task that would have intimidated many men was successfully achieved by Szek, as details of the German cipher were cautiously secreted into the waiting hands of C's agents. Szek's work was one of the leads which enabled Room 40 to break German codes, culminating in the deciphering of the famous Zimmermann telegram.

When the Germans embarked on a further bout of unrestricted U-boat warfare in February 1917 they were justifiably concerned that this might bring the United States into the war against them. One way of avoiding this was to give the Americans something else to think about and to this end, Zimmermann, the German Foreign Secretary, sent a telegram to the German Ambassador in Mexico proposing an alliance between Mexico and Germany should the United States declare war. In return for her help Mexico would be given the states of Texas, New Mexico and Colorado, which had all been part of Mexico until the nineteenth century. The full story of the telegram lies outside the scope of this book. Suffice it to say here that the British intercepted the telegram and were able to gain an important lead in decoding it thanks to Szek's work. The discovery of the German plot was instrumental in persuading the American President, Woodrow Wilson, to declare war on Germany. The American entry into the war irrevocably loaded the scales against Germany, so perhaps it is not stretching the facts too far to suggest that Szek's work helped directly to turn events towards timely ultimate Allied victory.

The Germans seemed slow to realize how badly their cipher had been compromised. Other Naval Intelligence coups, like the retrieval of a codebook from a sunken submarine, kept Room 40 on top. Unsure of how much the British knew, the Germans only attempted to alter their existing code rather than create a new one. For Szek, however, the situation was now extremely dangerous, and the danger would grow with every day that passed. The Germans knew that some part at least of their cipher was broken and it would be only a matter of time before they traced the leak. Both Szek and the British knew this so Szek used his only reasonable option and invoked the agreement whereby the British were to get him out if he was in jeopardy. He still held the final links to the German cipher which Room 40 badly wanted and, in a bid to ensure that the British kept their part of the bargain, Szek refused to deliver these until he was safely in London. To the British, the danger was quite different: if Szek were caught by the Germans there was every likelihood that he would give away his contact in Brussels and much else besides. One way or another Szek had to be extricated from his predicament and if possible without the Germans realizing that he had betrayed their cipher. Consequently Szek was got out of Brussels and successfully smuggled across the border into the Netherlands where he boarded the ferry to Britain. But that is as far as he got. Szek never reached his family in Croydon, and in such official papers as have been released one finds no further mention of him.

In view of what did take place this official silence should occasion no surprise. During the viva for the doctoral thesis upon which this book is based, the Szek case came under discussion. My external examiner was Professor M. R. D. Foot, the Official Historian of the operations of the Special Operations Executive in France and one-time officer of the SIS. In the course of discussion Professor Foot disclosed that Szek had indeed boarded the night ferry but, once out in the North Sea, he had been assassinated, his papers taken and his body dumped overboard: in time of war, one more body, if found, would excite neither suspicion nor comment.[1] British Intelligence clearly had doubts about Szek if left in Brussels, but wherein was he dangerous once in British hands? What alternatives were there to killing Szek? There is no evidence that Szek would have betrayed what he knew, but even so might he not have been effectively shut away until the end of the war or until whatever information he held became obsolete? Even the supposedly ruthless KGB did not kill Leopold Trepper, head of the brilliantly successful 'Red Orchestra' in the Second World War, but put him in prison until Stalin's death in 1953 without any complaint from Trepper, who knew only too well why it was

1 Conversation with Professor M. R. D. Foot, 14 October 1984. The comments noted above were witnessed by Mr T. A. Jones, MA (Cantab.).

necessary. After further harassment from the Poles in the 1960s, he was permitted in 1973 to emigrate to Israel, where he later died a peaceful death. Britain is not, of course, a totalitarian state and Szek's release would almost certainly have been enforced after the war. Yet there is likewise no shred of evidence to suggest that any such proposition was ever either considered or put to him. What is far more likely is that Hall judged it expedient to get rid of a potential embarrassment. Szek's successful attempt to bargain his safety for the final cipher links was, too, an action calculated to incur Hall's wrath. The conclusion seems inescapable that Szek was killed because he knew too much and had angered the wrong man.

SEVEN

Airborne Operations

As the war ground on, the Secret Services grew both in numbers and techniques and there emerged, slowly at first, a recognition of the kind of men and women most effective in Intelligence work. There remained the perennial difficulties of movement within occupied territories and of conveying information undetected.

As early as September 1915 C's men were sending reports in from Cologne, Aachen, Berlin, Dresden and Dirschau, but operations in the heartland of the German Empire were by no means confined to his service.[1] In his *History*, Drake maintains that GHQ was barred from operating in Germany, for that was the sole preserve of the War Office.[2] This flies in the face of the facts, for a subsection of the GHQ Secret Service was very active there. This subsection was in the hands of Captain (later Sir) John A. Wallinger, E. A. Wallinger's brother who, operating from Switzerland (traditionally another War Office preserve), had established train-watching posts at Koblenz and Cologne by June 1915, with posts in Frankfurt and Mainz and two in Treves (Trier) by November.[3] In 1916 Bonn and Kobern were added to the list and Major Wallinger himself now ventured into the forbidden territory with a new post at Strasburg and the annexation of brother John's posts at Koblenz, Treves and Frankfurt.[4] Some of these posts were directed by agents secreted into Germany via Switzerland, but others were run almost like private enterprises by native Germans such as Tasche Heinrich, who from September 1915 controlled cells at Frankfurt, Wiesbaden, Mainz and Darmstadt.

John Wallinger attempted to develop further systems through the Netherlands and Scandinavia but by the summer of 1916 most of these had collapsed. He had shown himself to be a poor judge of character, for the head of his Swiss-based system, known by the initials P.D.,

1 Kirke Diaries, op. cit., 6 September 1915.
2 Drake, op. cit., pp. 3, 9 and 15.
3 Kirke Diaries, op. cit., 13 June and 30 November 1915.
4 Ibid., 10 June and 16 August 1916.

had 'cold feet, is incapable, inspires no confidence, and only wants to remain *embusqué* until the end of the war'.[1] Furthermore, 'Bernard', his chief agent, had proved himself a swindler who defrauded I(b) of a large sum of money without sending in a single genuine report.[2] John Wallinger's efforts in the Netherlands were deemed to have been merely poaching from his brother's organization and his Scandinavian system achieved nothing, partly because of War Office antagonism: they feared he would upset their own systems. Kirke summed up his efforts thus:

> His organization is useless, and has as a matter of fact produced [only] one report of any real value. He has not the knowledge, nor time to make a success of military secret service work. Under such circs. it is our duty to reorganize, introduce new direction with the service, or abolish it.[3]

Ultimately GHQ merged John Wallinger's systems with those of his more capable brother and of the War Office, though after the reorganization of 1917 all systems operating in Germany were supposed to be under War Office control. This did not prevent the occasional GHQ incursion into Germany, for Best used to visit a café at Waals on the Dutch-German border, an ideal spot for agents and their controllers to meet and exchange information and directions.

Crossing the German frontiers had become increasingly difficult. Kirke recorded that the 'Germans [are] thoroughly investigating business of travellers. If they do not carry out the business for which German Consul has given them a passport they are promptly arrested.'[4] However, this sort of control fluctuated according to German sentiment towards their neutral neighbours. Nobody had ever pretended it was going to be easy and German restrictions did not cause any service to abandon the use of commerce as a cover, only to their taking extra precautions to avoid that cover being blown. Kirke's diaries reveal that one agent was a commercial traveller who visited both Lille and Gand (Ghent) and another worked for Heinemann, the Munich-based publishers; the merchant banking firm of Ralli Brothers was also approached. A Dutch merchant called Dreckmeyer

1 Ibid., 19 July 1916. *Embusqué* was contemporary slang for a person who had inveigled his way into a safe job and intended to stay there until the fighting was over.
2 Ibid., 28 February 1916.
3 Ibid., 19 July 1916.
4 Ibid., 13 May 1915.

lent his services, as did the representative of a sugar firm, and banking acquaintances of one Intelligence officer succeeded in persuading a Dutch glass firm with connections in Tournai, Valenciennes and other places where glass works still functioned to assist British Intelligence.

Once an agent is on the spot he or she can commence operations, but getting that agent to the required spot was ever a thorn in the flesh of Intelligence. For GHQ Intelligence, with its responsibilities fixed firmly on the theatre of operations, the problems multiplied once the trench lines had sealed the direct route into the enemy's camp. It was this hard, unalterable fact that forced GHQ to trespass on the War Office's land, and resort to the neighbouring neutral countries as a means of channelling agents and information in and out of the target area. Besides the organizational difficulties and bitter personal quarrels this touched off, other drawbacks swiftly made their presence felt. It was all very well for Intelligence traffic of whatever nature to pass through the Netherlands, but the practicalities of getting an agent across the closely guarded frontier into Belgium were time-consuming and prone to failure. An alternative did exist in the shape of flying the agents over in the new aeroplanes but, as was soon discovered, this means was beset by difficulties of its own.

The first British attempt to land an agent from the air, in November 1914, had been an unmitigated disaster: pilot, agent and aeroplane were all lost. This discouraged further attempts until successes by the French Fifth Army in the summer of 1915 stimulated GHQ to renew their efforts. The headquarters of the RFC were informed and Trenchard, now GOC, called his wing commanders to a conference on 9 September. He told them of Intelligence's interest in mounting the operation and stated that the French 'have done this twenty-eight times, twenty-seven of which were successful'.[1] Trenchard then asked the assembled officers for their opinion on the practicality of the proposed operation, giving them until 9 a.m. on the 11th to let him have their views.

It barely left time for mature consideration of the question but nothing daunted the wing commanders replied in the affirmative – or so one must conclude from the fact that in the early hours of 13 September, Captain J. W. M. Morgan left the aerodrome of No. 6 Squadron in his BE2c, carrying agent Van de Leene, a native of Courtrai, whom he was to land near the village of Oyeghem. The

1 'Agent Dropping by RFC, May 1928', PRO AIR1/675/21/13/1726.

operation was hardly one of the outstanding success stories of the war. Landing in semi-darkness at 4.45 a.m., Morgan struck a tree and tore a wing from his machine. Both pilot and would-be agent were badly injured in the crash, the unfortunate Van de Leene having both legs broken and suffering 'slight internal injuries', injuries that would have been far worse had it not been for the protection afforded by the basket of carrier pigeons he had carried in order to send his messages back to GHQ. Both men were captured by the Germans as they lay helpless amidst the plane wreckage, but thanks to the slow German arrival on the scene, local civilians had taken the two pigeons which survived the crash and hidden them.[1]

Undeterred, Intelligence determined to try again. On the morning of 28 September, Captain G. L. Cruickshank (No. 3 Squadron) left the British lines in a Morane Parasol with agent 'Leonard' aboard. This time there was no trouble when Cruickshank landed, near Quesnoy. Instead, as Leonard was getting out of the Morane he accidentally brushed the petrol switch with his sleeve, stopping the engine dead. In those days the engines of aeroplanes had to be started by someone standing beside the machine swinging the propeller. Leonard was understandably very anxious to make good his escape before the Germans arrived. Cruickshank was equally impatient to be away and resolved the dilemma by drawing his revolver and, with that pointed in Leonard's direction, forced him to restart the engine. Cruickshank escaped, but the luckless Leonard was very shortly caught and shot by the Germans.[2]

Both I(b) and the RFC seem really to have got the bit between their teeth after this and another agent was made ready for the drop on 4 October. The pilot this time was Lieutenant J. W. Woodhouse, a man who would make a name for himself through his skill, courage and cool nerve in a number of such special missions, in the course of which he was decorated with the DSO and MC. Unlike the other special missions, Woodhouse's take-off was timed for 4.30 in the afternoon as the light was thickening. He had a choice of landing places, all in the neighbourhood of Cambrai. The first choice, near the village of Serain, had German troops in the vicinity who fired on the plane, and wisely Woodhouse swung away north-west towards Bantouzelle. By now it was nearly 5.20 p.m., dusk was falling and a ground mist had

1 Ibid.
2 Ibid. and Kirke Diaries, op. cit., 28 September 1915.

begun to develop which, although they may have been flying hazards, helped to conceal the exact landing place from prying eyes. Woodhouse located his landing ground and touched down:

> The agent was very quick in getting clear with his pigeons into the wood, but owing to a steep glide in landing, the forward cylinders got too much oil, with the result that they cut out and the engine stopped. The throttle had been set so that the engine would just run with all cylinders firing.
>
> The agent meanwhile had reached the wood, but seeing that Lieutenant Woodhouse was in difficulties returned to his assistance. Lieutenant Woodhouse, however, insisted on his return to the cover of the wood, and after putting his own gloves into the air-intake pipes, sucked in petrol, and started the engine himself, getting into the aeroplane as she moved off.[1]

Woodhouse got away but within minutes had to land again to clear his engine from over-oiling, which he did by running it all out in short bursts. He eventually got back to the British lines, but it was now dark and he lost his bearings, ending up landing blindly in a field near Bayonvillers, breaking his propeller in the process. It was clear that both agents and pilots needed to be carefully selected for this kind of operation – preferably those with nerves of steel.

On 3 October 1915 an agent called Victor Marie had been landed near St Quentin. This man was a professional smuggler, one of several employed by Intelligence during the war, and his house was a typical smuggler's den, complete with hiding places concealed in the roof and walls and even a secret passage leading from the cellar. He was one of those characters who love to lead their lives at a swinging pace, audacious, arrogant and possessed of a bold self-confidence that can so often enable such people to outface other, less assured spirits. These qualities aside, he was not above double-crossing anybody and one of his favourite occupations in life was to run rings round those in authority. His experiences as a smuggler inclined him to be a loner and once dropped back behind German lines he developed the habit of hiding by day and emerging after nightfall to recruit his agents and collect their reports.

Marie's house was ideally suited for spying on the Germans, positioned as it was near the Belgian-German border and near the

1 War Diary of 3rd Wing, RFC, for October 1915, Vol. VIII, *Special Mission by Lieutenant Woodhouse 4.10.1915*. PRO AIR1/2170/209/12/8.

principal railway line linking Namur and Cologne. He rapidly became GHQ's top agent in eastern Belgium. Like the other agents, he took carrier pigeons into Belgium with him; when these were all released, more would be dropped by the RFC in baskets with parachutes attached, provided Victor had put out the required signal – a clothes line with washing on it – at the pre-arranged dates. Periodically he would return in person to GHQ via the Netherlands to give Kirke a detailed briefing and to discuss any problems, most of which were in connection with the air-dropping of pigeons. Everything appeared to be in first-class order during the first six months; Victor Marie was on the spot, his system was growing, and the pigeons were returning with valuable information about the location and movements of German reserves. So important had Victor Marie become to GHQ that, unusually, it was decided to decorate him; possibly, too, this was partly inspired by the perceived need to bolster his morale, which was beginning to show clear signs of strain on his last visit to GHQ. Thus, in July 1916, Haig himself decorated Victor Marie with the DCM in appreciation of his valuable services, describing him as a 'really bold plucky fellow'.[1]

But now things rapidly began to go wrong. Every attempt to fly Victor Marie over the lines came to grief because of German fighter aeroplanes or persistently bad weather. The entries in Kirke's diary began to reflect the serious concern felt at GHQ over these failures and the resulting dislocation of a successful spy ring: '. . . we can do no more, but I have misgivings and much fear that we may lose Marie, when the whole service will go phut'.[2]

The situation was not helped when the RFC had three of their machines from No. 60 Squadron shot down while trying to reconnoitre a proposed landing place near Estrées on 2 August. Eventually, however, Second Lieutenant Ridley took off with Victor Marie from Vert Galant early in the morning of the 3rd, accompanied by two more machines for the purpose of attracting anti-aircraft fire, which they did admirably for a time. One developed engine trouble, however, and had to crash land, fortunately on the British side of the line, and the other watched Ridley's machine head towards the earth into a ground mist. It failed to reappear. There was a deafening and worrying silence from Belgium about the fate of Victor Marie until 7 October, when news came from the Netherlands that Ridley had safely reached that

1 Haig Dairies, op. cit., 9 July 1916, Vol. 10.
2 Kirke Diaries, op. cit., 20 July 1916.

country. It transpired that his machine had crashed in the mist but that both men had escaped unharmed and Victor had smuggled Ridley across the border. However, in doing so he had been forced to use the help of other people and had left too many traces. The Germans picked up his trail and by the beginning of December had tracked him down and arrested him. True to character, Marie defected to their Secret Service, with the result that GHQ's Beverloo system was destroyed before Christmas.

It was a sickening body-blow but worse was to come. The loss of aeroplanes on their missions had dire side-effects for GHQ. One had been written off in crash landing, three shot down on reconnaissance, one forced down with engine trouble and two others damaged by 'archies'[1] – a whole squadron, No. 60, had to all intents and purposes been wiped off the active list. Unsurprisingly, Kirke found that the 'RFC [are] not approachable for the present'.[2] Trenchard, who had in fact always disliked using aeroplanes for helping Intelligence, could hardly contain his anger and now limited operations in support of I(b) to within fifteen miles of the front line and in 1917 prohibited them altogether.[3]

Relations with the RFC had always been thorny and Trenchard's attitude was unquestionably part of the problem. Prior to the great German offensive of March 1918, the reports of the Secret Services had been indicating precisely from which railway stations the German reinforcements from Russia were detraining. Macdonogh sent the then Lieutenant-Colonel Marshall-Cornwall to Trenchard, then Chief of the Air Staff in London, to ask him to bomb these stations rather than dissipate his strength in raids of dubious value on the Rhine valley. According to Marshall-Cornwall, 'Trenchard only boomed at me about the tremendous moral effect produced by these raids on the German peple, which I knew to be quite erroneous.'[4] Once Trenchard had his heart set on something he did not rest until he had got it and, to him, the largely ineffectual raids on German industrial towns were part of a far larger scheme (it came to be called 'strategic bombing' little more than twenty years later) and he was not going to see his resources wasted in attacking targets indicated by Intelligence.

Yet this was never the whole story, for there is evidence that the

1 RFC slang for anti-aircraft fire.
2 Kirke Diaries, op. cit., 3 August 1916.
3 Drake, op. cit., pp. 22–3
4 Marshall-Cornwall, *Wars and Rumours of Wars*, op. cit., p. 37.

commanders of the RFC and, later, the RAF in the field were deeply suspicious of secret operations about which they were told little and which did not present any prospect of obvious benefit to their service. The officer who delivered a lecture to the RAF Staff College on 'The Use of Aircraft in Connection with Espionage' in 1924 was moved to remark that 'this work was not calculated to make them take a great deal of interest in the doings of this [Special Duty] unit'.[1] The same officer rightly criticized the lack of effective liaison between the RFC/RAF commands and Military Intelligence, and the fact that the military and air authorities did not always see eye to eye. The ignorance displayed by Intelligence over the practical capabilities of aircraft and the effect of meteorological conditions, together with the unimaginative responses of the air service officers and an administration which meant that such flights fell under the control of the military authorities, also came in for heavy stricture.

The increased efficiency of German anti-aircraft fire lay at the root of the problem. Without that, the losses that had called forth the anger and resentment of the RFC would never have been sustained and as things stood in late 1916 it put daylight flights of this nature out of the question. But if daylight flights were no longer possible then neither was landing agents at all. Aeroplanes simply did not have night flying and night vision equipment – it had not been invented. Night landings were therefore out of the question unless there was a bright moon and a properly reconnoitred landing ground, facts Intelligence officers never seemed to appreciate, for they were still pressing for night landings in impossible country only a month before the Armistice.[2]

Intelligence would have to look elsewhere for a means of landing agents by air, at least temporarily. The idea of using an airship was raised but was rejected on the grounds that experiments had been made once before and had proved unsuccessful. That had been in July 1916, when a small submarine scout airship (SS40) had been borrowed from the Admiralty to see if it could drop agents by using a Calthrop 'Guardian Angel' parachute, one which was attached to the aircraft by a cord, with the parachutist's weight being used to pull the parachute out of its spring case. The airship, based at Boubers Sur Canche near Frévent, made several flights and successfully dropped dummies on parachutes. The next step was to test her in active service conditions

1 'The Use of Aircraft in Connection with Espionage', PRO AIR1/2399/280/1.

2 Interview with Captain Bruce, cited in 'Landing of Agent Over Line at Night Fitting of Parachutes DH4. 18 October 1918–10 November 1918', PRO AIR1/1997/204/273/245.

and to that end reconnaissances were made over the German lines on the nights of 28–29 August, 22–23 and 26–27 September. Although the airship got across the lines and returned safely, she was felt to be too vulnerable to anti-aircraft fire on moonlit nights and on dark nights was just as helpless as an aeroplane.[1] She had then been returned to Britain and there was no enthusiasm to use her again.

It had been as much desperation as anything else which led Intelligence to the use of free, gas-filled balloons carrying an agent in a basket slung underneath, which could be allowed to drift over the enemy lines when the wind was in the right direction, the speed of the wind and the amount of ballast carried determining where it would land. The idea took shape at the beginning of November with Trenchard's encouragement; after all, if Intelligence were playing with these toys they might leave the RFC to get on with its proper job. Things moved rapidly and without a hitch. Major Wallinger began experimenting with the balloons on 10 November and the Admiralty, in the shape of Admiral Vaughan-Lee and Commodore Sueter, arranged that one of his officers, Lieutenant Ivone Kirkpatrick, and another officer from GHQ should join a course in free ballooning at Wormwood Scrubs on 15 December. Not only the RFC were ready to help Intelligence; the Navy was actively encouraging the idea, even to the extent of sending Commander Pollock, their ballooning expert, over to France with two balloons at Christmas. The experiments went better than anyone had dared to hope, greatly helped by the fact that the prevailing winds on the Western front blew from the south-west and so into the occupied territories, and it was proved conclusively that it was possible to land agents with remarkable accuracy, provided wind and weather were favourable.[2]

Agents landed by this method were originally equipped with a new portable wireless designed by Captain Round, Marconi's chief inventor. His continuous wave set weighed 57 pounds complete, quite acceptable in a free balloon (less restricted by weight problems than an aeroplane) and light enough to be carried after landing. Drake relates there was 'considerable success' in landing accurately but that no intelligible transmissions were received due to 'a certain lack of interest on the part of the local technical experts'.[3] Round eventually

1 *See* 'The Naval Airship (SS40) on the Western Front, 1916', PRO AIR1/163/15/136/1; and 'The Use of Aircraft in Connection with Espionage', PRO AIR1/2399/280/10.
2 Drake, op. cit', p. 24.
3 Ibid.

discovered that the receiving apparatus was defective.[1] Drake concluded that 'This was a matter beyond the control of anybody working in I(b) as in such technical affairs one is obviously in the hands of one's experts.'[2] Use of this particular equipment was discontinued after the Germans captured one agent and his transmitter after an accident in landing, and executed him.

Nevertheless, seven balloon landings were made. After landing in the early hours of the morning, the agent would lie low until the population went about their daily tasks and then join them. In case he was seized by the German Army, Wallinger's service devised a scheme to ensure his speedy release. He was equipped with a bottle of Belgian spirits or some tobacco, both of which were contraband under the German government in Belgium. Naturally there was a considerable black market in these goods and once the Germans discovered such items, the person concerned would be transferred to the custody of the civil police, since the carriage of contraband was a civil offence. Any action which might have aroused suspicion in the first place would soon be accounted for and forgotten; the agent would be in a civilian gaol for a few weeks, after which he was free to resume his activities.[3]

Fortunately, since balloons were so subject to the vagaries of wind and weather, the RFC relented in its policy of non-cooperation and flights to land agents were resumed as necessary, with Woodhouse, now a captain, well to the fore. They were still not without their comic, even bizarre aspects. One such flight, in July 1917, was due to take off from Treziennes aerodrome when a 'large number' of German aeroplanes chose that precise moment to raid the airfield:

> During this raid, a gallant old Frenchman, who had volunteered to be dropped in a parachute over the enemy's lines, was strapped to the machine. Whilst a large gramophone at the side was playing the 'Marseillaise' the engine was run up and the machine took off, with the brave old Frenchman, garbed as a peasant, singing aloud to the accompaniment of the gramophone.[4]

Two new developments had taken place earlier that year which placed the air dropping of agents on a much sounder footing. The first, in February, proved that agents could achieve better parachute drops

1 Ibid.
2 Ibid.
3 Best Papers, loc. cit., 'Pinnacle 90'.
4 'A Short History of 'I' Flight RAF', PRO AIR1/163/15/136/1.

from an aeroplane than from an airship. This was good news for the RFC, for it meant that they could transport an agent to a desired locality without running the risk of losing aeroplanes and pilots by landing on unknown territory at night. Intelligence opposed the idea, largely on the grounds that it would be unnerving for the agents, and a lengthy wrangle ensued which lasted right until the end of the war. The RFC eventually had its way, since it held the trump card of being the arm of the service now responsible for these missions.

The second development was the establishment of the Special Duty Flight in April, with the specific purpose of carrying out these special missions by night. It was the first and only night flying unit on the Western front, though the idea caught on, with another such flight being formed by the British forces in Italy at the beginning of 1918. The SDF was a self-contained unit of 'about' 4 officers and 25 men, with 6 aeroplanes of varying types. It was equipped with its own stores and transport and could move to any part of the front where its services were required. For the purposes of administration it was attached to the 9th (GHQ) wing and for discipline it came under the squadron on whose aerodrome it happened to be at any given time.

Woodhouse inevitably served in this flight and soon established himself as its leading pilot. Despite the flight being blessed with one of the new parachute-equipped machines, it was still necessary on some occasions to land behind enemy lines, presumably on account of the agents' widespread distrust of this still novel means of descent. On one such occasion Woodhouse nearly repeated the incident of September 1915, in the only case of failure in a Special Duties Flight mission that I have been able to trace. Woodhouse had landed his BE2e at night and the agent was making off when, in turning his machine, Woodhouse accidentally stopped the engine. Again the agent returned to assist but this time Woodhouse decided to take the plugs from the engine and clean them. By the time this was complete dawn was upon them – and so was a German patrol. Luckily for pilot and agent the engine started first time and they were both able to fly to safety, though under fire from the thwarted German soldiers.[1]

Dropping an agent by parachute was not without its moments, either. As the aeroplanes had no provision for carrying a passenger the agent was normally mounted on a small seat placed on the rear spar of the lower port plane, facing the tail of the machine with his legs

1 'The Use of Aircraft in Connection with Espionage', PRO AIR1/2399/280/1.

dangling into space. To prevent him being swept away by the slipstream, a cord and belt held him to one of the aeroplane's struts. Halfway along this cord was a quick release, operated by string from the pilot's cockpit. Thus when the pilot yanked the string the agent was swept away by the slipstream whether he was ready or not. It may sound like something designed in a lunatic asylum but at least it worked – which is more than can be said for its intended replacement. That consisted of a wooden box made of three-ply and resembling a coffin (perhaps all too appropriately). This contraption was fixed to the lower port wing, parallel and close to the fuselage. It had no top and was open at the back end; in this the agent was to lie face-down, full-length and hold on by putting his fingers through a slit cut for the purpose in the bottom of the box. Then, or so the theory went, all he had to do when the aeroplane reached the desired locality, was to let go and slide backwards out of the box. This method was only ever tried once.

When the aeroplane in question, a BE12, was over the drop area, the agent lost his nerve. Instead of sliding out gracefully, the wretched man clung in panic to the edge of the cockpit and the pilot's coat. An amazing scene followed, reminiscent today of a sketch from a Buster Keaton film, with pilot and agent struggling fiercely while the machine plunged from 1,600 feet to about 900 feet. The pilot then drew his revolver and threatened to shoot the unwilling agent, but to no avail. Fearing that the machine would crash and kill both of them, he struggled to keep the plane level, while smiting the agent's knuckles with the butt of the revolver. This had the desired effect and the agent released his hold, to be swept away into the darkness. The aeroplane was by now very close to the ground. By the time the pilot had regained control and some height, there was no sign of the agent's parachute having opened. Shaken, the pilot returned to his aerodrome and reported that he thought the agent had been killed. However, by an amazing stroke of luck he had survived and, after a decent interval, wrote to the RFC apologizing for the trouble he had caused.[1]

Agents were successfully landed by parachute in 1917 but through one mishap or another several of them were captured and shot, frequently through failure to conceal the parachute, which was some 30 feet square. The agent was not equipped with tools for burying it and even if he had been, the discovery of freshly turned earth would

1 Ibid. *See also* 'A Short History of "I" Flight RAF', PRO AIR1/163/15/136/1.

be sure to put the Germans on his trail. However, any losses increased the distrust felt for the parachute by the Intelligence Corps, who decided it was too risky to continue using it and they again abandoned the idea in favour of having the aeroplane land.

The Independent Air Force, created for bombing German industrial targets, became involved in the dropping of agents but theirs were not the first bombers to have been so used. Sidney Reilly, reputedly the 'ace of spies', was always air-minded and in 1917 and 1918 he was several times dropped behind enemy lines, sometimes disguised as a peasant and sometimes, when in Germany, as a German soldier with papers to show he had been wounded and was on sick-leave from the front. Armed with these he was able to move freely throughout Germany, a fact of vital importance in gathering information.[1] It has also been claimed that he was dropped by parachute near Mannheim from an aeroplane ostensibly on a bombing mission. That was the winter of 1917–18, his task to discover as much as he could about Germany's offensive plans for 1918. He is supposed to have remained in Germany for several weeks and got the necessary information before being airlifted out by another bomber returning from a raid on Mannheim.[2] Although Reilly did undertake a number of audacious and exceptional missions while in British pay, this latter claim is in doubt. It was a possible feat, but the claim is made without evidence of any kind and is not confirmed by Reilly's most reliable biographer.

The air-dropping of agents was by no means confined to the Western front; records exist which confirm that the Balkans got their fair share of airborne British agents. Lieutenant Walter S. Scott, flying a BE2c from No. 17 Squadron twice dropped agents behind the Salonika front near Fotolievo in the Drama Valley, on 16 December 1916 and 1 January 1917. In the first case he was greatly aided by mist, as his report shows:

> Shut off engine at 6,000 feet and planed down. Found mist on the ground rising up to 200 feet. Managed to land – broke centre section wires. The Greek Spy got away unobserved as it was impossible to see more than 5 yards around the machine owing to mist.[3]

One of the first secret missions entrusted to Lieutenant (later Brigadier) George Hill was to land by aeroplane behind the Bulgarian

1 R. B. Lockhart, *Ace of Spies*, London, 1967, p. 59.
2 R. Deacon, *A History of the British Secret Service*, London, 1969, pp. 218–19.
3 'Report on SS Airships, Types and Certain Operations', PRO AIR1/727/152/5.

front. He was one of the first people to do so and building on his experience gained there he later served Military Intelligence in Russia where, amongst other things, he organized guerrilla units composed mainly from officers of the Tsar's Armies, to harry the Germans in an attempt to keep the Eastern front alive. He also managed to create a phenomenally efficient messenger service based on Lettish and Estonian couriers who succeeded in carrying messages throughout Russia under the very noses of both the Germans and the Bolsheviks.

It was one thing to get all these agents into the target areas and have them glean the desired information, but one major obstacle continually threatened to render all their efforts and the risks they took worthless. 'The fundamental weakness of most intelligence networks is the inability of the man in the field to get his message to the right people at home and/or to have that message acted on.'[1] It was in the field of communications that all the great disasters which struck the Secret Services occurred; the German interdiction of the ferry services in 1916 was a notable example. One ancient method of communication, though attended by certain difficulties, was in almost constant use; carrier pigeons accompanied agents into occupied territories, however they were transported there, and the RFC was engaged in supplying more pigeons to agents already *in situ* and within range. The flights were hazardous but at least the aeroplane did not need to land. The early pigeon drops by daylight had had to be replaced in 1916 by night flights to avoid the enemy's anti-aircraft defences. However the pilot had to be able to locate the dropping zone in the dark; usually it would only be marked by a white sheet or tablecloth so inevitably these ventures were restricted to bright, moonlit nights and even then the pilot would have to risk flying dangerously low – sometimes as low as twenty feet – to be sure of his mark.

An idea of both the precision needed and the perils encountered can be gained from details of a mission flown on the night of 24–25 July 1918, to drop birds to Victor Liagre of Rue Menin 14, Tourcoing, an agent of the French Secret Service. 'I' flight was given the job. Lieutenant J. Wingate, pilot, and Captain C. C. Cole, observer, were detailed to drop baskets of pigeons to Liagre in the cemetery at the Pont de Neuville. After flying their FE2B through searchlights and an anti-aircraft barrage, they reached a position a few miles to the north-west of their objective. Wingate wrote:

1 Best Papers, loc. cit., letter from 'David' to S. P. Best, 12 July 1974.

> I was then at 3,000 feet, and immediately shut off my engine and glided down in the direction of the objective. At this point I observed a heavy barrage of searchlights, A.A. Onions[1] and M.G. going up West of Tourcoing, where we had been a few moments before.
>
> Captain Cole now picked up our objective and we glided down over it without engine, apparently attracting no attention. We arrived over the Churchyard at a height of 2,000 feet, and I spiralled down directly over it to a height of 150 feet, then turned down wind and still without engine, glided down over the S.W. end, ultimately dropping my load at 11.15 p.m. with my Altimeter registering just over 50 feet, thus making absolutely sure of my attempt.[2]

Great nerve is needed to control an aeroplane in darkness, without power or night-flying instruments, and keep it right above a small objective at such a low height. As it was, Wingate and Cole were lucky to get back, since a strong wind made it impossible for them to gain much height immediately after the drop. Even so, they insisted on firing on transport on the Lille-Halluin road and dropping four 25 pound bombs on the railway near Comines, though at the expense of being picked up by searchlights and having to run a gauntlet of anti-aircraft fire and attacks by German aeroplanes on their way home.

The great advantage with pigeons was that they were so swift to return – Intelligence could normally count on them being back in their lofts about ten hours after being released by the agent. One machine dropped pigeons on a graveyard near Roubaix on the night of 24–25 August 1918, and the birds were back in their lofts between 9 and 10 a.m. the following day, with what was described as 'important information'.[3]

Aeroplanes were exactly what were needed to drop pigeons to agents in precise locations, but by early 1917 Intelligence were thinking of exploiting the attitude of the population in the occupied territories on a larger scale; finding in fact a substitute for the direct contact with friendly civilians that had been lost because of the trench lines. The development of the free balloon was the answer to their problems and these were used to dispatch pigeons in March 1917, four in a basket, to areas of particular interest to Intelligence. The basket descended by parachute released by a timing device: an alarm clock

1 A type of fireball used by the Germans as an anti-aircraft weapon.
2 'Report on a Special Mission by "I" Flight on the Night of 24–25 July 1918', in *Secret Service GS11, February–August 1918*, PRO AIR1/1068/204/5/1621.
3 'A Short History of "I" Flight RAF', PRO AIR1/163/15/136/1.

was set to go off when it was estimated the balloon would reach the designated area, the winding key releasing both basket and parachute. Since the prevailing winds on the Western front blew from unoccupied territory, the balloons could be launched on a high percentage of nights. From November 1917 fuses were used to release the basket after a specific time, but with both devices precise calculation of the wind speed and direction were required. Another method consisted of a canvas sponge-bag filled with water being attached to the balloon: a hole was punched into this immediately before launching and the resulting leak served as ballast to keep the balloon at its correct height. According to Kirkpatrick, the balloon apparatus was over 30 feet in height and difficult to handle in wind and darkness.[1]

The pigeons were accompanied by a questionnaire asking those finding the birds for information about the German forces in the area: the identity of enemy units; whether they were Active, Reserve, Ersatz[2], or Landwehr[3] (but Landsturm[4] were specifically excluded); their morale; where they had come from; where they were going; the strength of the companies; the quality of food; the staffs in the area; road and rail movements; train units present; and the construction of trenches and aerodromes. As Belgium had two languages, the questionnaires were printed in both French and Flemish. Each pigeon was accompanied by an aluminium capsule or a twelve-inch length of very fine but strong steel wire for the finder to attach the completed questionnaire, and also by several days' supply of bird food.

The Germans found the pigeons, once released, impossible to stop. They tried hawks and shotguns but Nicolai records that pigeons were shot down in only eleven cases – and all those carried important military information.[5] Other measures included decoy pigeons which would return to German lofts revealing the identity of the informant, 'with the inevitable consequences' for him or her, but this failed to

1 Kirkpatrick, op. cit., p. 13.

2 These were divisions created in 1914 from men liable for military service but who had not been called up; they were used to create duplicates of existing units.

3 The third line of troops in Prussia/Germany's system of conscription. Created in 1813 as a *levée en masse* of all reasonably able males to fight Napoleon, by 1914 they were men who had served their military service in the standing army and then the Reserve. After that they passed to the Landwehr, in the first *ban* (grade) to age 35, and in the second *ban* to age 45.

4 Essentially a home guard and not intended for active service. Composed of all males not in the standing army, Reserve or Landwehr. Used between 1915 and 1918 for policing occupied territories.

5 Nicolai, op. cit., p. 157.

deter the Belgians.[1] The Germans at Aachen then started to release birds carrying misinformation but this ploy was defeated by the British politely requiring the sender to supply not only his own name but the names of two friends in the unoccupied territories who could identify the handwriting. The British were greatly assisted by the fact that the breeding and racing of pigeons were popular pastimes in Belgium and northern France, providing a good cover for any visiting birds. The Germans, countered, or tried to, by promising fourteen days' leave out of turn to any soldier who shot down a pigeon, and resting troops were turned out at night to patrol the fields in the hope of seizing the air-dropped pigeon baskets. Such was the impact made by the pigeons on the Germans that a rumour gained credence that the British had trained flocks of pigeons to fly along the routes of the railway lines with miniature pre-set cameras in their tail-feathers to take photographs of the railway lines at frequent intervals.

It was originally calculated that I(b) would be lucky if 5 per cent of pigeons returned but in fact the average rate of return was 40 per cent and in some cases even higher.[2] From a flock of pigeons released from the Grande Place, Arras, on the night of 8 April 1917, 25 per cent had returned by breakfast time on the 9th, of which approximately half carried useful reports.[3] The balloons were usually launched at around 11 p.m. and many of the messages were received by 9 a.m. the following morning.[4] Some idea of the value of the pigeon service can be obtained from Drake's statement that the 'information in most cases was of a very high order and had the advantage of being fresh and rapidly transmitted'.[5] Wallinger too claimed that 'Much valuable information has been obtained by this means.'[6] An added advantage was that the accuracy of free ballooning enabled Intelligence to acquire information from areas where they had no agents. So rewarding were the results of this tactic that the RFC and later the RAF found themselves dropping pigeons on priority localities at short notice, especially during the Allied advance of the summer and autumn of 1918. For example, in August that year the Germans were being steadily forced back. Information was very urgently needed

1 Kell Papers, loc. cit., 'Lecture on Security Intelligence in the Field'.
2 Drake, op. cit., p. 26.
3 Kirkpatrick, op. cit., p. 130.
4 Drake, op. cit., p. 26.
5 Ibid.
6 Kirke Papers, loc. cit., letter from Wallinger to Drake, 6 February 1918.

about German forces on the line Lille-Douai and as there were no agents in that sector and the pressing urgency of the situation precluded the use of free balloons, 'I' Flight was called to the rescue. They parachuted 24 pigeons into the villages on the railway line linking the two cities but unfortunately the deed was badly timed for the civilians there had fled from the approaching guns and not one bird ever came back. As Captain Lawrence, then commanding the flight, wrote. 'This was a very unfortunate blow, for the majority of the birds were very highly prized.'[1]

Pigeons were generally in short supply on the Western front by late 1917 and an ingenious method known as the 'tin-pot stunt' was devised by Wallinger's service to replace them – 'small balloons for use by the inhabitants in lieu of pigeons, [were dropped] together with small tin canisters containing the necessary chemicals for the production of hydrogen or similar gas'.[2] These were again rained on the inhabitants of Belgium and northern France by free balloon but the results were disappointing to say the least. Only 1 balloon out of 100 returned from an experimental drop and that burst while crossing the German lines, the deflated balloon and attendant message ending up caught on the German wire. Fortunately for its sender who, despite specific instruction to the contrary, had been unwise enough to sign the message, the balloon was retrieved by a British infantryman from a raiding party, who had seen it fluttering limp and lifeless on the wire for a few days.[3] The reasons for the failure could only be guessed. Drake considered – rather arrogantly – that it was 'perhaps too complicated for the average peasant'.[4] A more likely explanation is that such easterly winds as existed at the time were simply not strong enough to return the balloons to Allied lines.

If the winter of 1916–17 had been the darkest hour in the history of the Secret Services, it was also the hour which heralded dawn. Under the terms of the reorganization of early 1917, the GHQ services were at last permitted to send two officers to the Netherlands to establish some sort of control and stability amongst the GHQ systems, Captain Verdon representing Cameron's service and S.P. Best that of Wallinger. Best was to have a profound impact on the situation and his

1 'A Short History of "I" Flight RAF', PRO AIR1/163/15/136/1.
2 Drake, op. cit., p. 27.
3 Ibid, p. 28.
4 Ibid.

active, fertile mind was soon grappling with the problem of getting reports across the frontier. Signalling by light was attempted. Best recalled:

> We had a man who had a big stove fairly close to the Frontier and he'd just walk across it so as to send signals by morse, standing in front for a while for a dash and for a moment if he wanted a dot.[1]

However, this was too slow to be satisfactory; something faster and more direct would have to be found. The first answer Best came up with was really another variation on methods already in use against the electrified wires, but it was both quick and efficient:

> A contraption which consisted of two longish pieces of wood with grooves lined with rubber, and, at the sides you had two pieces of wood hinged in the middle attached to the end of the longer side. It was so arranged that if you put them between two of the electric wires and straightened the side pieces, there was a gap left wide enough between the wires for a man to get through.[2]

Nevertheless, if the courier wore a long coat which was wet or if the weather was bad and his trousers wet, he would still receive a shock. So, 'One day when I was in my bath, I had an idea which solved the whole problem – simply thigh-length rubber boots and elbow-length rubber gloves. When a man put those on, he got through the wire without any trouble at all.'[3] Then again, besides written reports, Belgian women could conceal information in their knitting, plain stitches representing coaches carrying men and purl stitches those carrying horses; the finished product was again forwarded by hand.[4]

When Best arrived in the Netherlands, his work was made easier by the fact that, such was the need for fighting men, the occupying forces in Belgium were spread very thinly, as were the frontier guards. As early as July 1916 Kirke recorded that the number of German troops in Belgium was being reduced 'owing to the shortage of men'.[5] Nicolai supports this evidence of the effect of the war of attrition. It necessitated an increasing reliance on electric fences, while as to the men guarding them:

1 Best Papers, loc. cit., 'Pinnacle 90'.
2 Ibid.
3 Ibid.
4 Scotland, op. cit., pp. 43–4.
5 Kirke Diaries, op. cit., 17 July 1916.

> The old Landsturm soldiers on guard, too, were not always proof against the pleas of apparently harmless frontier people, and, as a result, they became unreliable. Sometimes it was their kindness; often they were heavily bribed; again they were persuaded by ever more and more tempting gifts of food.[1]

Unsuccessful attempts were made to communicate by wireless, an idea which originated with the Belgians in February 1915, for they had a transmitter at Baar-le-Hertoge, an enclave of Belgian territory in the Netherlands able to operate throughout the war as the Germans could not reach it without infringing Dutch neutrality.

Apart from the attempts made in conjunction with the free balloons, two others were made by Cameron's service. In May 1915 an unsuccessful attempt was made to establish a wireless in Gand but in September 1915 one, already mentioned, was established in the house of an abbé in Lille. This was done through the agency of 'Ramble' (Mademoiselle Louise de Bettignies), described by Sir John French as a 'regular modern Joan of Arc'.[2] Ramble was very highly thought of by GHQ Intelligence. She had started her espionage career disguised as a nun in a convent at Lille and received items of wireless equipment smuggled individually across the Dutch border until the complete wireless could be assembled. By the beginning of September 1915, the wireless was operating but only to receive messages, since the noise made by the generator made it recklessly dangerous to transmit. Nevertheless the wireless made it possible to arrange for at least one consignment of pigeons to be air-dropped to waiting agents. When the head of Ramble's system was arrested by the Germans, she was the obvious replacement and she led the Lille system with vigour and panache, sharing the risks of her agents and often taking on more than her fair share of work and responsibility. The picture of her that comes across from Kirke's diaries is of an utterly trustworthy and reliable individual who was a masterly judge of character and who drove her agents hard. The Lille system under her inspiring leadership might well have developed into the best system operated by GHQ during the war but in late 1915, disaster struck. At the very end of October the Germans discovered the wireless and mopped up the whole system, Ramble herself being arrested in Tournai at the beginning of November, though she did manage to swallow unde-

1 Nicolai, op. cit., pp. 173–4.
2 Kirke Diaries, op. cit., 7 October 1915.

tected the report she was carrying. Ramble was imprisoned by the Germans and died two months before the Armistice. In 1918 an attempt was made by the RAF to communicate with an independent group, based at Tournai, who had contacted the British saying they had a wireless and explosives and wanted to co-ordinate their activities with the British. An aeroplane was sent to try to get in touch with them by airborne wireless, but nothing further is recorded.[1]

From the combined efforts of the Secret Services, and from as early as mid-1915, there was rarely any doubt amongst the British high command of the locations of German units. The train-watching system allowed them to observe exactly what the enemy was doing with his forces and, when complemented by the study of the Order of Battle through I(a), this meant that it was impossible for the Germans to achieve any large-scale surprise that would win the war on the Western front. The location of their troops disclosed their intentions to the British at every step, for from that deployment it was possible to deduce its purpose. The importance of this was never more apparent than in 1918, the year of decision, when Germany assembled all her might for one last offensive intended to win the war.

The key to the success the Germans anticipated was the reinforcement they received from the collapse of Russia. Some 40 divisions were transported thence to the West in the winter of 1917–18, some of them (known as Force D), having been specially trained in new infiltration tactics which the OHL[2] thought would at last break the deadlock at the front. A special artillery group, known as 'Ludendorff's Siege Train', had been massed to prepare the way for the infantry and this too went towards the Western front. The artillery concentrated between Liège and Antwerp, and Force D around Fourmies and a place Kirkpatrick calls Chimies, though he presumably means Chimay. The whole German move from east to west and the subsequent concentration had been observed at every step of the way, permitting Kirke to state:

> Generally speaking in spite of efforts by the enemy to avoid observation by using circuitous routes the moves from the Eastern to

1 'The Use of Aircraft in Connection with Espionage', Appendix A, PRO AIR1/2399/280/1.
2 Oberste Heeres Leitung (Supreme High Command).

the Western Front in the winter of 1917–1918 were accurately noted by our agents.[1]

The Germans had travelled through and into areas watched by *La Dame Blanche* so their presence could hardly escape notice, especially since the training area of Force D was Fourmies, base for one of that system's cells. The movement, massing and training of the German reserves was all done under the eyes of British agents. The final evidence about the area of the coming offensive fell into place when, in February, the train-watchers reported the Germans concentrating in a region bounded by Valenciennes, Hirson and Douai, and then, in early March, the move of Ludendorff's Siege Train and Force D. Thus Macdonogh was able to predict the date, time and location of the German offensive with complete certitude and Lord Derby could write to Haig that, 'It looks now as if an attack might come within a very short time on your front, and on that part of the front of which Gough is in command.'[2]

In an unprecedented move Haig personally inspected the Fifth Army's front between 12 and 15 February and again between 7 and 9 March. On 6 March Macdonogh himself visited GHQ. Regrettably Haig's diaries do not disclose what they discussed, but it would be reasonable to assume that it was the German offensive given the timing and the fact that Haig visited the Fifth Army next day. Haig's diaries do show that Cox, the new BGGS(I), 'gave reasons why we think the enemy is preparing to attack on the fronts of our Third and Fifth Armies', and that General Salmond, commander of the RFC, reported on his plans to meet attacks on the Third and Fifth Armies.[3] The Secret Services had revealed much of the German plan of attack, something which I(a) – under the conditions in which it had to operate – could never have done, and in this respect it can be said that the Secret Services were decisive.

In view of British awareness of the German move it may be asked, why did Haig not stiffen the Fifth Army's slender reserves? It is not possible to debate that question fully in a book of this kind, but several points should be noted. The German plan envisaged more than one offensive and Haig rightly feared for the Channel ports in the

1 Kirke Papers, loc. cit., 'Lecture on Secret Service', 27 November 1925.

2 Papers of the 17th Earl of Derby [hereinafter Derby Papers], 27/2, correspondence with Sir Douglas Haig, Liverpool Record Office, letter from Lord Derby to Field-Marshal Sir Douglas Haig, 5 March 1918.

3 Haig Diaries, op. cit., 2 and 4 March 1918.

north. Moreover, the manpower at his disposal was reduced because the Prime Minister withheld troops in case Haig launched another offensive – as, indeed, he had intended to do. Also, Haig had been expecting reinforcements from the French on the southern sector of his front, but these did not materialize, since Pétain and French Intelligence believed the Germans were to attack them and ignored British Intelligence reports to the contrary. As late as 23 March Pétain 'said he was most anxious to do all he can to support me, but he expected that the enemy is about to attack him in Champagne'.[1] Furthermore, GHQ was surprised by the apparent ease with which the Fifth Army gave ground. On both 15 and 22 February Haig had noted that he expected the Germans to be able to penetrate the front positions of the BEF as the British had repeatedly done to the Germans in their offensives.[2] What he did not anticipate was the actual depth of the German advance made; Haig was certainly shaken by that and his diary shows the fact only too clearly:

> I was surprised to learn that his [General Gough's] troops are *now behind* the Somme and the R. Tortille. Men very tired after two days' fighting and long march back. On the first day they had to wear gas masks all day which is very fatiguing, but I cannot make out why the Fifth Army has gone so far back without making some kind of a stand.[3]

Haig, in his General Staff detachment, was making no allowance for the fog that had rendered the men of the Fifth Army helpless on that March morning and prevented them from seeing the enemy or firing at him.

The reasons for the retreat of March 1918 must clearly be sought elsewhere than in surprise or lack of preparation. The German offensives of 1918 are sometimes regarded as being great defeats for the Allies in that large areas of territory were lost, as were many men. This is a superficial view. Certainly, the German offensives were dramatic in those terms but the territory lost was essentially irrelevant unless it was decisive, and this it never was. The areas which might have given Germany a decision were Paris and the Channel ports, and it was certainly the German intention on 21 March to break the British

1 Ibid., 23 March 1918.
2 Ibid., 15 and 22 February 1918.
3 Ibid., 23 March 1918.

line and wheel northwards, rolling up the BEF and seizing those ports.

As it turned out, a skilful defensive, informed of the enemy's intentions by Intelligence, prevented this in spite of an initial setback. Haig was rightly willing to give ground on the southernmost sector of his front and could afford to do so, though there can be no doubt that he did not expect to have to give so much. The OHL made the error of reinforcing their success in this sector, where nothing decisive could be gained. When they finally recognized their mistake and endeavoured to retrieve it by launching the offensive's second phase ('Mars'), they were decisively beaten.

The observations of Major-General Davidson, Haig's Director of Military Operations,[1] on this effort are worth recalling, for the engagement on 28 March is virtually forgotten nowadays:

> On the 28th, early, the Germans with twenty-nine divisions delivered their assault, known as Operation Mars, against eight British divisions about the junction of the First and Third British Armies in the Arras sector and were heavily repulsed. The enemy recognized failure and this was the turning point of the whole battle.[2]

Indeed it was. Had the Germans succeeded in breaking the pivot of the British defences at Arras there can be little doubt that the BEF would have been split in two and defeated in detail, with the loss of the Channel ports. It is inconceivable that France would have been able to continue alone in those circumstances.

Although the Germans had other stages of their great offensive still in hand, their main thrust had been broken and at a cost they could no longer afford to replace. When they attacked in Flanders in April, Intelligence had again divined their intentions, though here the Germans were lucky in that their stroke fell on Portuguese troops who had no stomach for the fight and who fled. Nevertheless, the tide of German success was stayed by British Empire forces, notably the Australians, and Ludendorff had to abandon this part of the plan. He next turned against the French, but again Intelligence discovered the intention – only for their warnings to fall on deaf ears because yet again the French would not believe them. The next and final German attack was swiftly defeated; this time French Intelligence created

1 More accurately, for GHQ, he was BGGS(O), *see* Abbreviations, p. xv.
2 Major-General Sir John Davidson, *Haig: Master of the Field*, London, 1953, p. 127.

success by breaking the German wireless cipher and so reading the enemy's orders well in advance.

What was decisive about the failure of the German offensives of 1918 was that they cost Germany her remaining reserve and thus her last hope of victory. By the summer of 1918 German manpower resources were exhausted; the Germans were forced to break up numbers of divisions in order to maintain others, even at less than their proper establishment. What is certain is that the discovery of German intentions in March 1918 began the Allied victory.

The fact that the Fifth Army was hit so badly in spite of this foreknowledge throws the main drawback of the Secret Services into sharp relief. Despite their ubiquity and ingenuity they could never accomplish the acquisition of information from the battlezone. It was in that area that governments and generals alike were looking for a decision, a military decision gained by the overthrow of one of the armies that would end the war. Consequently, although the Secret Services could tell GHQ which area of front the German divisions were destined for, they could tell nothing of them once they got into the five- and later ten-mile cleared zone. Then it was up to I(a), labouring under all the burdens already noted, to try and inform the generals of what the Germans were doing.

It was this factor, about which nothing could then be done, that forced Intelligence to concentrate on the broader picture, a picture which helped the commanders up to a point but which left the troops to fight it out. That was what it came down to in the end, for while the Germans had soldiers who were prepared to fight, Intelligence could exert very little influence on events. It could neither force German soldiers to run away nor could it help the Allied armies except at the very forward edge of the battle area, and that was not enough to win the war.

Nevertheless, in their broader picture the excellence of the Secret Services – at least, the post-April 1917 vintage – did give the Allies an enormous advantage. Two men in a position to judge had no illusions about the contribution of secret Intelligence to final victory. Macdonogh, the man upon whom all the burdens eventually rested, wrote to Kirke that 'we got an immense amount from Secret Service'.[1] Kirke also had no doubts about its worth, having told his Staff College officers a year earlier: 'The most important source is Secret Service.'[2]

1 Kirke Papers, loc. cit., letter from Macdonogh to Kirke, 2 November 1925.
2 Kirke Papers, loc. cit., 'Lectures on Intelligence', 1924.

Their opinions are reflected in the increased budget the Foreign Office received from Parliament for the Secret Service. In 1914 it was £40,000. In 1918 its official budget had swollen to nearly £250,000 – a sixfold increase, and that just for the service run by C. Even if it could not place victory directly into the hands of a commander-in-chief, Intelligence could enable him to avoid defeat and help pave the way for eventual success.

EIGHT

A Riddle No More

THE fate of the Russian Imperial family – the Tsar, the Tsarina and their five children – has been the subject of debate and controversy from the time of their incarceration and presumed demise until the present day. In the course of researching the career of Richard Meinertzhagen, head of MO2, and his work during the First World War, some extraordinary evidence came to light which to all appearances linked both him and King George V directly to an attempt at rescuing the family from Ekaterinburg in 1918.

Like the Kaiser, the Tsar and Tsarina were cousins of King George. Family feelings as well as concern for a brother monarch would automatically have engaged the King's concern and sympathy for the Tsar, but at a time of some social unrest and of war between the three family empires his feelings would perforce have been limited in expression, publicly at least, by political considerations. An important entry in Meinertzhagen's diary indicates that not only did the King pursue his wish to rescue the Imperial family but that he did so in direct but undisclosed opposition to the veto of his Prime Minister, Lloyd George. By following every available lead it has been possible to piece together the formation of a complex plan of rescue and disguised identity for one survivor of the Imperial family, a plan which originated with King George V and which was executed without Government knowledge by members of British military Intelligence and of the court.

Central to the concealment of these roles has been the official stance on the question of Anna Anderson, who claimed to be the Grand Duchess Anastasia. Previous to 1976, tacit agreement was given to the official Russian statement that all the Imperial family and some of their servants had been shot in the cellar of Ipatiev House in Ekaterinburg in 1918, and that the bodies had been dismembered and burnt, the remains supposedly being dumped in a mineshaft.

In 1976 a book called *The File on the Tsar*[1] was published which

1 A. Summers and T. Mangold, *The File on the Tsar*, London, 1976.

presented a radically different version of the fate of the Imperial Romanov family. Written by two respected BBC investigative journalists, Anthony Summers and Tom Mangold, it argued that although Tsar Nicholas II and his young son had almost certainly been shot, the female members of the family had been secretly transferred from Ekaterinburg by the Bolsheviks; thus the story of violent massacre and bloody dismemberment rested on very shaky foundations. According to Summers and Mangold, their theory had drawn an interesting response from the House of Windsor in that 'a senior member of the British royal family conceded that the Romanovs may not have all died at Ekaterinburg'.[1] This remarkable qualified admission most certainly contains a germ of the truth.

Debate about the identity of the Anastasia claimant, Anna Anderson, was central to *The File on the Tsar*. Her story, as far as she revealed it, contends that she alone escaped from Bolshevik detention. The long investigation into her identity began in Berlin in 1922 with the report that a member of the Imperial family had been seen – an anonymous girl – among the patients at Dalldorf Insane Asylum. For some reason, she became known as the false 'Tatiana'. Over the ensuing months the royal families of Europe ranged themselves into lines of supporters and detractors.

Against a background of firm general belief in the deaths of the Romanovs at Ekaterinburg, Anna Anderson claimed initially to be the sole survivor of the massacre there; the exact date and route of her escape remained obscure. Later, however, she declared this account of her survival to be inaccurate and in 1974 she told Summers and Mangold: 'There was no massacre there . . . but I cannot tell the rest.'[2]

Witnesses recorded in *The File on the Tsar* had testified that one Grand Duchess had been rescued from Ipatiev House in July 1918, resulting in a house-to-house search in the town; a senior British Intelligence officer in Russia, Major Stephen Alley, 'knew one of the family had been saved'. Later testimonies make it appear probable that some time in the summer of 1918 the five Romanov women had been moved from Ekaterinburg to Perm, 200 miles to the north-west, where one witness, Natalya Mutnykh, spoke of seeing 'the former tsarina and three daughters'. She mentioned in addition an escape story concerning the Tsar's second daughter, Tatiana, and yet another story, corroborated, about a later escape bid by Anastasia, which

1 Ibid., 1978 edition, p. 354.
2 Ibid., 1976 edition, p. 239.

resulted in her recapture and injury and possibly in confinement apart from her family.

For some time negotiations had been taking place between Moscow and Berlin for the release of the Romanovs and it is possible that the family were *en route* for Moscow. But by September 1918 not only was it clear that Germany was losing the war, but the Red Terror was at its height: the fate of the Romanovs became of small account. The Bolsheviks eventually abandoned Perm to the advancing White Army at the end of 1918. Another witness, Yevgeniya Sokolova, testified that 'the tsarina and three daughters were evacuated from Perm to Glazov'. Thereafter, all trace of them vanishes.

These mentions of 'three daughters' are significant. Was Anastasia being detained separately or had she died of illness or injury? Or had there in fact been an escape – from Ekaterinburg? And if so, of whom? Summers and Mangold have deduced that both escape stories refer to Anastasia – to Anna Anderson – and in a new edition of their book (1987) put forward further and, I think, sound evidence to substantiate her claim to be a Grand Duchess. The purpose of this chapter is to demonstrate that in fact one Grand Duchess had left Russia before her and to pose again some unanswered questions – about the real reason for Anna Anderson's reluctance both to explain events at Ekaterinburg and to resolve confusion over the timing and route of her own later escape; and, most significantly, about the reason for the implacable opposition to her claim and the investigation of it by the royal courts of Europe.

The story is long and ravelled and the search back and forth through files and records for the many characters in it was triggered by one entry in a British Intelligence officer's diary.

Among much other valuable new evidence, *The File on the Tsar* revealed for the first time that plans had been laid at the highest level to rescue the Romanovs from their confinement at Tobolsk on the River Irtysh in Siberia. The agent for this rescue bid was to be the Norwegian explorer and adventurer Jonas Lied, who was mysteriously summoned to London in the early spring of 1918. Lied's diary, and conversations with Ralph Hewins, a close British friend of Lied,[1] disclosed a round of discussions with leading members of the British Intelligence hierarchy, among whom was Colonel Frederick Brown-

1 Ibid., pp. 257–9.

ing, C's right-hand man. Other high-flyers included Lord Robert Cecil of the Foreign Office and Captain Sir Reginald 'Blinker' Hall, the brilliant Director of Naval Intelligence.

Lied not only met Intelligence officers but also the Grand Duke Mikhail Mikhailovitch of Russia, cousin of the Tsar and a distant relative of King George V. Mikhail had been banished from Russia following his morganatic marriage; after many wanderings, he and his wife settled in England at Keele in Staffordshire, forbidden to live within easy reach of London. Both the banishment and residential restrictions were eventually lifted and the errant Duke moved to London, initially to Kenwood House in Hampstead and then, in 1917, to Cambridge Gate near Regent's Park. He and King George soon established a warm relationship, so much so that the King and Queen attended the wedding celebrations of Mikhail's second daughter at Kenwood in 1916 and permitted the use of the Chapel Royal at St James's Palace for the marriage of his eldest daughter in 1917.

When Lied met the Grand Duke he discovered that Mikhail was the director of a plan to rescue the Tsar: he had personally contributed £800 of his own money towards the operation costs, then a considerable sum; but, or so he told Lied, this sum was conditional on his part in the rescue attempt being kept secret.

The plan outlined to Lied had the whole Imperial family being ferried down the River Yenisey in central Siberia aboard one of Lied's cargo boats to a rendezvous with a Royal Naval torpedo boat at a sawmill depot where the Yenisey disgorges into the Kara Sea. The torpedo boat would then race north for the Arctic, via Novaya Zemlya, and thence to Britain. King George had given the plan his blessing and it was a thriving enterprise until the Prime Minister, David Lloyd George, cut the ground from under it.

On the face of it, the Prime Minister's veto appeared to destroy any plan to rescue the Imperial family, tolling the death knell of the King's hopes and quite possibly of the Romanovs too. King George would have had to be more than human – or less than human – not to smart at the terse curtailment of so much careful planning over what he saw as a family affair, not to feel increased anxiety about his cousin's fate, and not to harbour resentment against his Prime Minister. There is evidence of the King's anxiety over Lloyd George's degree of control in Britain in those early months of 1918. Field-Marshal Sir Douglas Haig was a close friend of the King who had married one of the Queen's ladies-in-waiting. Whenever Haig was home from the front the two men met and the meticulous Field-Marshal duly recorded each meeting in the pages of his diary. 11 February 1918 was no exception:

> I then went to Buckingham Palace and saw the King at 12 o'clock. He took me down in his lift to the garden, and we walked in the grounds till 12.45 about. The walk, H.M. said, is exactly one mile round, so he knows exactly what amount of exercise he takes! A terrible mechanical sort of exercise which cannot do one's whole system much real good! We discussed many topics. H.M. said he was really powerless and that Lloyd George was really Dictator! I assured H.M. that L.G. knew he was not so, really, at the same time Lloyd George had a very strong desire, in my opinion, to disintegrate the Army.[1]

Was the King really so impotent in the face of Lloyd George's unequivocal refusal to permit any official attempt at a Romanov rescue? What options were left open to him? In narrowly legal terms, the King had been driven into a corner. In fact it would seem that he made up his mind to act, and to act independently and without the knowledge of his Prime Minister.

The British sovereign is the supreme head of the armed services and it is to the sovereign that officers and other ranks alike swear fidelity and allegiance. Among the duties imposed by being head of the services is that of maintaining close contact with progress of their operations in the different theatres of war. To this end King George held private meetings each week with the different heads of section at the War Office, and this was no different in the case of MO2 and Richard Meinertzhagen.

Meinertzhagen's conspicuous abilities were recognized not only by the military establishment – in 1919 they earned him a place in the British Military Mission at the Paris Peace Conference. Here he made a deep impression on Lloyd George, who did not often look kindly on soldiers, and who committed his impressions of Meinertzhagen to paper in his *War Memoirs*:

> I met him during the Peace Conference and he struck me as being one of the ablest and most successful brains I had met in any Army. That was quite sufficient to make him suspect and to hinder his promotion to the higher ranks of his profession.[2]

1 Haig Diaries, op. cit., No. 122, vol. 25, 11 February 1918.
2 D. Lloyd George, *War Memoirs*, London, 1938 edition, Vol. II, p. 1923.

Meinertzhagen was a magnificent all-rounder who combined strength of character with humour and sociability, and decision with probity: an honest extrovert who was able and willing to accept formidable responsibilities and who was honourable and upright to the point where he would risk his military career by openly disagreeing with his commanding officers when he thought them wrong.

On visiting the palace to report to the King in the spring of 1918, Meinertzhagen 'found my friend Hugh Trenchard there. Part of my work in the War Office was organising an intelligence service devoted to happenings in Russia.'[1]

'Boom' Trenchard, the far-sighted 'Father of the RAF', was then serving as Chief of the Air Staff in London, a position in which he was uncomfortable, an alien amid the pedestrian bureaucracy and petty intrigue of a desk job at the Air Ministry. He shared some noteworthy qualities with Meinertzhagen: both were outspoken and decisive men of action, colourful characters in whom determination, resolve and judgement were nicely blended. But there the similarity ends. In stark contrast to the extrovert and outgoing Meinertzhagen, Trenchard was a more withdrawn, austere character. Born in 1873, he had been commissioned into the Royal Scots Fusiliers, with whom he served in the Boer War. He was severely wounded in the lung but recovered sufficiently to return to the fight with the Mounted Infantry in the Cape, the Transvaal and the Orange Free State. By 1903 he was serving with the West African Frontier Force in Nigeria, where, from being simply a rather awkward and inarticulate junior officer, he developed into a man of initiative with iron in his soul. His time in Nigeria imbued him with a deep and abiding interest in the continent, something again which he shared with Richard Meinertzhagen, and which remained with him all his life.

This period of Trenchard's life was overshadowed by the illness of his elderly parents and he found himself trying to care for and support them out of his Army pay at a time when private means were taken for granted and it was considered irregular for an officer to try to keep his own body and soul together simply on his pay. This constraint had a two-fold effect in that it forced Trenchard to be singularly abstemious and also to consider every service post which could promise a higher salary. On the eve of the First World War he joined the Royal Flying

1 Meinertzhagen Diaries, op. cit., Vol. 20, 18 August 1918, pp. 169–70.

Corps, completing his flying training by virtue of a last-minute appeal to his instructor shortly before the fledgling Corps took the field. His rise was rapid thereafter; as early as 1915 he was offered the chance to become Chief of Staff to the RFC. It was a chance he passed up: such a post clashed with his inclination to lead from the front and it was that capacity which eventually took him to command of the Corps. He could invariably see to the heart of any problem in an instant and that, coupled with a selfless devotion to duty and unimpeachable sincerity, made him a force to be reckoned with.

So Meinertzhagen, at the heart of MO2, and Trenchard, the power behind the British war effort in the air, were both at the palace to see the King together. Their joint presence was no mere coincidence and the meeting's true object was not long in being disclosed. Meinertzhagen's diary tells us that:

> King George opened the conversation by saying he was devoted to the Tsar (his cousin) and could anything be done about rescuing them by air as he feared the whole family would be murdered. Hugh was very doubtful as the family must be closely guarded and there was no information regarding landing facilities for aircraft. I said I thought I could find out about that and perhaps arrange for a rescue party to bundle at least some of the royal prisoners into an aircraft. But it was taking a great risk as failure would entail the murder of the whole family.[1]

The proposal was outrageously risky and not only for the Romanovs. With this closet conference King George risked constitutional uproar should such a venture, in direct contravention of a government decision, be discovered. It must be imagined, therefore, that the King's very human concern for his cousin's family and a more impersonal concern for the fate of a brother monarch in revolutionary times took precedence over any concern for his own position as constitutional monarch. The risk to the Romanovs he accepted, since the alternative was intolerable, and a covert operation held out the hope, however slender, of preserving at least some of the lives at stake.

Two officers, Meinertzhagen and Trenchard, had been selected who were well-fitted for their task, a task reminiscent of a quest undertaken by a Galahad or Lancelot instead of modern professional soldiers; but both men were suited by temperament and by the nature of their service for this real-life 'Prisoner of Zenda' rescue – they also

1 Ibid.

had ready access to all the necessary facilities they might need, and their discretion, it may be supposed, was unquestioned. It was an action characteristic of a late-Victorian attitude towards derring-do, of accepting and overcoming awesome challenges, a point illustrated by even a cursory glance at the pages of the *Boy's Own Paper*, W. H. Fitchett's *Deeds That Won The Empire*, or the novels of G. A. Henty. The concept was thoroughly inculcated in a generation of erstwhile empire builders and administrators, and has its adherents still.

But before the King's project could advance very far it was very nearly unhinged by one of those unforeseen difficulties which pervade all fields of human endeavour: Trenchard lost his job. As Chief of the Air Staff, resentful at being chained to a desk and trammelled by the coils of red tape, Trenchard's spirit had fretted for a more active command. Following a fierce dispute with the Air Minister, Lord Rothermere, one of the legion of press barons whom Lloyd George had handsomely bribed with ministerial office and a master of intrigue, Trenchard submitted his resignation with some feeling of relief. First, Rothermere begged Trenchard to delay his departure from the Air Ministry until he himself resigned, an action which, so Trenchard was assured, would not be delayed beyond the end of April. Then, without warning, on 13 April Rothermere suddenly accepted Trenchard's resignation, a manoeuvre which led to an unseemly semi-public row in which the politically naïve Trenchard came off second-best. The first King George knew of these events was the report in the Sunday newspapers; Trenchard was forthwith summoned to Buckingham Palace for consultations and it is worthy of note that Lord Stamfordham, the King's Private Secretary who saw Trenchard out after his audience, enjoined him to 'Say nothing to anyone.'[1]

Four weeks of unemployment followed for Trenchard until he was officially gazetted as 'Specially employed at HQ, RAF, France' on 17 May with effect from the 8th. In reality he had accepted command of the new Independent Air Force, formed with the object of conducting a long-range bombing offensive over Germany. Undoubtedly he would now exercise more authority over the movement of both aeroplanes and personnel than he could have achieved at his desk in the Air Ministry. As his biographer noted 'It was almost as if Trenchard regarded every cog in the machine as his personal

1 A. Boyle, *Trenchard, Man of Vision*, London, 1962, p. 278.

property, to be used for a purpose which he alone fully understood and therefore had the sole right to judge.'[1]

So the nucleus of a rescue team was back in place but the problems facing the would-be rescuers were daunting, a terrifying combination of burgeoning civil war and the known transfer of the Romanovs from Tobolsk to more rigorous confinement in the bitterly hostile city of Ekaterinburg. The commander of the guard at Ipatiev House, the 'House of Special Purpose', was Alexander Avdeyev, a 35-year-old former fitter who, from all accounts, was a coarse bully with a penchant for humiliating his prisoners. He was also a thief and a drunkard. Corruption and pilfering flourished under his regime and discipline crumbled away.

As spring wore into summer the situation became even more parlous. With the advance of Admiral Kolchak's White armies, spearheaded by the heroic Czech Legion, Ekaterinburg increasingly assumed the appearance of a town in the rear of a battlezone attended by all the chaos and confusion inherent in those discordant circumstances. Under these conditions opportunities would arise for the infiltration of agents into the locality and the chances were not left to go a-begging.

As a result of the publication of *The File on the Tsar*[2] it is known that Captain C.S. Digby-Jones was in Ekaterinburg during the critical period. The name 'Jones' appears scrawled in the margin of the fourth page of a report by Sir Charles Eliot, British High Commissioner for Siberia[3], adjacent to the passage describing the 'sounds of uproar and shooting [that] were heard in the house that night and that no traffic was allowed in the streets near it'. 'That night' was the night of 16–17 July 1918 when the murders of the entire Imperial family were alleged to have been perpetrated.

Jones ostensibly belonged to the British contingent at Murmansk under Major-General Poole, code-named 'Elope', one of only two formed bodies of British troops in Russia at the time (the other force, also in North Russia, was code-named 'Syren'). In the Public Record Office at Kew is a document listing all the officers serving in both these units.[4] Jones appears under the heading *Royal Engineer Officers*,

1 Ibid., p. 304.
2 Summers and Mangold, op. cit., 1978 edition, pp. 271–2.
3 PRO (FO 371/3977, Part I)
4 Nominal Roll of Officers 'Syren' and 'Elope' June-July 1918. PRO (WO 106/1151).

Field Engineers but his commission – a temporary and acting one – dates only from 1 June 1918. He does not appear in the *Army List* prior to June 1918 and both these circumstances give rise to the thought that Jones was using a cover. The document at Kew was despatched at 8.18 p.m. on 30 June, received at the War Office at 10.50 a.m. on 1 July and shows Digby-Jones firmly attached to Poole's command – whereas he was in Ekaterinburg on 1 July, watching the 'House of Special Purpose'.

There is another name scrawled in the margin of the sixth page of Eliot's report and in this instance the name is less distinct; it could be Toll, Ioll or Joll. A search of the *Army List*[1] for July 1918, however, establishes that it could only refer to Major Harry Howeis Joll, DSO, MC, of the Royal Regiment of Artillery, commissioned on 31 August 1915. After Joll's entry in the *Army List* there is a small italic *s*, denoting that this officer was on the Special Duties List, that he had special abilities in one field or another and was available for special employment should need arise. Some of the officers are so listed because of their expertise in a technical field or because of their linguistic ability, but others are there because they are suited for Intelligence work. These latter have traditionally provided the backbone of the Army's secret Intelligence as opposed to the official Secret Intelligence Service.

So it appears that at least two British officers were in Ekaterinburg at the critical time; but a two-man team could not possibly attempt or achieve the rescue of seven well-guarded prisoners. Who else could have been chosen by Meinertzhagen to play a part in such a desperate mission?

The *Nominal Roll*[2] in which Jones's name appears provides a clue. It lists a number of Intelligence officers, interpreters and RAF officers as part of Poole's command, but there is not so much as a hint that any of them might be involved in anything but their *bona fide* missions. Yet in the light of what must be regarded as the steps taken to obscure Jones's true purpose, there is solid justification to delve further into the list, and a check on the *Nominal Roll* discloses a further apparent cover-up.

Under the heading *Infantry* is the name of another Poole, Captain John Sanderson Poole, DSO, of the King's Royal Rifle Corps. A

1 *The Army List, July 1918*, op. cit., p. 526a.
2 PRO (WO 106/1151).

cross-check with the *Army List* for July 1918[1], reveals the initials *f.c.* beside his name, indicating that he had been transferred to the air service (on 17 February 1917) and was now commissioned in the newly established Royal Air Force. What is, perhaps, equally significant is the fact that the other officers listed in the *Nominal Roll* are shown to be elderly and retired by the *Army List*, having been brought back into the service to train the levies it was hoped to raise in North Russia. Poole (born 16 September 1896) was a mere stripling by comparison and the only one young enough to withstand the rigours of any genuinely 'active' service. This, coupled with the fact that his status as an officer of the RAF had been disguised, is the clearest intimation that he, like Jones, had another purpose for being in Russia: since King George clearly had rescue by air in mind, it follows that at least one member of the rescue team would have to be a pilot.

If a rescue bid was to have even a remote chance of success the Romanovs would have to be informed of developments. To communicate with prisoners under armed guard posed a formidable problem, but there is evidence to suggest that it was done. According to Carl Ackerman, a journalist from the *New York Times*:

> . . . news travelled to and from the Tsar through signals from the attic of the brick house across the street from the Ipatiev residence . . . when the observer under the roof of the house across the street saw the tsar in the garden he would phone 'the baggage is at the station' and then messages would be communicated to the Tsar.[2]

Ackerman had an excellent reputation and had been specially selected to cover the Romanov case. His book makes clear that his enquiries were both painstaking and thoroughgoing, and the tenor of his report carries conviction. He was not the sort of man to waste his readers' time with unsubstantiated irrelevancies. Another journalist known to have been in the region at the time was Robert Wilton of *The Times* who was also a member of MI1(c), experienced both at nosing out information and even, on occasion, at disseminating misinformation. He was so anxious to cover up the truth of events at Ekaterinburg that he shouted at Commandant Joseph Lasies of the French Military

1 *The Army List, July 1918*, op. cit., p. 1388a.
2 C. Ackerman, *Trailing The Bolsheviki*, New York, 1919, p. 100.

Mission that, 'Even if the tsar and the imperial family are alive, it is necessary to say that they are dead!'[1]

It seems, then, that the British had at least a four-man team in Ekaterinburg and would have been able to communicate with the Tsar. But even with the prevailing climate of sloppiness at the Ipatiev House no rescue attempt could be undertaken lightly. Upon closer examination Meinertzhagen found that '. . . the Tsar and his wife were too closely guarded'.[2] Time was beginning to press and he decided instead to attempt the rescue of the Tsarevitch, 14-year-old Alexei and the four Grand Duchesses: Olga, aged 23, Tatiana, aged 21, Marie, aged 19, and the youngest, Anastasia, aged 17. No details of the operation are given but Meinertzhagen's diary tells us how the rescue attempt ended:

> On July 1st everything was ready and the plane took off. Success was not complete and I find it too dangerous to give details. One child was literally thrown into the plane at Ekaterinburg, much bruised and brought to Britain where she still is. But I am sure that if her identity were known she would be tracked down and murdered as the heir to the Russian throne.[3]

This is the first reliable evidence we have that not all the Romanovs died in Russia, whether at Ekaterinburg or elsewhere, and it is the first reasoned explanation for the ending of the Romanov line in the persons of the Tsar and Tsarevitch. It is no longer just a question of debating whether Anastasia escaped from Russia and when and how, but of discovering how one of her sisters escaped from Russia before her, and of establishing that sister's identity.

Meinertzhagen had recognized when King George first mooted the idea that a rescue attempt might well entail fatal consequences for any Romanovs unfortunate enough to be left in Bolshevik hands. After a period of delay while presumably the rescue was reported to Moscow, we know that decisions were taken and the guard at the 'House of Special Purpose' was changed. The sealing-off of Ipatiev House and the sounds of gunfire and uproar emanating from it in the early hours of 17 July, undoubtedly reported by his Intelligence Officers, seemed to confirm Meinertzhagen's worst fears. The opening words to the key

1 Summers and Mangold, op. cit., 1978 edition, p. 103.
2 Meinertzhagen Diaries, op. cit., 18 August 1918.
3 Ibid.

entry in his diary confirm what he believed to be the true course of events that night: 'Russia and the Tsar. I have hesitated to record an exciting experience I had last month in connection with the murder of the Tsar and his family.'[1] He also refers to the move from Tobolsk to Ekaterinburg 'where they remained until their murder on July 16th 1918. Even now I feel it a bit dangerous to disclose detail.'[2] Finally there are his last words on the subject to close the diary entry: 'What bestial swine the Russians are, murdering little girls because they are the daughters of the Tsar.'[3]

When the officer in charge of the last-ditch attempt to rescue the unhappy Romanovs reported that those members of the family left in Bolshevik hands had indeed been murdered, one might expect this to be taken as conclusive evidence of the fact by the British royal family. This and the need for the safety of silence, both for the sake of the Grand Duchess and for the sake of King George's own position, would also explain and justify the royal family's unbroken and continuous opposition to Anna Anderson, the late Anastasia claimant, who could have revealed the rescue mission. Indeed, such was the strength of the opposition to her claims that the late Lord Mountbatten personally contributed a considerable sum of his own money towards the costs of defeating her in the German courts.

Since the most recent (1987) edition of Summers and Mangold's book presents further evidence that Anna Anderson's claim was genuine, the only statements she ever made public on the events of July 1918 take on new significance in the light of Meinertzhagen's disclosures. In the 1960s she told Prince Frederick of Saxe Altenburg that, 'Events in Ekaterinburg were quite different from what they say. But if *I* say that, they think I'm mad.'[4] Events there *were* very different from the commonly accepted version and the Anastasia claimant knew precisely what she was talking about – there is now *bona fide* evidence to prove it.

Sir Charles Eliot's official report for the Foreign Office on the events at Ekaterinburg is dated 5 October and it is clear from it that Eliot was not privy to the inner truth of the affair. There are sections of his

1 Ibid.
2 Ibid.
3 Ibid.
4 Summers and Mangold, op. cit., 1978 edition, p. 234.

report founded on rumour and conjecture, something Eliot admits to be the case. When writing of the uncertainties facing the Bolsheviks during the closing days of their rule in Ekaterinburg, Eliot noted an incident which, he considered, may have influenced subsequent events: 'There is some evidence that they [the Bolsheviks] were much alarmed by an aeroplane flying over the garden of the house and I fear it is comprehensible that in a fit of rage and panic they made away with His Imperial Majesty.'[1]

It is hard to believe that the Bolsheviks would have been driven to rage and panic, much less murder, by a solitary unidentified aeroplane which dropped no bombs, did no damage and might even have belonged to the Red Army. Aeroplanes were no novelty by 1918; the combatant powers used them on all fronts in their thousands and they were used by both sides in the Russian civil war. The aeroplane provided no reason, or even excuse, for murder *unless* considered in the light of the previous rescue. Far more probable was it that fear of another aerial rescue caused the local Soviets to quail, especially as they would almost certainly face a firing squad if any new attempt succeeded in any degree. Hence the hasty activity and bursts of gunfire within the walls of Ipatiev House.

Yet on the sixth page of his report Eliot states: 'On July 17 a train with its blinds down left Ekaterinburg for an unknown destination and it is believed that the surviving members of the Imperial family were in it.'[2] Eliot presents no definite facts to support his view but those seeking to prove that the Romanov women survived have seized upon this statement as key evidence in their case. No doubt the train could, as Summers and Mangold maintain, have been carrying living Romanovs from Ekaterinburg to Perm, but equally it could have been freighted with the bodies of very dead Romanovs being carried to an unknown destination. In either case the train theory would explain the absence of human remains at the infamous 'Four Brothers' mineshaft and it would conceal the fact that one member of the family had already escaped, thus saving the Bolsheviks from an acute embarrassment and avoiding the gift of a new figurehead and rallying point for the Whites.

In their discussion of the case of Anna Anderson, Summers and Mangold inform us that 'There are witnesses who testified that one

1 PRO (FO 371/3977 Part I), p. 7.
2 Ibid., p. 6.

grand duchess was rescued from the Ipatiev House,'[1] witnesses whose statements must surely now be accorded a respect previously denied. The most important of these witnesses was cited by Summers and Mangold who related how the German Vice-Consul in Leningrad, Dr Günther Bock, in 1926 asked Commissar S. L. Weinstein about the fate of the Romanovs: 'The official replied that all of the Romanov family were dead, with the exception of one of the women, who was known to have gone missing.'[2] Perhaps even more convincing evidence comes from the widow of Major Stephen Alley. Alley worked as head of the Russian section of MI1(c) after his return from Russia and was thus well-placed to know what was being done and would have been ideally placed to assist Meinertzhagen, at least in an advisory role. Mrs Beatrice Alley told Summers and Mangold that: 'He thoroughly believed Anastasia was still alive, because he knew one of the family had been saved.'[3] With all their research concentrating on Anastasia as a survivor and with no evidence to make these two suggestions of another escape credible, still less with any corroboration from Anna Anderson, Summers and Mangold merely recorded the comments and returned to their principal investigations.

But in the light of Meinertzhagen's diary entry, the sudden and dramatic changes at Ipatiev House shortly after 1 July must now be accorded a new significance. On 4 July, three days after the rescue and at the right time for the Moscow leadership to have learned of it and taken action, the venal Avdeyev and his deputy, Moshkin, were suddenly arrested without warning. A thorough inspection of the house was made by the chairman of the local Soviet, Alexander Beloborodov, in the company of other senior local communists. The local guard were then entirely replaced by Lettish, Austrian and Hungarian guards drawn from the elite units of the Red Army and numbered amongst the regime's most dedicated disciples.

Yankel Yurovksy was the new commandant and he confined the personnel of the original guard to the exterior of the grounds, strictly forbidding them to go upstairs to the Romanov quarters. Security was markedly increased. More guards and guard posts appeared, a machine gun was mounted in the attic and a sentry stationed in the back garden where none had been before. Such drastic steps were not taken without good reason. The pervading atmosphere of drunken-

1 Summers and Mangold, op. cit., 1978 edition, pp. 237–8.
2 Ibid., 1987 edition, p. 233.
3 Ibid., p. 233.

ness and harassment which had characterized the Avdeyev regime hardly constituted sufficient reason; it had not troubled the Bolsheviks in the preceding months and Lenin was not likely to lose any sleep over the misfortunes of a redundant Imperial family. Far more likely was it that the rescue of one Grand Duchess on 1 July had caused Chaya Goloshchokin, the regional commissar for war, to race to Moscow at the beginning of the month. He did not return to Ekaterinburg until 14 July and it is known that the Imperial family featured amongst his discussions in Moscow. The disappearance of that family just two days after his return points to a decision not merely to change the guard and increase security at Ipatiev House but to murder some or all of the family in Ekaterinburg or else move some or all of them to another, even more secure, place of detention.

The Lied mission had intended to make good the escape along the River Yenisey and there is evidence that an escape this way was still under active consideration in July 1918: the logistical requirements of the route would have been to hand, as would the requisite navigational details. But the Lied plan had been devised while the Romanovs were at Tobolsk; their removal to Ekaterinburg had vastly complicated the undertaking.

As one would expect, the documents in the Public Record Office maintain a sepulchral silence on the matter of the Romanovs throughout 1918; in fact, the Foreign Office files contain only one reference to them throughout the whole of the first six months of the year, in May 1918. Yet the War Office files (WO106 *Military Operations and Intelligence*) do not appear to have been consulted by others who have studied the Romanov case, a strange omission given that any rescue of the Imperial family would have necessitated some military involvement.

Interestingly, these files reveal a sudden and unexplained flurry of activity in Siberia from April 1918 onwards and several of the documents do shed a chink of light on the Stygian expanse of mystery. For example, amidst the scanty files of General Poole's mission which, through Digby-Jones, appears to have been implicated in the rescue, there is a message to the *Committee on Russian Supplies*, or Rusplycom as it was known from its telegraphic address. The message is dated 30 April 1918 and announces that:

> . . . commercial co-operation would at present be the best method of

> contact with Siberia and would open the road to further influence. We ought to act immediately and the assistance of everyone having a knowledge of Siberia is essential.[1]

Taken at face value this statement appears perfectly innocuous, but closer examination raises some awkward questions. Why would a body charged with supplying those Russians still fighting the Germans be seeking to penetrate Siberia, where the German Army was not operating? Why, in any case, would a British force carrying responsibility for the Murmansk area concern itself with Siberia? And to what end was Rusplycom endeavouring to exert 'further influence' in that region, aided and abetted by 'everyone having a knowledge of Siberia'?

The reason for Rusplycom's sudden and marked interest in Siberia can be divined from the circulation list of this particular document, which included the Director of Military Intelligence, MI0(a) and MI6. MI0 was a new section within the Directorate of Military Intelligence, formed in January 1918 as a result of Russia's impending exit from the war. It combined the functions of Intelligence and Operations and was formed from personnel drawn from MI2(d) and MO2, Meinertzhagen's section. It was responsible for all matters concerning Russia, Rumania, Siberia, Central Asia, the Caucasus, Persia and Afghanistan and would certainly have been the only section at the War Office capable of undertaking an operation of the sort called for by the situation at Ekaterinburg. So was Rusplycom, at least in part, a cover for Intelligence activities in Russia? Was the sudden upsurge of interest in Siberia in April the precursor to a bid to rescue the Romanovs?

Taken in isolation, this document does not represent conclusive proof of these possibilities, but the date on which the message is stamped as having been received in London, 18 March, is significant by virtue of the reply sent on 21 May:

> T.887 May 21st Cipher
> Hicks's telegram 00329 urging despatch to mouth of Yenesi of trading expedition. Plans in detail have already been considered by us for the despatch of vessels via Kara Sea re exchange goods from Siberia ports. Owing to lack of tonnage project has definitely been abandoned.[2]

1 MI0(a). North Russia. Box 23, File 18. General Poole's Mission Personnel. 1918 January-May. PRO (WO 106/1150).

2 Siberia 4. Correspondence and Telegrams. No. 454 Kara Sea Route. PRO (WO 106/1218).

Once again the circulation list makes interesting reading, with the Director of Military Intelligence, MI0, MI0(a) and MI6 all being party to it. What possible reason could there be for all the interest in the mouth of the Yenisey? There was no port there of any size and the hinterland comprised an undeveloped and sparsely populated region of bleak tundra and forest with a total lack of communications for any worthwhile trade in anything. Besides, who were they going to trade with? But once recall the commercial code employed in Ekaterinburg ('the baggage is at the station') and the wording of this telegram can be seen in a different light.

Nor is this all. The fact that the message is held in a file purportedly dealing with North Russia while the reply is lodged in a file relating to Siberia surely calls for some comment.

The Siberia files have their contents listed at the beginning of each folder. One document listed in *Siberia 4* is *No. 461 Irkutsk prisoners of war and Ex-Czar*. This title has been deleted in green ink, an ink habitually used by C, the head of the Secret Service. Beside the deletion appears the reference 'RM8480', also written in the tell-tale green ink.[1] Needless to say, the document has been extracted from the file, but it is at least arguable that the initials RM refer to Richard Meinertzhagen, the officer in overall command of the operation.

Between the files *Siberia 4* and *Siberia 6* one would reasonably expect to find *Siberia 5*, covering the months of July and August 1918. This, too, has vanished, not even being dignified with a listing in the general catalogue. The War Office files accomplish two things at the very least: they provide concrete evidence of the interest in Siberia and the Yenisey area, and they disclose that attempts have been made to conceal that interest.

According to Meinertzhagen, the escape from Ekaterinburg had been effected by aeroplane. The fact must be faced, however, that no aeroplane of the day could hope to reach the British-held areas in North Russia from Ekaterinburg unless it could refuel *en route*, hardly a practical proposition in an unknown country rent by civil war. Not even the long-range Handley-Page 0/400 bomber could accomplish the journey non-stop.

The emphasis on Siberia in those few files which have survived to reach the Public Record Office now acquires a further significance,

1 Siberia 4. Correspondence and Telegrams. Contents List. PRO (WO 106/1218).

because an alternative escape route did exist through Siberia, along the route of the Trans-Siberian Railway, most of which was then dominated by the famous Czech Legion. Open warfare between the Czechs and Bolsheviks had begun on 25 May 1918 when the Czechs seized Novonikolaevsk (today's Novosibirsk), a city lying on the Trans-Siberian between Omsk and Krasnoyarsk. By the end of June a huge tract of Siberia, including a large stretch of railway, several towns and, importantly, the port of Vladivostok, lay in Czech hands; and where Czech rule held sway the Whites shot up like mushrooms, proliferating to the point where no fewer than nineteen competing White 'governments' were struggling for power by the beginning of July 1918. Safe refuelling stops on a flight from Ekaterinburg to Vladivostok would certainly have made that a likely escape route, though the journey would have been a long and risky one.

The plan to move the rescued children through Siberia would be dangerous but it was safer than moving north or directly east of Ekaterinburg: the route would largely be in the hands of anti-Bolshevik forces whose co-operation in any secret British moves could be counted upon, and would provide opportunities for vital rest, fuel and provender in relatively safe areas. Perhaps even more to the point, Intelligence had men on the spot who could make arrangements. Omsk, shortly to become Admiral Kolchak's capital, appears to have been a centre of activity and the Rusplycom telegram[1] already cited states that the 'names of the two first-rate men at Omsk' would be sent to London. Quite apart from this, an agent of the Secret Intelligence Service's Stockholm section was also in Omsk during the summer of 1918 – agent ST12, who sent a report[2] to London on the activities of the Grand Duke Mikhail Alexandrovitch, living in the Governor's House at Omsk, flying the Imperial flag and endeavouring to start another counter-revolutionary movement.

Even more significantly, the British cruiser HMS *Suffolk* was stationed at Vladivostok from where she could provide secure communications or even a floating operational headquarters. The Admiralty Papers in the Public Record Office do refer to a number of secret telegrams sent by Captain Payne, the officer commanding HMS *Suffolk*, to the Admiralty,[3] but these telegrams are nowhere to be

1 MI0(a). North Russia. Box 23, File 18. General Poole's Mission Personnel. 1918 January-May. PRO (WO 106/1150).

2 Siberia 6. August and September 1918. No. 815 PRO (WO 106/1219) *and also* Siberia. Policy. July 1918. No. 44. (WO 106/1220).

3 *See*, for example, China Station. Telegrams, No. 329. 28 June 1918. PRO ADM137/766.

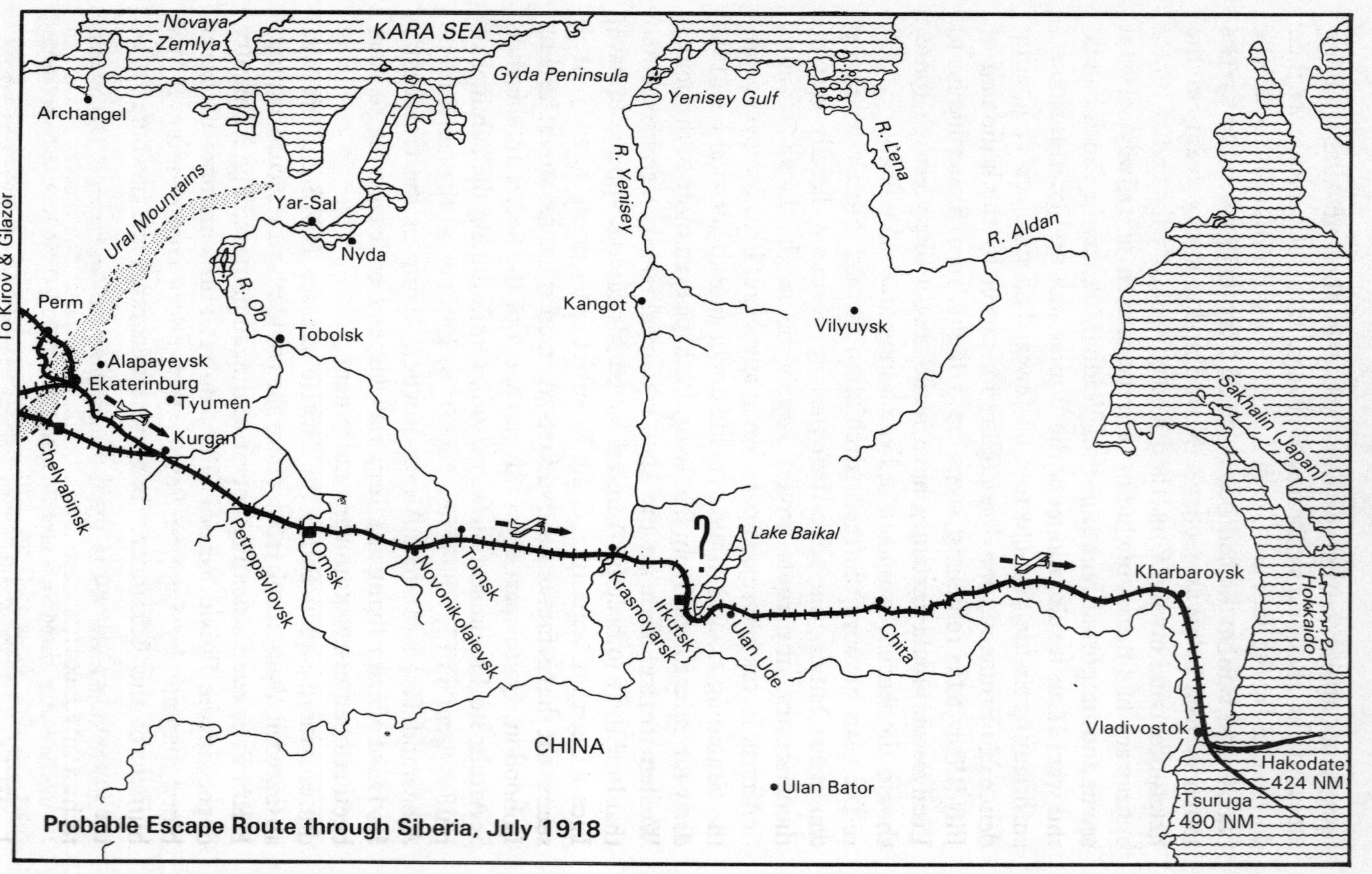

Probable Escape Route through Siberia, July 1918

found, appearing neither in the records of the China Station nor amongst the unedited General Letters.

Naval involvement of some kind would be essential if the Grand Duchess were to be 'brought to Britain' and the means of providing help once again involved the British royal family.

Concern had been growing in official circles in London over what seemed to be a loss of faith on Japan's part in Britain's ability to win the war. In order to counter this it was suggested that a Briton of sufficient distinction should travel to Japan, thereby restoring confidence in a British victory. King George V wished to confer the rank of Field-Marshal in the British Army on the Emperor of Japan and it was Lord Beaverbrook who suggested that the mission to confer the baton should be headed by a member of the royal family. Choice in this respect was distinctly limited, since only one member of the family was of a suitable age and bore the requisite military rank to undertake the venture, and that was Prince Arthur of Connaught.

A mission to Japan had first been mooted by Lord Beaverbrook at the beginning of March 1918, but the King had been unwilling to draw the Prince away from his service with the Canadian Corps on the Western front, where he had proved himself a capable officer.[1] At that time the King's hopes had still been vested in Jonas Lied but with Lloyd George's opposition and the collapse of the Lied venture it seems the King found good reason to bid Prince Arthur return to London at short notice.

Arthur of Connaught, who now seems forgotten by the British public, was born in 1883, the son of Prince Arthur William Patrick Albert, himself the third son in Queen Victoria's numerous brood and 1st Duke of Connaught and Strathearn. The young Prince Arthur had been pitched early on to the public stage, sharing many of the royal duties with the then Prince of Wales, later King George V, in the absence of any other royal male of comparable age. He had married HRH Princess Alexandra, co-heir to the Duchy of Fife and daughter of the Princess Royal, who held the duchy in her own right. Of royal blood himself, having married royalty and bearing many of the burdens of royal duties, he was in every aspect a perfect choice to head the mission to Japan and thus it was that the King sent a curt telegram to him in France: 'Please come home as soon as possible as I want to

1 Political. Japan Files 6083–9874. Nos. 56869 and 64446. PRO (FO371/3234).

see you and you had better bring your things with you.'[1] On his return the Prince found himself charged with the responsibility of leading a strong team to the Orient, his chief supports being Lieutenant-General Sir William Pulteney and Lieutenant-Colonel the Earl of Pembroke.

The 15th Earl of Pembroke had succeeded his father in 1913, was an officer in the Royal Horse Guards, the Blues, and had close links with the crown, maintaining the long-standing tradition of personal service to the monarchy which marked the Herbert family.[2] A carefree and buoyant personality, he was the life and soul of the mission party. He had completed his war service on the personal staff of General Pulteney, an old Etonian who had begun his own military career in the Scots Guards in 1881 with Prince Arthur's father, HRH Lieutenant-General the Duke of Connaught as his colonel. Pulteney fought during the Egyptian campaign of 1882 and later became an ADC to the Duke and a trusted friend of the King. Consequently Pembroke and Pulteney formed a close-knit team whose competence and discretion could be relied on utterly and who, for reasons of state, would now have a glorious opportunity to serve their King, under cover of the mission to Japan.

After paying his official calls in Japan and presenting Emperor Yoshihito with his brand new Field-Marshal's baton, Prince Arthur and his party took some leave in Nagoya and Kyoto from 29 June onwards, with the Japanese wishing to keep his movements after leaving Tokyo on the 29th absolutely secret.[3] The extra curtain of secrecy contrived by the Japanese about the Prince's movements gave rise to comment in Japan. After the royal visit, a correspondent from the Japanese newspaper *Jiji* gained an interview with Viscount Hatano, the Minister of the Imperial Household Department which had been heavily involved with the domestic arrangements for the Prince's stay in Japan. Hatano told the correspondent that

> . . . the secrecy observed as to His Royal Highness's programme of travel was objected to, but this secrecy was in accordance with a strict

1 Telegram from HM King George V to Prince Arthur of Connaught, 2 April 1918. Held in the folder 'Prince Arthur of Connaught's Mission, 1918', Royal Archives, Windsor Castle. RA GV PS 24190.

2 David Herbert, *Second Son: An Autobiography*, London, 1972, esp. p. 14.

3 Telegram from Sir C. Greene, British Ambassador in Tokyo, No. 681, 25 June 1918. Held in 'Prince Arthur of Connaught's Mission 1918', loc. cit., RA GV PS 24190. *See also* PRO (FO 371/3234 189 113242).

> request emanating from a certain quarter where extreme anxiety was felt. The programme of the royal journey was marked secret, and with the exception of the Reception Committee no-one, not even himself, could get an advance view of it. He had even complained but there was no help for it.[1]

With typical Japanese inscrutability the origin of the strict request is disguised, but the discreet reference to 'a certain quarter' in connection with a royal visit indicates that the request emanated from within the Imperial Household: it is all in keeping with what has been termed the 'Trade Union of Kings'. The British Ambassador to Japan, Sir Conyngham Greene, sent a telegraphed report to London, referring to a conversation between Prince Arthur and the Japanese Prime Minister, which read in part:

> His Excellency added it was evident in despatching Prince Arthur to Japan the King had something more in mind than ceremonial of handing of Field-Marshal's Baton.[2]

Clearly there were some aspects of the visit to Japan which could not be spoken of openly in the presence of the British Ambassador. The fact that Sir Conyngham Greene was being kept in the dark is reinforced by his ignorance about Prince Arthur's leave. In his report on the Prince's mission Greene lamented that:

> I have had to depend on the brief official programme and on the meagre records of the press for the following brief account of the Prince's movements after his departure from Tokyo. The silence of the press is of course the result of instructions to keep His Royal Highness's movements secret and not due to any lack of interest in them.[3]

Interestingly, the log book of HMS *Suffolk* at Vladivostok records the arrival and departure of several vessels of the Imperial Japanese Navy in this vital period of July. Their return to Japanese waters, where the movements of Prince Arthur were being kept secret, gives rise to some speculation. If a Japanese vessel formed part of the escape route chain, it would have been a death-blow to the King's hopes of keeping his rescue bid a secret from the Government had the Foreign

1 Political. Japan. Files 6083-9874. No. 276 140777, 15 August 1918. PRO (FO 371/3234).
2 Ibid. No. 198/99 115461, 1 July 1918.
3 Ibid. No. 162924, 26 September 1918.

Office learned enough, through the agency of the Ambassador, to become suspicious.

It had been decided that the Prince would pay an official visit to Canada, where the Duke of Connaught, during his varied career, had been Governor-General between 1911 and 1916 and where the family still had many connections. It seems that the decision to include Canada had formed no part of the mission's original plan; the visit was not added until the beginning of May 1918. The Japanese battle-cruiser *Kirishima* was assigned the task of carrying the mission's personnel to Vancouver. On board with them went two Foreign Office bags from the Tokyo Embassy for despatch to London.

At this point a screen of silence falls round the travels of the bags and round Prince Arthur's mission. In the *Canada Register* for 1918 to 1919 in the Public Record Office, against a brief statement about the documents that had been held there – including another reference to the Foreign Office bags – is written 'No. 36524S' in red ink. Someone, at some stage, has tried to blot out the 'S' with ink. Consultation with staff at the Record Office led to the discovery that the red ink and the letter 'S' meant that the subjects of those papers were secret and that the papers had probably been destroyed – indeed, stamped in the column to the right of the inscription in red was the legend: 'Destroyed Under Statute'.[1] There are two references to these *Canada Register* documents held in the papers of the Foreign Office and the Admiralty, but the documents themselves are lodged in neither place.

Given that Meinertzhagen's diary entry is truthful and given a certain amount of mystery and obfuscation encountered in investigating the likelihood of the events it indicates, a willingness on the part of the reader to pursue these ideas must be assumed.

Getting the rescued Grand Duchess from Ekaterinburg to the safety of Prince Arthur's mission would have presented problems but it would have been possible to fly from Ekaterinburg to Vladivostok over White-held Siberia in a matter of a few days. After that three distinct possibilities of route exist, but there is no sure evidence to confirm any one of them.

The first is that a Japanese destroyer carried the Grand Duchess from Vladivostok to Tsuruga in Japan, a mere 43 miles from Kyoto

1 *See* Canada Register 1918 to 1919, (IND 18846), Vol. 29, 29 July 1918. PRO (CO 335).

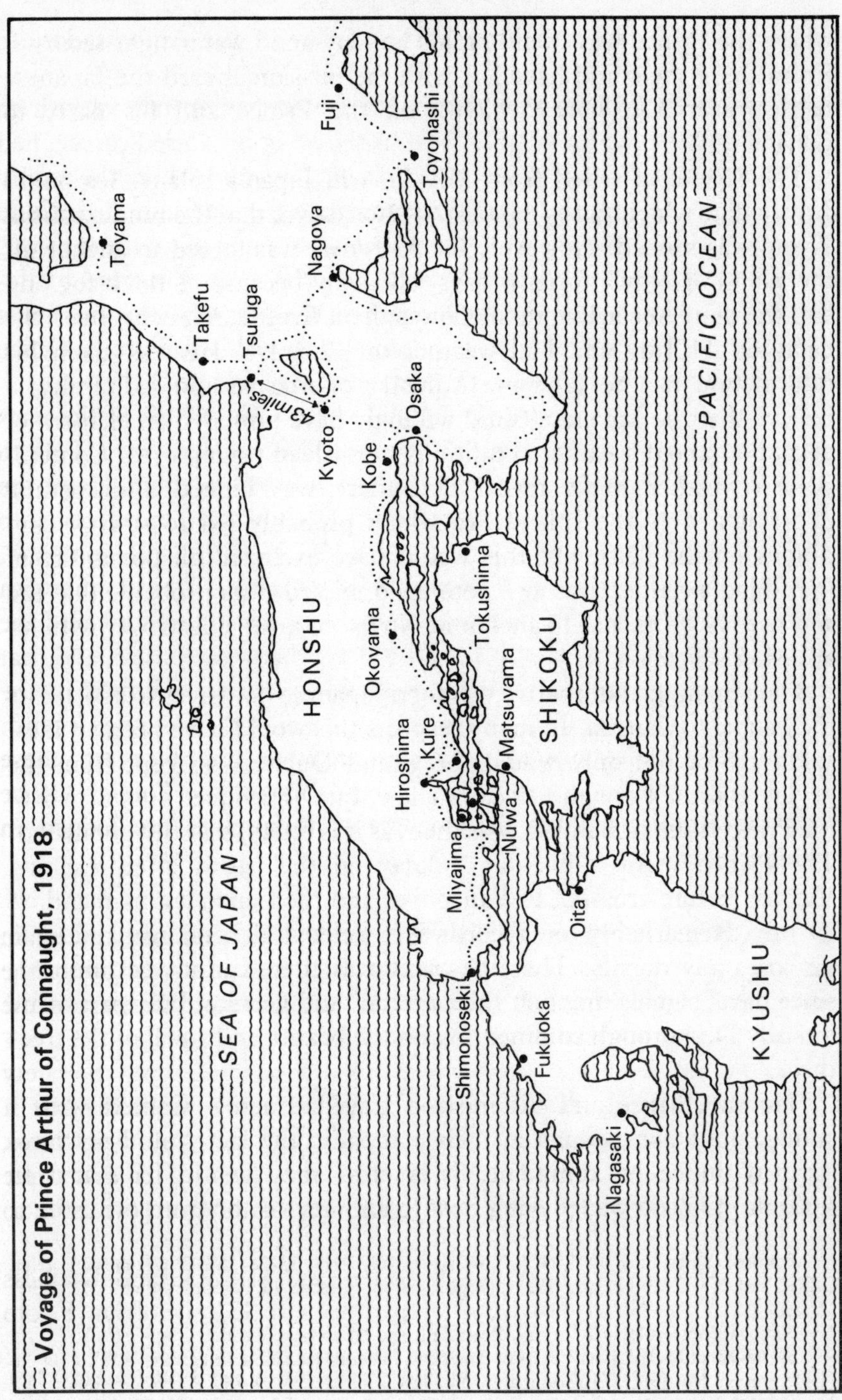

Voyage of Prince Arthur of Connaught, 1918

where the Prince was spending his holiday amid water-tight security. From there she could have left with the mission aboard the Japanese battlecruiser *Kirishima*, which took the Prince and his party to Canada.

The *Kirishima* sailed from Miyajima in Japan's Inland Sea on 10 July, a date which raises the second alternative, that the rendezvous at Kyoto was missed. However, the *Kirishima* was forced to anchor off the island of Nuwa for two days, allegedly because of thick fog and bad weather. According to Sir Conyngham Greene, fog occasioned the delay on 11 July and bad weather on 12 July.[1] He was given his information by the Japanese Ministry of Marine and Admiralty. I believe that the Japanese could willingly have provided an element of deception about weather conditions to mislead prying eyes. Contemporary weather maps reveal that there was indeed a deepening depression over the Inland Sea which probably led to stormy conditions on the 12th, but this would have excluded all possibility of fog.[2] Had a rendezvous at Kyoto been missed, it is probable that fog was used as an excuse to anchor at Nuwa, to meet a destroyer without arousing suspicion.

The remaining alternative was for a Japanese destroyer to slip across the Pacific to Canada. In many respects this would have been an ideal solution, for not only would the Grand Duchess be kept from the prying eyes of Foreign Office officials, but Vancouver Island, where the Prince's mission sailed, was then, as it is today, scantily populated. The Prince spent a five-day holiday on the island after reaching Victoria before crossing to Vancouver and the Canadian mainland on 29 July. Remarkably few records even refer to this sojourn and none discloses any details. That the party was there cannot be doubted, since naval signals mention their arrival[3] and General Pulteney wrote to Lady Desborough commenting on the beauty and smell of the trees there.[4]

Had the Prince and his mission travelled across Canada with a young, unknown woman in their company, the fact would not have escaped notice or comment. It is clear they would have had to separate. Canada was playing host to another visitor from the mother

1 Political. Japan Files 6083-9874. No. 212 (11 July 1918, 122284, Sir C. Greene to Foreign Office) and No. 222 (12 July 1918, 123503, Sir C. Greene to Foreign Office). PRO FO 371/3234.

2 National Meteorological Society, Bracknell, and 'Historical Weather Maps', USA.

3 *See* 'West and South East Coasts of American General Operation Telegrams 1918', 1 July to 31 December. No. 99 GSO Esquimault, No. 138, 25 July 1918. PRO ADM 137/960.

4 Grenfell Papers, loc. cit., letter to Lady Desborough, 1 August 1918, D/ERv C2130/162.

country at this time, one not so prominent as Prince Arthur and one whose movements would not attract untoward attention. The visitor was Armorel, the wife of Richard Meinertzhagen. It would have been a simple matter for her to meet the Grand Duchess and escort her across Canada to a port of embarkation, especially since her husband's maternal grandfather, Richard Potter, was the chairman of the Grand Trunk Railway of Canada.

Armorel Meinertzhagen crossed the Atlantic from Montreal in Cabin 14 of the Canadian Pacific Ocean Service Ltd's vessel *Corsican*. Occupying Cabin 13 was a 22-year-old Canadian masseuse called Marguerite Lindsay. The Merchant Shipping Act of 1906 and the Aliens Act of 1905 required ships' masters to furnish lists of all passengers disembarking at British ports to the port officers of the Ministry of Transport. No exceptions were made with the *Corsican*, which docked in London on 8 August 1918, easily meeting the timetable given in Meinertzhagen's diary. Passengers who were listed as having British possessions usually had their residential address listed; for example, 26-year-old Miss Laura Aikin was to live at 'Chertsey', Leatherhead, Surrey. Marguerite Lindsay was noted as having British possessions but the address given for her is clearly non-residential: the Bank of Montreal, 9 Waterloo Place, London.[1]

Apart from Marguerite Lindsay's age – just right for a daughter of the Tsar – and the fact that she appeared to be in company with Richard Meinertzhagen's wife, there is another interesting fact to register about the *Corsican* passengers; among them was numbered Miss Henrietta Crawford, aged 44, a Principal Matron from the War Office. The Tsar's daughters were all taken ill during their confinement at Tobolsk and the rude circumstances of their captivity at Ekaterinburg could have further weakened them. For this Grand Duchess, there was the additional possibility that she had sustained some injury during the rescue or subsequent flight. The presence of a suitably reliable and senior nurse in Canada would have been a sensible and perhaps necessary precaution.

It is unfortunate that all of Armorel Meinertzhagen's papers relating to the period of her marriage to Richard Meinertzhagen have disappeared; they might just have thrown light on this episode. Conclusive evidence that her 'companion' was not who or what she said she was appears to surface in the records of Canadian births.

1 *See* 'Passenger Lists, Inwards', August 1918. PRO BT26/648.

Research among Canadian birth records was undertaken for me by Dr John A. Houlding of Toronto. There is no record for the birth of any Marguerite Lindsay for the period during which her stated age suggests she would have been born. It has been possible to run a further check on Canadian births through the Church of Jesus Christ of Latter Day Saints in Exhibition Road, London, with the same result. Searches among the Birth Registers for the United Kingdom in London, Edinburgh and Dublin again show that no Marguerite Lindsay was ever born at the time in question. The conclusion must be that whoever entered the country with Armorel Meinertzhagen was not who she claimed to be.

All trace of Marguerite Lindsay now vanishes. There is no record of where or with whom she might have been living in Britain: the Bank of Montreal does not keep customer records for 70 years. If, as I contend, the Lindsay identity disguised a Grand Duchess, a number of questions remain. Was her identity changed again? Did she live, and for how long? Did she marry? Did she have children? Is there still a direct claimant to the crown of all the Russias alive and living, perhaps, in Britain? But the pieces of jigsaw so far collected do begin to form a convincing picture: the disguised presence in Russia of British Intelligence; Meinertzhagen's known mission and its partial success; the possibility of a route across Siberia; the Japanese ships returning to Japanese waters; Prince Arthur's journey to Japan and thence secretly to Kyoto and on to Canada aboard a Japanese warship; Armorel Meinertzhagen's unexplained voyage across the Atlantic, hazardous in wartime with the seas infested with hostile U-boats and mines; the mysterious Miss Lindsay; and a host of mysteriously vanished papers.

In the folder of papers covering Prince Arthur's mission at Windsor Castle, document No. 81 has vanished, its place being taken by a sheet of plain paper upon which is written: 'Colonel Wigram has taken a paper out of this file. 10.7.18.'[1] Colonel Wigram was Colonel Sir Clive Wigram, close assistant to Lord Stamfordham, the King's Private Secretary and who succeeded Stamfordham in that office when the latter died in 1931. Why such a degree of secrecy surrounding much of the mission's activities, if there is nothing to hide?

The identity and means of concealment of the Grand Duchess have proved predictably difficult to establish but the papers of members of

1 'Prince Arthur of Connaught's Mission 1918', loc. cit., 10 July 1918, RA GV PS 24190.

the Japanese mission seemed an obvious source to investigate. The only papers relating to General Pulteney so far discovered are a lengthy series of letters to Lady Desborough, held in the Hertfordshire County Record Office. The General continued his correspondence throughout the Connaught mission, but one letter is of particular interest. It was written on 1 August 1918 and contains the words: 'You will have got my letter written from the Pacific.'[1] Needless to say, this letter has also had the magic wand waved over it and has disappeared from an otherwise complete and meticulously catalogued correspondence. Given the timing and location, is it possible that Pulteney was less than totally discreet in the missing letter about the Russian aspect of the mission? If so, someone has taken the trouble to ensure that this indiscretion was never made public.

Nevertheless, if a document disappears the historian can accept that such things do happen – papers get lost, accidents happen and individuals will destroy compromising documents. If two documents belonging to different people involved in the same events vanish, their disappearance might conceivably be attributed to coincidence. But in this case the complete loss of all the rest of Prince Arthur's papers, which were never deposited in the Royal Archives, the disappearance of General and Lady Pulteney's papers and the silence all requests for information about them produces, the disappearance of the Grand Duke Mikhail's papers, the withholding of the papers of the Duke of Connaught and the Earl of Pembroke, the extraction of a document in the *Siberia 4* file in the Public Record Office, the disappearance of *Siberia 5*, the destruction of documents in the *Canada Register* and the absence of documents in the Foreign Office files all surely point to something more than mere coincidence.

The shield of secrecy around the Meinertzhagen mission has been unfalteringly maintained and there are reasons for this with which it is impossible not to sympathize. The late Lord Mountbatten of Burma put his finger on the problem very precisely when he tried to dismiss the idea of an attempted rescue with the words, 'I do not say it would have been inconceivable. But in the light of the government's attitude, and the fact that King George V was a constitutional monarch, it would have been virtually impossible.'[2]

To embark on a private operation in the face of governmental

1 Grenfell Papers, loc. cit., letter to Lady Desborough, 1 August 1918, D/ERv C2130/164.
2 Summers and Mangold, op. cit., 1978 edition, p. 354.

opposition was a bold move indeed, for it is a staple of British political life that the sovereign's prerogatives are only exercised on the advice of duly appointed ministers responsible to Parliament, and the Romanov rescue clearly violated the accepted convention. The Crown could not accept the risk of discovery; the political scene would have been riven quite as gravely as in the clash between the two Houses of Parliament in 1910 and 1911, a clash which in 1918 would have been relatively fresh in everyone's minds. Mountbatten, of course, was anxious to preserve the position of the Crown to which he was so closely related and that was reason enough to discourage further research along this line.

The case appears to be that King George used his position as sovereign head of the armed services to engineer this rescue and thereby circumvent his chief minister's opposition. As head of the armed services he was perfectly entitled to give orders to his officers, all of whom had sworn allegiance to him and not to any transient cabinet: no loyal officer could conceivably refuse such a request from such a source. There is a constitutional dilemma here and the King would have been squarely caught on its horns. The Crown is supposed to be apolitical, to refrain from taking political steps without governmental advice – but the monarch is the legal head of the armed services and lawful commands must be obeyed. Everything hinges upon how the word 'political' is interpreted. Did the partially successful rescue have political consequences? It certainly has political implications but in the event there were no consequences – though there undoubtedly would have been had the Grand Duchess become the focus and inspiration for a Romanov restoration movement.

It might be argued that a constitutional monarch would not dream of instigating a private enterprise behind the back of the government, but constitutional monarchs do dream of such activities and sometimes put their dreams into practice. There have been two instances of such exploits this century and they are denied by nobody. The first was the rescue of Prince Andrew of Greece and his family, including the present Duke of Edinburgh, in 1922. Here King George V used his influence directly with the Foreign Office to engineer the rescue and equally directly employed the Royal Navy. On the King's instructions, a special emissary was despatched to Athens post-haste to parley with Pangalos, the Greek dictator, while the cruiser HMS *Calypso* was ordered to the Piraeus in a show of force. Pangalos caved in and Prince Andrew and his family were quietly embarked on the

Calypso at dead of night and thence to safety. The second instance was the employment of the now notorious Anthony Blunt, who, when an officer in MI5, was sent on a secret mission to Germany by King George VI at the end of the Second World War. The nature and purpose of this mission has never been revealed.

Had the truth about the Meinertzhagen mission been made public the King would have faced a barrage of criticism from those who would accuse him not only of a consitutional misdemeanour but of wilfully gambling with his relatives' lives, and thus responsibility for the murder of the unluckier members of the Romanov family would be said to rest at the door of the House of Windsor. Faced with such a prospect, the King's wish to smother the truth can readily be understood. In this regard the opinion expressed by the Queen of Denmark when pressed about Danish files on the Romanovs is interesting. She briskly replied that 'It is a family matter, and nobody else's business.' That, of course, is hardly the case. The Tsar and his family were public figures whose words and deeds deeply influenced the lives and fortunes of many millions. To pretend that the fate of such a family is entirely private borders on the disingenuous. In any case, the events outlined here happened more than 70 years ago and the protagonists are long since dead. This is now fairly and squarely a matter of history, and thus is fair game for the historian.

Faced with the understandable desire of the King and royal family to protect both their privacy and the secrecy of the mission, we should expect relevant documents to be missing from collections and those that survive to be designed to maintain the shield of secrecy.

But the question of sources must necessarily raise the issue of how much trust can be placed in Meinertzhagen's diary. The historian knows that sources such as diaries have no inherent monopoly on the truth; everything ultimately depends on the character and intent of the diarist. Can any imputation of being economical with the truth be levelled at Meinertzhagen over this issue? It is a diary held under restricted access in one of Britain's leading libraries and appears to be consulted but little, as most of Meinertzhagen's life is covered in his published books which are based on that diary. Why, then, should this particular Russian episode be omitted from his published books?

In 1918 he was working at the very nerve-centre of the British High Command, involved in matters too sensitive to be risked in the published diary. He comments: 'For 19 years I have kept this diary without a break, until February of this year when I entered the War

Office. I there found that my work brought me in contact with so much very secret matter, and that whatever my opinions were they were based on essentially secret information. In view of this I thought it preferable to keep silent, than to submit to paper whatever views I held.'[1] Therefore, his diary contains no entries at all between 17 March and 3 August 1918. The attempt to rescue the Romanovs, however, was not on quite the same level of secrecy, since it did not jeopardize national security. Even so, there were elements that demanded some degree of security. He wrote: 'Even now I feel it a bit dangerous to disclose detail.'[2] Apart from the possibility of a constitutional storm engulfing his Royal commander-in-chief, the rescued Grand Duchess could quite possibly be endangered too, for 'I am sure that if her identity were known she would be tracked down and murdered as the heir to the Russian throne.'[3]

As we have seen, Meinertzhagen's words do not stand alone. His diary entry is corroborated by Major Alley, another senior Intelligence officer who was in a position to know if anything out of the ordinary had happened in Ekaterinburg.

In general, it seems that no doubts were felt about Meinertzhagen's veracity. His diary was used as a source by the British Official Historian of the campaign in East Africa, who had no qualms about the high standards of accuracy and reliability he found in it. For a statement to constitute a lie it has to be told to someone, and Meinertzhagen kept this Russian affair hidden in the recesses of a diary and did not make it public. What possible motive could there be for falsehood in a private diary, for unless he published all he knew what was there to be gained? And can Meinertzhagen convincingly be accused of perpetrating a deliberate fabrication when his whole life portrays a man of probity who was honourable, upright and honest to a fault?

Neither can the crucial diary entry be attributed to fantasy. If that had been the case, how is it that fantasy never manifested itself elsewhere in the diary and that the entry was never expunged once the writer had recovered his wits? Can one credibly maintain that the outstanding chief of Intelligence in East Africa and Palestine, now being groomed to become head of Intelligence on the Western front, was living even occasionally in a world of make-believe?

1 Meinertzhagen Diaries, op. cit., Vol. 20, 11 November 1918, p. 186.
2 Ibid., 18 August 1918, pp. 169–70.
3 Ibid.

Yet Meinertzhagen's diary is challenged by the King's diary where, on Saturday, 31 August 1918, the King recorded that news from Russia indicated there was a strong probability that *all* the Romanov family were murdered together with the Tsar. So there are two diaries, Meinertzhagen's and the King's, the contents of which are at complete variance. One of the entries is certainly a fabrication.

The King had the motive, the means and the opportunity to initiate the mission, and he also had good reason to cover his tracks. The historiography of Royal papers shows that the King was well aware of the likelihood of his own diary eventually being opened to the inspection of scholars and this represented the soundest of reasons to lay a false trail, though the King, an essentially honest man, must have thought long and hard before the momentum of events told him there was no other choice. The historiography of royal papers over the course of this century also reveals that interference is widespread, with documents of considerable historical value – but probable royal embarrassment – being put to the torch. King Edward VII had his mother's correspondence with Lord Granville destroyed and also removed her letters to Disraeli from Lord Rothschild's safe-keeping, destroying all letters about the royal family and the correspondence between Disraeli and members of the royal family.

Queen Victoria's diary, which would have been a document of tremendous importance, fell into the hands of her youngest daughter, HRH the Princess Beatrice. The Queen had instructed her daughter to copy the contents of the diary and this she dutifully did, destroying the precious originals in the fire as she went. But Princess Beatrice did not copy out the full diary – she is known to have destroyed a considerable part of it without making any copy and also to have debased the value of the remainder by altering much of the material she transcribed. King George V, when Prince of Wales, was well aware of what was happening and objected without success, though he did succeed in saving material relating to his grandmother's girlhood. With this example in front of him, the King could not fail to realize that diaries would not always remain private but that questions about their veracity could be readily warded off. Moreover, George V himself ordered the destruction of many papers in the Royal Archives dealing with George IV; and, when his mother, Queen Alexandra, died in 1925, her papers were put to the torch, again with the King's knowledge. On these grounds alone, therefore, there is a strong case that argues that the King's diary is open to question on this point. The extraordinary circumstances facing both the King and his cousin's family in 1918 were grounds enough for him to act out of character on that occasion. And it must never be overlooked that although King George, a devout Christian, attended a memorial service for the Tsar after his murder was announced, no memorial service was ever held for the Tsar's family, much less attended by the King, in spite of the official stance adopted towards their death. Perhaps the King's diary entry gives him an escape clause. The wording is sufficiently uncertain to allow of it: in all probability his relatives had all been murdered. A probability rather than an established fact, something of which he had been informed but with no suggestion that the information was reliable – he recorded it but refrained from elaborating it.

The King's information – or perhaps misinformation – came from General Poole at Murmansk and reached the King from the DMI. Poole's telegram, also dated 31 August, records 'that there is every probability' that all the Imperial family were murdered. The telegram survives but we do not know the source on which he based it – one which he 'had no reason to doubt'.[1] There is at least the possibility that Poole's information was sent back and recorded in order deliberately to conceal the truth.

Meinertzhagen became increasingly concerned about what was to become of his diaries: 'I have left them to Dan [his elder son, killed on active service] and trust he will see that they are not mutilated. Should he or Anne ever wish to make a connected story of my not uninteresting life I hope they will do so.'[2] Thirteen years later he wrote with obvious concern:

> I do not know what will happen to my diaries. I am leaving them to my executors who can hand them to Ran [his only surviving son, R. R. Meinertzhagen] when he is a little older. But they must not be mutilated or become the possession of some irresponsible person. To me they have been a wonderful safety valve and record and they should prove interesting to my descendants.[3]

On a different note, what is one to make of the sudden rush of public positions offered to Meinertzhagen in the post-war period? Some of these were undoubtedly founded on his superlative military record, such as Head of the Secret Service in Ireland in February 1921, which

1 Summers and Mangold, op. cit., 1987 edition, p. 81.
2 Meinertzhagen Diaries, Vol. 52, 21 January 1944, p. 114.
3 Ibid., Vol. 67, 29 March 1957, p. 114.

the DMI advised him to refuse as he was getting married the following month. He was also offered the job of Head of the Special Section of the Metropolitan Police, with responsibility for the safety of the royal family and Government ministers and alternatively, a seat in Parliament – both of which he also refused. In 1924 it was proposed that he accept the Governorship of the Falkland Islands with prospects of a larger colony later, a proposal which was again rejected, this time in his wife's interest.

Posts like these are not offered to anybody, only to those who have proved themselves in Crown service. They are certainly not offered to liars or fantasists. Meinertzhagen's is the diary of a senior officer of British Military Intelligence, the very body which would have had to be involved in any Romanov rescue mission, and his honesty cannot reasonably be called into question. As his only biographer, John Lord, stated: 'Above all, he was never afraid of being honest, and that may be a saving virtue in any time or place.'[1]

I said earlier that all trace of Marguerite Lindsay had vanished after her arrival in England. However, the mystery comes into focus again in 1919 in the shape of a hasty one-line note scribbled by General Pulteney to Lady Desborough. The note is very simple: 'What was the name of the doctor at Harrogate please?'[2]

Why should Pulteney want a doctor when neither he nor his wife was ill – they had no children – and why a doctor from Harrogate, of all places? If a Grand Duchess were in hiding in Britain and possibly ill or injured the answer must be either that the doctor in question was a specialist in a particular field, or was particularly discreet and trustworthy, or both. Spanish influenza was raging throughout Europe at the time, claiming more deaths than the war, but the fact that the doctor came from Harrogate is perhaps significant; the wording of the note, too, would seem to indicate that a need for a doctor had been discussed before. In the early years of this century Harrogate was still a famous spa town, patronized by royalty, peers and eminent figures; discretion in treating a sensitive case could be assured. Interestingly, the town already had connections with the Romanovs: the Grand Duchess George Mikhailovitch and her daughters had taken the waters there in 1913 and had established two

1 Lord, op. cit., p.xi.
2 Grenfell Papers, loc. cit., letter to Lady Desborough, 11 March 1919, D/ERv C2130/164.

hospitals for wounded officers there during the war. At Knaresborough, on the outskirts of Harrogate, was a well-known sanatorium. Perhaps the doctor was an expert on tuberculosis?

Had the Grand Duchess been ill, King George V and those involved in the plot were indeed in a quandary: what does one do with a seriously ill Grand Duchess whose true identity must be kept secret? She would not be kept near the King in such a condition and in any case treatment of an unknown woman at court by necessarily expensive experts could have led to dangerous speculation. Meinertzhagen disclosed that the Grand Duchess was living in the British Isles under a false identity, both to shield herself and her Royal protector. As another royal refugee expressed it, 'You see, it was a very large family and there were always plenty of relatives and places to visit.'[1] Not only would there have been the royal family and their relatives and close friends, there were also the Grand Duke Mikhail and his two married daughters, and the Grand Duchess George and her two daughters. Any of these could have absorbed an extra family member, bound to silence as they would have been about her identity, by loyalty and even perhaps oath, while she built a new life. If the Grand Duchess were hiding among the exiled Russians or with a British family, where in Britain could she be?

There is a fine irony in the thought that in Europe and America a Grand Duchess was trying to establish her true identity while in Britain there may already have been another forced to conceal hers. And so the story seems to end. One Grand Duchess rescued from Ekaterinburg, flown to Vladivostok, there transferred in all probability to a Japanese vessel and carried to safety in Prince Arthur's train to Canada and thence to England. The Tsar and his son shot but the rest of the family transferred to Perm and Glazov, where all trace of them vanishes. Except for Anastasia.

It is my belief that the rescued Grand Duchess was Tatiana, a belief not merely based on the disclosures made about an escape from Ekaterinburg and the references to Tatiana already noted and the unlikelihood, given Anna Anderson's story, that Anastasia escaped at that time, but based on something more. Two of the parties to the plot had strong Irish connections: the Earl of Pembroke owned large estates in Ireland and drew much of his income from there, and

1 HRH Prince Philip, the Duke of Edinburgh, to Richard Hough. *See* R. Hough, *Mountbatten, Hero of Our Time*, London, 1981, p. 111.

General Pulteney of Prince Arthur's mission and the vanished 'letter from the Pacific' had married into the prestigious Arnott family, who owned estates in Dublin and Cork. One small clue to the Grand Duchess's identity does perhaps exist in the Arnott family. For some reason the uncle of the present baronet, one-time heir-apparent to the baronetcy, chose to name his daughter Tatiana. Was that a courtesy to the living or a remembrance of the dead? I believe the latter. It would surely have been impossible to prevent a surviving Grand Duchess from somehow meeting the Anastasia claimant, a claimant who knew more than she would ever tell, especially if visiting her among the many other members of the British, German and Russian royal families who did so. Some hint of such a meeting must have leaked out or been recorded had it ever taken place.

Despite its tragic ending, perhaps because of its web of deception, the Meinertzhagen episode stands as a fine example of the courage and ingenuity of the officers of British Military Intelligence. There was no other formation in the world that could have planned and conducted such a remarkable and daring operation. Perhaps now that the truth about other deaths in Russia, like those of the Polish officers at Katyn, seems likely to be established, it may be possible for the truth about the Imperial family at last to be revealed by Russian sources. Only two things appear certain as yet: that one Grand Duchess was secretly rescued by British Intelligence acting on King George V's direct orders, and that the truth about the fate of all the Romanovs has yet to be admitted.

NINE

Behind the Scenes

THE hand of British Military Intelligence played no less a part in the German revolution of 1918. To grasp the extent of British machinations in the affairs of the enemy state, one must take the story back to 1915. It was in that year that Intelligence discovered how valuable left-wing dissidents within Germany could be – some German socialists had already shown themselves only too ready to betray their country. Even before that, however, the Directorate of Military Intelligence had divined potential weaknesses within the opposing Empire.

In the intoxicating summer of 1914 the German people had been swept into the war on a magnificent tide of euphoria which had united the political parties of the Empire behind the national effort. The Kaiser's statement, 'I recognize no more parties, only Germans,' found a ready response among all significant factions. Normally at loggerheads with each other, they resolved to bury their usual differences for the duration in an internal peace pact known as the 'Burgfrieden' or 'Fortress Truce'.

The Burgfrieden was by no means the only new political fact of life which the people of the Empire had to digest. On the outbreak of war the Prussian Law of Siege came into force throughout all the Kaiser's domains in a calculated attempt to enforce the required degree of national unity. This law restricted political rights and activity severely, depriving people amongst other things of the right of assembly, but beyond this it placed the Army in a position where it could legally intervene in domestic politics. Germany was divided into districts, each of which was responsible for raising and maintaining an army corps; when the soldiers left for the front, the Deputy Commanding General of each corps forthwith assumed command of his corps' district. Under the Law of Siege these gentlemen found large areas of civilian life coming into their purview, matters in which they had no experience and where they were inclined to meddle in order to provide stop-gap solutions to the problems thrown up by the war, solutions which not infrequently exacerbated the problems and caused bureaucratic chaos. The Law of Siege was, predictably, one feels like saying, geared to the conditions of 1870–1 and could not cope with a long and brutal total war which speedily came to invade all aspects of life.

One of the most sinister aspects of the First World War was the way in which millions of citizens, in every participating country, were pushed in one direction and pulled in another by the warring governments. This totalitarian experiment in social control began with efforts to control and direct the actions and passions of the population through both legal and moral agencies. The legal pull was exerted through the laws which governed how the citizen should act to support the war effort, whether or not he or she agreed with it; in Britain the Official Secrets Act and the Defence of the Realm Act were and are examples of this, but they were mild, almost genteel, in comparison with the Prussian Law of Siege and the Auxiliary Service Law on conscripted labour. The moral push was engineered by a propaganda campaign depicting the Allied enemies as something worse than the devil and therefore unworthy of anything other than the nastiest treatment that could be devised. People's passions were excited by calls to arms which ranged from patriotic appeals, through chivalric sentiments, to shaming those who would not go and fight. The unknown citizen's efforts, his money, his body, were now needed as never before.

Beside the nobility of the Burgfrieden ideal were set new political and social issues. The biggest single political issue was the lack of democratic rights in Germany, a Germany where the Chancellor – the head of government – was appointed by the Kaiser, nominated his own ministers and owed no responsibility to the elected Reichstag. The latter's only means of exerting political influence was through a partial control of the budget. A symbol of the frustration of many Germans lay in the Prussian three-class franchise, established in 1848, which contrived to place a disproportionate weight of political power in the hands of the great Prussian landowners and aristocracy. In 1914 these issues were very much alive, if for the present masked by a superficial unity. It was an age-old recipe for trouble, for as the great Greek historian Thucydides wrote, '. . . war is a stern teacher; in depriving them of easily satisfying their daily wants, it brings people's minds down to the level of their actual circumstances'.[1]

The actual circumstances in Germany after two years of total war

1 Thucydides, *History of the Peloponnesian War*, London, 1979 (reprint), Vol. I, p. 313.

were empty bellies, deprivation of political rights, heavy losses and declining hope, a formidable combination guaranteed to try the strongest of unities. The Burgfrieden had never been that and the coffin-lid was really nailed down on it by the Somme campaign of 1916. By now both sides recognized that what they were facing was less a struggle between armies of men than the pitting of men against enormous industrialized material power.

In the grim autumn of 1916 the discredited Falkenhayn was replaced as Chief of the German General Staff by the hero of Tannenberg, Feld-Marschall Paul von Hindenburg and Beneckendorff, with his inseparable *éminence grise*, General-Leutnant Erich Ludendorff. This partnership, which had sprung to fame on the Eastern front, presided over the latter stages of the Somme holocaust and was deeply impressed by the material supremacy of the British. The knowledge brought about a new approach in German strategy: the Eastern front was now to be the springboard to victory, while the Western front would be held by a dour defensive based on a shortening of the line. The Germans would withdraw to a new and formidable defensive line constructed over the winter of 1916–17, called erroneously by the British the Hindenburg Line.

Manpower was Germany's most critical problem and the staggering bloodletting of 1916 left Germany's new military masters with the problem of reducing demand on Germany's shrinking reserves by shifting the burden onto weaponry and munitions. Yet to achieve this, industry, too, had to have more men in order to expand production: it would have to compete directly with the army for manpower. The solution reached by the Knights of the Eastern Front fell into two parts, the Hindenburg Programme and the Auxiliary Service Law. The Hindenburg Programme sought to establish new factories to produce weaponry and munitions on an equal footing with the Allies, and the Auxiliary Service Law was intended to provide conscripted labour both to man the new factories and to mine the coal which powered them. The decision was made in the knowledge that compulsion would increase the danger of conflict between the state and the industrial workers; the trade unions would be certain to demand important concessions in return for their co-operation. By forcing the Imperial Government to pin its hopes of continuing the war on the co-operation of the unions and industrial workers, the balance of domestic political and social power could be shifted: if requiring support from the people, it could not reasonably deny them a voice in the affairs of state.

The Auxiliary Service Law, with its plans for compulsory civilian mobilization in support of the industrial war effort, was duly presented to the Reichstag and was duly passed, sweeping away many of the hard-won rights of the trade unions and workers, such as their 'Freizügigkeit' or freedom of domicile. The Socialist Party, the SPD, eventually came round reluctantly to support the Law and thereby made themselves an easy and inviting prey for the extremists. Under the colossal strain of the war the extremists had been growing in strength and numbers, and becoming steadily more vociferous and radical. As early as March 1916, seventeen of the SPD Deputies had voted against the war credits in the Reichstag and a further fourteen had abstained. The seventeen rebels then formed themselves into a loose grouping called the Social Democratic Labour Fellowship. They were joined by some trade union leaders and under their aegis, a huge peace meeting was held at Frankfurt on 1 October 1916, attended by a crowd 30,000 strong, at which a resolution was passed demanding immediate peace on the basis of the status quo.

Such menacing rumbles of discontent continued throughout the hard winter of 1916–17, known in Germany as the 'turnip winter' as much of the populace was reduced to the most basic of diets. The first six months of 1917 shattered any remaining illusions of domestic repose within Germany. A steady drift to radicalism was punctuated by a series of major strikes in Berlin, Leipzig and other industrial centres, but far more ominous was the open breach in unity witnessed in the Reichstag. The outbreak of revolution in Russia in March and the establishment of the Provisional Government marked the advent of a new instability, for the events in Russia fired the imaginations of the Left throughout Europe. With the Bolshevik coup in November, the Empire of the Tsars had been swept into the dustbin of history and the radical programme of the new rulers of Russia shook the old states of Europe to their foundations, commanding widespread sympathy and support especially from those upon whom the burdens of war bore hardest. The new Bolshevik state towered over war-shattered and exhausted Europe like a colossus attired in the garb of freedom, offering to liberate poverty-stricken workers from the shackles of injustice, servitude, war and capitalism. According to communist theory, war was the constant handmaiden of capitalism, and to extirpate war from the human condition it was therefore essential to destroy capitalism. The working classes of the warring states were fighting the wrong enemy: they were pitting their pitiful lives against the workers of other countries, when the real enemy, the class enemy, lay all the time at home. It is, perhaps, difficult now to imagine the dramatic effect of the Bolshevik cry on the war-torn and starving populations of Central Europe, but in the last fifteen months of the war the new credo of internationalism was stronger than it has ever been since, and it sounded in the air like a tocsin.

Germany was potentially Bolshevik Russia's most deadly enemy on two counts. Firstly, the German armies had advanced deep into Russia and, had they chosen to do so, they could have advanced to Moscow without fear of serious opposition and put paid to Bolshevik pretensions in short order. Secondly, it was the continuation of the war that had doomed the unhappy Provisional Government; and besides, Lenin needed peace with Germany to devote his attention to destroying his class enemies within Russia.

What followed was a classic demonstration of Lenin's dictum 'take one step backwards in order to take two steps forward'. Negotiations for the urgently needed peace were put in hand, but while they progressed, no stone was left unturned in the attempt to riddle German soldiers with Bolshevik ideas. Ultimately the German hard-line policy forced the Bolsheviks to sign a humiliating peace treaty at Brest-Litovsk in March 1918, but once the peace was signed the road was open for Bolshevik propaganda to pour into Germany, not least through the return of thousands of prisoners-of-war who had been thoroughly imbued with Bolshevik ideals. Moreover, the blatantly annexationist nature of the peace fuelled the war aims debate within Germany, alienating not just the radicals but more moderate socialists who had hitherto supported what they saw as a struggle against 'Tsarismus'. By one of those curious ironies of history, Bolshevik propaganda sought the same short-term goals as did that which would emanate from MI7(b).

Thus, in 1917, the whole continent seethed with a vigorous new discontent which, by the end of year, had found expression in each of the major warring powers. The French armies were racked by mutiny during which numbers of the mutineers displayed all the alarming symptoms of revolution; France, like Germany, was beset by serious strikes, and also the Bolo Pasha/Malvy treason cases. Russia was plunged not once but twice into the turmoil of revolution and in Britain Ramsay Macdonald appealed to the working classes to follow the example of their brothers in Russia. There were serious strikes, leading Sir William Robertson, CIGS, to write to Haig that:

> I am afraid there is no getting away from the fact that there is some unrest in the country now as a result, partly, of the Russian revolution. There have been some bad strikes recently, and there is still much discontent.[1]

In the far Antipodes a newspaper published a notice reading:

> To arms, capitalists, parsons, politicians, landlords, newspaper editors and other stay-at-home patriots. Your country needs you in the trenches. Workers, follow your masters!

The printer and publisher of this witty polemic were convicted of 'circulating statements likely to prejudice recruiting' and were fined £50; the alternative was six months' imprisonment with hard labour.[2]

In the absence of basic political rights and the presence of starvation caused by the blockade, Germans were inclined to listen all the more avidly to the new medley of change. The Russian revolution both frightened and emboldened the moderate SPD and lent a new virility to the malcontents of the Social Democratic Labour Fellowship who, by the spring, felt themselves strong enough to form their own radical political party, the Independent Social Democrats (USPD), dedicated to peace without annexations or indemnities, and to the democratization of German politics with the overthrow of capitalism. The majority socialists, the SPD, inspired partly by the urge to retain their position as the mouthpiece of the German working man, took a leaf from the USPD's book and laid before the Reichstag a Resolution calling for Germany publicly to offer peace proposals with no annexations or indemnities.

The July Peace Resolution was the first really considerable open breach in German political unity, not simply because the largest Socialist party had broken ranks, but because thereby they gained the support of bourgeois parties like the National Liberals. In response to this new challenge, the parties of the Right, still pursuing the dream of a victorious peace with extensive annexations in Belgium, France, Poland and parts of Austria which would leave Germany supreme in Europe, rallied to form the Vaterlands Partei, dedicated to fighting off the threat posed to their ambitions by knock-kneed weaklings of the Left.

The split in the Burgfrieden was thus irrevocable and all the pre-

1 Field-Marshal Sir William Robertson, *Soldiers and Statesmen*, Vol. I, p. 313.
2 M. Rickards and M. Moody, *The First World War: Ephemera, Mementoes, Documents*, London, 1975, p. 25.

war political strife resurfaced with renewed vigour. The split over war aims dovetailed with demands for political reform, including a Government responsible to the Reichstag, and the political divisions were now both sharper and bolder than they had ever been, running through every province in Germany. If those divisions had remained largely confined to the political parties they would be of only passing interest, a footnote in the study of nations under stress. But the USPD and the avowedly revolutionary Spartacists were intent on widening their sphere of influence. The Spartacists were the followers of Karl Liebknecht, taking their name from the heroic leader of the slaves' revolt against Imperial Rome. They sought outright rebellion and tried their hand at propaganda with pamphlets like 'Der Deutsche Soldat als Hanker der Freiheit', and 'Kameraden Erwacht!', aimed specifically at the men in the German Army. Nevertheless, for all their struggles, the Spartacists remained little more than a highly vociferous minority group until the end of the war, lacking both the respectability and popular appeal to convert an essentially conservative working class into full-blooded revolutionaries. With serving men the activities of both groups were more successful and culminated in a serious mutiny in the German Navy at Kiel in July. The Imperial Government responded to this challenge with brutal efficiency and the mutiny was suppressed, but not before emergency measures were taken: at one stage Naval officers were permitted to carry small arms ashore with them to protect them from the assaults of the matelots and dockers.

Reports on the mutiny were soon in the hands of Mansfield Smith-Cumming. Hitherto all riots and strikes in Germany had been due to food shortages, with little real political undertones. But the Naval mutiny was different. It was a fully fledged political move, engineered by would-be revolutionaries, in which physical violence had been directed against officers. Its significance was not lost upon C, who hurried to the Director of Military Intelligence, Major-General George Macdonogh, with the news.

Little is known directly about this fascinating man, for none of his private papers or effects seem to have survived him, most being destroyed in the Blitz in 1941. His life was in any case kept very private, so the impression left to later generations is of an enigmatic man, such information as exists coming from official documents, hearsay and the imprecise reminiscences of his contemporaries.

George Mark Watson Macdonogh was born in 1865, the son of a

Deputy Inspector of Royal Naval Hospitals, and joined the Army in 1884. He was a retiring and diffident man who shrank from argument with more aggressive characters. This diffidence concealed an iron will and a superbly analytical and penetrating mind. He had been commissioned in the Royal Engineers; it is interesting to note how high a proportion of the best Intelligence officers of the First World War came from the more technically minded corps of the Engineers and Artillery. Macdonogh was certainly in his element in the Engineers and soon found himself a captain and on his way to Staff College. Here his fellow students included officers like the future Official Historian of the war, James Edmonds, another Engineer who was to be closely involved with the creation of an efficient, professional Intelligence service. Others included the future Field-Marshals Haig and Allenby. Macdonogh was also a keen student of law, combining this successfully with his military career, being called to the Bar at Lincoln's Inn in 1897. In each sphere discipline, attention to detail, analytical ability, a calculating mind and the study of hard evidence are required, so Macdonogh's early careers laid a sound foundation for his work in Intelligence.

The Macdonogh family were converts to Roman Catholicism from the Methodist Church and, in 1918, after Macdonogh had become Adjutant-General and was within striking distance of the highest ranks in the Army, pressure was put on him to change his religion. Sincere in his beliefs, he refused, and thereby blighted his chances of further promotion, to his country's great loss.

His marriage to a Finnish lady, Aline Borgström, exerted a considerable influence on his life, endowing him with a love of Scandinavia and stimulating him to study Swedish and Finnish; he became proficient in both languages. Marriage, however did not incline him to be any more socially outgoing and his brother officers saw little of Aline, the two of them apparently content to live almost in retirement. In later life Macdonogh chose to represent Finnish interests, numbering amongst his many legal and commercial activities Presidency of the Anglo-Finnish Society, the Vice-Presidency of the Finland Fund, and membership of the Finnish Aid Bureau. The Macdonoghs' only son died in 1915, a loss that troubled them both deeply, and led to Macdonogh spending some considerable time away from the front. Even under the burden of his great grief, however, he still maintained the same stolid, unflinching, capable exterior.

He had few close friends and those he had were all killed during the war, after which he set his face against letting people get too close to him, though he was universally respected and liked. As often in such cases he developed a deep understanding of his fellow man, with all his weaknesses and imperfections. In all, he was formidably equipped for the part he was to play as Director of Military Intelligence in striking at his adversary's weakest point.

As early as the spring of 1915, GHQ Intelligence had been running an extremely useful information system. This was the Briefeinfall (invasion or incursion by letter) system. It was the brainchild of a Russo-German Jew code-named 'Romulus', an 'idealistic socialist' and an 'enthusiastic anti-Boche socialist'.[1] Like others of his persuasion, Romulus considered that German victory would put back the socialist clock by years and had to be averted at all costs. The lynchpin of his system was another German socialist named Schmidt who lived in exile in Switzerland, from where he ran a socialist newspaper. Schmidt was actively trying to engineer a socialist coup in Germany and, in order to help him do so, his colleagues in Germany sent Schmidt military information by letter to enable him better to judge his opportunity. These letters were sent to Switzerland six days a week to Swiss socialists who believed them to be purely political and so forwarded them to Schmidt without further question. Schmidt, of course, promptly turned them over to Romulus who gave them directly to British Intelligence.

Save for a small amount for expenses, none of the socialists received payment; Romulus held that they worked better for an ideal and many of them, of course, had no idea that they were aiding the official enemy. The system was scattered the length and breadth of Germany and, as the only central control was Schmidt, the chances of the Germans destroying the network appeared slim. Not that it would worry the British unduly if they did, for there were nearly a thousand men working for Schmidt. As the officer in charge at the British end remarked, 'If men are caught and shot, it is so many bosches the less, and we don't mind how many they shoot, provided others remain to carry on the good work.'[2]

By June 1915 the Briefeinfall system was prospering and reports were being received every other day from places as widespread as

1 Kirke Diaries, op. cit., 20 June and 30 November 1915.
2 Ibid., 30 November 1915.

Mainz, Mannheim, Nürnberg, Stuttgart, Bremen, Frankfurt, Koblenz and Treves. In fact the Germans did become suspicious and arrested some of Schmidt's men for spreading pacifist propaganda. Discovering that they were communicating with Switzerland, they hurriedly imposed a ban on sending such material between the two countries. The effect on Schmidt was devastating. It was as if the rattle of the firing squad's rifle bolts was already ringing in his ears. Quite unlike a man preparing to be the hero of a revolution, he simply lost his nerve and by December had dropped both his plans and his colleagues. The system came apart at the seams and since there was no one ready to hand to take over, GHQ decided to allow the dust to settle before renewing this approach. By 1916 when they came to restart it they found Schmidt's ring had completely dispersed and neither its former scope nor its former value could be recaptured.

The Briefeinfall system was but one of several which relied on disaffected socialists. The Scandinavian Section of the Secret Service, under Commander Stagg RN, ran a similar operation through Denmark under the command of Major Holme RA known as the Nemesis system. This comprised another party of dedicated socialists with revolutionary ambitions who not only supplied information to the British but performed minor acts of sabotage on their own initiative and at their own expense. They claimed to be responsible for several railway accidents and to have sabotaged artillery rounds and small arms ammunition,[1] but their doings pale into insignificance beside the campaign which was to be hatched in the shadowy recesses of the War Office in the autumn of 1917.

By August, when the crises within the Fatherland were germinating, Macdonogh had shown himself to be alert to the potential for revolution in a sober report on 'The Man-Power and Internal Conditions of the Central Powers'.[2] At this juncture Germany's plight was not yet so critical that hopes of real revolution could be entertained: indeed Macdonogh thought that 'it may be safely said that at present no revolution can be expected in Germany'.[3] The key words are 'at present', for they show that the likelihood of such an eventuality was very much in his mind, especially if its development

1 Ibid., 17 April 1916.

2 W.P.49. Cabinet Committee on War Policy. 'The Man-Power and Internal Conditions of the Central Powers', by the Director of Military Intelligence. 31 August–1 October 1917. PRO WO 106/312.

3 Ibid.

was judiciously fostered by the British. While ready to concede that German morale was not yet ready to wither, Macdonogh could draw the Cabinet Committee on War Policy's attention to the fact that it had been shaken. The failure to bring Britain to her knees by the unrestricted use of U-boats had contributed mightily to this shaking, for the U-boat campaign had been launched in a blaze of publicity which forecast that Britain would not survive for more than three months, and the failure to realize this over-optimistic promise undoubtedly dented German confidence. So too had the failure to drive the British from Baghdad, the slowly increasing American strength and the thoroughly unexpected, if temporary, revival of the Russian Army. These setbacks were bad enough in Macdonogh's view but they were as nothing compared to the 'further defeats on the Western front where she has not scored a single victory against her chief opponents since May 1915, and where she has been forced to relinquish a large amount of territory and has lost heavily in men and guns'.[1] Nevertheless, while the Germans had reserves in hand and while opposing Governments held fast to the idea of total victory and dictated peace, fighting would continue.

In summing up the situation in August, Macdonogh argued that:

> While the morale of the German people is as yet far from being broken and while the economic situation cannot yet be depended on to bring Germany to terms, transportation is daily becoming more inefficient and public opinion is undoubtedly becoming highly sensitive, disappointed and suspicious. At the same time it must be remembered that further military successes against German troops, combined with a very stringent blockade will alone cause the German people to lose confidence in their rulers.[2]

Macdonogh's paper raised another aspect of the struggle which few others had as yet recognized, and that was the link between military operations and the home front, the first real attempt to exploit the underlying social forces so omnipresent in total war. What Macdonogh had recognized was that the struggle between the great nations was not to be decided solely on the battlefield, but in the factories, dockyards, marshalling yards and slum tenements of industrial Europe. In Macdonogh's view the aim of operations was to be less the destruction of the enemy's army than to be part of a much broader

1 Ibid.
2 Ibid.

attack on his whole national will to fight. Such a war was not being fought merely to defeat the enemy, but to crush him utterly. It seems that Macdonogh alone was prepared to voice this view, to focus on the possibilities of further internal crises in Germany and to study the situation in order to take full advantage of events.

If German confidence had been shaken in August, by October it had been eroded to a lamentable condition and Macdonogh's judgement told him that now German morale was sufficiently depressed to justify attacking it directly. The great and bloody battles of 1917 may not have broken the German Army, but they had succeeded in weakening morale at home to the point where any further failures, coupled with a deliberate campaign of subversion, could bring the war to a halt. By early October Macdonogh had discussed his ideas with that arch-intriguer, Lieutenant-General Sir Henry Wilson, the future Field-Marshal and Chief of the Imperial General Staff. Wilson thought Macdonogh's ideas important enough to record the outline of the conversation in his diary:

> Macdonogh came over to the Horse Gds at 11 o'c., and we had a long talk. He doesn't believe in breaking the German Army but he does believe – perhaps in the next 12 mos. [months] – in breaking the heart of the German people.[1]

It was not long before it was being recommended to the War Cabinet that military operations should be aimed at bringing further pressure to bear on the German home front rather than directed solely against the German Army. After reviewing the internal difficulties Germany had been subjected to during the year, Macdonogh urged that full pressure ought to be maintained on the battlefronts since 'Further [internal] crises are imminent and, apart from the pressure which the Entente can exert by maintaining a united front as regards war-aims and by repeating calmly and dispassionately through the medium of our leading statesmen the reasons for our refusal to treat with the present leaders of Germany, we can by maintaining at full strength our military pressure on the German Armies in the Western Theatre hasten the crises and accentuate internal dissensions.'[2]

The objective of renewed military operations is here made crystal

1 Diary of Field-Marshal Sir Henry Wilson [hereinafter Wilson Diary], 12 October 1917, IWM.

2 'Effect of Military Operations on the Political Situation in Germany', by the Director of Military Intelligence. 14 October 1917. PRO WO106/313. (Reprinted at Appendix III.)

clear. The Directorate of Military Intelligence had recognized something true of all conflicts: it is not the gun that counts, but the man behind it. Weapons are only lethal when wielded by people prepared to use them. It is in the minds, hearts and spirits of people that the solution to all conflict lies, not in the various tools and artefacts they employ to aid the conflict. Intelligence came not so much to engage in direct opposition, but to induce Germans to question what they were fighting for and throw their weapons aside. They engaged in manipulation of a whole population, a different front altogether. That it was a front is denied by nobody and it was recognized as such at the time: the phrase 'home front' passed into the English language during the First World War. It was used freely in the Second World War and was a phrase which everybody understood. There is an intimate connection between a military situation and propaganda and it was a fact of the greatest significance that Macdonogh recognized this connection, seeing military operations not simply as a search for victory in the field but as a more insidious attack on enemy morale. According to Macdonogh, the two elements were complementary for, 'if our military pressure at full strength is maintained, the feelings of apprehension will increase, the infallibility of von Hindenburg and Ludendorff will be further questioned, and pacifist tendencies will be strengthened'.[1] The final arbiter of victory in the long-drawn-out clash of juggernauts was to be less the defeat of the German Army than the breaking of spirit of the German people, culminating in a revolution which would overthrow the Kaiser and German General Staff. Military operations had brought the German people to such a pass that it was feasible to think in these terms, and they were to be the main weapon in bringing the revolution to fruition, but they were not to be the only weapon.

The neutral Netherlands, lying just across the North Sea, provided the nearest safe haven for German political refugees, deserters from the German Army and pacifists opposed to the war, and by mid-1917 the country was fairly infested with these escapees, eking out a precarious and monotonous existence. The Netherlands was also, of course, one of the favourite safe havens for the British Secret Services.

One of the political refugees was a man called Carl Minster, a native of the industrialized Ruhr whose heady outspokenness against both the war and the Imperial regime had made Germany too hot for him.

1 Ibid.

As well as being a revolutionary, Minster was a skilled journalist who had produced a radical newspaper, *Der Kampf*, in Duisburg. He had fled when the police began to close in on him and, with the aid of his revolutionary friends, had been smuggled into the security of the Netherlands. He unfurled his banner anew in Rotterdam, from where he maintained his links with his partners in Germany, resurrected *Der Kampf* and founded two political organizations for fellow exiles, 'Der Freie Arbeiter' and 'Arbeiter Vorbildungsverein Deutscher Zunge', both breathing hate and fire against the Hohenzollerns and all their works and pomps. Minster's unconditional aim was to inspire revolution in Germany, establish a socialist republic and thereafter peace.

Groups of all political persuasions had been founded by the exiles, but most were dominated by the Left. After Minster's groups the most important ones were the organizations of the deserters from the German Army, who, being otherwise alone, bored and frustrated in a foreign country and by their desertion having forfeited all claim to consideration by the Imperial Government, had largely to rely on their own resources. These men were in an especially awkward position. Many had not deserted from political conviction but from fear of death or simply because they could not stand army discipline and the war; but desertion was a capital offence in Germany and they could never have returned to their homeland had Germany won the war. Moreover, the only fellow Germans in the Netherlands who could or would associate with them were the radical exiles, so inevitably they fell easy prey to the revolutionaries.

When the armies of the First World War are thought of collectively, the image conjured up by the imagination is one of great faceless masses of conscripts, of uniform identity, as stereotyped and unindividual as the battles in which so many of their humble, expendable lives were lost. Because the war itself was so massive, the soldiers so numerous, and the casualty lists so harrowingly long, it is all too easy to forget that these armies were composed of men with feelings, pride, political beliefs of their own, men with secret terrors and men with social needs. These are the factors which influence men who are not constrained by law or discipline. Left to their own devices in the Netherlands, such men were temporarily free to be individuals again and seek the fellowship of others drifting just as aimlessly. One of the major deserters' clubs, led by a man called Rohbach, forged close links with Minster and swiftly became embroiled in his work and designs.

It seems probable, however, that both Minster's and Rohbach's organizations would have been left to flounder in poverty and insignificance had it not been for C's old naval colleague, Captain Richard Bolton Tinsley of His Majesty's Secret Service. Tinsley was a born intriguer with a crafty and complex mind. He also had a bent for adventure, and was unswervingly loyal and discreet. As has been seen, he did not work at all well with any but his closest colleagues, being frequently imperious, secretive and quarrelsome, nor did he like the idea of sharing what he regarded as his own special responsibilities with others. Nevertheless, he had imagination and this he could share with subordinates, inspiring them through that one personal trait to overcome obstacles which might otherwise have daunted them. Minster and Rohbach passed Tinsley enormous amounts of small-scale but vital information, giving him access to new deserters and permitting him to pump these men for information about the location and movement of units, the feelings of the soldiers and the civilians within Germany, the distribution and quality of foodstuffs, and tactical changes in the Army. Information of this calibre, constantly renewed by fresh adherents to the deserters' organizations, represented a major breakthrough by any standards.

The organizations of Minster and Rohbach were extensive, well-founded, enjoyed their own secret and secure communications with Germany and, most significantly, were composed entirely of Germans. They were men whose aims coincided with those advocated by Macdonogh, but what was needed was a means to subvert the German people. That means was propaganda. Not only were the organizations used as channels for British propaganda but they also produced their own propagandas independently of the British, which they pumped directly into Germany's industrial heartland and into the Army. When funds ran short Tinsley stepped in and used Secret Service funds to subscribe to 9000 copies of *Der Kampf* and so ensured its survival.[1] The infiltration of the German organizations in the Netherlands was vital because propaganda does not say the right things to the right people automatically, as if guided by some higher law. It has to be directed to its target, to the men and women who will read it and be convinced by it, and to convince these people effectively it must give them a message which is both credible and which appeals to them.

During his last months in France before his return to the War

1 Bruntz, op. cit., p. 74.

Office in December 1915, Macdonogh had been investigating the possibilities of persuading German soldiers to surrender or desert and he now expanded this idea. Within a short time of becoming DMI he created a new section, MI7(b) under Colonel W. E. 'Farmer' Davies, concealed behind the title 'Press, Publicity and Propaganda'. Davies was an officer of the regular army who had been seriously wounded and was no longer fit for active service; he was champing at the bit in his enforced idleness and ready to jump at any chance which gave him the opportunity to do something useful. Davies issued an invitation to the Army calling on all men with any literary experience to contact him. Kitchener's Army was full of men of talent in various fields and 'some thousands' from all ranks responded, composing their contributions when not engaged in the trenches. From these, twenty men were selected who, like Davies, were no longer fit for active service and these became the full-time staff of MI7(b).

The first major achievement of the new section was the creation of *Le Courier de l'air*, a newspaper designed to raise the morale of the civilians in occupied areas and keep them informed. By the spring of 1916 the section was already preparing and producing leaflets to be air-dropped on to German troops but with the advent of the subversive campaign the section's work and importance changed dramatically. As the internal situation in Germany worsened, the section extended its range to concentrate on exploiting the growing political and social divisions there in a campaign that would, in 1914, 1915 or even in 1916 have been seen as a wasteful irrelevance.

The section operated in complete secrecy, hence little is heard of its work compared with the extravagant claims voiced on behalf of Lord Northcliffe and Crewe House to the credit for the successful propaganda offensive. In a letter to the Official Historian, Davies wrote, 'The point is that MI7 did the real thing and, as with Secret Service, kept it completely dark. Even Macdonogh himself knew very little of the details and often said "I don't know what MI7 are doing but I do know there is no section can land me in a worse mess". He was satisfied implicitly to trust me and my successor (Julian Fisher). It was particularly necessary to keep the real doings hidden from anyone likely to blab or be got at even in the Section. Even I did not know all the doings that were done.'[1]

1 Edmonds Papers, loc. cit., VI/8, letter from Colonel W.E. Davies to Edmonds, 6 March 1943.

With all its work shrouded at the time in such secrecy it comes as no surprise to find that the official documents of MI7(b) were destroyed after the armistice on the grounds that they 'would have been too incriminating'. Secrecy was so closely maintained that the members of MI7(b), in the best traditions of the darker corners of British officialdom, remained silent about their work even after the publication of *Secrets of Crewe House* by Sir Campbell Stuart in 1920. This boastful book is widely accepted as the standard study of the propaganda offensive and has succeeded in establishing the claim that Crewe House, under Lord Northcliffe's direction, was responsible for its success. This claim is perfectly fictitious. The propaganda offensive was part of a much broader and deadlier strategy, masterminded by Macdonogh, who took the unprecedented step of writing to the Official Historian, recommending that, 'I hope you won't get Campbell-Stuart or Beaverbrook to write the history of it [propaganda]. "The Secret of Crewe House", as I once told C.S., was that it did nothing but use the material the War Office provided.'[1] Coming from the one man who should have known the truth if anybody did, this statement must carry weight.

The activities of the other parties engaged in propaganda – Crewe House, Lord Northcliffe, the Foreign Office, John Buchan, Masterman and Lord Beaverbrook – did little more than provide MI7(b) with necessary cover. The claims of Crewe House will not withstand even cursory examination, chiefly because in the length of time they were operating on the Western front it would have been impossible for them to achieve all Stuart claims for them. In the spring of 1918 MI7(b) was already distributing approximately one million leaflets to the Germans every month. In June they dropped 1,638,758; in July 2,292,699; in August 3,874,468; up to 27 September 3,270,754; in October 5,360,000; and in November until the armistice, 1,400,000. By the time Crewe House began to investigate the possibilities of attacking German morale, MI7(b) had already distributed no fewer than twelve million leaflets. The first Crewe House leaflets were not issued for distribution until 4 September 1918 and were not released until the 6th. In the light of these facts are we seriously to believe that Northcliffe and Crewe House destroyed German morale in barely two months? It is simply not credible. The very most they could have

1 Edmonds Papers, loc. cit., VI/8, letter from Lieutenant-General Sir George Macdonogh to Edmonds, 27 January 1932.

Major Edmund A. Wallinger.

AVIS

En vertu du jugement du Conseil de guerre de la Commandanture d'Etape 158 du 8.2.18. ont été

I. Condamnés à mort

1.) le maître d'école **Legrand** Henri, de Thiers,

2.) le tisseur **Beauvois** Nicolas, de Rieux,

3.) le garde municipal **Thuillez** Pierre-Joseph, de Rieux,

pour avoir recueilli un pigeon voyageur laissé tombé par l'ennemi et avoir relaché ce pigeon avec des nouvelles destinées à l'ennemi, au lieu de le remettre à l'autorité allemande.

II. Condamné à 10 ans de travaux forcés

le maire **Boudaillez** Edouard, de Rieux, complice de ce crime.

A. H. Qu., le 23 Février 1918.

Le Général-Commandant en Chef

gez. von der Marwitz

General der Kavallerie und Generaladjutant.

Sigismund Payne Best, 1918.

Lieutenant-General Sir George Macdonogh with Marshal Foch (*left*), saluting the coffin of the unknown warrior at Boulogne as it travelled to London, 1919.

(*Opposite*) German proclamation of death sentences for French subjects caught in possession of Allied carrier pigeons.

The daughters of the Tsar. *Left to right*: Marie, Tatiana (*seated*), Anastasia, Olga.

(*Left*) HRH The Grand Duke Mikhail Mikhailovitch.

HRH Prince Arthur of Connaught.

Lieutenant C. E. S. S. Eccles, 5th KRRC and 41st Light Mortar Battery, 1917.

(*Opposite*) The Grand Duchess Tatiana.

Brigadier-General John Charteris, Haig's chief of Intelligence.

achieved was the hastening of a process already far advanced. The credit really belongs to MI7(b) and the Directorate of Military Intelligence and stems directly from Macdonogh's decision in October 1917. The greatest propaganda success enjoyed by Lord Northcliffe and Crewe House lay in deceiving the British public who, lacking any other evidence, were only too ready to credit Stuart's spurious claims.

Despite the loss of the official papers belonging to MI7(b), there is one collection of documents which enables us to trace the section's progress and some of the details of its work.[1] This collection consists of the papers of Colonel A. N. Lee of the Sherwood Foresters who served as the section's representative in France, where he worked with Colonel Church who commanded Special Intelligence for GHQ. A high proportion of his papers are in fact official MI7(b) documents, suggesting that the colonel made use of the opportunity provided by the destruction of official files to 'liberate' many of those held at GHQ.

These papers show clearly that the section was seeking to sow revolutionary feelings as early as July 1917, for one document lists the propaganda pamphlets available at 28 July. These include a tract on 'The Revolution in Russia' and another, 'Was England zu dem Deutschen Friedensvorschlag denkt', which argues that Imperial Germany was a state founded on oppression. Even at this stage two documents were returned to MI7(b) on the grounds that they were 'inflammatory'; 'Kaiser und Krieg oder Republik und Frieden' and 'Republik bedeutet Friede und Freiheit!' Another, 'Das Freie Deutsche Wort', was returned because it was 'inflammatory in some parts'.[2]

The question of what constituted inflammatory propaganda and what did not is worthy of more detailed examination. The return of the offending pamphlets was in response to a complaint by the German Foreign Office to contents which attacked the Kaiser personally, depicting him as a warmonger and a coward bent on driving his people to death and ruin to preserve his own position. The German protest was merely the first round fired in an increasingly bitter war of words. The propaganda leaflets of 1917 were air-dropped and it was only a matter of time before an aeroplane on such a mission was brought down. On 17 October Lieutenants Scholtz and Wookey of

1 The Lee Collection, Department of Printed Books, IWM.
2 Ibid., P. 15, If29, 'Inflammatory Propaganda'.

No.11 Squadron, RFC, were shot down south-west of Cambrai. The leaflets they had been carrying, 'Deutsche Gefangene', 'S Konigs Klaroen', and *Le Courier de l'air* were in no sense 'inflammatory' but the Germans were alarmed by this new form of warfare and showed precisely what they thought of what they deemed uncivilized conduct by court-martialling both men before the Mobile Court of the German Commandant of the region on 1 December 1917[1] and pronouncing on them prison sentences of ten years. To make the point more strongly, they treated the officers as common criminals, which meant that they were deprived of the normal rights and dignities usually accorded to prisoners-of-war.

The German action was responsible for a considerable rethink within British Intelligence and on 3 February 1918 orders were issued to Headquarters RFC to halt the distribution of all propaganda until further notice. In fact Intelligence appear to have been on their guard since the return of pamphlets in July 1917 and the use of aeroplanes to drop inflammatory propaganda had been stopped immediately following the downing of Scholtz and Wookey. On 19 October, Colonel Church had written to the Brigadier-General Intelligence, John Charteris, proposing that shells and mortar bombs should be developed to replace aeroplanes as a means of transmission: 'The method suggested would be useful, especially as "inflammatory" material cannot now be distributed by 'plane and the amount which can be sent over by balloon is limited.'[2]

Far from being prepared to stop revolutionary propaganda, Intelligence simply imposed a temporary halt while seeking a safer method of delivering it. Shells and mortar bombs were studied far into 1918 and in October it was finally agreed that a mortar bomb would be the best means of firing propaganda across. However by then MI7(b) had developed a satisfactory alternative. Wireless had been considered but was abandoned due to technical difficulties and (remembering that private wireless was unavailable at the time) the unlikelihood of any German official making public any propaganda transmission that was received.

In the end Intelligence returned to their faithful standby, the free balloon, despite Church's reservations. The balloons then being used

1 Ibid., P. 62, If964 & 1044, 'Discontinuance of air distribution of propaganda by aeroplanes. Scholtz & Wookey Case'.

2 Ibid., If/P.33A, I(f)451, 'Experiments made to ascertain possibilities of finding out if propaganda can be fired over lines by shells, mortar bombs or grenades.'

by Intelligence were of fabric; in war-time conditions this was neither as plentiful nor as cheap as Intelligence could desire and anyway all available fabric balloons were already being pressed into service for carrying pigeons or agents. The answer to the problem was simplicity itself: paper was to replace fabric as the skin of the balloon. The paper balloons could be easily mass-produced to lift up to four pounds in weight and, as with pigeon baskets, a fuse cut to length according to wind speed and direction released the pamphlets as the balloons passed over their target.

It all took time. The loss of aeroplanes as a means of transmission could not immediately be made good. As late as 16 May 1918 Major the Lord Kerry of MI7(b) was having to tell Colonel Church that

> . . . the cause of the delay over the two P/W [prisoner of war] photograph Post Cards therein quoted was due to the fact that all printing of propaganda for aerial distribution was suspended from the time that distribution by aeroplane ceased, until paper balloons were available. They would have been sent to you rather earlier than was the case, but for your notification some month or so ago, that the immediate need was 'inflammatory' pamphlets.'[1]

Thus, within the bounds of the policy laid down – that propaganda could be inflammatory and actively seek to foment revolution, but should refrain from personal attacks on the Kaiser – it cannot be reasonably doubted that MI7(b) was bent on fanning the flames of internal discontent. The surviving examples of their aerial leaflets make this abundantly clear.

Leaflet AP11 'Soldaten Deutschlands' was revolutionary and anti-monarchist, emphasizing the futility of the German war effort and focused on the undemocratic nature of German politics. 'Die deutsche politische Reform dem Kriege zuzuschreiben – Die innere Zerklüftung Deutschlands' was not simply revolutionary but also commented on the growing divisions in Germany while contrasting this with the unity of the Allies and the increasing numbers of American troops in France. AP7, 'Deutsche Soldaten!' was calculated to be socially divisive, stressing how poorly fed and paid the German workers were in comparison with the industrialists and war profiteers. 'Sind Wir Freie Männer Oder Sklaven?' posed the question of whether the Germans were free men or slaves, while 'Die Sklaverei des deutschen

1 Ibid., P. 15, If29 'Inflammatory Propaganda', Kerry to Church C.P.(c)881 & 900.

Volkes' really answered this question by proposing that the Germans were slaves and should free themselves by revolution. There are many others in the same vein.[1]

It was one thing to bombard the Germans with this mighty weight of paper, but how could its influence be assessed, especially when set against other influences, such as Bolshevism? The way MI7(b) tackled this problem was to turn to the nearest source of first-hand evidence – German prisoners-of-war. The Lee Collection shows plainly that this was done and that questionnaires on political issues were devised in conjunction with MI2(e) to discover the best types of propaganda and to evaluate the appeal of existing leaflets. The earliest such questionnaire in the Lee Collection dates from May 1918[2] and the questions were successively updated as the war ground on. Part of one from August 1918 is clearly trying to discern the political awareness of the German soldier:

Lichnowsky.
Was the Lichnowsky memorandum discussed in your regiment?
Had you heard of it before it was published in 'Vorwärts' and the other papers?
What do you think of its effect?
Did it effect [sic] your views at all?

Max Harden.
What is his present position and influence?
Is the 'Zukunft' much read?

Moral and Political.
Have you heard of the crew of the 'Derfflinger' throwing their officers overboard, or of other mutinous movements in the Navy?
Is there any *organization* of a seditious character in the army?
Do you think the present offensive will finish the war?
Of which member of the Reichstag do you think most highly?
Have you ever seen any of the Spartacus letters and pamphlets?
Do you think the people at home are any easier in their minds than they were a year ago?
Is it true that investment in war loans is one way of getting leave?
Are civilians compelled to invest in war loans?

1 All examples are from the Aerial Leaflet Collection, 1914–1918, File No. 3 (41:43) Numeric, and File No. 3 (41:43) Uc, IWM.

2 Lee Collection, loc. cit., P. 65 C.P.(c) 1003 'Interrogation of Prisoners re – Propaganda effects', I(g)170/125, Questionnaire on Political Matters.

> Have you had any experience of air-raids, in the war-zone, or outside it?
>
> What is the effect on the civilian population?[1]

The results of the propaganda offensive were assessed in monthly evaluations, based on returns from each army in the line. In some cases prisoners felt that inflammatory propaganda was a waste of time and this was reflected in the analysis that 'political cartoons and discussions of German political intrigue and of their responsibility for the war have little value' and 'it is held that the average leaflet though neat and convincing is rarely read and that revolutionary leaflets fail to effect much. This is twice stated.'[2]

On 5 November, Lieutenant-Colonel Ryan of the First Army sent in a bleak report which poured cold water on the idea of fomenting revolution in Germany:

> Leaflets laying too much emphasis on a revolution (as in Russia) do not seem to have had the effect desired. The German soldiers are afraid of a revolution and would fight against it.
>
> Leaflets pointing out the need of a change in the German Government before they can obtain peace are good, but the prisoners want a peaceful change of Government and not one as in Russia.[3]

Naturally, one should not expect all the prisoners to speak with one voice, but there were a greater number of prisoners whose opinions ran utterly counter to those cited above. For example, the same report which doubted the value of revolutionary propaganda also noted, 'The betrayal and deception of men by their leaders. This is twice put forward,' as was 'The hardships of German families at home, owing to the continuation of the struggle.'[4] One German soldier, from the 15th Reserve Infanterie Regiment, stated on 19 October that: 'The leaflets treated most seriously are those pointing out the interests of Capitalists in the war.'[5]

The officer compiling the report, Captain E. N. Hale, observed that 'nearly every prisoner interrogated mentioned this subject voluntarily' and 'They also read with interest arguments and advantages of Representative Government. They are firmly convinced that nearly all

1 Ibid., 58B, I(g) 170/125, 25 August 1918.
2 Ibid., P.74 C.P.(e) 1724, 'Suggestions by Corps and Divisions regarding balloon Propaganda'.
3 Ibid. First Army No.448 (IG).
4 Ibid., 58B, I(g) 170/125, 25 August 1918.
5 Ibid., P.74 C.P.(e) 1724, 'Suggestions by Corps and Divisions regarding balloon Propaganda'.

the German populace have no special desire to retain the Hohenzollerns.'[1]

Other men from the 88th Infanterie Regiment and the 115th (Baden) Liebgarde Regiment left their interrogators firmly convinced that 'In reading reports sent in it is noteworthy that the prisoners interrogated on the subjects of propaganda talked freely of internal and future problems in Germany.'[2]

Even more important is another report from the First Army which contrasts boldly with Lieutenant-Colonel Ryan's dismal conclusions:

> Propaganda dealing with the subject of militarism are [sic] much discussed by German soldiers with British prisoners of war, and have made a great impression on the former. German soldiers say, however, that the facsimile letters from German prisoners of war in England are not considered genuine.[3]

Further evidence is apparent in a letter written by Captain H. Miller to Captain Hazeldine of I(b), which reported that:

> The German soldiers in Roubaix are very badly fed at present and are making great complaints aginst the capitalists, who, according to them, are responsible for the war.
>
> *Note*. This appears to be a matter to be harped upon in British propaganda.[4]

Other information for directing the propaganda campaign and assessing its effect came from *repatriés* who had recently been living amongst the Germans. One citizen of Bruay picked up leaflets at Grand Han and Eneille

> . . . inciting German troops to join in a general revolution against the continuation of the war. It appears that many papers of this nature are now being distributed throughout Belgium. Informant did not know whether this was Allied propaganda or internal propaganda by revolutionary Germans.[5]

Another, from Halluin, repatriated on 7 September, revealed how deep the cleft was in German ranks:

1 Ibid., P.74, C.P.(e) 1724, 'Suggestions by Corps and Divisions'.
2 Ibid.
3 Ibid., P.24, C.P.(c) 'Reports on the working of Allied Propaganda behind the line', First Army No.448 (IG).
4 Ibid., Captain Miller to Captain Hazeldine, I(b)1319 C.416, 7 October 1918.
5 Ibid., I(b) 1319/C.401, 22 September 1918.

> Before informant left a considerable number of leaflets were thrown by aeroplane. They certainly demoralised the troops, and there were frequent brawls between those who were demoralised and those who remain patriotic.[1]

The balance between the reports saying that revolutionary propaganda was having minimal effect and those showing that it was having very considerable effect comes down massively in favour of the latter. No doubt there were particular zones where loyal, dedicated troops still fought with the spirit of patriotism and dedication, but the mass of the German Army had simply had enough and were turning to revolution as an escape from hell. The assessments made by the MI7(b) officers at GHQ bear this out. Their records of prisoners' statements led them to the conclusion that balloon propaganda was creating a considerable effect, as much by the number of leaflets as by their contents. They could report that:

> Nearly all prisoners state that the leaflets are eagerly sought for and discussed and, while many maintain that this is only out of curiosity or for the purpose of souvenir hunting and state that they disbelieved or laughed at the contents, others say that they have sent the leaflets home to Germany, that these put new ideas into their heads about the Allied views on the war and show them the other side of the picture.[2]

A brisk evaluation of the effect of revolutionary propaganda on the front of First Army, dated 5 September, summed up the situation:

> A prisoner of the 15th Reserve Division, who was recently on leave in Germany, when in company with some Bavarians, was shown a number of revolutionary pamphlets which he states have been widely circulated amongst Bavarians. They were all violently anti-Prussian and appealed to the men to refuse to fight.
>
> A number of prisoners captured recently have spoken of the distribution of pacifist and revolutionary pamphlets amongst the troops.[3]

Perhaps the best way of all of measuring the impact of British revolutionary propaganda is to look at the reaction of the German authorities. They were terrified. Many of the leaflets were sent home

1 Ibid., I(b) 1319/C.412, 28 September 1918.
2 Ibid., T.7. 'Report On Prisoners' Statements Relating to Propaganda', n.d.
3 Ibid., P.65, C.P.(c)1003, 'Interrogation of Prisoners re-Propaganda effects, Extracts from First Army Summary No.1330, Revolutionary Propaganda'.

to Germany and this alarmed the German command more than any other single aspect. They protested through their Foreign Office, they imprisoned two officers of the RFC, and they issued strict orders to the Army that men finding such leaflets were to hand them in forthwith. The orders were ignored and reports reaching the British from occupied Gembloux related that the Germans 'feared the consequences of these leaflets being taken home by the troops.'[1] Attempts to stem the flood were useless, as can be seen in the complaint of Colonel Nicolai, who wrote that 'no fewer' than 300,000 pamphlets were surrendered in one army area alone in July 1918 and 'the number of those not delivered could not have been small'.[2]

The subversive campaign, controlled and directed by Intelligence, was nothing less than a deliberate, calculated attempt to transfer the power to make peace or war from the Imperial Government to the people. In focusing on the social dimension, Macdonogh had gone straight to the heart of the matter. In the War Ministry in Berlin, General-Major von Wrisberg, Director of the National War Department, complained sourly that reports received at the ministry indicated that 'It is almost certain that there is in Germany a secret committee of central authority, which works under English authority and unlimited English financial aid in conjunction with the radical elements of the Social Democrats for a revolution among the German working class.'[3] Like Nicolai of the German Secret Service, he realized that a considerable amount of subversive material was both written and distributed by Germans. A case in point is a letter sent in April 1918 from Malmö in Sweden to an address in Sumatra. It enclosed the seventeenth in a series of four-page pamphlets printed in Switzerland and entitled 'Das Freie Deutsche Wort' (German Free Speech) and was intercepted by the Royal Navy's East Indies Station. The pamphlet is violently anti-Prussian, almost pro-Ally in sentiment, and its socialist bias is transparent. It begins with the following heavy-type introduction:

> The number of German Republicans, Democrats and Socialdemocrats, who have had to flee to neutral countries for fear of arrest, increases daily. Others who on account of their political views and in

1 Ibid, P.24, CPc 'Reports on the working of Allied Propaganda behind the line', Avian. 403/18/9/18. I(b) 1319c.
2 Nicolai, op. cit., pp. 162–3.
3 Bruntz, op. cit., p. 79.

> spite of age and infirmity have been put into the fieldgrey uniform have gone over to the enemy; they have been treated well and have found freedom there. They all have but one single wish: to acquaint the German people with the truth, to snatch the bandage from their eyes, etc . . .[1]

The pamphlet closes with another heavily typed paragraph bearing the threatening message:

> We have succeeded in having the following impressed upon all French soldiers: whoever gives himself up as prisoner (i.e. to the French) and mentions the password 'Republic' will be treated with the greatest kindness. If he wishes, he will be allowed to work for the Freedom of Germany with compatriots who are of a like mind.
>
> To our kin at home: Spread the truth, spread this paper, agitate for the German Republic.[2]

In Zurich, in neutral Switzerland, the British Consulate used the services of a naturalized Swiss called Wolfsohn, in actual fact a renegade Prussian named Mendelbaum, to propagate the word. Mendelbaum was a convinced socialist who, in common with Romulus and the members of the Briefeinfall ring, passionately believed that the road to the triumph of socialism ran through the ruin of Prussian militarism. Under his aegis several liberal and socialist 'confidants' within Germany were used to spread the seeds of doubt, despair and rebellion, and his British paymasters – perhaps puppeteers would be a better word – ensured that he wanted for nothing in the pursuit of the common goal. An American who worked under Mendelbaum, John Kern, summed up the motive force when he wrote,

> It is right that the authors of the printed materials should be mostly Germans who are trying to democratize their country. In Germany we possess many confidants, namely under the Socialists and among the working class, who are working hand in hand with us. The circle is getting larger. We hope for success soon and then for peace.[3]

Other Germans co-operated for less noble reasons. Herr Grohmann, a tailor in Hamburg, struck a bargain with the British whereby he was able to circumvent the blockade and smuggle rubber into Germany, in return for which he also accepted propaganda and distributed it in Hamburg and its environs. His motive was simplicity itself: handsome

1 'General Letters No. 131, April 1918', PRO ADM 125/66.
2 Ibid.
3 Bruntz, op. cit., p. 183.

profits. Rubber was otherwise unobtainable and the little that could be smuggled in fetched huge prices, especially on the black market.

Far more dangerous than any individual, however, was the increasingly militant stance of the radical parties. The main extra-parliamentary weapon of the USPD was strike action in the factories. They had made an all-out effort in January 1918 with a great national strike which they hoped would paralyze Germany to the extent where the Imperial Government would be forced to stop the war against the infant Bolshevik Russia. The Government broke the strike and arrested the USPD activists behind it, calling them up and sending them to the front in the process. The USPD had both to cope with its failure and the more extreme members of the party, now convinced that strikes alone could not force the Government to its knees and advocating the use of arms. One of their leaders, Ledebour, speaking at the General Congress of Workmen's and Soldiers' Councils of Germany in December 1918, said:

> They obtained weapons, they enlisted recruits, and we others who co-operated with them to a certain extent, influenced our workmen . . . Besides, we had not only made preparations in Berlin but had established relations with all the provinces.[1]

His colleague, Vater, speaking at Magdeburg in December 1918 also made it plain that 'the revolution did not come as a surprise to us. We had been systematically preparing for it since January 25, 1918.'[2]

These extraordinary, even unnatural proceedings, are entirely contrary to the standard of behaviour one might expect from a country's inhabitants in a time of severe trial. But not only was the age when entire populations could be manipulated by outside propaganda just dawning; the powerful example of the Bolshevik revolution appealed to many Germans.

Two of the battalions which went to form the Red Army when it first came into being were recruited from German socialists, who marched and fought together as such. At the first-ever parade of the Red Army in Moscow in April 1918, these German battalions proudly took their place alongside their Russian comrades. One of the spectators watching the parade was Count von Mirbach, the German Ambassador to the Soviet State, who was driven to paroxysms of rage

1 Ibid.
2 Ibid.

and anguish on witnessing his fellow countrymen marching under the Red Flag.[1] Before the year was out thousands more of their comrades would be fighting alongside them under the same banner, men who were instrumental in blocking the advance of the Czecho-Slovak Legion and Kolchak's White Army. The Bolsheviks, driven by the vision of worldwide revolution, emphasized the German connection – after all, had not the founding fathers of communism, Marx and Engels, both been born German, and had not Marx prophesied that Germany would be *the* country in which the world revolution would start? Lenin was clear about his expectations in this direction. Before leaving for Russia he had spoken to the Swiss workers at the beginning of April 1917, telling them that 'We will . . . carry on a revolutionary struggle against the Germans . . . the German proletariat is the most trustworthy, most reliable ally of the Russian and the world proletarian revolutions.'[2]

The strikers' directorate in Berlin which co-ordinated the struggle in January 1918 did indeed set forth revolutionary demands, including the relaxation of food restrictions; an amnesty for political offenders; the restoration of political rights abolished by the Law of Siege, such as the right of political assembly; the democratization of the Government; immediate peace on the basis of no annexations and no indemnities; and the participation of workers' delegates at the peace negotiations. These demands were unashamedly and unequivocally political and, had they been met, would have established an entirely new political and social balance of power within Germany, entirely uprooting and destroying the mastery of the landowners, industrialists and Hohenzollerns just as effectively as any revolution. Of 772 strikes in 1918, Helmut Koch has found that 531 were political strikes as opposed to 241 which were economically motivated; 7,396 factories were affected, of which 6,302 fell victim to political strikes and only 1,094 were disrupted by economic strikes; 5,227,982 working days were lost, 3,776,456 through political action compared with 1,451,526 which can fairly be attributed to economic grievances.

The great German spring offensive of 1918 can now be seen in a new light. Some members of the German General Staff were only too well aware of what was happening to their country and knew that only victory in the field could stave off revolution. It had to be now or

1 *See* R.B. Lockhart, *Comes the Reckoning*, London, 1947, p. 233.
2 Lenin, *Collected Works* (English edition, 1930), Vol. XX, pp. 85–7.

never: Germany could not withstand another year with her long-suffering people spreadeagled on the cross of starvation and internal dissent. This was the main motive for their last desperate gamble, and they knew that if the dice rolled against them the consequences would be dire indeed. At the beginning of the final year of the war German morale received a tremendous supercharge from the collapse of Russia and the prospect of a swift victory in the West. An almost mystical enthusiasm bordering on the excesses of August 1914 fired the faithful in the German Army. At the War Office Richard Meinertzhagen had no hesitation in divining the motives behind Germany's last throw:

> I believe the whole situation is an effort to stave off revolution. If Germany fails she gets her revolution for a certainty, if she succeeds, both we and France and Italy will suffer from Civil disturbances which will cripple us and enable the Hun to trample us under foot, a game he can play right well and which he will not be slow to avail himself of.[1]

The Spartacist, Ernst Meyer, wrote to Lenin on 5 September 1918:

> In the army resistance is increasing, and among the workers the realization is growing that the old methods of parliamentary opposition and demonstrative resistance are no longer sufficient. The events in Russia have taught a lesson and provided an example which cannot be overlooked.[2]

The Allies introduced a new chorus to the opera of confusion by announcing their adherence to the Fourteen Points of President Wilson, which had been presented on 8 January. In the mind of the idealistic President, his structure for a new world, founded on principles of justice and national self-determination, was the way forward to a new enlightenment where peace and integrity would dictate the course of international relations. The President's Allied counterparts took a cynical view of the new commandments. Clemenceau, Prime Minister of France, contemptuously exclaimed upon hearing of them: 'Quatorze commandements! C'est un peu raide! Le bon Dieu n'en avait que dix!' Although the points were not designed as a propaganda ploy, they proved to be propaganda of an eminently astute kind, firing the flagging emotions of a dreadfully fatigued world whose people had grown sick of war without end and despair without redemption. For all their high-mindedness, the fourteen points sounded especially plausible and convincing to the exhausted

1 Meinertzhagen Diaries, op. cit., 12 February 1918.

2 Cited by H. Koch in 'Collapse of Germany', Purnell's *History of the First World War*, London, 1968-70.

people of Germany, offering as they did an honourable way out of their predicament.

The German Army had only one card left to play, and they had to play it; the great spring Offensive of 1918. With the defeat of this final bid, all that Meinertzhagen had prophesied and Macdonogh had worked for welled up to defeat the German war machine.

Picture the plight of the Germans in the summer of 1918 – bewildered, battered from all sides, torn this way and that by competing forces which were too large and complex to be comprehended when their immediate concerns were empty bellies, starving children, shoddy clothing and the challenge of an awesome array of scintillating new ideas which promised justice, peace and plenty to a spiritually enervated people. Pulled in one direction by their instinctive patriotism and the blandishments of a General Staff which continued to assure them that all was well, pulled in another by enormous losses and obvious defeats, and in still another by the flourishing communist ideals fed and watered by subversion and the propaganda of MI7(b). Something had to give. With the defeats that summer it was the anxious hope of relief through victory that snapped, bringing in its train confusion and bitter resentment. The tendency of people to hope against hope, even in desperate situations, is one of the most endearing of human attributes. Hope makes all the difference in outlook between a long stretch in purgatory and an eternity in hell; deprived of their last hope, millions of Germans decided that the latter prospect was one they could not and would not bear.

It was the will of the ordinary soldiers, the Poor Bloody Infantry, which gave first. Yet the term 'soldiers' was a misleading one by mid-1918. These men were not the disciplined and well-trained professionals of August 1914, but citizens-in-arms, many of them with only six weeks' basic training behind them. Many, too, were very young, little more than boys – so serious had the German manpower situation become that Ludendorff even considered the conscription of fifteen-year-old boys from the German-occupied Ukraine. Young and impressionable, they were familiar with the propaganda prepared by MI7(b). Before the war the rank and file of the German Army had been drawn largely from the rural areas of the Empire, tough, healthy, trustworthy countrymen who were used to obedience, hard work and long hours. David Nash of the Imperial War Museum describes exactly the change in character of the men in the German Army:

> The Army set its face against recruiting men from industrialized areas for the stated reason that the countryman was better physically suited to military life. Bernhardi even went so far as to dismiss town dwellers as weaklings and drunkards. The true reason for the unpopularity of these recruits, however, was that they tended to be socialist in inclination and belief, and they were seen as a disruptive element in a solidly conservative Army . . . The war injected into the Army the very element that it had tried to exclude, and it could be argued that one of the reasons for its disintegration in 1918 was the widespread revolutionary propaganda that was spread throughout its structure by some of these conscripted malcontents.[1]

Not only were the rank and file discontented. The Imperial Government had indeed thought to break strikes by conscripting many of the ringleaders, but this ploy backfired on them. Such men promoted mutiny, dereliction of duty and desertion. They were actively involved in distributing revolutionary propaganda amongst the troops and harvested their reward in the summer of 1918. As late as 1922 some of those who had carried the message of despair and revolution into the ranks of the Army were still gloating over their achievement. At a meeting of the USPD in Andernach on 5 February 1922, the party's secretary, Rosendal boasted: 'Even I myself did nothing since 1918, when I had already been sent to the front three times, but try to work as leaven and undermine the front.'[2]

The results are well known. Desertion and shirking were rampant, with tens of thousands of men slipping away en route to the front, exacerbating Germany's already grave shortage of men. Heinrich Brüning, a member of the moderate Centre Party and one of the last Chancellors of the short-lived Weimar Republic, was an infantry lieutenant in 1918 and wrote of his surprise when, towards the end of the war, he found that desertion did not occur as isolated instances but as a mass phenomenon. Hordes of deserters infested the German rear areas, skulking in attics in Brussels and other Belgian cities. Officers' patrols were even sent into Namur in a bid to round up miscreants there, because the Military Police were unable to cope with the size of the problem.

1 D.B. Nash, *Imperial German Army Handbook 1914–1918*, London, 1980, p. 19.
2 R.H. Lutz (trans. by W.L. Campbell), *The Causes of The German Collapse in 1918*. Sections of the officially authorized report of the Commission of the German Constituent Assembly and of the German Reichstag, 1919–28, the selection and translation officially approved by the commission, Stanford University Press, 1934 (reprint by Archon Books, 1969), p. 139..

At the front the situation was, if anything, even worse. Men surrendered to the Allies in droves, thus explaining how the British Army captured over 188,000 Germans in the last great offensive of the war. It is well-known, too, how the German reserves, moving up to retrieve the situation on 8 August, were greeted by retiring troops with shouts of 'Blacklegs! Strikebreakers! War-Prolongers!', terms normally the hallmark of industrial disputes rather than military mutinies. It speaks volumes about both the spread of the rot within Germany and the character of the men serving in the Army. It was this refusal to fight on which led Ludendorff to call 8 August 'the Black Day of the German Army' and forced him to recognize that German fighting power had declined beyond all doubt. Germany had introduced the concept of 'the nation in arms' to the world and now the German nation was no longer willing to bear arms against those whom the Imperial Government classed as enemies.

It is a home truth of every revolution that revolutionaries are defeated if the armed forces of the state stand against them. In the Germany of 1918 the Army actually became the spearhead of revolution. It was not the Stars and Stripes, the Union Flag or the Tricolour which was hoisted at Kiel and Berlin in that grey, dank November of 1918, but the Red Flag. It was not Allied soldiers from whom the Kaiser and the petty princelings of Germany fled, but their own people in arms against them.

There are those who affect to pretend that the German collapse owed nothing to internal conditions but was due solely to defeat in the field, the revolution only bothering to raise its head once everything had been sealed and settled at the front. Such an attitude betrays a lack of insight into the nature of total war, omitting as it does the social dimension of the conflict and the fact that revolutions have to be planned and prepared.

Military operations were but one side of the coin, the internal stresses of German society the other. George Macdonogh and the staff of British Military Intelligence had the wisdom and the wit to ensure that the two walked hand in hand. Military Operations came to be regarded as a necessary adjunct to a very much wider struggle. They were used to create the first chink in the armour of German morale; after that subversion and propaganda were the points inserted to prise that armour open, together with the Allied refusal to treat with the Imperial Government. Together with the collapse of Germany's allies, it was the fact that the people of Germany would no longer fight, irrespective of whether they were soldiers or civilians, that ended the war in 1918. Without this collapse the war could easily have dragged on into 1919. Even the later Allied victories on the battlefield were themselves the fruit of Germany's moral decay, and those victories achieved still greater results through their effect on the home front. Had not the subversive campaign tilled the soil, the German revolution which ended the war – just as Bloch had said it would – could never have taken place and the OHL could have continued to fight.

They certainly proposed to continue the fight, for due to the faltering of the Allied advance they could anticipate the necessary breathing space for regrouping and fighting on in order to obtain better armistice terms. In November the OHL had decided to fall back on the Antwerp-Meuse line, a formidable position from which they could reasonably expect to hold off the Allies. Reasonably expect not simply on the grounds that the position was a strong one, but because the Allies were by this time running into considerable difficulties through fatigue and that bane of all generals, logistical problems. It is a moot point whether the pursuit could have been pressed any further at that time. One need only look at the British Second Army after the armistice to appreciate the difficulties encountered. Following four days' rest immediately after the armistice, the Second Army began to move towards Germany. It was the only British army advancing since more troops were unnecessary now that the fighting had stopped, so it did not have to compete with other forces for road or rail space or for food. Nor did it have to contend with the systematic demolition of roads, railways, bridges and water supplies which retreating armies leave in their wake to embarrass their pursuers. It sounds a simple task. Yet the Second Army's War Diary reveals that it was anything but easy, and it ought to be remembered that War Diaries tend to be bland and factual and do not give a reader any impression of what it was like to march over a blasted, cratered landscape burdened with pack, rifle, ammunition, rations and wearing a jock-strap. The Diary relates how 'the narrow one-way roads in the area through which the advance was carried out and the slippery state of these roads made it essential to reduce to the greatest extent that the tactical situation allowed, the number of troops to be supplied in the forward area, if the advance was to continue undelayed'.[1]

The Second Army was forced to leave all the heavy artillery several

1 Second Army War Diary, PRO WO 95/277.

days' march behind the leading Corps: supply trains were reaching the advance railheads 48 hours behind schedule. Thus the 1st Canadian Division had to cancel its march on 29 November since it had no supplies for its men. How could an army in this condition ever have hoped to wrest the fortified Antwerp-Meuse line from dedicated defenders? They would have needed all the artillery and engineering stores they could get, and many more men than they had. By the time these necessities had reached the front and a major assault been prepared, winter would have closed in and made further effort that year worthless. As it was, the German General Staff had to accept defeat as best they could. The subversive campaign had converted defeat into irretrievable disaster for the Germans, for which the credit belongs to Macdonogh, to British Military Intelligence and to those Germans who aided and abetted them.

The propaganda campaign of 1917–18 was the greatest the world has yet seen, in scale, in scope and in achievement. There has never been anything like it before or since, and subsequent campaigns have been naïve in comparison. One of the chief reasons for this has been that propaganda has always been studied in isolation, whereas it should be seen as part of a much wider campaign of subversion in economic and social matters within which military operations are an integral part. It should exploit existing conditions rather than attempt to create them.

Macdonogh was one of those characters who, throughout history, have worked quietly in the background, attracting very little public scrutiny yet affecting the fate of millions. It was his genius which rose above the war of masses – massed infantry, massed artillery, mass reserves, mass sentiment, mass bureaucracy and massive industry. In modern total wars there is rarely an opportunity for any individual to be a Caesar, a Frederick or a Napoleon, to influence the fate of nations at the decisive moment. Yet here is a case where the right man was in the right place at the right time, a man who unseen was able because of his insight to turn the great struggle on to a new axis.

Lip service is usually paid to Macdonogh as the 'best DMI this country has ever had'[1] but there is rarely a word as to why he should have been so. His greatest achievement lay in his recognition that the war was a total war and therefore incredibly complex, with all the factors being inter-related and inter-dependent. Neither operations

1 Marshall-Cornwall interview, loc. cit.

nor subversion could win the war alone. Certainly, the military collapse of the German armies preceded the internal collapse, but the fact that there was such a military collapse owed everything to Intelligence. It was Intelligence that had recognized the drift of the German domestic crisis and perceived that the German Government was incapable of surmounting the barriers erected by a political society it was neither able to control nor, because of its conservative proclivities, able to transform. Though nothing can or should detract from the heroic sacrifices made by most of the German people, the country's deep internal schisms existed and were brilliantly exploited with great foresight by Intelligence over the period 1917–18.

The effect of this strategy travelled well beyond the First World War. Most immediately it helped sow the seeds of grave political instability throughout Europe, though it was by no means solely responsible for this. The strains of total war, the near-starvation, the strength of the Bolshevik influence, all played their part in bringing the old order crashing down. The revolutionary ferment which gripped the Central Powers was neither entirely home-grown nor accidental, but spread in great part through the powerful catalyst applied by British Military Intelligence. As Major-General J. Pilch, later head of Hungarian Intelligence, wrote: '. . . subversion did not operate or occur in isolation – British Military Intelligence has supported it to a very significant extent.'[1] Pilch's book, a massive three-volume work, addressed an intelligent and educated audience, written as it was for limited circulation among the officers of Hungarian Military Intelligence. A few years after its publication the British sought to resurrect identical tactics to bring Hitler down. Thus it was that one of the veterans of the Secret Service in the First World War, Sigismund Payne Best, went to Venlo on the Dutch-German border in 1940 to meet German dissidents who allegedly wished to overthrow Hitler and the Nazis. The Germans were on the alert and this led to the famous Venlo incident, when Best and his associate, Captain Stevens, were kidnapped by the Gestapo and their Dutch escort shot dead. Not only did this temporarily discredit the Secret Service but it helped provide the Germans with an excuse to invade the Netherlands, on the grounds that British Intelligence were operating there.

So taken with the success of the First World War's subversive

1 Major-General J. Pilch, *The History of Intelligence and Espionage*, 1935, Vol. III.

campaign were the British that in 1938 a new section of the Secret Service had been formed, Section D, with the specific objective of managing sabotage and subversion in enemy states. Unfortunately it was formed too late, was provided with hopelessly inadequate resources and lacked a full-time staff with the necessary expertise. It could not hope to outface an enemy prepared by bitter experience to meet this sort of attack. Not only that, but conditions had undergone a fundamental change since 1917. The enemy was now a ruthless, totalitarian, one-party fascist state where all forms of overt political opposition were viciously and effectively suppressed. Nevertheless Section D later developed into a new group, the Special Operations Executive, which brought to a fine art a practice which the Secret Service had been intending to use in Belgium in 1918, that of fostering armed resistance to an aggressor.

Perhaps even more important was the enforced separation of Propaganda and Intelligence. As has been shown, the propaganda offensive of the First World War was the brainchild of George Macdonogh and 'Farmer' Davies, and the misreading of the lessons of this campaign was a monumental blunder. Placing the propaganda campaign in the Second World War in the hands of the press barons, *à la* Campbell Stuart, set the offensive off on quite the wrong foot. While British propaganda was naturally effective with the peoples in territories occupied by the Nazis, it failed to strike so much as a spark of resistance amongst the people who really mattered, the Germans themselves. Only they could actually overthrow Hitler from within (and thereby save the lives of many Allied servicemen) and the chance went a-begging.

The story of the 'stab in the back', in which the heroic German Army of the First World War was supposed to have been treacherously betrayed by the cowardly civilians and 'November Criminals', made excellent propaganda for Hitler, but his was an extreme position. The Allies, however, swung dramatically to the opposite extreme which was equally absurd, denying that there had ever been anything other than a purely military victory in 1918. They went out of their way in 1945 to overrun Germany physically by force of arms, irrespective of the cost, to ensure that such a story could never again be used as an excuse by any future German dictator. They achieved their aim, but Germany is today divided and the Red Army is on the River Elbe. There is an old Latin tag which translates as 'Who benefits?' Certainly not those Germans who actively opposed Hitler.

When all is said and done, the subversive campaign of 1917–18 remains a model of its kind which can be said to have shortened the war by at least one year. Macdonogh and his lieutenants have never been given due credit for this, something all the more strange since it stands as one of the few examples in a war of masses (in which circumstances habitually ran away with the men caught up in them) of far-sighted men actually seizing circumstances by the scruff of the neck and forcing them to a conclusion.

Even more significantly, the propaganda campaign may be regarded as the true beginning of centralized society, where the lives and fortunes of citizens are made subject to state authority, with all which that means in terms of the erosion of civil rights and liberties. During the First World War the idea of total state control was established everywhere. Intelligence, both offensive and defensive, was the key to this terrifying new departure. The control and direction of vast numbers of people, often against their better judgement and inclination, is a legacy of the war which is still very much a part of our lives today, a legacy which all post-1918 governments have contrived to fasten ever more thoroughly onto the backs of their citizens. It was the experience gained during the First World War that ensured internal cohesion and the crushing of free will in the Second World War if expressed in opposition to the government, and the continued manipulation of people's wills into the Cold War. Propaganda is still the most potent weapon in the arsenal of any state, totalitarian or otherwise.

TEN

Haig and Charteris

AMONG the broad themes discussed in this book, two in particular come together to some degree in this chapter: the idea of a General Staff Mentality and the disagreements between various British chiefs, whether among the various Intelligence sections or between Intelligence and Operations. The question considered here concerns the stance of Field-Marshal Sir Douglas Haig chiefly during the period 1917-18 and the influence exerted on him by his head of Intelligence, John Charteris.

Charteris has had many critics who have attributed to him an extensive and nefarious influence, the most prominent and influential of them being General Marshall-Cornwall who served on Haig's Intelligence Staff as a GSO2 in 1916 and 1917. He wrote that after arriving at GHQ,

> I soon discovered that the views held by Charteris, and reported by him to Sir Douglas Haig, regarding Germany's manpower reserves, morale and economic resources, differed widely from the estimates made by the Director of Military Intelligence at War Office, Major-General George Macdonough [sic], and submitted by him to the CIGS, Sir William Robertson. Macdonough [sic], assisted by Colonel Edgar Cox, the head of MI3, combined the best Intelligence brains at the disposal of the country. Charteris, however, with breezy optimism, disregarded the sounder and more cautious forecasts which emanated from the War Office and were submitted to the War Cabinet. Consequently the GHQ Intelligence Summaries seemed designed to bolster up our own morale rather than to present a true picture of the enemy's strength and fighting qualities.[1]

Charteris, Marshall-Cornwall claimed,

> . . . had an almost mesmeric influence on Haig who was fascinated by his quick-witted humorous form of talk, being rather a shy and reserved person himself and he gradually became a slave to Charteris's

1 'Experiences of an Intelligence Officer in World Wars 1 and 2, The Memoirs of General Sir James Marshall-Cornwall, KCB, CBE, DSO, MC', Chapter III, p.3., unpublished manuscript, ICMA.

> influence . . . [Charteris] was a very nimble-minded, quick-witted person, he had the gift of the gab, very persuasive and all wrong-headed in the way that he always felt that his main object in life was to maintain the morale of his Commander-in-Chief who trusted him implicitly.[1]

He believed that 'Haig tended to turn to him rather than to his own Chief of General Staff, the rather colourless Sir Launcelot Kiggell, as a personal adviser on all matters.'[2] Marshall-Cornwall's view was that Charteris' main objective was to maintain Haig's morale: 'He felt that his principal duty was to sustain the morale of his chief by painting the situation in the rosiest colours and ignoring unpleasant factors. This motive inevitably led to a combination of *suppressio veri* and *suggestio falsi*.'[3] According to Marshall-Cornwall, Charteris deliberately misled Haig but 'honestly thought that by suppressing all pessimistic evidence about enemy potential, moral and physical, he was strengthening his chief's determination to win the war'.[4]

In the view of another historian, Haig was similarly drawn to Sir Hubert Gough, Commander of the Fifth Army, in whom Haig 'saw a man able to establish quickly and easily a relationship with anyone, and there are indications that this facility fascinated him. He admired his wit, not least when it was a touch ironical.'[5]

Any assessment of Charteris's influence in determining Haig's strategy must consider whether or not Charteris genuinely believed what he was saying; whether or not Haig was as optimistic as Charteris; and whether or not Haig had his own ideas about the course of the war over which Charteris had little influence. On the face of it Haig does not seem the sort of man who would permit such intervention. As Charteris wrote to Liddell Hart:

> He had deep confidence in his own judgement on facts within his own knowledge or which (lacking knowledge) he accepted from others; but he never closed his mind to an addition to these facts and was always ready to amend his previous judgement in the light of further facts. He did not resent, in any way, the expression of a judgement contrary to his own from those he trusted; but while he did not resent it, it very rarely altered his own confidence in his own judgement.[6]

1 Marshall-Cornwall interview, loc. cit.
2 Marshall-Cornwall, *Haig as Military Commander*, London, 1973, p.214.
3 Ibid., p. 241.
4 Marshall-Cornwall, letter to the author, 9 February 1981.
5 A. Farrar-Hockley, *Goughie*, London, 1975, pp. 164–5.
6 Papers of Field-Marshal Lord Haig [hereinafter Haig papers], letter from Charteris to Liddell Hart, 11 October 1935, 3/55/357, NLS; and Papers of Captain Sir Basil Liddell Hart [hereinafter Liddell Hart Papers], I/259/94, KCL.

Marshall-Cornwall, too, received the impression of Haig that: 'Although invariably courteous, he was slow of speech and frigid in manner. One felt it would be difficult to alter his pre-conceived ideas. There was no doubt of his determination to pursue these to the end.'[1] It has even been suggested that Charteris was in such awe of Haig that he was chary of imparting 'distasteful' information to him.[2]

Field-Marshal Wavell, Commander-in-Chief Middle East for part of the Second World War, throws further light on Haig's character. Wavell had served on the General Staff in France under Haig and then on Allenby's staff in Palestine and so was well placed to observe both men at close quarters. They were of nearly the same age, they had both lost their fathers early in life and both had been brought up by their mothers. Wavell recognized that both had essential qualities of greatness:

> . . . absolute courage, moral and physical, strength of purpose and constancy, a high sense of duty, and a fine generosity of spirit. Both were hardy and enduring of body and handsome of face and form. Both, though self-reliant, were reserved and aloof, both in their different ways somewhat alarming to approach. Both were liked and admired by women for their strength, and welcomed by children for their gentleness. Neither took any notice of women's admiration, but both adored children.[3]

Yet Wavell considered that Allenby, despite his nickname of 'The Bull', had the finer perception and greater general knowledge. Haig was intensely professional and his mind lacked interests outside soldiering, thoroughly immersed in the GSM. In contrast to Allenby, with his love of nature, Haig's mind tended to be narrowly concentrated on the problem directly in front of him, and perhaps he was technically the more efficient of the two. He would probably have earned the deep respect of the German Chief of Staff, Graf von Schlieffen, of whom it was said that when out riding in East Prussia, a captain on his staff drew his attention to the magnificent view presented by the River Pregel, glittering like a silver ribbon in the early morning sunlight. The single-minded von Schlieffen is reputed to have crushed his romantically inclined subordinate with the cold

1 Marshall-Cornwall, *Memoirs*, op. cit., p. 4.
2 J. Terraine, *Douglas Haig, The Educated Soldier*, London, 1963, p. 101.
3 General Sir Archibald Wavell, *Allenby, A Study in Greatness: The Biography of Field-Marshal Viscount Allenby of Megiddo And Felixstowe, GCB, GCMG*, London, 1940, p. 62.

retort: 'An insignificant obstacle, Captain.' Many stories have been told about von Schlieffen over the years and this one may be no more truthful than most of the others. What it does display, though, is the intensity of the man in following his path in life and his single-minded determination to exclude all else. That was equally applicable to Haig, who pursued his strategic vision unflinchingly, with a solidity of purpose and courage in the face of enormous difficulties which excites our respect and admiration – but must also occasion a degree of concern, since it also argues a lack of toleration and flexibility.

Would such a purposeful and determined, not to say dedicated man, so solemnly sure of his course, allow his personally chosen subordinates to exert undue influence over him? Haig chose his closest staff officers, including Charteris, because they would support his ideas, not the other way around. Charteris can be criticized for supporting his chief's known views and his confidence in the correctness of his theory, and in that respect can be said to have kept up his morale, but Haig was an optimist and neither his views nor his personality appears to have required undue support.

Haig recognized that he was an optimist. He wrote to his wife on the first day of the German counter-attack at Cambrai:

> You will think I am a terrible optimist! Even when we suffer a check. The truth is that I know and feel that our own troops, man for man, are better than the German and that given a fair chance our fellows will come out 'on top'.[1]

After speaking with Lloyd George, Geoffrey Dawson, editor of *The Times*, noted that he had professed great admiration for Haig, 'commending especially his courage and optimism'.[2] Haig wrote in his diary on 8 August 1918: 'Everywhere else [i.e. other than III Corps' front] the situation developed more favourably for us than I, optimist though I am, had dared even to hope.' Indeed, Haig even went so far as to advocate optimism as policy, writing to Robertson that:

> The only point I am not in accord with you on is the desirability of issuing such pessimistic estimates from your Intelligence Branch. They do, I feel sure, much harm and cause many in authority to take a pessimistic outlook, when a contrary view, based on equally good

1 Haig Diaries, op. cit., letter from Haig to Lady Haig, 30 November 1917, 3155/148.
2 J. E. Wrench, *Geoffrey Dawson and Our 'Times'*, London, 1955, p. 153.

> information, would go far to help the nation on to victory. Personally I feel we have every reason to be optimistic and if the war were to end tomorrow, Great Britain would find herself not merely the greatest power in Europe, but in the World.[1]

Optimism was necessary to carry through such a war. One Intelligence officer, Captain (later Major-General) Hotblack trenchantly observed,

> If they [GHQ] had not been optimistic and if they had more accurately forseen the course of the War, they would doubtlessly have collapsed and told the Government that the War could not be won without the help of a new and powerful ally; a political rather than a military matter.[2]

One can only imagine the effect of such a message on the Government. Charteris, too, was an optimist and once he had formed a conviction, he too supported it through thick and thin. In a lecture on Intelligence in 1916, he advised his students:

> I will only say now that in making these deductions, always have the courage of your opinions. Do not be afraid of critics telling you afterwards that your deductions were not correct. Be accurate in the facts, logical in your deductions, but having made these deductions stand by them.[3]

A close friend, who had known Charteris for 53 years, referred in his obituary to 'his tenacity in holding onto a conviction in which he truly believed'.[4] A newspaper article, probably written by W. H. J. Wilkinson, one of Charteris's subordinates, shows a shrewd assessment of his character and suggests what lay behind his optimism:

> . . . he was also too much of an optimist – a victim of his own sanguine exuberance – while he liked to deal too starkly in blacks and whites with not enough toning in between.
>
> Yet I cannot help thinking that had my chief paid less attention to his notorious graph of enemy man-power, which seemed to obsess him (possibly from contact with higher officers) and been more accessible to

1 Papers of Field-Marshal Sir William Robertson [hereinafter Robertson Papers], Haig to Robertson, 13 August 1917, I/23/44, KCL.
2 Hotblack Papers, loc. cit.
3 Charteris Papers, loc. cit., 'Lecture on Intelligence', 4 February 1916.
4 Charteris Papers, loc. cit., obituary by Sir Ronald Charles, *Royal Engineers' Journal*, March 1946.

the many brilliant 'civilian' Intelligence brains in the BEF, the results might have been happier.[1]

The graph referred to estimated enemy losses from captured pay-books, a matter of Intelligence evaluation discussed more fully in the next chapter. However it will do no harm to note here that Charteris misinterpreted the heavy German call-up of 1917; it was not simply to replace casualties but to build and maintain the new divisions Germany was creating. Charteris, who had no training or experience in Intelligence, lacked the perspective necessary to recognize the heavy call-up for what it was. He had never served in the War Office and had received his staff training at Quetta, generally regarded as very much the poor relation to the Staff College at Camberley.

The controversy over Charteris stems largely from the general question of his influence over Haig and in particular his conduct before the Battle of Cambrai in 1917.

Another of Charteris's contemporaries, Colonel Woolrych, said Charteris's reports were 'All eyewashes . . . and once too often', and that 'Charteris was always dangerous because of his optimism'. His influence was attributed to the fact that Haig 'was a personal friend of Charteris'.[2] It is certainly true that Charteris had been on Haig's personal staff since 1908 and that both had belonged to the same masonic lodge in India. Sir Henry Wilson discusses the two men in his diary:

> What an amazing mentality! [Haig.] And I attribute most of this to that fool Charteris, who, I fancy, was the real author of that wonderful order Haig issued after the first attack on the Somme last July when, in substance, he said the Boches were beaten + we had nothing to do but reap the fruits of Victory![3]

Wilson also refers to Macdonogh's opinion of Charteris:

> I had a long talk with Macdonagh [sic]. He is quite of my opinion that Charteris is a dangerous fool because of his ridiculous optimism and because he is also untruthful. He thinks that Boches can take a punishment of another million before being in difficulties.[4]

1 Charteris Papers, anon., 'Misuse of the War's Greatest Surprise', *The Pioneer*, (Allahabad), 27 June 1929.
2 Woolrych interview, loc. cit.
3 Wilson Diary, op. cit., 13 May 1917.
4 Ibid., 8 June 1917.

Wilson also noted that Lloyd George 'cursed Charteris heavily which amused me', that over dinner at the Carlton 'Rawly [General Rawlinson, GOC Fourth Army] also said that Charteris is a public danger', and six days later that Lord Milner 'thought Charteris *must* be kicked out over all this business'.[1]

In his *War Memoirs* Lloyd George was just as critical and in his sketch of the man also paid off a few scores against Intelligence in general:

> General Charteris, who was an embodiment of the Military Intelligence which he directed, glowed with victory. For him the news was all good. If there were any elements that might have caused doubt in more discriminating minds, at least General Charteris had not discerned them. And if he had, he was proof against their maleficent influence. He could not help his hopeful reports. His computations were not mathematical, but temperamental. From the mass of information that came into his office he chose his facts and figures by attraction and not reflection. He could only be caught by a bright fly. That he swallowed up to the gut.[2]

Prior to the British offensive the Germans had moved three divisions into the Cambrai area from the Russian front, and the fact was reported to Charteris by Marshall-Cornwall. According to Marshall-Cornwall:

> Charteris had already informed his Commander-in-Chief that there were no German reserves behind the spot we were going to attack. We had no reserves either,[3] but Charteris said 'Well, it's alright, carry on, we will go through with the tanks and push the cavalry through.' A week later, I think about the beginning of December, the Germans counter-attacked, from Cambrai, at Bourlon Wood and these three divisions drove us back to our original front-line.
>
> When I produced the documentary evidence that these three divisions had arrived, Charteris said 'This is a bluff on the part of the Germans to try and put us off attacking, and as I have already informed the Commander-in-Chief that there are no reserves behind the German front I do not propose to upset his morale by giving him this

1 Ibid., 16, 20 and 26 October 1917.

2 Lloyd George, *War Memoirs*, London, 1933–6 edition, Vol. IV, p. 2224.

3 This is inaccurate. A French Infantry Corps and a French Cavalry Corps, both commanded by Général de Goutte, were in reserve for the battle. See Haig Diaries, op. cit., for 20 and 25 November 1917 and also the Edmonds Papers, loc. cit., III/13/1–14.

> information. You are not to put these divisions on the intelligence map.'
>
> Just before the battle, when I got this Intelligence and Charteris had rejected my information and said it was a bluff on the part of the Germans, I was so horrified that I went straight to his [Haig's] Director of Military Operations, General Sir John Davidson and told him about the arrival of these reserve troops which Charteris had refused to believe, and I said I could not go on working with my own boss any longer and wanted to go back to regimental duty. So I was told to stay where I was and to let him [Davidson] know privately what the real situation was.[1]

According to Marshall-Cornwall's view, the view that has been accepted by historians ever since, the three German divisions, news of whose arrival Charteris had suppressed, effectively cheated the British Army of a wonderful victory and were then responsible for throwing the British troops back beyond their original front line. If these allegations are true then John Charteris was criminally culpable for the completely useless loss of thousands of British lives. Marshall-Cornwall's testimony has been accepted without further investigation not only because he was there, as part of Haig's Intelligence Staff, and was a man of unimpeachable integrity, but because his explanation of events provides a perfectly good reason for the failure of an apparently brilliant idea – a surprise attack by massed tanks to destroy the entrenched deadlock.

But there is evidence that strongly indicates that the Battle of Cambrai did not follow the sequence of events described by Marshall-Cornwall. At the time he was only a major on the General Staff and therefore without the seniority to know all that transpired either on the battlefield or in the innermost recesses of the high command. We have already seen that his evidence is at fault on two counts, the first being his apparent ignorance that two French Corps were in reserve and anxiously awaiting the chance to sweep into the German rear, and the second his apparent ignorance of the tank breaking the Canal Bridge at Masnières (see pp. 68–9) which effectively stopped any attempt to exploit the tanks' initial success, something which cannot be laid at John Charteris's door. Nor was the success of the German riposte derived from any failing by Charteris. Marshall-Cornwall unequivocally claims that the reserve divisions he brought to the

1 Marshall-Cornwall interview, loc. cit.

latter's attention were responsible for the devastating German counter-attack, but this is not so. By the time the Germans went over the top on 30 November, those three divisions had faced ten days of stiff fighting in the course of which they had suffered terribly. The troops who counter-attacked so splendidly that autumn morning were fresh troops, such as the 3 Garde Division, and had been drawn from other sectors of the Western front.

That is, however, a side-issue compared with the fact that the German counter-attack was expected; indeed the main thrust, directed against the left of the new salient at Bourlon Wood, was repulsed with heavy losses. Corps commanders were certainly aware of the impending blow. On 4 December Haig visited Lieutenant-General Snow of VII Corps, and recorded:

> He expected the attack because enemy had thrown 7 new bridges, and made approaches and he particularly did his best to prepare his left flank to meet the blow. He personally went, the day before the attack, to Villers Ghislain [sic] (where he expected to be attacked) and arranged for 13 extra m[machine] gun posts.[1]

Edmonds, the Official Historian, supports this and places the responsibility for permitting the German success squarely on the shoulders of General Sir Julian Byng, commanding Third Army:

> Many warnings of its being in preparation were sent into the Third Army headquarters, notably by the VII Corps (Snow), which stood fast as the pivot on the right of the attack. Nothing, however, was done to meet the counter-attack as Byng and his Chief of Staff were convinced that the Germans were far too weak to attempt such an operation. A suggested bombardment of the enemy concentration area in the Scheldt valley was not carried out. Another suggestion, to take the enemy's thrust in flank, was also ignored, and the reinforcements were used to meet it frontally. This I say from personal knowledge as I paid several visits to General Snow . . .[2]

Edmonds also privately noted in his personal papers that Byng was known to his contemporaries as 'Byng the Bungler'.[3] Byng had massed his own reserves to face the main thrust of the German attack against the north face of the salient, which was the correct General Staff solution to the military problem he was facing. It was not,

1 Haig Diaries, op. cit., 4 December 1917.
2 Edmonds Papers, loc. cit., III/13/1–14. Winter 1917–18.
3 Ibid.

however, that thrust which did the damage. The critical blow fell on the southern flank of the salient, sweeping the defenders away. This attack was a subsidiary effort but it fell on divisions which Byng had not supported, and incompetent generalship did the rest. Basil Liddell-Hart, the military critic and historian, had a habit of jotting down the conversations he had with people who supplied him with information about the armed services. He noted one conversation with Edmonds on 7 October 1927, in the following terms:

> Jock Stuart's remark at time of Cambrai – 'Our generals are so stupid that even when they get opportunities they don't know how to use them.' Reference to Snow's wish to counter-attack against German flank, whereas Byng directed cavalry straight at Germans (Burnett-Stuart was BGGS to Snow). Snow had full knowledge of German counter-attack coming, but Byng refused to credit it. Snow had asked Pulteney to concentrate his guns on the Crevecoeur hollow where Germans were massing, but Pulteney would not.[1]

The case against Byng grows stronger with the knowledge that GHQ were also aware of the impending attack. Haig telegraphed to Robertson after the blow had fallen, stating specifically that the attack had not come as a surprise, listing the indications GHQ had of the growing menace and the steps they had taken against it.[2] Furthermore, the inevitable official enquiry into the reverse concluded quite unequivocally that, 'The Reports of the various commanders forwarded by Sir Douglas Haig indicate that an attack by the enemy on or about the 30th November was not unexpected, and they show that steps had been taken by those commanders to meet the eventuality.'[3]

After the war Byng could hardly be publicly criticized by the Official Historian since he was by then one of the victorious commanders and a peer to boot, so Edmonds's comments in the volume which deals with Cambrai are restrained. What is abundantly clear is that Byng's subordinates had early evidence of the German stroke and they had forwarded it. GHQ may be blamed for not assisting Byng by sending him reinforcements, but John Charteris was not responsible for operational decisions of that nature. Nothing can exculpate Byng

1 Liddell Hart Papers, loc. cit., 11/1927/17.
2 Haig Diaries, loc. cit., 18 December 1917.
3 CIGS Memorandum forwarding to S of S Reports of Enquiry Regarding the Events of 30 November 1917, PRO WO106/314.

from turning a deaf ear to the reports, from mishandling his reserves or from neglecting the southern face of his position.

What is equally certain is that Charteris did err greatly in not informing Haig of the arrival of German reinforcements beforehand. He subsequently endeavoured to cover his tracks by writing: 'It is a tremendous responsibility for D H and for the first time in the war "I" has been for holding back and "O" has been for going on.'[1] He made a similar claim in his biography of Haig.[2] Marshall-Cornwall says of this: 'I think the Operations Branch felt it was too late to countermand the offensive. Charteris's claim is quite fictitious.'[3] The lie is surely given to Charteris's claim by Edmonds in his obituary of Davidson: 'Only once did he disagree with his chief, and that was in 1917 over the decision to carry out the Cambrai operation.'[4]

It will be helpful here to consider Haig's general theory and outlook on the war and the way he believed it would be fought, in order to assess how much Charteris's opinions may have influenced him and also how the information given him by Charteris may have affected his views.

Haig held the theory, developed while he was in India, that battle consisted of four necessary phases: 1. The manoeuvre for position; 2. The first clash of battle; 3. The wearing-out fight, of varying duration; 4. The eventual decisive blow.[5] It seems that almost alone with Kitchener, he had foreseen a war lasting at least three years, which would place 'the eventual decisive blow' squarely in late 1917.

Haig maintained this view throughout the war, as is revealed by his directions to his Intelligence Branch:

> At the Council of War on August 5th [1914] he had pointed out that since Great Britain and Germany were fighting for their existence the war would inevitably be a prolonged struggle, and would require the development of the full force of the British Empire to achieve success. The Battle of the Aisne, which enabled him to gauge the fighting qualities of the German troops, confirmed his belief that man-power would ultimately decide the war, and he directed his staff to begin the study of the man-power which the German nation could effectively

1 Brigadier-General J. A. Charteris. *At GHQ*, London, 1931, p. 269.
2 Brigadier-General J. A. Charteris, *Field-Marshal Earl Haig*, London, 1929, p. 282.
3 Marshall-Cornwall interview, loc. cit.
4 Edmonds Papers, loc. cit., V/2, obituary of Major-General Sir John Davidson. 19 February 1954.
5 J. Terraine, *The Smoke and the Fire, Myths and Anti-Myths of War 1861–1945*, London, 1980, p. 58.

employ in the field . . . the studies of the man-power of the German Army – commenced during these early months at First Corps Headquarters – were developed at each successive stage of Haig's progress in the war, and he rarely allowed more than a day or two to pass without himself inquiring into the developments of this investigation.[1]

In his final despatch Haig argued that the great battles of 1916 and 1917 should be seen as part of the same continuous engagement. The war was inevitably long because:

> In the stage of the wearing-out struggle losses will necessarily be heavy on both sides, for in it the price of victory is paid. If the opposing forces are approximately equal in numbers, in courage, in morale and in equipment, there is no way of avoiding payment of the price or eliminating this phase of the struggle.
>
> In former battles this stage of the conflict has rarely lasted more than a few days, and has often been completed in a few hours. When armies of millions are engaged, with the resources of great empires behind them, it will inevitably be long.[2]

Haig had formed his opinion on the way the war would be fought before it started. It would be a war of military exhaustion. In May 1917 he considered more time was required in phase three:

> The enemy has already weakened appreciably; but a long time is required to wear down such great numbers of troops composed of fine fighting material and he is still fighting with such energy and determination that the situation is not yet ripe for the decisive blow.[3]

There is no evidence of Charteris's optimism here. Yet little more than a month later Haig's position had begun to shift:

> After careful consideration of all available information I feel justified in stating that the power of endurance of the German people is being strained to such a degree as to make it possible that the breaking point may be reached this year.
>
> Despite the distress in Germany and the short rations in the German Army we must still reckon on desperate efforts being made by the enemy to hold on in the hope of outlasting the determination of the Allies. But we have already overcome similar efforts on the Somme, on the Ancre, and at Arras. We are able to do so again. Every success

1 Charteris, *Field-Marshal Earl Haig*, op. cit., p. 110.
2 J. H. Boraston, *Sir Douglas Haig's Despatches*, London, 1919, p. 320.
3 OAD 428, 'The Present Situation and Future Plans', 1 May 1917, cited in J. Terraine, *The Road to Passchendaele*, London, 1977, p. 85.

> brings us nearer to the end of the long and desperate struggle and we are now justified in believing that one more great victory, equal to those already gained, may turn the scale finally, and, at the least, will have an even greater effect than previous victories in Germany and on the world's opinion generally.[1]

One week later his view had become a degree more optimistic:

> According to reports, the endurance of the German nation is being tested so severely that discontent there has already assumed formidable proportions. The German Government, helped by the long disciplinary training of the people, is still able to control this discontent; but every fresh defeat of the German armies, combined with a growing realization of the failure of the submarine campaign, increases the difficulty of doing so, and further defeats in the field may have unexpectedly great results, which may come with unexpected suddenness. The German Army too, shows unmistakeable signs of deterioration in many ways and the cumulative effect of further defeats may at any time yield greater results in the field than we can rely on gaining.[2]

By the end of June Haig was beginning to believe the German Army could be defeated in the field that year, that it was possible to reach phase four. Harington relates that:

> Sir Douglas Haig warned us in a memorandum on 30th June shortly after Messines that the fundamental object of the operations was the defeat of the German Army and that this could not be achieved in a single battle and that we must make preparations for 'very hard fighting lasting perhaps for weeks' and that we must arrange to deliver a series of organized attacks on a large scale and on broad frontages.[3]

In short, Haig believed phase four was close enough to justify such an effort.

June 1917 also saw a paper produced by Charteris. In it he argued that there appeared 'no reason to anticipate that Russia will make a separate peace' and concluded: 'It is a fair deduction that, given a continuance of circumstances as they stand at present and given a continuation of the effort of the Allies, then Germany may well be forced to conclude peace on our terms before the end of the year.'[4]

1 Haig Diaries, op. cit., OA799, Haig to Army Commanders, 5 June 1917.
2 OAD 478, 'Present Situation and Future Plans', 12 June 1917, PRO WO106/312.
3 Major-General Sir C. Harington, *Plumer of Messines*, London, 1935, p. 109.
4 Ia/35273, 'Note on the Strategical Situation with Special Reference to the Present Condition of German Resources and Probable German Operations', 11 June 1917, PRO TI73/829.

This was wildly over-optimistic. While the War Office recognized the gravity of the situation facing Germany nobody there considered that Germany would be forced to make peace at such an early date. Robertson was sufficiently alarmed to request that Haig refrain from circulating this paper to the War Cabinet, as it clashed with the War Office estimates they had already received. Yet when he met the War Cabinet, Haig told them that:

> Germany was nearer her end than they seemed to think, that *now* was the favourable moment for pressing her and that everything possible should be done to take advantage of it by concentrating on the Western front *all* available resources. I stated that Germany was within 6 months of the total exhaustion of her available manpower, *if fighting continues at its present intensity*.[1]

Charteris's comment on Haig's statement is noteworthy:

> DH gave the definite opinion that if the fighting kept up at its present intensity for 6 months, Germany would be at the end of her available man-power. This is going rather further than the paper I wrote to DH on the 11th June (Ia/35273). It depends on Russia . . . But my words were 'It is a fair deduction, given a continuance of the effort of the Allies, etc., etc.' That includes Russia, but it does not differ materially from DH's bolder statement.[2]

Charteris had indeed included Russia in his paper. Haig had omitted this qualification and elaborated on Charteris's paper of his own accord.

It has been alleged that Charteris

> . . . was unable to impart to Haig the very real misgivings and qualifications with which he regarded much of the information that he gathered. All through the year [1917] there was a discrepancy, sometimes very substantial, between what Charteris thought privately and what he proffered Haig as a basis for the latter's plans.[3]

If Charteris's letters to his wife may be construed as private thoughts, they reveal that he was firmly convinced that the Germans were on the verge of defeat. On 29 July 1916 he wrote: 'I believe the war is going to be over quicker than you think.'[4] On 13 August: 'I am so

1 R. Blake (ed.), *The Private Papers of Douglas Haig 1914–1919*, London, 1952, p. 240.
2 Charteris, *At GHQ*, op. cit., p. 233.
3 Terraine, *Douglas Haig*, op. cit., p. 311.
4 Private Papers of Brigadier-General John Charteris, courtesy of his grandson, Lieutenant-Colonel J. A. Charteris, MC [hereinafter Charteris Private Papers].

convinced that the war will be over before this time next year'[1] and on 18 August:

> I believe the Germans are absolutely sick of the war and may take heroic measures any day now. It is, I think, about even chances whether the war is over before Xmas or after next winter. Anyhow Germany must know now that she is beaten and she will not want to fight it out when we are throtling [sic] her. I hope we shall go on till she is absolutely beaten.[2]

The same views are expressed throughout 1917. As late as 1 November he wrote:

> In spite of the success of our own battle we cannot help being a bit depressed at the Italian news. It is so like the Sisyphian stone – just as we get in sight of the top of the hill, another of our Allies crumbles up and down goes the stone half way down the hill.[3]

Those at the War Office were regarded as 'professional pessimists'.[4]

Part of Haig's four-phase theory was reinforced for him by the experience of the first Battle of Ypres. Haig had commanded I Corps which bore the brunt of the losses; the old BEF was destroyed. Edmonds wrote: 'In December 1914 we touched bottom in depression.'[5] The battle made a great impression on Haig; perhaps it even exerted the same kind of influence on him as another defensive battle, Verdun, had on Pétain, for Haig was always fascinated by Ypres thereafter.[6] Giving up when the going got rough was one thing that Haig firmly set himself against and, though he might genuinely feel for the losses his armies suffered, he would persevere until victory was his. The influence of Kiggell should not be underestimated here, for he carried greater weight with Haig than is normally attributed to him. He was in full agreement with Haig's theory and fully supported him over the Flanders offensive.[7] He may not have been a dramatic or colourful character, but this should not lead anyone to discount his influence, as does Marshall-Cornwall.

Kiggell's papers reveal that he and Haig enjoyed a close relation-

1 Ibid.
2 Ibid.
3 Ibid.
4 Charteris Papers, loc. cit., letter from Mrs N. Charteris to Sir Ronald Charles, 25 February 1946.
5 Liddell Hart Papers, loc. cit., I/259/94, Edmonds to Liddell Hart, 9 November 1934.
6 Alistair Horne, *The Price of Glory*, London, 1962, pp. 227 and 289.
7 C. A. C. Repington, *The First World War*, London 1920, pp. 101–3.

ship. Haig considered him a man of ability and sought his advice on a number of matters, including which books Kiggell thought he should read. In 1911 Haig wrote: 'I am ready to go anywhere in the good cause, provided you help and support me and don't go making yourself ill by overwork.'[1] In October 1914 he wrote: 'I must send you a line to thank you for yours of 8th and to say that you *must arrange* to *come out here in some capacity soon* . . . Hoping to see you soon. This is just a line to encourage you [to] come out.'[2] Following Kiggell's dismissal in December 1917, Haig wrote to him:

> I wish you most heartily the best of good luck for this New Year and I can never thank you sufficiently for all you have done to help in the year that has gone. I am sorry to see that my recommendation to promote you to general has not been accepted by War Office.[3]

Charteris did not receive such a tribute from Haig. As late as May 1918 Haig was still writing to ask Kiggell for his opinion on the situation of the Western front.[4] Charteris himself had no doubt about the influence of Ypres on Haig or its connection with his theory:

> One small suggestion I make to you. Haig's persistence in attacking was not wholly or even mainly optimism. His studies had led him to the definite view that premature abandonment of a plan had been a most fruitful cause of failure, both from a material as well as a psychological aspect. The errors of the Germans in 1914 had confirmed this conclusion – at which he arrived long before 1914. I am not referring to Passchendaele in this suggestion.[5]

After the first three weeks of the Flanders offensive, Haig informed the War Office of the state of the German Army:

> Some of his units are still fighting almost as well as ever, especially in defence; but the signs of deterioration in others are well marked, and it's noteworthy that even on our present limited front of attack he has failed to provide staunch troops on a considerable part of his line. In front of the XIV Corps a large proportion of the defending troops are reported both by our own men and by prisoners, to have run away. Such weak portions of a position must result eventually in compromis-

1 Papers of Lieutenant-General Sir Launcelot Kiggell [hereinafter Kiggell Papers], letter from Haig to Kiggell, 5 April 1911, I/8, KCL.

2 Kiggell Papers, loc. cit., I/39, letter from Haig to Kiggell, 12 October 1914.

3 Kiggell Papers, loc. cit., II/14/1, letter from Haig to Kiggell, 1 January 1918.

4 Kiggell Papers, loc. cit., II/18, letter from Haig to Kiggell, 14 May 1918.

5 Haig Papers, loc. cit., 3155/337 and Liddell Hart Papers, loc. cit., I/259/94, letter from Charteris to Liddell Hart, 11 October 1935.

> ing the whole of it; and even though, for a time, the rents made may be filled up by throwing in other troops, this entails a very heavy drain, as well as discontent and loss of morale amongst the troops so thrown in owing to the untrustworthiness of their comrades.[1]

Haig's view of the shaky morale of some German units was based upon a report by Charteris on 21 August 1917. Evidence for the report from the Fifth Army – or at least parts of it – consisted of captured documents from the 226th Reserve Infanterie Regiment, 450th Infanterie Regiment, and the 9th Company of the 358th Infanterie Regiment, all of which alluded to evasion of duty and indiscipline. Also cited were examples of large-scale surrender and indiscipline in the 79th Reserve Division and the 6th Bavarian Reserve Division; prisoners of the 49th Reserve Division and 36th Division also reported low morale and indiscipline.[2]

Haig had already mentioned the low morale of the 6th Bavarian Reserve Divison in his diary on 1 August. Charteris did not state that the Germans were on the point of collapse, but his evidence was such that Haig would, given his strategic theory, have interpreted it as bearing out his idea. Once again, Haig had gone further than Charteris, for the latter neither stated nor implied that the situation would lead to 'discontent and loss of morale' amongst fresh German troops. Haig's theory returned to the fore at the end of September and beginning of October, when he considered the time might be ripe for the fourth phase, the decisive blow. At a meeting with Gough and Plumer, commander of the Second Army, he:

> . . . urged the necessity for preparing to exploit our success after the attack following that of the 4th October. I am of opinion that the enemy is tottering and that a good vigorous blow might lead to decisive results.[3]

At another conference four days later, Haig expressed the view that:

> Continued defeats, combined with the long duration of the war, had tended to lower the enemy's morale. The condition of certain hostile divisions was known to be bad. The time may come shortly when the enemy's troops will not stand up to our repeated attacks, or when he

1 OAD 602, 21 August 1917, in 'Correspondence between General Staff, War Office and GHQ France', PRO WO106/407.
2 Ia/38607, 'Note Regarding German Man-Power, Casualties and Morale', 21 August 1917, PRO WO106/1514.
3 Haig Diaries, op. cit., 28 September 1917.

> may not have sufficient fresh troops immediately available to throw into the battle. The enemy failed to take advantage of his opportunities on 31st October, 1914, and did not push forward when his repeated attacks had exhausted the British forces on the YPRES front. We must be careful not to make the same error.[1]

The German Army was not yet ready to collapse, but there were indications which suggested it might be on the path dictated by Haig's theory.

It is also worth noting what others, closely engaged in the battle, felt about German morale. Harington, CGS to Plumer, observed that several German units were displaying poor morale although most still offered stubborn resistance.[2] Geoffrey Dawson, editor of *The Times*, wrote to the Bishop of Pretoria on 7 November about the feelings of the General Staff and regimental officers after a visit to the front:

> They were all in fine spirits – perhaps a little more so than the regimental officers, though there's not the slightest despondency anywhere. The latter are inclined to resent the over-optimism of GHQ about falling German *morale*, etc., and there are doubts of the wisdom (at this stage and with these numbers) of set-piece battles as against the trench raid business.[3]

Repington, correspondent for the *Morning Post*, noted a conversation with Plumer to the effect that 'the Huns still fight well, and Plumer is rather sarcastic about Charteris's optimism'.[4] This however, should not be construed as meaning Plumer was opposed to the Flanders offensive. Harington observed, 'I can say without any hesitation that my Chief, General Sir H. Plumer, welcomed and endorsed the plan.'[5] He repeated this in a letter to Edmonds: 'I feel as regards LG [Lloyd George] that my job begins and ends with clearing Plumer from LG's assertions that he disagreed with Haig over Passchendaele as he certainly did not.'[6] This was in response to Lloyd George's argument in his *War Memoirs* that Plumer had opposed Haig's plans for an offensive in Flanders, neither the first nor the last time the ex-prime

1 Haig Diaries, op. cit., OAD 645 'Record of a Conference held at Second Army Headquarters, Cassel, at 11 a.m., 2 October 1917'.
2 Harington, op. cit., pp. 122–3 and 128–9.
3 Wrench, op. cit., p.154.
4 Repington, op. cit., Vol. II, p.99.
5 Harington op. cit., p.109.
6 Edmonds Papers, loc. cit., 1/2B, letter from Harington to Edmonds, 21 November 1934.

minister traduced the facts. Repington further noted on 14 October: 'I found Plumer heart and soul for the Flanders offensive.'[1]

Undoubtedly in the late summer and early autumn of 1917 both Haig and Charteris were over-optimistic, but early in October both men recognized that the chance of reaching a decision in 1917 was lost and were counting upon renewing the offensive in 1918. One prime reason for abandoning the earlier high hopes was that the Navy informed GHQ the Channel was too rough to permit the amphibious landing on the Belgian coast which had been intended as part of the Flanders offensive. That Haig recognized the Flanders offensive was not going to achieve its stated aim is shown in his letter of 8 October. He wished to send

> . . . as many officers and men as possible on leave between the cessation of this offensive and the commencement of the next. The armies have undergone almost superhuman exertion and hardships during the last few months, and unless the demands made on them during the winter are reduced to a minimum they cannot be expected to respond fully to the further heavy calls entailed by a renewal of the offensive next year.[2]

In November Haig urged Robertson not to imperil the prospects for an offensive in 1918 when he spoke to him at St Pol, and again in writing three days later.[3] Charteris, too, accepted that no decision was possible in 1917. Repington recorded on 14 October that he 'motored to Advanced GHQ to have lunch and a talk with Charteris, the head of Haig's Intelligence. I find that he is strongly set upon continuing the Flanders offensive next year, and is most optimistic as usual.'[4]

It is reasonable to ask why Haig continued the Flanders offensive beyond early October 1917 if he saw no prospect of success then. There could be several reasons. The state of the French Army could have exerted an influence, but the extent of this would depend upon what Haig knew of its problems, and this is by no means clear, although Farrar-Hockley suggests that the French mutinies did have a bearing.[5] The attraction of German reserves to Flanders in order to

1 Repington, op. cit., p.99.
2 Haig Diaries, op. cit., OAD 652, 8 October 1917.
3 Haig Diaries, op. cit., 10 November 1917, *and* OAD 702, 13 November 1917, PRO WO 106/1516.
4 Repington, op. cit., p. 98.
5 Farrar-Hockley, op. cit., p.224.

decoy them away from the Cambrai attack is certainly another reason, and the desire to secure a good line for the winter is another. Nor can the continuation of Haig's 'wearing-out' phase be discounted. Whatever the reason, Haig clearly felt impelled to continue, as a conversation with Gough reveals. Gough informed Haig on the night of 16–17 October that 'tactical success was not possible, or would be too costly under such conditions, and advised that the attack should now be abandoned'. Haig replied, 'But, my dear Hubert, we have no alternative. We must continue.'[1]

After the setback at Cambrai, Government wrath was initially directed against Haig. Lord Derby, Secretary of State for War, had however had Charteris in his sights for some time. On 7 December 1917 Derby wrote to Haig: 'You will remember that I have before suggested to you the desirability of replacing Charteris . . .' and again on 11 December:

> I have mentioned to you on more than one occasion that he was doing you an infinity of harm by his optimism and by what I consider his inaccurate information, and I have begged you to make a change. You tell me that you invariably make an allowance for the optimism of Charteris. That may be so, but I cannot think that you make sufficient allowance, and the best proof I have of that is your letter of October 8th. That letter is clearly based on wrong information, and for that, although signed by you, I cannot hold you responsible.[2]

Haig wrote to his wife on 14 December:

> It is over a year ago since Derby and the War Office have set their faces against poor Charteris. And although he has done his work admirably and his Intelligence branch is in excellent order, I feel that it would be wrong of me to keep an officer at this time who seems really to have upset so many people and have put those who ought to work in friendliness with him against him.[3]

It appears in fact that it was in February 1917 that Derby began his attack; there is no hint of criticism before then. On 1 February Haig had held a press conference with some French journalists in which he said 1917 would be the decisive year, and waxed enthusiastic on the impending defeat of Germany. His statements were given much publicity in France and were reproduced in *The Times*, where the

1 Ibid.
2 Derby Papers, loc. cit., 920 DER (17), 27/2.
3 Haig Papers, loc. cit., 3115/149.

optimistic views expressed angered Lloyd George. Charteris should have censored the journalists' reports, but was about to go on leave and neglected to do so, leaving the originals unchanged. The upshot was that Derby wrote to Haig on 20 February saying that the interview had 'created an atmosphere of expectation of complete victory which will cause a great feeling of despondency if the offensive does not produce, and produce immediately, the highest results':[1]

> This leads me to what is really the object of this letter, namely, as to the course you should pursue with Charteris. You will get an official letter on the subject, but I cannot help saying I think Charteris's action in passing this interview for publication without first submitting it to you is absolutely unjustifiable. He has let you down very badly, and let you down in a respect which you in France can hardly realise at the moment. He has destroyed in this country all confidence in his judgement, and everything which passes through his hands as having been approved by him will be the subject of suspicion.
>
> I therefore feel that, in your own interest (which I know as a matter of fact, you would never for one moment consider), but far more in the interests of the country, that you should consider making a change, but while leaving him to do any intelligence work which, so far as I know, he is capable of performing as well or better than others, this question of the proof-censoring of similar statements to the one in question should be entrusted to other hands.[2]

This is significant, for Derby quite clearly states that he had no quarrel with the rest of Charteris's work. Nevertheless it is from this time that confidence in him is lost and 'everything which passes through his hands' becomes suspect. Here the seeds of future trouble were sown, for as Derby's official biographer says, Derby was 'inclined throughout his life to give as much attention to small matters as to great and this lack of a balanced sense of proportion must be considered one of his defects'.[3] It is a defect which raises its head on other occasions, most notably in the private vendetta he waged against Curzon, remorselessly pursuing him over the trivial matter of an official car once used for private purposes. There is little room for doubt that henceforth Derby waged such a campaign against Charteris, and his deception over the German reserves at Cambrai in

1 Draft in the Derby Papers, loc. cit.
2 Ibid.
3 R. S. Churchill, *Lord Derby, 'King of Lancashire'*, London, 1959, p. 259.

December 1917 sealed his fate. Derby acknowledged in both his letters that Haig would have made allowance for Charteris's optimism:

> I can believe that you realise he may exaggerate and give unduly optimistic opinions, and that you will endeavour to make allowance for this failing, but at the same time it is hardly possible for you to avoid being influenced to some extent by his opinions, though probably unconsciously so.[1]

Derby denies Charteris is being made a 'whipping-boy' in his letter of 11 December, yet initially Lloyd George had intended to dismiss Haig and it was only the intervention of Derby which redirected his wrath. Derby gives the game away towards the end of that letter: 'Much as I dislike giving you an instruction which I know to be repugnant to you, I look upon you as a National asset and I cannot allow your loyalty to a subordinate to affect your position.'[2] In other words, the subordinate officer had to be sacrificed in order to preserve the position of the National asset. When Haig felt it to be a choice of Gough or himself being dismissed, he decided that Gough was the more dispensable.[3] On the basis of the available evidence one may be justified in concluding that not only Charteris but most of Haig's senior staff were to some extent made scapegoats in order to preserve Haig's position.

Sir Philip Sassoon was Haig's Military Secretary and as such privy to all that transpired at GHQ, both official and confidential. In December 1917 he wrote to Lord Derby: 'About C [Charteris]. I *think* it will be alright. But it would be bad policy as well as unfair to make out that he is going in any sense of the word as a scapegoat for Cambrai.'[4] Nevertheless, Haig's staff went and so sprang up the myth that Haig had been misled by the departed staff officers, notably Charteris, rather in the way that those opposed to the policies of medieval kings always took care to blame all the misfortunes facing the country on the king's 'evil advisers' when they raised the standard of rebellion: it was the only way to bridle the king's power without appearing treasonable. Viewed in that light, the attacks on Haig's staff can be seen as an attack on the Commander-in-Chief and his strategy.

1 Derby Papers, loc. cit., letter from Derby to Haig, 11 December 1917.
2 Ibid.
3 Farrar-Hockley, op. cit., p. 324.
4 Derby Papers, loc. cit., letter from Sir Philip Sassoon to Lord Derby, undated, marked 'Private and confidential' in response to Derby's letter of 26 December 1917 to Sassoon. 920 DER (17) 27/3.

If the Government and the War Office wanted to undermine the strategy being pursued on the Western front, then their action was well directed, for that strategy was the child of Haig's own thought rather than the fruit of poor or deceptive advice. Haig had chosen his staff, including his much-derided Chief of Intelligence, on several grounds. Personal friendship and trust occupied an important place but none so important as the fact that he knew he could rely on them to carry out his every wish in relation to his strategic theory, a theory which he had formed long before the war and which owed nothing to the influence of his staff. In this case the advisers were supporting the king's chosen position rather than shaping it and their culpability is proportionately diminished.

Like every other commander of every other army to fight in the war, Haig had been set the task of bringing the enemy to his knees by destroying his armies in battle. Neither Haig nor any of his contemporaries could achieve this unless there was a considerable disparity between the contending armies in numbers, weapons or morale. The successes the Germans achieved against the weaker members of the Allied nations, the Serbians, Roumanians and, ultimately, the Russians, were all the fruits of such disparities and these disparities did not exist on the Western front. A commander faced with an insoluble problem of this nature needed optimism to be able to continue to face it and try to overcome it. If Haig was to go on, he had to have the confidence that he could bring about the defeat of the enemy and, Charteris notwithstanding, he had resolved the question of how he was going to do this in his own mind well before he accepted the command of the BEF. His theory was in many respects typical of the GSM, especially in the way in which it pushed the question of the cost in human life into the background. It was a theory which Haig's staff supported and carried out rather than directed and controlled.

Haig disagreed violently with Macdonogh's view of the morale and fighting potential of the German Army and people expressed in WP49. There is more to this disagreement than the differing perspectives of the War Office and GHQ. On 15 October 1917 Haig had noted 'another instance of insubordination in the German Army' and added:

> Yet it is stated in a note by the DMI War Office dated 1st October (WP49) 'that morale of the troops in the field gives no cause for anxiety to the German High Command'. I cannot think why the War Office Intelligence Department gives such a wrong picture of the situation except that General Macdonagh [sic] (DMI) is a Roman Catholic and is

(perhaps unconsciously) influenced by information which doubtless reaches him from tainted (i.e. catholic) sources.[1]

Haig expressed his feelings against both Roman Catholics and Jews on other occasions.[2] Haig was a devout Scots Presbyterian and such views were typical of some sections of that Church.[3] It sounds as though Haig were desperately attempting to attribute some reason to Macdonogh's refusal to share his views rather than admit that Macdonogh had facts at his disposal which were as good as Haig's. Charteris shared Haig's religion and also his views on Catholics. On 17 November 1917, he wrote to his wife about the criticisms being directed against GHQ:

> My chief opponents are the Roman Catholic people, who are really very half-hearted about the whole war and have never forgiven DH unjustly for being Presbyterian. However as you will see in the papers the Army is not without its defenders in the Press and even in Parliament, and I have hope that LG's incompetency may be exposed very soon now . . . There is no secret of who are attacking DH. They are *Lord French* a jealous and incompetent old fool; *Winston Churchill* seeking his own glory and with no judgement to control a vivid imagination; *Henry Wilson* a military blackleg and a quite incompetent soldier, who is an Irishman and an intriguer. Macdonagh [sic] takes a hand against both DH and me, he is a Roman Catholic and a pessimist of the deepest die [sic].[4]

Given the background of distrust and dislike, amounting almost to hatred, of Catholics by some Scots Presbyterians, it would appear natural for both men to distrust Macdonogh. The fact that Macdonogh did not fall in with Haig's theory or consider the defeat of the German Army likely could merely be a rationalization of Haig's disagreement, a case of guilt by association. In either respect it shows Haig was not a man to tolerate contradiction of his existing ideas, so convinced was he that his way was the only way to win the war.

Charteris had no illusions about the extent of his influence over Haig. After the German spring offensive had begun in 1918 he wrote in a letter to his wife:

1 Haig Diaries, op. cit., 15 October 1917.
2 Ibid., 4 August 1918, 3155/66 and a letter to his sister Henrietta, 23 June 1895.
3 *See*, for example, H. MacPherson, *Scotland's Debt to Protestantism*, Edinburgh and London, 1912.
4 Charteris Private Papers. *See also* letters of 21 and 22 October 1917 and 15 November 1917.

> I do not suppose I could have done anything had I been in my old job to have prevented it. Anyhow I had not a chance. When you have time at the Hallams [his home], read some of those notes of mine which I took home in January. They will show how I urged certain measures. I took the notes home with some foreboding that this might happen. Perhaps for you and the boys it's well that I am no longer in a position that any one hereafter can say that I had great influence at this period.[1]

In December 1917, at the height of the attacks on him over Cambrai, he had confided to his wife that:

> The War Cabinet attribute to me however, far greater power and influence than I really possess and are frightened. It will make no real difference to me. I will get another similar job, I expect, somewhere, and I have told them all that if any attempt is made publically [sic] to associate my name in any way with any reverse at Cambrai then I will hit back and damned hard. Provided no such attempt is made I am quite content.[2]

Marshall-Cornwall claims that Charteris's eventual replacement, Brigadier-General Edgar Cox, felt Haig was continuing to rely on Charteris's advice in 1918 rather than his own:

> The extraordinary thing was that even after Charteris was transferred in December to be number two to Sir Eric Geddes at the transportation organization, Haig was still depending on him for advice about the strategy of the war, and the unfortunate Cox, Brigadier Edgar Cox, who had replaced Charteris, was absolutely in despair, because he said that the Commander-in-Chief really does not take my advice at all, he still relies on the advice he gets from Charteris.[3]

In this case Cox is likely to have been mistaken. In his new post as Deputy Director General Transportation, Charteris spent most of his time on the lines of communication and was rarely present at GHQ, much less Advanced GHQ. It would have been difficult for the two men to meet, and meeting would have been necessary for Charteris to exert any influence. When asked if he could give an example of where and when Haig took Charteris's advice in 1918, Marshall-Cornwall replied, 'No I cannot.'[4]

1 Charteris Private Papers, letter from Charteris to his wife, 25 March 1918.
2 Charteris Private Papers, letter from Charteris to his wife, 11 December 1917.
3 Marshall-Cornwall interview, loc. cit.
4 Ibid.

Study of both Haig's Diaries and Charteris's private letters reveal that the two met on six, possibly seven, occasions in 1918 (Charteris wrote that he 'saw' Haig on 18 June, but does not appear to have spoken to him). Meetings did take place on 10 January, 12 March (both these were in Britain), on 29 May, 20 and 27 July and 24 August. 29 May appears to have been the only occasion when strategy was discussed in any detail. Charteris wrote:

> It was a very pleasant dinner, DH, Lawrence, Sir A. Sloggett, a couple of ADCs and myself. DH was very nice and sent all manner of kind messages to you. We walked round the garden together after dinner and then had a long conference *tête-à-tête* in his room. I will tell you sometime about that. Then Lawrence and du Cane from Foch's staff (who arrived after dinner) came in and we had a more formal council. Quite like old times.[1]

With one exception this is the only occasion to record discussion of military business. Given Charteris's character it is highly unlikely he would have omitted to mention further such discussions to his wife. This exception was 24th August, when Charteris had been ordered to Baghdad in a position with less pay than he had had on leaving India in 1911. He went to see Haig officially about this and Haig promised to take the matter up strongly. Charteris was to provide a written statement which Haig would forward with remarks to the War Office. Haig noted, 'He seems almost a sort of Dreyfus in the eyes of our War Office authorities.'[2]

Haig may not have been far wrong. If there was such an attitude at the War Office it might well have stemmed from Macdonogh, now Adjutant General. In Charteris's Personal Service Record there is a note which reads: 'The Adjutant General has given me certain verbal instructions in regard to Brig. General J. Charteris. Have you any objections to our [word illegible] telegraph IA please.'[3] This is dated 5 September 1918, after Charteris's meeting with Haig, and it could suggest some sort of intrigue against Charteris within the War Office. There is, naturally, no record of the 'certain verbal instructions'. That such intrigues were possible is supported by Meinertzhagen, who recorded that when he was at the War Office in 1918 he was in violent

1 Charteris Private Papers, letter from Charteris to his wife, 29 May 1918.
2 Haig Diaries, op. cit., 24 August 1918.
3 Personal Service Record of Brigadier-General J. A. Charteris, Ministry of Defence [hereinafter Charteris Personal Service Record], courtesy of Lieutenant-Colonel J. A. Charteris, MC.

disagreement with the whole of the General Staff save his immediate chief, Lieutenant-General Thwaites, then DMI. According to Meinertzhagen, Thwaites said:

> The trouble with you, Meinertzhagen, is that you look just a little further ahead than most of us, you know you are right and you persist in telling us all that we are wrong. On this occasion I feel you are right, but if the team is to work smoothly your unorthodox views must take second place even if they are perfectly correct. And if you can't fit into the War Office machine you run small chance of getting on.[1]

I believe it is right to question much of the apparently hard 'evidence' which has been levelled against Charteris over the years. Marshall-Cornwall's claim (*see* p. 325) regarding the views which Charteris had allegedly been feeding Haig is based on events which were supposed to have taken place in April 1916 when Charteris was in fact on sick leave, suffering from pneumonia: 'In his absence it fell to me to report personally to Douglas Haig each morning on the Intelligence situation.'[2] This is not borne out by Haig's Diary, which shows that Marshall-Cornwall's commanding officer, the head of I(a), Colonel B. W. Bowdler, took the daily Intelligence reports to Haig in Charteris's absence. I wrote to the General to query the discrepancy, and in a letter dated 3 May 1983 he admitted that: 'I may have exaggerated when I said I reported to Haig "each morning".'

If that was 'exaggeration', the claim about Charteris's actions that April would appear to be downright falsehood. I have no direct evidence but I feel that Marshall-Cornwall's words were prompted by personal dislike at least as much as by conviction, a belief reinforced by the General's oft-repeated and completely unprompted protestations, both in his conversation with me and in several letters, that he bore Charteris no personal ill-will. Whatever the case, the General has done Haig's, Charteris's and his own reputation a grave disservice, to say nothing of the historical implications.

A further matter raised by Charteris's Personal Service Record is the fact that throughout most of 1917 he was a sick man. The Record reveals that a duodenal ulcer had been diagnosed in March 1917 and was aggravated by the conditions of active service.[3] Meerloo writes:

> Stomach ulcers . . . may arise when the body manufactures too

1 Meinertzhagen, *Army Diary*, op. cit., p. 296.
2 Marshall-Cornwall, *Wars and Rumours of Wars*, op. cit., p. 25.
3 Charteris Personal Service Record, Army Form A45, Medical Report on a Disabled Officer.

> much hydrochloric acid, which is necessary for the digestion of food. The stomach ulcer patient is a person who reacts to strong emotions, especially repressed hostility, with an excessive secretion of hydrochloric acid. The innate secretion reflex, favourable for the digestion in case of hunger, grows into an unfavourable condition reflex where hunger and aggression mutually increase the hydrochloric acid secretion. Gradually more and more of the sour fluid is manufactured until finally the patient finds himself suffering from ulcers.[1]

Dr Robert Beatty, a qualified clinical psychologist, believes that such an ulcer would have been very painful and although it would not affect the victim's judgement, it would lead to abnormal haste in any activity. This might go far towards explaining Charteris's curious action over the censoring of Haig's French press interview before going on leave. Charteris's treatment of events in his published books requires some comment, especially in the light of a letter from Edmonds to Liddell Hart:

> I am sorry that you have quoted Charteris's 'diary' but you may have done it with malice aforethought. It is whispered among the initiated that it is a fake. *Before* the event he was invariably wrong. So it is amusing to read how wise he is like critics of the Belloc school after it. In some cases he reverses what is in the written contemporary record.[2]

This comment refers to Charteris's book, *At GHQ*. Charteris did not in fact keep a diary and he clearly states this in the Preface: the book was chiefly composed from the letters he sent home to his wife, and he wrote nearly every day, sometimes more than once. Edmonds should have known this as he proof-read the book.[3] It is typical of the malice that sometimes governed the Official Historian. For example, his papers show that he was engaged in a conspiracy with Field-Marshal Montgomery-Massingberd to smother the views of J. F. C. Fuller in the inter-war years, even to the extent of preventing his historical works becoming part of the course at the Staff College.

Yet undeniably Charteris did sometimes try to disguise the facts. His statement that Intelligence was opposed to the Cambrai offensive is a case in point. The fact that some passages of *At GHQ* did not reflect his true optimism has led many of Haig's supporters to the

1 Joost A. M. Meerloo, *Mental Seduction and Menticide*, London, 1957, p.42.
2 Liddell Hart Papers, loc. cit., I/259/76.
3 Edmonds Papers, loc. cit., II/2/243, Charteris to Edmonds, 28 March 1931.

conclusion that Charteris deliberately deceived Haig and that there was a difference between his view and that of Haig. However this is not true of the bulk of the book, which for the most part reproduces Charteris's contemporary views. Edmonds overstates the case, and while there is some case against Charteris, it can do without such distortions.

Charteris believed:

> I was only attacked as a means of getting at DH and by some of my rivals at the WO who joined in the hunt. But I am not really worried about it. I have always done my best and it has been good on many occasions. Nothing else matters as regards myself.[1]

He was in many respects ill-equipped to be head of Intelligence, as is suggested by his miscalculations, yet these were honest errors and Charteris saw his reports as the truth. It was his misfortune that his optimistic and buoyant nature was matched by a lack of understanding and experience of Intelligence work, apparent in his errors of judgement over estimates of German reserves and morale. The evaluation of the morale of large groups is intricate and subtle, and Charteris was not at home with these complexities.

1 Charteris Private Papers, letter from Charteris to his wife, 17 November 1917.

ELEVEN

Evaluation

UNTIL all the material extracted from prisoners, documents, aerial observation, patrols, wireless and the other sources covered has been weighed and categorized by the Intelligence Staffs it is merely information, not Intelligence. The process of weighing and cross-checking is known as evaluation, a process in which very few senior officers were engaged. Macdonogh wrote to Kirke to say that not more than one per cent of Intelligence officers were involved in evaluation.[1] In essence evaluation is a matter of judgement and sense of proportion. It enables sound decisions to be made which will achieve given ends in the most economical manner in relation to observed facts. That kind of judgement is not the same thing as common sense, knowledge or understanding, though all three play a part.

In the First World War the Intelligence Staff was hamstrung by the problems faced in getting accurate information at the trench-bound front and even more by the difficulties in getting it back from the trenches. Consequently much of the advice the Intelligence Services were able to offer the Commander-in-Chief and the CIGS, and through them the War Cabinet, was no more than deductions based on probabilities. But the difficulties referred to were not the only or necessarily most influential problem. Evaluation was the province of the chosen few but even those few were subject to the vagaries and prejudices of human nature. However stringently those men were chosen, their judgements would still be influenced by what psychologists call 'noise', interference from matters not immediately connected with the subject, such as prejudice, personal differences, jealousy, illness, optimism, pessimism or the wish to stick to a preconceived plan. Conflicting evidence was a common problem. In July 1918, there were doubts about evidence from prisoners and deserters, about the location of artillery positions and dumps and the fact that the Army Group of Kronprinz Rupprecht of Bavaria still had

1 Kirke Papers, loc. cit., letter from Macdonogh to Kirke, 2 November 1925.

a large number of uncommitted divisions in Flanders. Haig mused in his diary:

> Will the enemy go on with his attacks about Rheims, or will he withdraw such of his reserves as are left and add them to Rupprecht's Reserves for a blow against the British? Evidence seems to be accumulating of an attack against the Hazebrouck-Ypres front about the 20th. A captured Officer under special examination stated that his trench mortars had to be in position in the Kemmel sector by the 16th. Another prisoner stated that an attack is to be launched on that front between the 18th and 20th.[1]

In this case the dilemma went unresolved until the Germans had the initiative brusquely torn from their grasp by the French General Mangin's counter-attack at Villers Cottérêts on 18 July.

Situations like this demanded that those officers charged with the task of evaluation resort to deduction, albeit deduction informed by experience and training. In the short term the enemy's immediately available strength, his dispositions and known inclinations were important, but beyond that his ability to take the strain depended in the end on his reserves of manpower, on the strength of his industry and the moral stamina of his people. A case in point is the British view of likely German action following the replacement of von Falkenhayn as Chief of the Great General Staff by Hindenburg and Ludendorff. Falkenhayn's offensive at Verdun, designed to bleed the French Army white, had succeeded in haemorrhaging the German Army too, and the Allied offensive on the Somme, supposedly forestalled by Falkenhayn's stroke at Verdun, made Germany's manpower situation perilous. To cap it all, the Russian Brusilov offensive tore a gaping hole in the Eastern front, a wound soon aggravated by Roumania's declaration of war. Germany's new helmsmen came straight from the Eastern front and had several options open to them. The British General Staff were forced to admit that 'An investigation of the enemy's intentions, being necessarily speculative, often fails, and while three courses may seem open to him he frequently selects a fourth.'[2]

The options deemed open to the Germans were to renew the offensive at Verdun, to attempt to defeat Roumania, to launch offensives on either the Russian Northern or Southern fronts, or to

1 Haig Diaries, op. cit., 16 July 1918.

2 'Possible action of the Central Powers During the Autumn and Winter of 1916', 9 September 1916, PRO WO106/310.

attempt an invasion of Britain. An offensive on the Russian Northern front was considered unlikely: winter conditions were harsh and German troop strength there had been reduced to send help to the Austrians, reeling from the Brusilov offensive. An offensive on the Russian Southern front would have no worthwhile strategic objective: Kiev, the nearest city of any importance, was some 250 miles from the present front line. An invasion of Britain was considered improbable since it would afford no relief to Austria, the season was too far advanced and anyway command of the sea was required if the forces landed were not to be isolated and defeated, and this the Germans did not have. The remaining options were to attack Roumania or to re-open the Verdun offensive. It was surmised (correctly) that Hindenburg as an 'Easterner' had opposed the Verdun venture from the outset, and an effort at Verdun would not alleviate Austrian distress. It was consequently considered that Germany was most likely to attack Roumania, which in fact was what happened. Correct evaluation did little to help Roumania, however, since neither the British nor the French Army could offer direct assistance: therefore renewed assaults on the unyielding trench lines in France was their only realistic response. Thinking never progressed far enough to consider all the German options after dealing with Roumania. The DMI estimated in November 1917 that Germany's most likely course in 1918 would be to knock Italy out of the war.[1]

Such deductions did not figure prominently in the decisions that shaped the way the war was fought overall. The slaughter of 1916 marked a turning point, for it drew a new dedication to the struggle from the belligerent governments who, rightly or wrongly, decided they could not turn back after sustaining such horrific losses unless they could offer complete victory to their peoples. It was in Germany that the most vigorous reaction to these circumstances was found and in February 1917, the CIGS, General Sir William Robertson, offered it as his considered opinion that Germany was preparing to make a supreme effort that year 'which, as she has not the men required to maintain in the field for a long period all the new divisions she is forming, seems to be directed to obtaining an early decision of the war'.[2] In the same paper the CIGS observed 'all indications go to show that the campaign of the coming summer will govern the final

1 *See* respectively, 'German Plans for the Winter of 1917–18', PRO WO106/1511 and 'Note by the DMI,' 17 November 1917, PRO WO106/1516.
2 'Germany's Intentions', 23 February 1917, PRO WO106/1512.

issue of the war' and it was therefore necessary to 'give the enemy a sound beating'.[1] Robertson also cautioned that 'We must, however, carefully guard against jumping to the conclusion that a sound beating is the same thing as winning the war outright this year.'[2] By March Robertson noted that there was 'every indication that this year's campaign will prove decisive', but that victory was likely to be reached 'not by the breaking of the German line or the retirement of the German armies, but by the exhaustion of the Central Powers, and nothing would be more fatal than to give the impression that we are staking everything on the result of one battle or on our ability to win a great strategical victory. It is certain that the war is entering on a phase which will impose a far severer strain on all the belligerents than they have yet had to bear, and victory will rest with that side which displays the greatest resolution and endurance.'[3] Attrition would be slow and require a large and indefinite number of men; a breakthrough would require the British to take a far larger share in the offensive than they had hitherto, and would equally require a large number of troops.

In the view of the General Staff at the War Office, based on evidence from Intelligence operations on a global scale, the focus had shifted from simply defeating the German Army in the field to a slow and expensive struggle of exhaustion, much as Bloch had forecast. Yet the chosen military path was a painful one which most politicians and some soldiers were reluctant to tread. A great, decisive, traditional-style victory in the field would relieve them of the need to go that way. If the victory could not be won on the Western front, might it not be won elsewhere?

Haig felt there was every chance of just such a victory if he were given the men and guns he needed to bring it off. He accepted that it would take time to achieve and that it would only come through the exhaustion of the German Army's physical and moral powers of endurance, but still he felt that the prospect was realistic. His approach, and the difference of emphasis with the War Office, was shown in his assessment of June 1917 (*see* p. 337).

Haig believed that the only way to win a war of endurance was to concentrate on wearing out the German Army on the battlefield in order to win the great victory the politicians wanted. In command of

1 Ibid.
2 Ibid.
3 'A General Review of the Situation in All Theatres of War', 20 March 1917, PRO WO106/1512.

the largest Army Britain had ever put into the field, he can hardly have been expected to tell the Government that such a victory was unattainable. In November he told the CIGS:

> I am convinced that the peace we aim at can be attained only by the defeat of the German armies; that by concentration of effort and full development of our resources we can defeat them, the time required depending to some extent on the amount of assistance given by our Allies.[1]

There was a sharp difference in emphasis between the War Office and GHQ over the way in which Germany was to be beaten. GHQ, as was its job, held that victory in the field, *à la* Napoleon, was the only way to force Germany to sue for peace. A circle of brighter minds at the War Office did not exclude victory in the field from their picture but they placed it in perspective as one part – albeit a key part – of a very much broader equation. The differing approaches originated to some degree in the evidence supplied by the different Intelligence branches upon which those judgements were based, their respective manpower and morale studies.

Manpower studies comprised two inter-related sections, one dealing with the strength and losses of the hostile armies in the field, and the other with reserves in the homeland who could serve with the armies in the field. The War Office and GHQ employed different means of assessing these factors. The former allotted a fixed percentage of casualties to every battalion the enemy had engaged in a specific action. To give an example, a paper by Macdonogh on German losses in the Somme offensive up to 30 September 1916 stated that, since 1 July, 380 individual battalions had been engaged by the enemy on the British section of the Somme, of which 35 had been used twice and 25 others had remained in the line for the whole three months. Macdonogh considered it safe to assume that these 25 battalions had received 100 per cent drafts over this period: it was German practice to replace losses in active and reserve units without battalion movements. Consequently the number of battalions engaged was 380 + 35 + 25; giving a total of 440. The German official casualty lists (at this stage belated and incomplete) showed an average loss of 43 per cent in infantry. Macdonogh considered that 'We shall therefore probably not be taking too high a figure if we assume an average of 50 p.c. casualties

1 OAD 702, letter from Haig to Robertson, 13 November 1917, PRO WO 106/308.

in the 440 infantry battalions engaged.'[1] These calculations put German losses at 220,000 men, to which an estimated 40,000 was added for losses amongst supporting units, such as artillery and pioneers. As the French were heavily engaged in the offensive as well, a similar calculation was made for their section of the front. This figure, added to that on the British section, gave a total of 884 German battalions engaged and a total estimated German loss of 522,000 men. This was only an estimate and Macdonogh admitted 'it is of course not possible to give as yet, any exact estimate of the German losses on the Somme'.[2]

While not pretending to be exact, this method of estimating enemy losses continued to be used. When the Germans were relieving their divisions more frequently, as in Flanders in 1917, it became necessary to take a somewhat lower figure as a basis of loss. The estimated percentage was reduced to 2000 men per division, or approximately 17 per cent, with losses of supporting arms being estimated at a fifth of this. On this basis the total German casualties on the British front in 1917 were estimated at 976,000 men. The rest of the Western front was considered to have cost the Germans 800,000 men and the Eastern, Balkan and Italian fronts a further 300,000. The gross German casualties on all fronts in 1917 were estimated to be a staggering 2,000,000 men.[3]

By contrast GHQ arrived at its estimates of German losses through the study of captured paybooks. Although these provided a sound record of the wastage of conscription classes they were by no means precise enough to render a sufficiently detailed guide to losses in a specific engagement: for that they needed to be regarded with a healthy degree of caution. They were, however, the basis for the June 1917 statement by Charteris that:

> A reliable informant has given the total casualties suffered by the German Army in the battles of Arras, Champagne and the Aisne up to the beginning of this month [June 1917] as 400,000.[4]

Charteris argued that the total casualties suffered by the Germans since the beginning of April 1917 were not less than 500,000 men, an

1 'German Casualties in the Somme Fighting', 30 September 1916, PRO WO106/310.
2 Ibid.
3 'Estimate of German Casualties on the British Front and on the Other Fronts in 1917', MI3 11 December 1917, PRO WO 106/313.
4 Ia/35273, 'Note on the Strategical Situation with Special Reference to the Present Condition of German Resources and Probable German Operations', 11 June 1917, PRO T173/829.

average of nearly 250,000 a month. The War Office held that German losses at Arras from 9 April to 16 May had been only 132,000 men.[1] The discrepancy between their figures and those of Charteris – no fewer than 368,000 Germans – would have had to be accounted for by wastage and French efforts. This was clearly excessive for a period of barely two months; two months, moreover, which had seen the French Army racked by widespread 'collective indiscipline', as the mutinies of early 1917 have been called.

Charteris constructed a graph showing the decline in enemy reserves from the information contained in the paybooks. Reliance on this method prompted Haig's reply to Smuts's query about GHQ estimates of German losses: he said 'they had the evidence of the captured company rolls [the roll numbers in the paybooks], which all pointed in one direction'.[2] The author of the *Pioneer* article mentioned earlier stated that in London's view:

> Battles were being fought principally to cause a drop in the curve of that graph – showing a further decrease in enemy man-power. It was decided that it wasn't good enough (even given that the graph was accurate, which the wretched thing never was).[3]

Charteris, however, was convinced he was right and that his graph proved his case that Germany was nearly beaten. His sincerity in this respect is clear from a statement by Kirke in August 1916 on the war's probable duration:

> Personally I see no reason why the war should end for another year as K [Kitchener] foretold, though there are a number who think it's nearly over now, including Charteris. I think they are wrong. Things are going quite nicely on the whole for those who don't expect miracles.[4]

Nevertheless, Charteris's figures could give no indication of how many of the 'missing' men had been transferred to other formations or were on leave or absent for any other reason.

GHQ were persuaded to think again about reliance on German paybooks, the shortcomings of which were bluntly underlined in the

1 'Table showing comparative British and enemy casualties on the battle fronts of Arras, Messines and the Third battle of Ypres (to 5 October 1917)', 17 October 1917, PRO WO106/313.

2 Terraine, *The Road to Passchendaele*, op. cit., p. 85, citing the 'Cabinet Committee On War Policy', 11 June 1917, PRO CAB 27/6.

3 Charteris Papers, loc. cit., *The Pioneer*, 27 June 1929.

4 Kirke Papers, loc. cit., letter from Kirke to his mother, 27 August 1916.

debates surrounding Haig's proposals for an offensive from Ypres that summer. In August 1917 GHQ adopted a means of estimating enemy casualties which closely resembled the War Office system. After observing that the 1918 Class provided between 17 and 25 per cent of prisoners taken (which corresponds to the information in the Bosworth Papers), GHQ proceeded to estimate enemy losses in Flanders and at Lens by classifying divisions as 'exhausted' when withdrawn from the line after losing 3,200 men, all arms. On this basis GHQ estimated the German losses in Flanders up until 21 August as 90,000 men and a further 10,000 at Lens.

Following the change of method at GHQ, in December 1917 both the War Office and GHQ submitted papers on German losses in the course of the year. The War Office estimated the Germans suffered 662,000 battle casualties on the British front and a further 314,000 through wastage, a total of 976,000 men. GHQ estimated the German loss as 710,500 battle casualties and 285,120 through wastage, a total of 995,620 men.[1] Estimates, however, are only that. When GHQ's estimates were formally called into question by Sir Henry Wilson in the paper (WP61) he had prepared for the Cabinet Committee on War Policy, in which he challenged not only Haig's strategy but the figures it was founded on, Haig could justifiably confound him by replying:

> As to my estimate of 100,000 as the average net German monthly loss, the casualty lists published until recently by the enemy show that their average loss has been greater than that, and up to the date when my paper [OAD 652, 8 October 1917] was submitted both the French authorities and the Intelligence branch at the War Office agreed that 100,000 was a safe estimate.[2]

That the Germans had suffered heavy losses could not be doubted; during 1917 the BEF alone had captured over 72,900 prisoners and 527 guns on the Western front.[3] Had the British armies suffered such a loss in prisoners alone it would have been regarded in Whitehall as a major defeat. However, the true significance of these losses lay in the implications they had for German reserves and Germany's ability to continue the war.

The reserves available to the Germans had a considerable bearing on British strategy. The War Office Review of March 1917 had estimated

1 PRO WO106/313 and OAD 726, 10 December 1917, PRO WO106/3133.
2 OAD 702, 13 November 1917, PRO WO106/308.
3 'Our Military Effort During 1917', PRO WO106/308.

these reserves at 2,100,000 men, some 700,000 of whom would probably be required for the fresh divisions being raised, leaving 1,400,000 to replace losses.[1] It was considered these reserves would not last beyond the winter of 1917–18. The Review states:

> By the end of November 1917, therefore, and assuming that the rate of permanent casualties is as before, [120,000 men per month] the whole of Germany's present available reserve will be reduced to under half a million, and she will have in addition the youths of the 1920 Class, about 500,000 in number.[2]

In June Charteris presented a far more optimistic view. He argued that classes up to 1916 were exhausted as a source of drafts, that the 1917 Class was at its maximum and fielding between twelve and fifteen per cent of the fighting infantry and would provide few more reserves, that the 1918 Class was in the process of coming to the front in large numbers and was already providing the bulk of immediate reserves in the advanced field depots, and that the 1919 Class was in the home depots. He also argued that returning wounded might provide some 50,000 more men each month, indicating that the balance needed to replace the losses in the anticipated heavy fighting would have to be found from the younger classes. He concluded that:

> The question of man power may be summed up in one sentence, viz:– Germany is now within four to six months of the total exhaustion of her available man power, if the fighting continues at its present intensity. At the end of this time, it can be definitely asserted, she will be unable to maintain the strength of her field units at even their present reduced establishments.[3]

Once GHQ changed their method of assessing losses through captured paybooks, which exaggerated the estimate for monthly wastage in the German Army to more than twice the War Office estimate, such dangerous foundations for actions were largely eradicated.

The course of the Flanders offensive of 1917 led Lloyd George to seek the opinions of Field-Marshal Lord French and Lieutenant-General Sir Henry Wilson on the future strategy to be adopted. This raised the question of German reserves once again, for the basis upon

1 'A General Review of the Situation in all Theatres of War', 20 March 1917, PRO WO106/1512.
2 Ibid.
3 Ia/35273, 11 June 1917, PRO TI73/829.

which French and Wilson formed their judgement was an assessment of the situation by Macdonogh. He stated that Germany had 620,000 reserves in her home territories but that the 1920 Class was still to be called up and that might yield a further 550,000 men, although these were unlikely to be in the field before the spring of 1918. His final assessment was:

> It should be noticed that if fighting continues on the western front with the same intensity as during the last year Germany may not enter 1918 with more than 200,000 men in reserve in addition to the 1920 Class. She will probably hold back her 1921 Class as long as possible, and it seems highly unlikely that more than a quarter of a million of that class could be made fit for field service during 1918. If, therefore, casualties continue at their normal rate the whole available reserve would be exhausted during that year.[1]

Macdonogh recognized German reserves were running out and at this stage the difference between his and Charteris's view is measured in months rather than years. By the time Macdonogh's paper was presented, the GHQ figures were already out of date. Towards the end of August, Haig was already beginning to temper his views, telling Robertson only that 'The time is fast approaching when [the enemy] will be unable to maintain his armies at their present numerical strength.'[2] As time wore on, so the degree of change at GHQ became greater and in his reply to the criticisms of French and Wilson, Haig's view was closely aligned to Macdonogh's:

> The considerable wastage imposed on the enemy by a continued offensive may be expected to leave at the end of the year but a small balance, if any, of the 500,000 men in the reserves he now has available, and he is likely to commence the new year with only some 500–600,000 reserves at his disposal including the whole of the 1920 Class which, judging by the experience of the 1918 Class, will be of low fighting value. At the normal rate of wastage, therefore, since the 1921 Class will not be fit to take the field next year, the enemy's man power will be running out next May or June at the latest.[3]

There was still some difference between the views of the War Office

1 W.P.49, Cabinet Committee on War Policy, 'The Man-Power and Internal Conditions of the Central Powers', Note by the Director of Military Intelligence, 31 August – 1 October 1917, PRO WO106/312.
2 OAD 602, 21 August 1917, PRO WO106/407.
3 Haig Dairies, op. cit., OAD 652, 8 October 1917.

and GHQ, but the gap had narrowed considerably. Robertson commented:

> As regards the reserve available on October 1st, there is a difference between the calculations of Sir Douglas Haig and the Director of Military Intelligence respectively of 720,000 less 500,000–220,000. It is not altogether surprising that two different officers should arrive at two different conclusions, and the difference is not great seeing that Germany has a population of 68,000,000.[1]

Both the War Office and GHQ expected the war to continue into 1918 and both expected that Germany's reserves would run out then. What altered the equation altogether was the collapse of Russia, which permitted the Germans to transfer more than 40 divisions to the Western front.

Views on Russia, both War Office and GHQ, were subject to some uncertainty. The prime minister, David Lloyd George, had requested Haig's views on the role of the British armies in the event of Russia being unable to maintain an active part in the war, in conjunction with the weakened condition of France and Italy. Haig still considered that there were sufficient prospects of success in the West to justify a continuation of the offensive. He dismissed the very idea of sending large reinforcements to fronts other than the Western on the grounds that under the conditions postulated by the prime minister, 'my armies might be reduced to the defensive'.[2] When that was written the Bolshevik coup had not yet thrust its menace upon the world and Russia was still at war with Germany. Haig could still observe that:

> I am confident that if the measures I have advocated are adopted success on the Western front is within our power, even though Russia should collapse entirely and despite the weakened state of France and Italy . . .
>
> So far the enemy has brought but few divisions from Russia to this side and those he has brought have in most cases been replaced by divisions exhausted in the fighting here. Evidently, therefore, he does not expect any immediate total collapse in Russia . . .
>
> The German forces transferred to the Western front would in all probability be limited to, at the most, the thirty-two more efficient

1 Letter from CIGS to Secretary War Cabinet, 26 October 1917, PRO WO106/1515 and WO106/308.

2 Haig Diaries, op. cit., OAD 652, 8 October 1917, PRO WO106/407.

> divisions above mentioned, giving Germany a total of a hundred and seventy-nine divisions on this front.[1]

Haig also considered it possible that Russia might not collapse, arguing that future developments in Russia were so uncertain that the possibility of Russia being able to hold the present number of German divisions on the Eastern front could not be ignored: 'Russia may prove capable of more than has been reckoned on, since the alternative for her is to submit to a separate peace on Germany's terms, and to forfeit the friendship of her allies and the respect of the world.'[2] Not having to confront the difficulty at first-hand and balance the requirements of the BEF in France against the demands of the Navy, the mercantile marine and industry – all of which were absolutely essential to Britain's war effort – GHQ comfortably left the War Office and the Cabinet to solve the sticky problem of the supply of men.

Uncertainty about Russia was not confined to GHQ. The War Office had been closely watching events in Russia throughout 1917, and presented studies to the CIGS and War Cabinet at various stages. The paper on 'Military Effect of Russia Seceding from the Entente' of 9 May showed that the War Office was alive to the risk that Russia might collapse. 'The Present Military Situation in Russia and its Effects on our Future Plans' of 29 July noted that the Russians no longer had the will to fight, but cautioned: 'On the whole we ought not to jump to the conclusion that Russia is out of the war for good and all.' But on 17 November the 'Note by DMI' on military action to be taken in 1918 considered that Russia was incapable of mounting a serious offensive in 1918 and could not remain in the war into 1919. Macdonogh went so far as to support the GHQ view that an offensive in the West was the best way of meeting the threat. The choice, wrote Macdonogh, lay between attacking strongly or defending strongly 'and there can be little doubt that the offensive will produce far better results than the defensive': it could lead to victory in 1918 with Germany collapsing before the harvest of that year had been gathered in.[3]

Once Russia did start negotiations for peace, GHQ was swifter than the War Office to recognize the implications, for not only did GHQ Intelligence note the likelihood of a German offensive in the

1 Ibid.
2 Ibid.
3 *See*, respectively, PRO WO 106/1512, 1513 and 1516.

West, but also predicted when the offensive would begin. The realization of the changed circumstances in Russia first became apparent at the beginning of December 1917. Haig recorded the content of a conversation with Kiggell, his CGS, as follows:

> With the fact of Russia entering into negotiations for peace without consulting us, it is possible that Germany may start a big offensive on this front next Spring. We ought therefore to make our front as strong as possible and avoid having weak points.[1]

As early as 6 December Charteris presented his opinion that the Germans would attempt to deliver such a blow on the Western front in the early spring, not later than the beginning of March, as that would force a decisive battle before the American Army could have an effect.[2] Haig observed on 20 December that 'C [Charteris] thought that the enemy's big blow would not fall until March.'[3]

Kirke, who served in GHQ Intelligence under Charteris and was then at the War Office, was never a friend of Charteris, resented what he regarded as the latter's ill-informed meddling with his own work and was quite scathing about the optimism of his chief. Nevertheless, he was too much a professional to permit his personal feelings to muddy the waters of his judgement. His professional approach was reflected in one of his lectures to his Staff College students:

> You may say that the efforts of the Intelligence were not worth much in the war, for the highly optimistic estimates formed at GHQ in '16 and '17 of the waning strength of the Germans were proved to be all wrong. Personally, I do not draw that particular conclusion. The Germans were undoubtedly very near the end of their tether up to the moment when the Russian Revolution upset all calculations. The mistake made at GHQ was in not recognising the enormous effect caused by the Russian Revolution.[4]

Prospects of victory did not solely depend on estimates of losses or on available reserves, but on the will to fight of the men who made up those reserves. Evaluation of the enemy's morale was a very influential factor in deciding whether to aim for a struggle of endurance or victory in the field, and it was over the evaluation of German morale

1 Haig Diaries, op. cit., 2 December 1917.
2 Haig Diaries, op. cit., Ia/42726, 'Note on German Intentions', 6 December 1917.
3 Haig Diaries, op. cit., 20 December 1917.
4 Kirke Papers, loc. cit., 'Lecture on Secret Service', 27 November 1925.

that the Intelligence branches of the War Office and GHQ differed most considerably.

The conduct required of a soldier in the field is to fight as long as he has the means to do so, even though he risks being killed or wounded in the process. Soldiers who fight until disabled by death or wounds are doing their duty to the full and can be said to have good morale. Soldiers who desert or surrender readily in large numbers while still capable of fighting are not doing their duty and display poor morale. How widespread this conduct is within an Army as a whole dictates whether any evaluation of morale as poor can have general application. Morale on the home front can be considered good if the bulk of the population actively support the national war effort, or at least refrain from hindering it.

All groups are composed of sub-groups and when a nation is the primary group under consideration, its component sub-groups are its racial and political elements. Thus Germany had sub-groups which could be described as Saxons, Alsatians, Majority Socialists and Independent Socialists, among others. Intelligence battened onto several of the more fragmentary of these sub-groups and used them to good effect on several occasions during the war to cause deeper and deeper cracks in the façade of German unity. To a great extent the unity of any group depends on the confidence group members have in their leadership and its ability to attain group goals. In a united group relatively few people will dispute the general drift of policy, or have the confidence to disagree openly with the view of the majority. Yet any disturbance of unanimity increases the confidence of individuals and minorities in offering a challenge to group decisions and this can lead to a decisive shift in opinion.[1] This was precisely what Macdonogh was seeking to bring about, basing his assessment expressed in 'Effect of Military Operations on the Political Situation in Germany' on the growing, dangerous and ever more overt rifts in German society and political life. Once these divisions had come into the open in wartime conditions they would be impossible to heal, especially if external pressure continued to build up the momentum. In Macdonogh's view, military efforts on the Western front would apply the bulk of the pressure, aided and abetted by a campaign of subversion and propaganda.

1 A. Pepitone, 'The Determinants of Distortion in Social Perception' in H. Prochansky and B. Seidenberg, *Basic Studies in Social Psychology*, London 1969, p.398 ff.

That cohesion was recognized as symptomatic of sound morale is demonstrated in a paper by Major-General C. H. Harington, widely regarded as one of the best staff officers in the war. He stated that the power of the enemy's armies to maintain the struggle depended on three primary factors: (a) Man Power; (b) Material Resources; (c) Moral Cohesion.[1] It is worthy of note that factor (c) is not entered as 'morale' alone. In a perceptive and accurate paper on Austro-Hungarian morale of July 1917 the two sides of the morale question in a total war were clearly recognized:

> In examining the 'morale' of any belligerent it is necessary to distinguish between the army in the field and the rest of the nation, including the troops in depots and garrisons in home territory.[2]

The paper then listed the sources for evaluating the army in the field as: (a) The behaviour of the troops in action; (b) The examination of prisoners; (c) Captured documents. The relative importance of these sources was assessed, and the conclusion drawn as follows:

> It must be admitted that the behaviour of Austro-Hungarian troops in action, which is by far the most important criterion, shows little evidence of loss of morale. In the recent fighting on the Isonzo and in the Trentino they fought as well as at any previous period of the war. The examination of the prisoners taken in the recent fighting on the Isonzo showed that, although the standard varied greatly in different units, the general average of both physique and morale was good.[3]

The importance of deserters and captured documents was put into perspective:

> There is not sufficient evidence, however, to state that the morale of the Austro-Hungarian troops in the Eastern Theatre has deteriorated since 1916. It is true that the numbers of deserters have increased during the last few months, and that these deserters have reported a certain lack of discipline in their units, but this is probably due to the open fraternization that was encouraged until recently between the opposing armies.
>
> There is, however, a considerable amount of evidence of loss of morale in captured letters on both fronts, but it must be remembered that similar letters have been found on German prisoners since the first

1 'Evidence of war-weariness and desire for a separate peace in Austria-Hungary', 7 July 1917, PRO WO106/1513.
2 Ibid.
3 Ibid.

> battle of Ypres in 1914. The worst type of soldier in every army will always write despairingly of his hardships and it would be unsound to infer a general lowering of morale from such complaints and protests.[1]

Thus the temptation to over-estimate moral decline because of one particular aspect, however consistent that may be, was avoided. The morale of the Austro-Hungarian Army was summed up thus:

> While there are undoubtedly discontented elements among the various nationalities represented in the army and a spirit of war-weariness prevails among individuals, there is yet no evidence of such a spirit developing into organized revolt, nor are there indications of a marked or widespread deterioration in the morale of the troops.'[2]

The morale of the nation was assessed from: (a) Captured documents; (b) Reports of neutral travellers; (c) Reports of agents; (d) The enemy press; (e) Indirect evidence from political changes. Many captured documents revealed evidence of war-weariness, with discussion of peace prospects being prevalent in February and March due to the rigours of the hard winter of 1916–17. Shortages of food and fuel were the subjects of numerous complaints, but again these had to be put into perspective since 'it must be noted, however, that similar expressions of complaint and despair are found in letters on German prisoners, and, according to the enemy wireless news, on Allied prisoners as well'.[3]

While the desire for peace was widespread in Austria-Hungary, a caution was included against assuming this was greater than elsewhere in Europe simply because of captured correspondence. On the other hand, 'The reports of neutral travellers, however, indicate that the feeling of war-weariness is more pronounced in Austria-Hungary than in Germany,'[4] and the 'reports of agents tend to confirm the impression of general war-weariness'.[5] War-weariness could take an active form, too: in June 1917 alone there were reports of explosions at the Skoda munitions factory in Pilsen, the dynamite factory at Pressburg, the ammunition factories at Budapest, Steinfeld and Bloeweg and a major strike at the Skoda works.

Politically, significance was attached to the Emperor summoning

1 Ibid.
2 Ibid.
3 Ibid.
4 Ibid.
5 Ibid.

the Reichsrat and granting an amnesty to Czech political prisoners, despite fierce opposition from Germans in both Austria and Germany. Pacifist speeches in the Reichsrat and similar expressions in the officially inspired Press drew forth the conclusion that:

> There is ample evidence, therefore, that the feeling of war-weariness in Austria-Hungary has reached a point at which the Government is forced to attempt to counteract it by conciliating the various nationalities and by convincing the people as a whole that, as far as the Government is concerned, there is no obstacle to an honourable peace.[1]

However, Austria was not prepared for peace at any price:

> Although there are many indications that Austria-Hungary is anxious for peace, and that certain sections of the people are possibly willing to accept any terms, there are no signs that the people as a whole is ready to accept the terms as defined in the Entente reply to President Wilson in January, 1917.[2]

Austria was still prepared to fight as Allied conditions for peace 'offered her no future except at the price of her dismemberment and have undoubtedly had the effect of strengthening the resistance of the people'.[3]

The fear of harsh peace terms grew stronger in all combatant nations through the severity of the peace inflicted on the weak and helpless Bolshevik Russia at Brest-Litovsk and remained strong throughout the war with governments on both sides insisting on winning an absolute victory. This underlay all the peace initiatives made throughout the war; they were unrealistic because each government insisted on maintaining fantastic and often ridiculous war aims to crush their enemies politically and economically. The only alternative to such a peace was to fight. It was on this basis that Macdonogh assessed German morale in his W.P. 49 of 31 August 1917, summing up:

> While the morale of the German people is as yet far from being broken and while the economic situation cannot yet be depended upon to bring Germany to terms, transportation is daily becoming more inefficient and public opinion is undoubtedly becoming highly sensi-

1 Ibid.
2 Ibid.
3 Ibid.

tive, disappointed and suspicious. At the same time it must be remembered that further military successes against German troops, combined with a very stringent blockade will alone cause the German people to lose confidence in their rulers.[1]

Haig wrote in blue crayon on his copy of the paper: 'In my opinion a most inadequate statement of the existing state of the German forces on the Western front,' initialling this statement and adding the date, 14 October 1917.[2] Haig replied with a paper which revealed how GHQ evaluated German morale, adding a covering note saying:

> The statements referred to [in W.P. 49] appear to me to represent the situation in a far more unfavourable light than is justified by evidence contained in various captured orders, letters and other documents, by prisoners' statements, and by the experience of our officers and men in recent fighting.[3]

The evidence GHQ relied upon to evaluate German morale came from several sources: German troops who had surrendered readily (men of the 19th Reserve Division); large numbers of prisoners (from the 20th Division); prisoners' statements suggesting poor discipline, near mutiny and dereliction of duty (men from the 45th Reserve Division, 10th Bavarian Division, 6th Bavarian Division, 79th Reserve Division and 206th Division); captured documents (from the 19th Reserve Division and 369th Infanterie Regiment); and evidence from British troops of 'numerous instances of a willingness to surrender on the part of the larger bodies of German troops, and there is a remarkable unanimity of opinion in our ranks as to the marked and steadily growing deterioration in the enemy's fighting qualities and morale'.[4]

In comparison with the War Office paper on Austro-Hungarian morale, GHQ showed no sign of placing the evidence cited into its perspective. Haig's letter to Robertson of 13 August 1917, underlines this fact:

> In this Army we are convinced we can beat the enemy provided units are kept up to strength in men and material. Our opinion is based on actual *facts* viz: the poor state of German troops, high standard of efficiency of our own, power of our artillery to dominate enemy guns,

1 W.P. 49, op. cit., PRO WO 106/312.
2 Haig Diaries, op. cit., papers relating to 15 October 1917.
3 Ibid., papers relating to 16 October 1917.
4 Ibid., *see also* PRO WO 106/313.

> etc. etc.. An occasional glance at our daily intelligence summaries would convince even the most sceptical of the truth of what I write. Moreover I have been in the field now for three years and know what I am writing about.[1]

The underlying problem was that GHQ took too narrow a view of German morale, basing their evaluation on the troops opposite active sectors of the BEF. Prisoners captured under such conditions could be expected to display signs of demoralization and Macdonogh was fully prepared to concede German morale would be 'naturally shaken in sectors of great hostile activity'.

A study of the morale of the BEF, based on its correspondence in the winter of 1917–18 is worth noting in this context. The study concluded that the morale of the Army as whole was sound. Nevertheless:

> There is a very striking difference between the results of the examination of the Second Army which at the time was bearing the brunt of the fighting, and that of the other Armies, and it must be admitted that in the former the favourable and unfavourable letters were almost evenly balanced; but taking into consideration the stress both mental and physical under which letters were written by men who are in the thick of the struggle it would be an injustice to the men to suggest that no mental reaction will take place under less strenuous circumstances, any more than that the high morale of the troops in the quieter sectors would die away when they are moved to more lively positions. In the other armies the favourable extracts greatly exceeded the adverse. In all armies a very large proportion of the letters specially examined contained no passages directly bearing on the subject, but were merely cheery ordinary letters which taken as a whole may be regarded as a favourable sign. It is not desired to gloss over or minimise the unfavourable aspect of this all important subject. War weariness there is, and an almost universal longing for peace but there is a strong current of feeling that only one kind of peace is possible and that the time is not yet come.[2]

It is a pity that the qualifications emphasized in this extract were not stressed equally when dealing with German correspondence. They underline Macdonogh's perhaps obvious view that the morale of

1 Robertson Papers, loc. cit., I/23/44.

2 'The British Armies in France as Gathered from Censorship', 18 December 1917, PRO WO 106/401.

troops in sectors of great activity would be shaken to a far greater extent than in the rest of the Army.

Men will usually fight if they perceive a reasonable chance of success or of serving a useful purpose. Consider the statement by the officer commanding 41st Trench Mortar Battery about his capture on 21 March 1918. Lieutenant Eccles wrote:

> The enemy had come up unobserved in the fog under cover of his bombardment; and before the mortars could reach the prepared dumps we were overwhelmed. It was a case of surrender or being shot down without chance to hit back.[1]

Writing of the same battle, the historian Martin Middlebrook draws the conclusion:

> Men in Western Armies do not normally fight on to certain death, although the award of posthumous medals and the official honouring of dead heroes is usually done to encourage men to hold out longer in hopeless situations. The real limit of a Western soldier's resistance is that point at which he feels his individual honour is satisfied. If they cannot be certain of coming out of a battle safely, then most men are prepared to put up a resistance that varies in length of time according to the circumstances, but the average soldier inevitably thinks of surrender when he feels that he has satisfied his own standards of honour.[2]

Though the War Office proved better at evaluating morale than GHQ, they were not infallible. Kirke observed:

> As showing the reverse side of the picture our chief agent in Holland has been deceived so often that in August and September 1918 he did not send in a large number of reports indicating the rapid deterioration of the Germany Army and the prospect of a speedy break-up.[3]

Lack of liaison appears to lie at the root of the problem between GHQ and the War Office as was the case with the Secret Services. There was scant exchange of details between the two bodies and on occasion Robertson seems to have been desperate for information. As early as January 1916 he had recognized this danger and had written to Haig: 'We must rigorously avoid forming into two separate parties. Each

1 'Statement of Circumstances Which Led to Capture', Personal Service Record of Lieutenant C. E. S. S. Eccles, 41st Trench Mortar Battery (5th K.R.R.C.), courtesy of the Mr M. A. C. Eccles.
2 Middlebrook, *The Kaiser's Battle*, op. cit., pp. 335–6.
3 Kirke Papers, loc. cit., 'Lecture on Secret Service', 27 November 1925.

must know all about the other's difficulties. I found while with you that even in the short time that has lapsed I have got out of touch to some extent.'[1] For whatever reason it seems he was unsuccessful, for the papers of Kiggell, Haig's CGS, reveal that throughout 1917 Robertson had to press for information he was not getting. For example, in January 1917 he had to request information on Haig's plans for Flanders, and in August 1917:

> I do not wish to be given any secrets you do not care to entrust me, then I cannot give them to the Cabinet or to anyone else, but I would like to have a few lines occasionally giving your opinion as to how matters are progressing – of course with the knowledge of the Commander in Chief. Not unnaturally the Cabinet ask me my opinion every morning as to how matters are going and it is rather difficult for me to say much as I have nothing to rely upon but the Communiqués and the slight additions you occasionally send to me. It would well be worth while for you to drop me a line once or twice a week during operations and give me such information as will enable me to show that things are going on satisfactorily.[2]

Quite apart from the deplorable lack of liaison revealed here, there are indications that the War Cabinet was only told what the Army felt it needed to know. Possibly the optimistic views expressd at GHQ were designed to assist in this ploy and so maintain political support for the Army's strategy, but that is only conjecture.

A policy of long-term solutions and wearing out the enemy's manpower and morale had little relevance to the men at the sharp end. They were interested in beating the Germans and getting back home unharmed. The optimistic Intelligence Summaries which appeared in the trenches every week, glowing with tales of how the Germans were weakening and what great successes the Allies had won, became targets of derision for men who, through their own bitter experience, knew that the Germans still fought only too well and had not given up one yard of ground without a stiff fight.

The difference that good Intelligence could make to men in the trenches is best shown by comparing and contrasting occasions when Intelligence failed and when it delivered the goods. The German gas attack which opened the Second Battle of Ypres is one case where

1 Robertson Papers, loc. cit., I/22/18a, letter from Robertson to Haig, 24 January 1916.
2 Kiggell Papers, loc. cit., IV/6 and IV/8, *see* respectively letters from Robertson to Haig, 26 January and 2 August 1917.

Intelligence managed to gain news of the new horror, but fatally miscalculated its likely effects. The first intimation of the coming attack was received from a French agent who reported that an attack was to be made on the Ypres Salient on the night of 15–16 April.[1] Next, a prisoner from the German 234th Regiment, XXVI Corps was captured by the French near Langemarck on 14 April; he informed his interrogators that an attack had been intended for the 13th – reserves had been brought up and passages for the assaulting troops cut through the wire. Routes had been prepared for the artillery which was to support the attack.[2] As a result of these indications the British liaison officer with the French Détachement under General Putz forwarded a report to GHQ:

> The Germans intend making use of tubes with asphyxiating gas, placed in batteries of twenty tubes for every forty metres along the front of the XXVI Corps. This prisoner had in his possession a small sack filled with a kind of gauze or cotton waste which would be dipped in some solution to counteract the effect of this gas.[3]

Some half-hearted attempts were made to gain confirmatory evidence, but aerial reconnaissance revealed no sign of German reinforcements and a lack of artillery ammunition prevented a raid being made, so it was concluded that the prisoner had been planted by the Germans, and that his story was a ruse. Agents had, in addition, reported the collection of cotton fabric by the Germans but it was assumed that this was for bandages and was not connected with gas.[4] The idea that it was a ruse was apparently confirmed by another prisoner captured by the French. He carried a mask which, he said, was for protection against Allied gas. He stated that there were no gas bottles in his area and the French considered that this negated the earlier report.[5] The British did receive further information from the Belgians but although it was put on the Intelligence files at GHQ no further action appears to have been taken.[6] As it was thought that any attack would be directed against the French (as indeed it was), the British were not unduly concerned, though in the British V Corps Lieutenant-General Plumer passed on the warning of an attack 'for what it was worth'.[7]

1 Edmonds, op. cit., *1915*, Vol. III, p.163.
2 Ibid.
3 Ibid., p. 164.
4 Kirke Papers, loc. cit., 'Lectures on Secret Service', 27 November 1925.
5 Elliot, op cit., p. 27.
6 Edmonds, op. cit., p. 164.
7 Ibid.

Superficially, it is easy to condemn Intelligence and the General Staff for doing no more about the information they had. But the information held by the British in April 1915 was at best circumstantial evidence of something no one knew anything about. Gas warfare is familiar to everybody these days either through history books or its renewed use in the Gulf War, but to the men of 1915 the words conveyed nothing more than something like a 'Chinese stinkpot'. As Edmonds wrote, 'It was presumed, no doubt, that the effect of gas would be trivial and local.'[1]

In contrast, during the limited German offensive between Boesinghe and Wieltje in the Ypres sector at the close of 1915, the movement of German reserves was observed and reported by agents at the beginning of December: the German 26th, 25th Reserve and 6th Reserve Divisions moved westwards to Flanders through Liège. Raids were undertaken and prisoners captured and aerial reconnaissance located gas stockpiles. GHQ were able to alert Second Army to expect an attack in this sector before the end of December. The Germans were planning to experiment with a new gas, phosgene, deadlier by far than the chlorine gas employed at Ypres in the spring and which, they hoped, would inflict severe losses on the British. Thanks to Intelligence warnings, Second Army was ready and waiting, its troops prepared with special anti-gas drills.[2] The Germans were prevented from leaving their trenches in any strength by a pre-arranged shrapnel barrage and, in the end, they only succeeded in pushing forward some twenty fighting patrols which were soon shot down by the waiting British infantry. From the German point of view the effort had been a complete flop. Their new gas had not lived up to expectations, at least had not been properly tested, and they had suffered severe losses in comparison to the British. Plumer, commanding the Second Army, personally thanked Macdonogh for his timely warning which had been decisive in beating off the attack.[3]

It was a fine end to Macdonogh's work on the Western front, for shortly he was to return to Britain to begin the work on the subversion campaign that had such an impact on the war. Alas, it was generally by things like the erroneous Intelligence Summaries that most fighting men judged Intelligence, as they knew nothing of behind-the-scenes operations. Unsurprisingly, when peace forced her time-honoured

1 Ibid., p. 165.
2 Edmonds, op. cit., *1916*, Vol. I, pp.158–62.
3 Kirke Diaries, op. cit., 12 and 19 December 1915.

rigid economies on the Army, the Intelligence Corps was a prime target, becoming an ever-smaller part of the Army of Occupation and vanishing entirely when the British withdrew from Germany.

APPENDIX I

Examination of German Deserter, Private Paul Sacksteder

Who gave himself up to the 3rd Division just east of ST ELOI on the night 10–11 April 1915.

1 Prisoner, who is 23 years of age, is a recruit who was rejected on medical grounds on first inspection and then posted to the 145th Regiment (XVI Corps) at METZ and transferred to the Ersatz Battalion of 4th Bavarian Infantry Regiment. Prisoner is a native of METZ, and speaks French better then he does German.

2 *METZ.* He remained at METZ with the Ersatz Battalion 4th Bavarian Regiment from 21 October until 7 March. He says that there are very few troops at METZ and that he does not think it so strong as is generally believed. METZ belongs to the Etappenabteilung VON STRANTZ. The forts have only small garrisons. The only fort that has been in action is FORT WAGNER near VERNY, which received a few shells.

German GHQ is on the railway between SEDAN and MONTMEDY, but the name of the station is carefully obliterated.

The gasometers at DIEDENHOFEN (THIONVILLE) have 'GOTT STRAFE ENGLAND' painted round them in enormous letters.

3 *Arrival at the Front.*
On 7 March prisoner was posted to 22nd Bav. Regt., 3rd Division (II Bav. Corps) and entrained from METZ to LILLE (La Madeleine Station). From LILLE he marched on the 8th to COMINES (Headquarters of II Bav. Corps and 3rd Bav. Div.?). There he was given a rifle, but he had to give up his iron rations.

4 *Enemy's distribution and defensive organization.*
The 22nd Bav. Regt. was then on the extreme right of the II Bav. Corps, with its right resting on the Canal. North of the Canal is the 99th Regt., XV Corps (G.O.C. VON DEIMLING). The 22nd Regt. then extended from canal to near ST ELOI, with the 23rd on its left.

About a week ago however the 22nd Regt. was withdrawn and sent elsewhere (said to be to ARRAS). Prisoner was transferred to 23rd Regt.

which then took over the whole front occupied by 22nd and 23rd (i.e. from Canal to just S.W. of ST ELOI – Mound. Order of Regiments right to left 23 – 17 – 18.

When the 23rd Regiment attacked ST ELOI on 14 March the 22nd merely demonstrated with rifle fire. They were told that the attack had succeeded 'without losses' but afterwards learned that there were 800 killed, wounded and missing. At that time he spent twelve days in the trenches, but the normal routine is three days in trenches, three days in support and three days in rest billets, though the periods are varied. His battalion (3rd) billets at BOUSBECQUE, the 1st and 2nd Battalions at WERVICQ.

The trenches are in good condition, and also the communication trenches. They are floored with planks laid on piles. There are loop-holes every four or five yards, mostly oblique to the front, and no dummy loop-holes. Our wire is as good as theirs. They do not work in front of the trenches much, but throw out knife-rests made by the pioneers.

5 *General.*

The 22nd Regt. used to wear a cap cover which hid the red cap-band. Shoulder-straps are seldom worn now. They have no trench mortars in his battalion. Plenty of hand grenades, but very few men know how to use them. They are of two patterns, a spherical one thrown by pioneers, and one fastened to a stick which has a fuse which has to be lit first.

6 *Artillery fire and targets.*

British Artillery fire very good, especially the field gun shrapnel, which bursts just the right height above the trench, and splinters fly back. Many of the larger shell of 10 cm (4.5″ Howr. ?) are blind, or the head merely blows off. Artillery waste ammunition by shelling second line trenches as these are unoccupied. The supports are in huts or dug-outs varying from 500 to 1500 metres behind the front line.

The German artillery is very strictly limited as regards ammunition. There are no guns in HOLLEBEKE Château Park, they are further South behind a wood, probably near OOSTTAVERNE.

The route taken by his battalion from the rest billets is BOUSBECQUE – WERVICQ – GODSHUIS – KORENTJE – HOUTHEM (Canal Bridge) – HOLLEBEKE – then due West. There is a Pioneer Park on the N.E. side of the road about 300 yards N.E. of HOUTHEM, and the field cookers are kept at the Western exit of HOLLEBEKE Village.

7 *Enemy's Distribution and Reserves.*

The distribution of regiments is normally two battalions in front and one in rest-billets. Prisoner had seen no other troops about except Train, 2nd

Pioneer Battn. a squadron of 3rd Bav. Chevaux-Legers (Divisional Cavalry who take their turn in the trenches and wear pink cap-bands), and the 47th Saxon Landwehr (47th Landwehr Brigade ?). The latter are in WERVICQ. He does not think Germans have any reserves near, and that an attack which went through the first line would have no further trouble.

Commander of 23rd Regt. is STETTIN, other commanders' names unknown. The brigade formation is no longer adhered to.

8 *Inhabitants.*

No inhabitants remain in HOUTHEM or West of it. They are in a very miserable condition, and heavily taxed. They can only get bread on producing bread tickets. This is worse than the soldiers' and has no yeast, and is very heavy. It is bran and potato meal mixed.

9 *German Morale.*

The Germans are confident of ultimate victory, but trust that the decisive battle will be won on some other portion of the line. They seem to have no notion of attacking here. The Bavarians are very good soldiers, better than the Prussians, and very fond of fighting – 'c'est leur grand plaisir'. Their discipline however depends on fear of their officers who treat them badly. They have great contempt for their officers who have little experience or ability, mostly promoted 'Einjahriger'. Their food is very poor and scanty. Beans and coffee, very little meat and bread.

The 'Iron Cross' is despised by the fighting troops, it is given to fawning deadheads on the lines of communication, regimental serjeant majors, etc. who never hear the sound of a bullet; 30,000 were distributed even before the fall of LIEGE.

The Kaiser and Hindenburg are popular heroes, but the Crown Prince has lost caste through his propensity for looting châteaux.

10 *English Prisoners.*

The English prisoners are very proud and obstinate. They refuse to work at all and so are kept strictly guarded in camps though not actually ill-treated. They will not resign themselves like the French and Russians who are mostly working in fields, factories and mines.

English prisoners are not allowed to work in the fields as the Germans fear they might make an organized attempt to escape.

English prisoners always refuse to salute German officers.

A well known English officer is said to have escaped from the Camp at WAHN; it is officially reported that he has been shot, but he is generally believed to have made good his escape.

11 *Credibility of evidence.*

SACKSTEDER is a native of LORRAINE and his native language is French, which he speaks better than German. He is a well educated man and he appeared to be telling the truth. He has no German sympathies.

J. H. M. Cornwall
Captain, GS

2nd Corps.
11 March 1915

APPENDIX II

GHQ Memorandum Instigating Raids

General Staff. GHQ
British Army in the Field,
Operations Section,
No. OA 447
Date, 5th Feb. 1915

First Army.
Second Army.
Cavalry Corps.
Indian Cavalry Corps.

1. The Field-Marshal Commanding-in-Chief desires me again to draw attention to the importance of constant activity and of offensive methods in general in dealing with the enemy immediately opposed to us.

2. For reasons known to you, we are for the moment acting on the defensive so far as serious operations are concerned, but this should not preclude the planning and making of local attacks on a comparatively small scale, with a view to gaining ground and of taking full advantage of any tactical or numerical inferiority on the part of the enemy. Such enterprises are highly valuable, and should receive every encouragement, since they relieve monotony and improve the morale of our own troops, while they have a corresponding detrimental effect on the morale of the enemy's troops and tend in a variety of ways to their exhaustion and general disquiet.

3. Further, as you are well aware, enterprises of this nature constitute the most effective form of defence, since by throwing upon the enemy anxiety for his own security, they help to relieve our own troops from the wearying and demoralising effects produced by expected attacks on the part of the enemy.

4. These minor operations should, of course, not be of an aimless character but should be based on a specific object, have a reasonable chance of success, and be commensurate with the losses likely to be entailed. They should be methodically initiated in accordance with the instructions of the Army

Commanders, and must invariably be well thought out beforehand, and careful preliminary arrangements made for their execution.

5. By the publication to neighbouring troops of short accounts of successful and meritorious work, by promptly bringing to the notice of the Commander-in-Chief the brave deeds of individuals, and by other similar means, the endeavour should be to create throughout the different formations and units of the Army a keen spirit of rivalry and emulation.

6. The Commander-in-Chief would be glad if you would give this matter your special attention, and issue the necessary instructions to give effect to his wishes.

W. R. Robertson.
Lieut.-General.
Chief of the General Staff.

APPENDIX III

Effect of Military Operations on the Political Situation in Germany

1. There can be no doubt that there is at the present moment a serious political crisis in Germany. As proofs of the existence of this crisis may be cited the fall of von Bethmann-Hollweg, the so-called 'Peace Resolution' passed by the Reichstag on 19 July, the formation of the Fatherland (or National) party which has been created to combat the Peace Resolution, and the recent attacks on Helfferich (the Vice-Chancellor), Michaelis (the Chancellor), Admiral von Capelle (Secretary of State for the Navy) and General von Stein (Minister for War), which are likely to result in the resignation of the three former officials.

2. The following extracts from moderate papers show how bitter the feeling is at present: The '*Vossische Zeitung*' describes Admiral von Capelle's attack on the Independent socialists as 'a deplorable, illegitimate trick on the part of the Government. Michaelis, as head of the Government, is responsible for the unhappy affair, which follows the unfortunate Helfferich incident.'

The '*Vorwärts*', in an article entitled 'Michaelis before the end', says 'The assertions of von Capelle have in an unspeakable manner converted the Reichstag into a theatre of the wildest scandal.'

The '*Kölnische Volkszeitung*' says 'Crisis is undoubtedly again in the air, a vote of want of confidence against the Chancellor being spoken of, and his fall, as well as that of the Vice-Chancellor, hinted at . . . We must get the better of this critical unrest, which is in such crying contrast to our brilliant military position.' The '*Kölnische Zeitung*' says 'The National Party is working against the Government. Unity is the need of the hour.'

3. The causes of the crisis may be summed up in the one word disillusionment. The German people feel that they have been misled by the predictions of the result of the U-boat campaign, by the forecasts of the harvest, by the promises of large quantities of grain and oil from Roumania, by the assertions that America would remain neutral, and above all by the prophecy of a brilliant strategical success after the retreat from the Somme, of the impossibility of a serious British offensive on account of the diminution of our munition supply through the action of the submarines, and more recently of the early collapse of the British offensive in Flanders.

All these promises and predictions were either made by the Government or were published in the officially inspired Press, and all have been proved false. The result is a widespread feeling of deep distrust which shows itself in political ferment.

4. The following statements by a German of considerable standing who was a witness of the crisis that resulted in the fall of von Bethmann-Hollweg, are noteworthy:

'Consternation and chaos reigned in the Government Departments in Berlin. It was fully expected that bureaucracy had seen its last day . . . A panic ensued and the fate of the German Empire was looked upon at that moment as almost sealed. Had a German Kerensky arisen, the Reichstag and the whole nation would have been behind him, perhaps for all time. Anything might happen in Germany now. The people have the power in their hands and intend to use it. Something has gone wrong in Germany. Another year of rationing, further disappointments in the U-boats, more heavy casualty lists, and the breaking strain will be reached.'

5. It is true that the July crisis was tided over by the intervention of von Hindenburg and Ludendorff, but the repeated heavy blows which the British Armies have dealt in the Western Theatre, combined with the unscrupulous efforts of the Pan-Germans to identify the Higher Command with their opposition to the Reichstag Majority, have undoubtedly begun to sap the confidence of the German people in their military leaders. Further crises are imminent and, apart from the pressure which the Entente can exert by maintaining a united front as regards war-aims and by repeating calmly and dispassionately through the medium of our leading statesmen the reasons for our refusal to treat with the present leaders of Germany, we can by maintaining at full strength our military pressure on the German Armies in the Western Theatre hasten the crises and accentuate internal dissensions. On the other hand, if this pressure is relaxed or transferred against one or other of Germany's Allies, the Higher Command may be enabled to restore confidence in the invincibility of the German Armies, to unite the warring factions and to reconcile the German people as a whole to the necessity of another year of war, supported by the conviction that by holding out they can win the peace that has been promised them.

They may even be enabled to win this winter an easy, spectacular victory similar to those of the Serbian and Roumanian campaigns in the winters of 1915 and 1916, by allowing them to withdraw troops from the Western Theatre and to concentrate them by means of their superior railway communications against one of our weaker allies before we could take the necessary steps to prevent a disaster.

6. But if our military pressure at full strength is maintained, the feelings of

apprehension will increase, the infallibility of von Hindenburg and Ludendorff will be further questioned, and pacifist tendencies will be strengthened.

The German Government will then be faced with one of two alternatives. They may attempt a *coup d'état* and dissolve the Reichstag, or they may throw over the Pan-Germans and endeavour to conciliate the Reichstag Majority. If the *coup d'état* is attempted, the resulting unrest will undermine the war spirit more quickly than we can dare to hope for at present, while, if a Moderate policy is adopted, we can depend upon the Pan-German to use their control of the heavy industries and agrarian interests to force a conflict with the rest of the nation.

In either case, therefore, a struggle between the bulk of the nation and a powerful and aggressive minority would be inevitable, and although it is not suggested, in spite of the recent revelations concerning the German Navy, that the majority would attempt a revolution, it is conceivable that, if the minority could not be brought to reason, the weapon of the general strike might be used.

7. To sum up, although it may be argued that the German armies cannot be decisively beaten in the field, the German nation is very vulnerable politically. The best weapon to take advantage of this weakness is military pressure for it will more than anything else accentuate the internal dissensions and contribute more rapidly than any other measure to the undermining and final breaking of the German war spirit which is our foremost war-aim.

G. M. W. Macdonogh,
DMI

General Staff,
War Office
13-10-17.

Secretary War Cabinet,
Please circulate to War Cabinet.

W. R. Robertson,
CIGS

14.10.17.

APPENDIX IV

Charts of War Office and GHQ Intelligence Organizations

Official titles in organizational charts of Intelligence can be misleading. For example, in the Directorate of Military Operations, MO2 was responsible for Intelligence in Russia, while in Egypt MO4 served as a cover for the Secret Service. Where such disguises can be recognized in the Directorates of Military and Special Intelligence, the official euphemism is contained in inverted commas and the genuine responsibility follows after a dash.

Key to charts:

DORA – Defence of the Realm Act
FO – Foreign Office
GS – General Staff
GSO – General Staff Officer; number denotes grade
IA – Indian Army
KRRC – King's Royal Rifle Corps; the 60th Foot
p.s.c. – Passed Staff College
RE – Royal Engineers
Res. of Off. – Reserve of Officers
RIR – Royal Irish Rifles
RN – Royal Navy
Temp. – Temporary
TF – Territorial Force (i.e. Territorial Army)

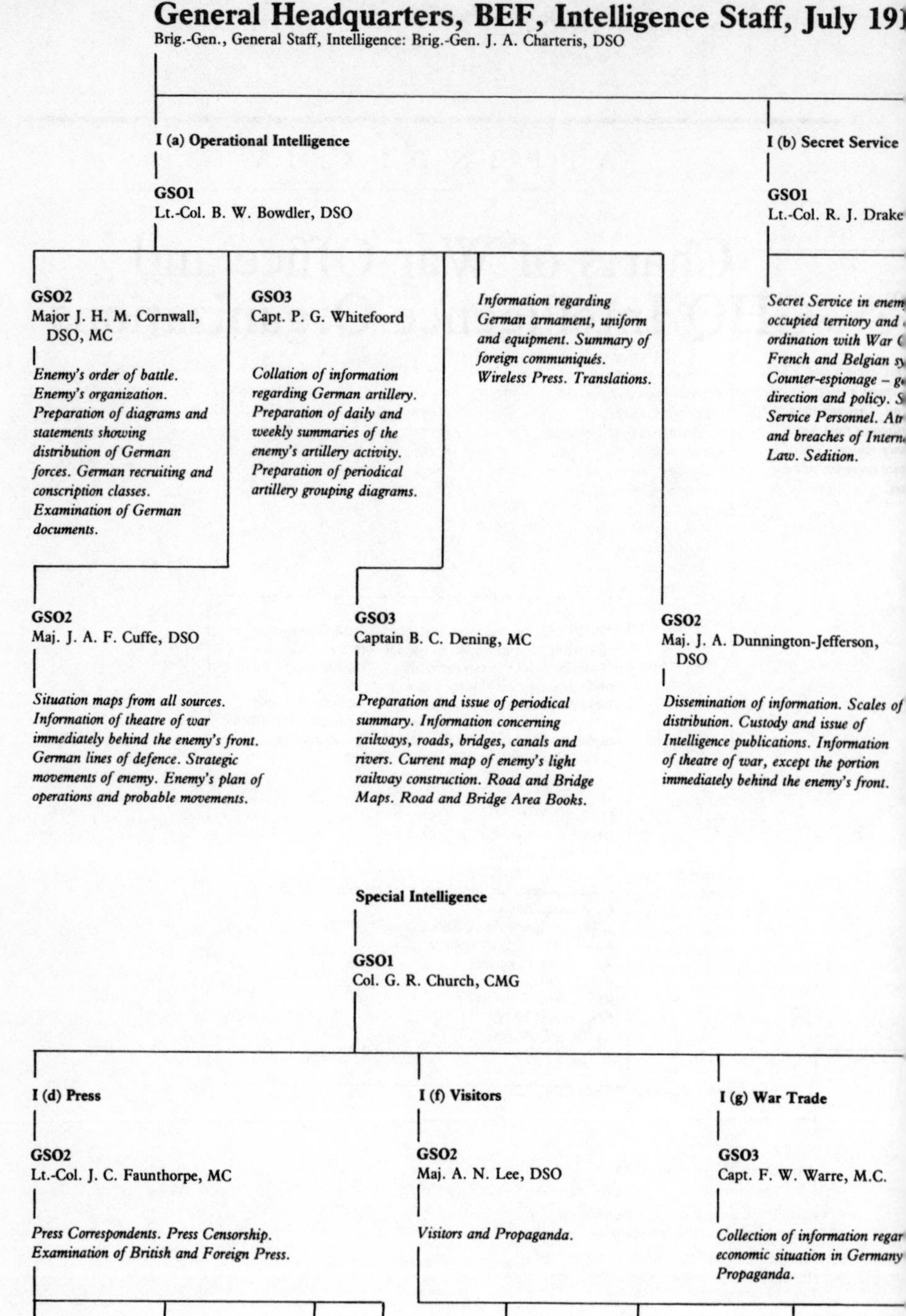

General Headquarters, BEF, Intelligence Staff, July 19
Brig.-Gen., General Staff, Intelligence: Brig.-Gen. J. A. Charteris, DSO
I (a) Operational Intelligence
GSO1
Lt.-Col. B. W. Bowdler, DSO
GSO2
Major J. H. M. Cornwall, DSO, MC
Enemy's order of battle. Enemy's organization. Preparation of diagrams and statements showing distribution of German forces. German recruiting and conscription classes. Examination of German documents.
GSO3
Capt. P. G. Whitefoord
Collation of information regarding German artillery. Preparation of daily and weekly summaries of the enemy's artillery activity. Preparation of periodical artillery grouping diagrams.
Information regarding German armament, uniform and equipment. Summary of foreign communiqués. Wireless Press. Translations.
I (b) Secret Service
GSO1
Lt.-Col. R. J. Drake
Secret Service in enem
occupied territory and
ordination with War
French and Belgian s
Counter-espionage – g
direction and policy. S
Service Personnel. At
and breaches of Intern
Law. Sedition.
GSO2
Maj. J. A. F. Cuffe, DSO
Situation maps from all sources. Information of theatre of war immediately behind the enemy's front. German lines of defence. Strategic movements of enemy. Enemy's plan of operations and probable movements.
GSO3
Captain B. C. Dening, MC
Preparation and issue of periodical summary. Information concerning railways, roads, bridges, canals and rivers. Current map of enemy's light railway construction. Road and Bridge Maps. Road and Bridge Area Books.
GSO2
Maj. J. A. Dunnington-Jefferson, DSO
Dissemination of information. Scales of distribution. Custody and issue of Intelligence publications. Information of theatre of war, except the portion immediately behind the enemy's front.
Special Intelligence
GSO1
Col. G. R. Church, CMG
I (d) Press
GSO2
Lt.-Col. J. C. Faunthorpe, MC
Press Correspondents. Press Censorship. Examination of British and Foreign Press.
GSO3
Capt. C. R. Cadge
British Press.
GSO3
Maj. Hon. N. Lytton
Allied Press.
Censor.
Photography. Cinematography.
I (f) Visitors
GSO2
Maj. A. N. Lee, DSO
Visitors and Propaganda.
GSO3
Capt. W. C. Scott
War Office Parties.
GSO3
Capt. H. C. Roberts, MVO, DSO
Foreign Office Parties.
GSO2
Col. B. R. James
the War Office
Military Attachés.
I (g) War Trade
GSO3
Capt. F. W. Warre, M.C.
Collection of information regar
economic situation in Germany
Propaganda.

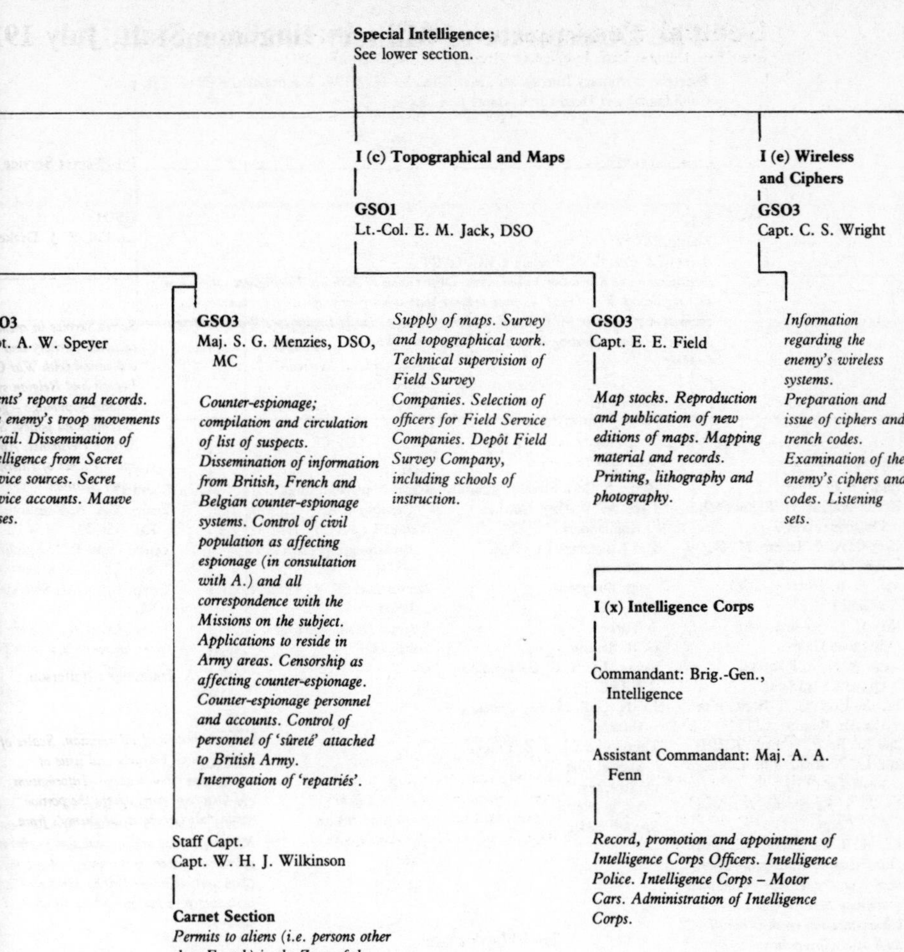

Special Intelligence;
See lower section.

I (c) Topographical and Maps

GSO1
Lt.-Col. E. M. Jack, DSO

Supply of maps. Survey and topographical work. Technical supervision of Field Survey Companies. Selection of officers for Field Service Companies. Depôt Field Survey Company, including schools of instruction.

GSO3
Capt. E. E. Field

Map stocks. Reproduction and publication of new editions of maps. Mapping material and records. Printing, lithography and photography.

I (e) Wireless and Ciphers

GSO3
Capt. C. S. Wright

Information regarding the enemy's wireless systems. Preparation and issue of ciphers and trench codes. Examination of the enemy's ciphers and codes. Listening sets.

I (x) Intelligence Corps

Commandant: Brig.-Gen., Intelligence

Assistant Commandant: Maj. A. A. Fenn

Record, promotion and appointment of Intelligence Corps Officers. Intelligence Police. Intelligence Corps – Motor Cars. Administration of Intelligence Corps.

O3
pt. A. W. Speyer

ents' reports and records. e enemy's troop movements rail. Dissemination of elligence from Secret vice sources. Secret vice accounts. Mauve ses.

GSO3
Maj. S. G. Menzies, DSO, MC

Counter-espionage; compilation and circulation of list of suspects. Dissemination of information from British, French and Belgian counter-espionage systems. Control of civil population as affecting espionage (in consultation with A.) and all correspondence with the Missions on the subject. Applications to reside in Army areas. Censorship as affecting counter-espionage. Counter-espionage personnel and accounts. Control of personnel of 'sûreté' attached to British Army. Interrogation of 'repatriés'.

Staff Capt.
Capt. W. H. J. Wilkinson

Carnet Section
Permits to aliens (i.e. persons other than French) in the Zone of the Armies. Control of circulation by rail in Army areas.

I (h) Postal and Telegraphic Censorship

GSO1
Lt.-Col. H. W. Holland, DSO

Compilation and revision of censorship regulations. Issue of censor stamps. Postal and Telegraphic censorship and breaches of rules governing same. Co-operation with allied censorships. Control of censor personnel (under GOC, Lines of Communication Area).

3
F. H. Norie,
O
ican Visitors.

The Directorate of Military Intelligence 1917

Director of Military Intelligence, Maj. Gen. Sir G. M. W. Macdonogh, KCMG, CB, p.s.c.
Confidential and Head Clerk, Capt. J. A. Kellett

MI1
Room 226
Brevet Lt.-Col. C. N. French CMG, GSO1
Organization of Service of Information. Distribution of Military Intelligence other than that regulating War Trade. Correspondence with other Government Departments. Co-ordination of work in MI1, 2 and 3. Compilation of Daily Intelligence War Summary. Military Policy regarding Submarine Cables and Wireless Telegraphy. Ciphers.

MI1 (a)
Room 254
Brevet Maj. R. G. Ritson, 6th Dragoons, GSO2
Cap. C. A. L. Irvine, MVO, Res. of Off., GSO3
Maj. C. B. Hornby, DSO, attached
Maj. C. S. Goldman, 4th Dragoon Guards
Capt. A. N. S. Roberts, Queen's Regiment
Lt. the Hon. O. S. Brett, 16th London Regiment (TF)
2nd Lt. E. T. Tatham, KRRC
2nd Lt. A. Read, 13th London Regiment (TF)
Lt. A. R. Rawlinson, Machine Gun Corps
Lt. M. R. K. Burge, The Buffs
Distribution of Intelligence other than War Trade. Routine business concerning MI1, 2 and 3. Communication on their behalf with other Government Departments. Distribution and despatch of Intelligence telegrams and their filing and record. Distribution of Intelligence reports and telegrams. Distribution and filing of Foreign Office telegrams except Trade & Treaty Series.

MI1 (b)
Room 5, Cork Street, Piccadilly
Capt. M. V. Hay, Gordon Highlanders
2nd Lt. (temp. Lt.) G. G. Crocker, 6th Dragoons
J. Fraser
J. Turner
G. B. Sansom
Temp. Lt. H. C. G. Tyndale, KRRC
Lt. H. C. S. Maine, Grenadier Guards
Temp. 2nd Lt. S. E. Fryer, Special List
O. Strachey
J. St. V. Pletts
Special Duties

MI1 (c)
Capt. Mansfield Smith-Cumming, RN
Temp. Lt.-Col. F. H. Browning, Special List, GSO1
Brevet Maj. T. B. Traill, DSO, GS03
'Special Duties' – Secret Intelligence.

MI1 (e)
Room 417
Temp. Maj. A. Simpson, RE, GSO3
Temp. Capt. P. J. Edmu
Temp. Lt. H. Matthews,
Temp. Lt. N. H. Swinste
RE
Temp. Lt. R.N. Hawes,
Duties in connection with W
Telegraphy.

MI1 (d)
Room 424
Capt. A. M. Gibbes, Res. of Off., GS
Temp. Lt. G. H. Booker, Special Lis
Military Policy and information regardi
submarine cables and wireless telegraphy
Questions regarding British Military Cip
including preparation and distribution of
ciphers.

MI3
Brevet Lt.-Col. E. W. Cox, DSO, RE, GSO1
Duties as MI2 with analysis of military information concerning the undermenti
countries.

MI3 (a)
Maj. G. D. Symonds, Res. of Off., GSO2
France and Belgium except parts occupied by enemy. Morocco except Tangier and part occupied by Spain.

MI3 (b)
Temp. Capt. E. M. B. Ingram, Special List, GSO3
Temp. Lt. G. Alliston, General List
Temp. Lt. E. O. Coote, Special List
Austria-Hungary, Switzerland, Netherlands and operations of Austro-Hungarian troops.

MI3 (c)
Brevet Maj. O. E. Wynne, RE, GSO2
Capt. J. S. Wilson, KRRC
Temp. Lt. T. A. Joyce, Special List, graded GSO3
Temp. Lt. J. L. G. Elliot, Special List
Temp. Lt. S. G. R. Baker, General List
Germany, Grand Duchy of Luxembourg. Operations of German troops.

MI3 (d)
Maj. C. L. Cobb
43 Regiment, IA, GSO2
Lt. A. K. G. Cr
East Surrey Regiment
Norway, Sweden, Denmark.

MI2
Room 223
Brevet Lt.-Col. B. T. Buckley, GSO1
Analysis of military information concerning the undermentioned countries (including colonies and protectorates) and their armed forces and correspondence with the Military Attachés accredited by these states to the Court of St James. Filing and recording of incoming telegrams and reports. Correspondence with British Military Attachés except on the subject of munitions.

MI2 (a)
Room 376
Brevet Maj. G. P. Tharp, Res. of Off., GSO2
Maj. R. G. T. Baker-Carr, MVO, GSO3
Maj. F. A. C. Hamilton, Cameron Highlanders, Res. of Off.
Maj. J. K. N. V. Bunbury, Queen's Regiment
Temp. Lt. H. W. V. Temperley, Fife and Forfar Yeomanry
The Americas (less Canada), Spain, Portugal, Italy, Liberia, Tangier, Balkan States, operations of troops of the Balkan States.

MI2 (b)
Room 227
Brevet Lt.-Col. W. H. Gribbon p.s.c., King's Own, GSO2
Maj. C. E. Foster, Kings Own, Capt. Res. of Off.
Capt. H. G. Money, Middlesex Regiment
Capt. D. J. Montagu-Douglas-Scott, Royal Scots
Ottoman Empire, Arabia, Sinai, Abyssinia, N. Africa except French and Spanish Possessions. Information emanating from Egypt and the Sudan. Western Persia – districts in which Russian or Turkish troops operate or are likely to operate.

MI2 (c)
Room 328
Capt. F. H. Kisch, DSO, RE GSO2
Maj. L. R. Hill, RFA, GSO3
Temp. Lt. the Hon. B. Brabazon-Ponsonby, Grenadier Guards
Persia (except districts allotted to MI2 (b)), Afghanistan, Chinese Empire, Empire of Japan, Korea, Siam and information from India and Burma.

MI2 (d)
Maj. P. H. du P. Casgrain, CMG, Res. of Off., GS02
Lt.-Col. A. G. Medley, IA
Russian Empire

MI4
Room 342
Col. W. C. Hedley, CB, CMG, GSO1
Collection and distribution of topographical information. Preparation of maps required for military purposes. Organization of geographical work for the Army. All matters connected with frontier questions, boundary delimitations and Demarcation Commissions. Selection of officers for survey and geographical work. Issue of maps for war. Selection of Staff Officers for topography with an army in the field. Colonial Survey Committee.
Map Room. General Staff Library.

MI4 (a)
Room 342
Lt. C. Romer, MC, RE, attached
Preparation, storage and issue of maps for home defence, overseas wars training and manoeuvres. Supply of Ordnance Survey maps. All defence scheme maps.

MI4 (b)
Room 340
G. H. Chilcott, Map Curator
Reception, indexing and storing of all published topographical maps in the world, also of all geographical material received. Providing geographical information for sections.

MI4 (c)
Room 45
F. J. Hudleston, GS Librarian
W. T. Baldry, Asst. Librarian
2 temporary women clerks
General Staff Library. Printed books and papers. Selection of English and foreign books, annuals and periodicals. Examination of English newspapers. Answers to miscellaneous queries, and provision of information for sections. Compilation of War Office Library Catalogue.

MI5
Brevet Lt.-Col. (temp. Col.) V. G. W. Kell, CB, ret. pay, Res. of Off., GSO1
Counter-espionage. Military policy in dealing with civil population, including aliens.

MI5 (a)
Capt. (temp. Maj.) H. E. Spencer, Res. of Off., GSO3
Capt. E. B. Powell, 8th London Regiment
P. F. N. Toulmin, Indian Police
Baron A. Sadoine
Monsieur J. Beer
Military Policy connected with employment of alien workmen on war services.

MI5 (b)
A. Marr, ICS
S. Newby, Indian Police
Duties connected with counter-espionage in British possessions in the East.

MI5 (d)
Capt. (temp. Maj.) F. Hall, Res. of Off., GSO2
Temp. Capt. F. Jackson, General List
Duties connected with counter-espionage in British possessions overseas other than in the East.

MI5 (e)
Maj. C. E. Dansey, Monmou Regiment, GSO2
Control of civilian passenger tr and from the UK. Passes and for the 'Zone des Armées'. Port Intelligence.

Military Permit Office.
Temp. Maj. R. D. Waterhou General List, GSO3, Milita Permit Officer

MI6 (a)
Military policy regarding restriction of enemy supplies and sources of supply. Black List Questions. Distribution and filing of FO, Trade and Treaty telegrams.

MI6 (b)
T. A. W. Gifford, graded GSO3
Collection analysis and distribution of information from military sources concerning the restriction of enemy supplies and sources of supply.

MI6 (c)
Brevet Lt.-Col. A. V. Jenner, DSO, GSO2
Provision of Intelligence Personnel. Questions regarding Interpreters, Censors the field, Intelligence Corps and Cipher Officers.

MI7
Brevet Lt.-Col. J. L. Fisher, DSO, Royal Fusiliers, GSO1

MI8
Col. A. G. Churchill, CB, p.s.c., GSO1, Chief Cable Ce
Cable Censorship.

MI7 (a)
Maj. H. W. Knox-Niven, GSO3
Policy regarding Press control and Press correspondents. Press censorship. All communications with official Press Bureau and issue of official Press communiqués. Military personnel of official Press Bureau.

MI7 (b)
Temp. Capt. the Earl of Onslow, Special List, GSO2
Capt. C. Montague Johnstone, Scots Greys
Capt. A. W. Foster, Royal Horse Guards, GSO3
Temp. Capt. C. Sandeman, General List
Capt. P. Chalmers Mitchell, FRS (TF Res.)
Temp. Maj. B. R. Cooper, General List
Capt. E. P. C. Amphlett, Worcestershire Regiment
Temp. Capt. A. J. Dawson, Border Regiment
Capt. A. F. Basil Williams (TF Res.)
17 Writers, 3 Artists, 8 Clerks, 4 S/hand Writers
'Policy regarding Press propaganda' — Propaganda in hostile countries and armies.

MI7 (d)
Lt-Col. E. St. A. Wake, retd. IA, graded as Censor
Study of Foreign Press and compilation of Daily Foreign Press Review.

MI7 (c)
Lt-Col. W. R. Greene, DSO, (TF Res.)
26 Translators, 1 S/hand Writer.
Military Translations.

MI8 (a)
Major Lord Arthur Browne, Res. of Off., GSO2
Policy and correspondence regarding the censorship of private and commercial cables and wireless messages overseas.

MI8 (b)
Temp. Maj. G. I. Phillips, GSO2
Co-ordination of policy c Central Telegraph Office and Cable Companies in regard to trade telegrams Compilation and issue of Cable Censors' Handboo

MI10
Col. B. R. James, p.s.c., Res. of Off., GSO2
Responsibility for Foreign Officers and reception of Foreign Military Missions. Liaison duties in this resp with GHQ, France. Correspondence regarding speci visits to France and all military establishments at ho

Director of Special Intelligence and Sub-Director of Military Intelligence. (Merged with Directorate in 1918.)

Director of Special Intelligence, Room 226, Brevet Col. (temp. Brig.-Gen.) G. K. Cockerill, CB, Royal Fusiliers, p.s.c.
GSO3 – Capt. C. Potts, Unattached List (TF)

MI5 (f)
Brevet Maj. E. E. B. Holt-Wilson, DSO, Res. of Off., GS02
Military Policy in dealing with the civil population, including aliens. Aliens Restriction Orders and DORA Regulations affecting Special Intelligence Duties. Intelligence Passes.

MI5 (g)
Maj. J. F. C. Carter, IA, GSO2
Special duties connected with counter-espionage.

MI5 (h)
Brevet Maj. M. M. Haldane, p.s.c., Res. of Off., GS02
Military records of aliens. Miscellaneous duties.

MI6
Capt. (temp. Maj.) G. L. Hoare, Res. of Off., GSO2
Questions of military policy connected with Trade War, traffic in arms, and martial law. International Conferences and Law. Provision of Intelligence Personnel. Questions regarding Interpreters, Intelligence Corps, Cipher Officers. Interior economy of Military Intelligence Directorate.

MI6 (d)
Capt. H. L. Gifford, RIR, GSO3
Traffic in arms. DORA Regulations 30, 30A and 31.

MI6 (e)
Capt. J. A. Kellett, Quartermaster
Interior economy of Directorate.

MI6 (l)
J. F. More, graded GSO3
1 clerk
Military International Law. Policy in connection with martial law. Compensation claims affecting General Staff or involving points of international law. Municipal law as affecting defence schemes etc. Consideration of draft Bills affecting General Staff.

MI9
Temp. Col. G. S. H. Pearson, CMG, graded GSO1, Chief Postal Censor

MI8 (c)
Maj. E. W. K. Money, Censor
Distribution of telegrams and information derived from Cable Censorship.

MI8 (d)
Col. H. R. B. Donne, CB, p.s.c., Deputy Chief Censor, graded as GSO2
Executive Censorship Duties at Central Telegraph Office and private Cable Companies in the UK.

MI9 (a)
Maj. A. S. L. Farquharson, Unattached List (TF), GSO2
General policy and correspondence regarding censorship of letter mails in UK and overseas and parcels for prisoners of war. Relations with Allied censorships. Censors stamps, except as regards distribution.

MI9 (b)
J. W. Scobell-Armstrong, attached, graded as GSO2
Policy and correspondence regarding use of the postal censorship in commercial and financial matters.

MI9 (d)
H. Claughton, graded as GSO2
Issue of permits under DORA Regulations 24(B) and (C). Policy and correspondence regarding control of printed matter and parcels.

MI9 (c)
F. V. Worthington, Deputy Chief Censor
Executive duties of postal censorship. Censorship of private terminal correspondence (including prisoners of war correspondence) except American mails. Censorship of private terminal correspondence with America, and supervision of Liverpool Censorship Office. Censorship of all non-terminal correspondence, private and trade. Censorship of parcels.

Select Bibliography

I. PRIMARY SOURCES

Interviews

Barks, Private H., 1/5th Battalion, North Staffordshire Regiment, 46th (North Midlands) Division, 30 October 1981

Castle, Lance-Corporal F.S., Intelligence Police, 17th Lancers, 25 March 1982

Few, Private H. J., Royal Army Medical Corps, 53rd Division, and Royal Engineers (Signals), 3 November 1982

Gyton, Corporal S. H., Royal Engineers (Signals), 29th Division, 30 October 1982

Lloyd, Mr, Royal Navy, 16 May 1982

Marshall-Cornwall, General Sir James H., Intelligence Officer, 3rd Division II Corps; GS03 (Intelligence) II Corps; GS02 (Intelligence) General Headquarters; MI3, War Office, 10 September 1980

Murray, Leading Seaman J., Hood Battalion, 63rd (Royal Naval) Division, 15 June 1982, 20 September 1986 and 28 February 1987

Pennell, Regimental Sergeant-Major G., 2nd Battalion, Royal Fusiliers, 29th Division, 1 May 1981

Piper, Corporal George, 6th East Surrey Regiment, 12th Division, 29 September 1986

Rackham, Brigadier B. B., Sub-Lieutenant, Hawke Battalion, 63rd (Royal Naval) Division, 27 February 1982

Woolrych, Lieutenant-Colonel S. H. C., Intelligence Officer, 7th Division, II Corps; Intelligence Officer, First Army; I(b), General Headquarters; Head of I(b), Second Army, 19 March 1982

Zealley, Sergeant P. R., 10th Battalion, the Royal Fusiliers, 10 August 1981

County Record Office, Chichester, Sussex

Papers relating to Lieutenant-Colonel G. E. Leachman, CIE, DSO

The Intelligence Corps Museum, Templer Barracks, Ashford, Kent

Papers of Captain S. P. Best

The Bosworth Papers

Papers of Brigadier-General J. A. Charteris

Papers of Private F. Cunnington, MM

Papers of Major-General F. E. Hotblack, DSO, MC

Papers of General Sir Walter Kirke

Papers of General Sir James Marshall-Cornwall, KCB, CBE, DSO, MC, including Experiences Of An Intelligence Officer in World Wars One and Two. Extracts From The Memoirs of General Sir James Marshall-Cornwall, the General's unpublished memoirs

Papers of Lieutenant-Colonel S. H. C. Woolrych, OBE

Papers of Lieutenant M. R. K. Burge. Burge served with MI 2(e) and his papers include History of The British Secret Services In HOLLAND; History of British Intelligence (Aland Islands, Russia, Spain-Germany and Palestine); and entries on Sweden, Spain, Austria, Petrograd and Mesopotamia

The Imperial War Museum, Lambeth Road, London

Department of Printed Books, Aerial Leaflet Collection, 1914–1918

Department of Documents, Papers of G. C. Andrews, 23 Observation Group, 4 Field Survey Battalion, Royal Engineers (Intelligence)

Papers of Captain S. P. Best

Papers of Captain F. G. Bird

Papers of Guy Buckridge, Royal Engineers (Wireless)

Papers of Captain L. C. Carus-Wilson, Second Army, Signals

Papers of Corporal F. G. Cousins, DCM, Special Company, Royal Engineers

Diary of Corporal O. H. Davis, MM, Royal Engineers (Signals)

Diary of D. H. Doe, Royal Engineers (Signals), 51st Signal Company, 19th Division

Papers of Sir Vernon G. W. Kell, KBE, CB

Diaries of General Sir Walter Kirke (The diaries are of great value in providing an important first-hand insight into the work of I (b) and also into the rivalries between the different Secret Services.)

Papers of A. G. Pepperell, Royal Engineers (Signals), BX Cable Section

Diary of Sapper A. Smith, Royal Engineers (Wireless)

Diary of Corporal W. A. Smith, MM, Royal Engineers (Signals)

Diary of A. E. Thomson, Royal Engineers (Signals)

Diary of Field-Marshal Sir Henry Wilson

Papers of *La Dame Blanche* (two boxes)

Papers of Colonel A. N. Lee

The Liddell Hart Military Archives, King's College, London

Papers of Brigadier-General Sir James Edmonds

Papers of Lieutenant-General Sir Launcelot Kiggell

Papers of Captain Sir Basil H. Liddell Hart

Papers of Field-Marshal Sir William Robertson

Liverpool Record Office

Papers of the 17th Earl of Derby

The Ministry of Defence

Personal Service Records of Brigadier-General J. A. Charteris and Lieutenant C. E. S. S. Eccles (These do not contain as much information as might be expected.)

National Library of Scotland, George IV Bridge, Edinburgh

Papers of Major-General Sir John Davidson
Diaries and Papers of Field-Marshal Lord Haig
Papers of General Sir Herbert Lawrence

Rhodes House Library, Oxford

Diaries of Colonel R. M. Meinertzhagen

Papers in Private Possession

Papers of Brigadier-General John Charteris, courtesy of Lieutenant-Colonel J. A. Charteris, MC (These are of the greatest importance in understanding the views and work of Brigadier-General Charteris.)
Papers of Captain L. McA. Gordon, courtesy of Mrs Springall
Papers of Charles Clarke, Valet to the Grand Duke Michael until 1916, courtesy of his granddaughter Mrs. P. Cullis

Documents in the Public Record Office, Kew

A number of very helpful documents are held in AIR 1 which throw useful light on the use of the air arm in connection with Intelligence. They could serve as the basis for a much-needed academic thesis or a book on the subject. Budding postgraduates take note.

AIR 1/149/15/98. Proposal to Attack and Destroy by Fire Enemy Wheatfields 12–26–4–1915
AIR 1/163/15/136/1. A Short History of 'I' Flight RAF
AIR 1/675/21/13/1726. Agent Dropping by RFC May 1928
AIR 1/720/42/9/1. 1918 November – Aerial Missions
AIR 1/727/152/5. 1915–18 Report on SS Airships, Types and Certain Operations
AIR 1/737/204/2/3. No. 3 Squadron RFC War Diary (Intelligence Summary) Period 1 January to 26 August 1915
AIR 1/1068/204/5/1621. 1918 February-August. Report on Special Flights. Secret Service GS11
AIR 1/1513/204/58/38. 1916 March–1918 April. Special Missions involving pigeons
AIR 1/1665/204/98/42. 1918 March. Dropping of pigeons and agents from the air into enemy territory
AIR 1/1768/204/143/2. North Russia, Syren Force. Observers' Reports June-September 1919 & Nominal Rolls (all ranks)
AIR 1/1938/204/245/9. 1918 June–October. Operational Instructions and Reports
AIR 1/1985/204/273/98. Report & Correspondence re. – Question of Using Balloons for Carrying Incendiary Bombs for Destruction of Enemy Crops. May and August 1918. I.F.G. 25/2
AIR 1/1997/204/273/245. 1918 October–November. Landing Agent Over Line At Night And Provision of Parachute DH4

AIR 1/1997/204/273/253. Independent Force Royal Air Force. Record of Special Operations Detailed to Units 20 June 1918 – 26 September 1918

AIR 1/2170/209/12/8. 1915 October – War Diary, 3 Wing RFC

AIR 1/2250/209/47/1. War Diary of 'X' Flight RFC Akaba. November 1917

AIR 1/2250/209/47/2. War Diary of 'X' Flight RFC Akaba. December 1917

AIR 1/2360/226/6/1–8. War Diaries of 'X' Flight RFC/RAF (Middle East) February–September 1918

AIR 1/2399/280/1. Lecture Paper On The Use of Aircraft in Connection with Espionage. 1924

Admiralty Papers

ADM 53/34428. Ship's Log HMS *Attentive* August 1917 to December 1918

ADM 53/61631. Ship's Log HMS *Suffolk* June 1918

ADM 53/61632. Ship's Log HMS *Suffolk* July 1918

ADM 53/61633. Ship's Log HMS *Suffolk* August 1918

ADM 125/66. China Station Records. Vol. LIX. General Letters Nos. 99–162

ADM 137/504. North America and West Indies. General Letters of the Commander-in-Chief. September 1916 to November 1918

ADM 137/718. China Station. General Letters

ADM 137/766. China Station. Telegrams

ADM 137/768. North America and West Indies General Operation Telegrams 1918, 1 May to 30 June

ADM 137/883. White Sea General Telegrams. January to June 1918

ADM 137/903. North America and West Indies General Operation Telegrams 1918, 1 July to 31 August

ADM 137/960. West and South East Coasts of America General Operation Telegrams 1918, 1 July to 31 December

ADM 137/961. Australia, China and East Indies including Persian Gulf. General Operation Telegrams. 1918 1 July to 30 September

ADM 137/963. White Sea Telegrams. July–December 1918

ADM 137/1619. North America and West Indies. Various Subjects 1918. Registered Papers

ADM 137/1620. Halifax. Convoy Letters. 1917, 1918

ADM 137/1623. North America and West Indies. Orders. Various Convoy & Wireless Telegraphy. 1916 to 1918

ADM 137/1630. Intelligence. 1918

ADM 137/4646. Pink Telegrams. July, August, September 1918

ADM 186/611. A History Of The White Sea Station, 1914–1919

The reader/researcher is warned that the Admiralty Papers are enormous in scope and quantity and the organization, sensibly arranged for operational requirements, vastly increases the amount of time and study involved in research. Anybody wanting to study these papers must be prepared to spend a lot of time pursuing leads through many different files and anticipate an unusual degree of frustration.

BT32/7. Ships Inward, 1915–1918

BT26/648. Incoming Passengers, Port of Arrival – London

Canada Files

CO 335/29. [IND 18846] Canada Register 1918 to 1919
CO 42
CO 714

Foreign Office Documents

FO 262. Japan: Correspondence
FO 262/1324. Foreign Office Commercial
FO 262/1331. Telegrams 151–300
FO 263/26. Consular Correspondence Register
FO 371/3181. Political. China Files 2567
FO 371/3234. Political. Japan Files 6083–9874. Account of Prince Arthur's visit
FO 371/3977. Part One: Report by Sir C. Eliot to Mr Balfour
Part Two: Report sent by investigator Sokolov to the British Government, 1920 (This is the official compendium of lies upon which the Ekaterinburg massacre story is founded.)

War Office Documents

The papers held in the War Office files normally skirt Intelligence carefully, but nevertheless there remain several documents of extreme importance. Those seeking to follow the relationship between Intelligence and action will find 'Military Operations and Intelligence' (WO 106) well worth their attention. It is, however, a massive collection and only those papers which proved most useful are listed below.

WO 32/10776. History of Military Intelligence Directorate During The Great War, 1914–1919

ARMY WAR DIARIES. WO 95

These are vital documents and form the basis of the official histories of the war. They are a day-by-day (in some cases week-by-week) record of the occurrences in the zone of each of the British Armies in the field and contain an enormous mass of information about very nearly everything, ranging from full-scale battles and the minutely detailed preparations made for them to visits from the Commander-in-Chief.

First Army	– WO 95/154–182,
Second Army	– WO 95/268–280,
Third Army	– WO 95/357–380,
Fourth Army	– WO 95/430–442 and WO 158/327–331,
Reserve/Fifth Army	– WO 95/517–525

Some War Diaries are more comprehensive than others. Generally speaking, the First Army War Diary is the most detailed.

WO 106/45

History of Intelligence (B), British Expeditionary Force, France. From January, 1917, To April, 1919. Colonel R. J. Drake. (A very helpful short account of the work of the I(b) Secret Service in the last two years of the war, but one that suffers from unreliability at certain points. A copy is lodged at the Intelligence Corps Museum, Ashford.)

WO 106/60

Turkestan Union. Turkestan War File, Document No. 6

WO 106/308

1. Committee Of Imperial Defence. The War. Suggestions As To The Military Position. 1 January 1915
2. General Staff. Note On The Situation. 30 November 1915
3. Suggestions As To The Manner In Which Diplomacy May Render Assistance In The Conduct Of The War
4. CID Paper No. 947. Note Prepared For The War Committee By The Chief Of The Imperial General Staff On The Question Of Operations On The Western Front. 5 January 1916
5. A General Review Of The Situation In All Theatres of War. 20 March 1917
6. 0.1/129/369 CIGS To Secretary War Cabinet. 26 October 1917
7. History Of The Organization And Development Of The Military Operations Directorate, Since December 1915
8. Our Military Effort During 1917
9. OAD 702 Field-Marshal Sir Douglas Haig To The Chief Of Imperial General Staff, Remarks On The Reports Of Field-Marshal Lord French And Lieutenant-General Sir Henry Wilson. 13 November 1917

WO 106/310

1. Appreciation Of The Existing Situation In The Balkans And Dardanelles With Remarks As To The Relative Importance Of This Situation In Regard To The General Conduct Of The War. 9 October 1915
2. The Present And Prospective Situation in Syria And Mesopotamia. 19 October 1915
3. Recommendation Of The General Staff On The Question Of The Action To Be Taken At Gallipoli. 21 October 1915
4. Provision Of Men To Win The War. Paper By The Chief Of The Imperial General Staff. 27 December 1915
5. The Situation In Mesopotamia. February 1916
6. The Sherif Of Mecca And The Arab Movement. 1 July 1916
7. German Casualties In The Somme Fighting. 30 September 1916
8. A General Review Of The Situation In All Theatres Of War, Together With A Comparison Of The Military Resources Of The Entente And of The Central Powers
9. Possible Action Of The Central Powers During The Autumn And Winter of 1916. 9 September 1916
10. Note On Our Future Military Policy In The Event Of The Failure Of The Entente Powers To Obtain A Decision In The Main Theatres During The Coming Summer. January 1917
11. A General Review Of The Situation In All Theatres of War. 20 May 1918
12. General Review Of The Situation With Especial Reference To The Possibility of Obtaining An Eventual Military Decision

WO 106/311

1. Note On Our Future Military Policy
2. Return Showing Percentage Of Rifles to Ration Strength Of British, French And German Armies On The Western Front. 4 January 1917
3. Assessment Of The Current Situation. 23 February 1917
4. Note On Forthcoming Operations On The Western Front. March 1917
5. Germany's Intentions
6. Précis Of 'Review Of Present Situation On The Western Front With Special Reference To The German Withdrawal On The Somme'. 2 March 1917
7. A General Review Of The Situation In All Theatres Of War. 20 March 1917
8. Situation At Salonika. 1 April 1917
9. Military Situation On Salonika Front. March 1917
10. Military Effect Of Russia Seceding From The Entente

WO 106/312

1. The Military Situation In Macedonia. 2 June 1917
2. OAD 478 Present Situation And Future Plans. 12 June 1917
3. Sir Douglas Haig Gives His Opinion Regarding The Prime Minister's Views In Regard To The Future Course Of The War
4. The Present Military Situation In Russia And Its Effect On Our Future Plans. 29 July 1917
5. Extract Of A Report On Captain Lawrence's Journey. 11 July 1917
6. Casualties Of The British Expeditionary Force In France From The Beginning Of The Offensive In April 1917 to 16 September 1917. 21 September 1917
7. W.P.49. Cabinet Committee On War Policy. The Man-Power And Internal Conditions Of The Central Powers. 31 August – 1 October 1917. (A very important document reflecting Macdonogh's views on the endurance of the Central Powers.)

WO 106/313

1. Occupation Of Jaffa-Jerusalem Line. 9 October 1917
2. Prisoners And Guns Taken And Lost By The British Armies On All Fronts Of The Period 1 January – 30 September 1917. October 1917
3. Effect Of Military Operations On The Political Situation In Germany. 13 October 1917 (An important document which marks the final stage in Macdonogh's switch to the view that an attack on the German Home Front was the way to win the war.)
4. Transfers Of German Infantry Divisions Between The Theatres Of War Since The 1 September. October 1917
5. Table Showing Comparative British And Enemy Casualties On The Battlefronts In The Battles of Arras, Messines And The Third Battle Of Ypres: Also The Numbers Of Prisoners And Guns Taken By The British, And The Extent Of Allied Territory Recaptured. October 1917
6. OA 216 Field-Marshal Sir Douglas Haig To The CIGS. Statement Showing The Comparative British And German Wastage By Divisions In The Flanders Battle. 16 October 1917
7. Italy. 21 October 1917

8. Report From Sir Douglas Haig Regarding Exceptional Weather Conditions In Flanders During The Last Three Months. 23 October 1917
9. General Military Policy. The Present State Of The War; The Future Prospects; And Future Action To Be Taken. Chief Of Imperial General Staff's Memorandum Re. Reports By Lord French (W.P.60) And Lieutenant-General Sir Henry Wilson (W.P.61). 26 October 1917
10. Movement Of Enemy Reinforcements To The Italian Front. 29 October 1917
11. Summary Of Information As To General Cadorna's Views Received By The British General Staff And Action Taken By Them. 29 October 1917
12. British Casualties On The Western Front In October 1917. 1 November 1917
13. Situation In Turkey. 15 November 1917
14. Note On Operations On Palestine Front. 17 November 1917
15. Strengths Of Allied And Enemy Forces On 5 December, 1917. 5 December 1917
16. Estimate Of German Casualties On The British Front And On Other Fronts In 1917. 11 December 1917
17. OAD 726 Field-Marshal Commanding-in-Chief, France To Chief Of The Imperial General Staff. 10 December 1917
18. Alleged Breakdown Of Egyptian Intelligence Branch Referred To In W.C.296/5. 14 December 1917

WO 106/314

1. Battle Of Cambrai – CIGS's Memorandum Forwarding To S. Of S. The Reports On Enquiry Regarding The Events Of 30 November 1917. 1 January 1918
2. Received Report Of Enquiry From Field-Marshal Sir Douglas Haig; Considered By CIGS, DMO And Major-General Callwell
3. General Military Situation On Italian Front During December, 1917. 13 January 1918
4. Weekly Summary 17 January 1918. Prime Minister's Comments On Information, Regarding Balance Of Strength Of Enemy On Western Front, Contained In Weekly Summary 17 January, 1918 – Chief Of Imperial General Staff's Statement Showing Revised Figures
5. Strengths Of Allied And Enemy Forces. 11 March 1918
6. Distribution Of Troops On Western And Italian Fronts, Central Powers And Allies. 12 March 1918
7. Report Of Eighth Visit Of Lieutenant-Colonel E. A. Plunkett, General Staff, To Salonika Front, 9 February – 24 March 1918. 28 March 1918
8. Comparative Statement Showing Situation Of French, British And German Reserves. 17 April 1918
9. Germany And Holland. 26 April 1918

WO 106/315

1. Man-Power Situation. Memorandum By The Army Council. 24 October 1918
2. Appreciation Of The Situation. 26 October 1918
3. Appreciation Of The Situation. 30 October 1918
4. Reinforcements For The British Army In France
5. Comparisons Of Reserves In Man-Power

6. British Military Effort During The War

WO 106/317

1–5. Appreciation By The General Staff Of The Actual And Prospective Military Situation In The Various Theatres of War, 2 October 1918, 9 October 1918, 16 October 1918, 30 October 1918, 6 November 1918

WO 106/322

1. Conditions In Austria. 1917
2. Department of State, Washington, D.C. Confidential Weekly Report On Matters Relating To The Central Powers. 19 November 1917

WO 106/346–348

Intelligence Summaries

WO 106/359

1. Organization Of Intelligence Section, General Staff. July 1917
2. Organization Of General Headquarters
3. Organization Of Intelligence Section, General Staff, GHQ. 3 May 1918

WO 106/360

Re-Organization Of The General Staff Branch, General Headquarters. April 1918

WO 106/390

Loos. 1915 September. 21 October 1915

WO 106/401

British Armies In France – General And Miscellaneous. The British Armies In France As Gathered From Censorship. Winter 1917/18

WO 106/402

Canadian Corps Report On Operations Against Vimy Ridge. 9–16 April 1917

WO 106/404

1. A Traveller Coming From Salzburg (Austria). 6 December 1917
2. Telegrams. General Spiers, British Mission Paris To War Office

WO 106/405

1. Telegrams. General Spiers, British Mission Paris To War Office
2. Note For Military Intelligence (British Mission Paris). March 1918

WO 106/416

British Expeditionary Force, France. Question Of Maintenance Of Touch With The French; And Covering The Channel Ports; Action Of The British Army If Compelled To Fall Back. 1918

WO 106/520

Notes On The American Army

WO 106/573

Operations In East Africa. 1915

WO 106/576

Memorandum. Précis Of Situation In BEA And Uganda. 20 November 1914

WO 106/577
East Africa. Communications War Office To Major-General Wapshare

WO 106/578
Extracts From German Military Report On German East Africa. 20 August 1915

WO 106/588
German Forces In South West Africa. 27 June 1916

WO 106/593
1. Notes On General Delme-Radcliffe's Views On The State Of The Austrian Army. 16 May 1918
2. Notes On DMI's Letter Dated 8th May. 12 May 1918

WO 106/637
German Cameroons. 20 September 1910

WO 106/638
1. German East Africa. December 1915
2. Comparison Of German East Africa And German South West Africa

WO 106/645A
Conquest of Cameroons. To June 1915

WO 106/645B
Copies Of Papers On The Military Situation In The Cameroons

WO 106/646
Operations In The Cameroons

WO 106/647
Cameroons

WO 106/654
Cameroons. Intercepted Despatches From German Governor Of Cameroons To Colonial Office, Berlin

WO 106/655
Troops In The Cameroons. Colonial Garrisons. Egyptian Army. 20 December 1915

WO 106/656
Intercepted Reports On Operations In The Cameroons By German Prisoners Released From SS *Appam* By German Auxiliary Cruiser *Möwe*

WO 106/660
1. Plans Of Offence Against Tsingtau (Kiaochow). 26 March 1913
2. Tsing Tao. 27 December 1912
3. General Staff Officer, North China Command. 2 January 1915

WO 106/661
German Defences At Tsing Tao

WO 106/667
Copies Of Reports By Brigadier-General N. W. Barnardiston, MVO, On The Operations At Tsingtau

WO 106/679
Czech War File. Document No. 19. MIO(a)

WO 106/680
Czech War File. Document No. 4, MIO(a).

WO 106/682
Czecho-Slovak Army In Russia. Papers By Professor Masaryk

WO 106/683
History Of The Czecho-Slovak Army In Russia

WO 106/684
Czech Troops. MIO(a) Document No. 7. August 1918

WO 106/704
Signals–Gallipoli. Account Furnished By Major H.C.B. Wemyss, DSO, MC, Royal Signals

WO 106/706
Sir Ian Hamilton's Despatches (with appendices)

WO 106/1098
General Knox's Report And Attendance At Versailles Conference Re. Expedition to Archangel. March 1918

WO 106/1149
Extracts From A Report On The Murmansk District. 24 May 1918

WO 106/1150
MIO(a). North Russia, Box 23, File 18

WO 106/1151
Nominal Roll Of Officers 'Syren' And 'Elope'. June–July 1918. MIO(a)

WO 106/1152
Military And Political. January – October 1918

WO 106/1190
South Russia, Ukraine. 1919

WO 106/1218
Siberia 4. Correspondence & Telegrams. 1918. Siberia April 1, July 18

WO 106/1219
Siberia 6. Nos. 739–873. 9 August & September 1918

WO 106/1220
Siberia Policy. July 1918

WO 106/1232
MIRA. Siberia. Document No. 145

WO 106/1318
Siberia Administration. August 1918

T173/829
1. Ia 35273. Note On The Strategical Situation With Special Reference To The

Present Condition Of German Resources And Probable German Operations. 11 June 1917 (A very important paper by Brigadier-General John Charteris, representing the high-water mark of GHQ optimism in 1917.)
2. Review Of The Enemy's Operations And Changes Of Disposition Opposite The II Corps Front During August 1917

Papers Deposited In The Public Record Office By Lieutenant-General Sir George Macdonogh, D.M.I.

WO 106/1510
1. Note By The General Staff On The Changes In The German Order of Battle In The Western Theatre Since January 1916
2. Memorandum On The Intelligence Service In Mesopotamia. June 1916
3. Operations. From GOC-in-C, Egypt To CIGS. 26 June 1916
4. Note On The Campaign In East Africa. 7 August 1916
6. Possible Action Of The Central Powers During The Autumn And Winter Of 1916. 9 September 1916
7. Report Of Agent 'R.16'. 27 June 1916

WO 106/1511
1. Estimate Of Turkish Resources In Personnel. 5 October 1916
2. Strength Of The Turks In Various Theatres. 5–6 October 1916
3. German Plans For The Winter 1917–18
4. Despatch Of An Expeditionary Force To Rabegh. November 1916
5. Note On Proposed Operations On The Eastern Frontier of Egypt. 12 December 1916

WO 106/1512
1. Return Showing Percentage Of Rifles To Ration Strength Of British, French, And German Armies On The Western Front. 4 January 1917
2. Germany's Intentions. 23 February 1917
3. Despatch Of Reinforcements From The Western To The Italian Front. 23 February 1917
4. Note By The General Staff On A Hostile Offensive Against Italy. 19 March 1917
5. A General Review Of The Situation In All Theatres of War. 20 March 1917 (A document which marks a significant stage in military policy.)
6. General Staff Tabular Statement: Entente And Enemy Man-Power. 30 March 1917
7. Instructions For The Field-Marshal Commanding-in-Chief, Home Forces. March 1917
8. Situation At Salonika. 2 April 1917
9. Notes Received From Captain Hartley, Chemical Adviser Third Army, Regarding The Effect Of Counter-Battery Work Carried Out On Third Army Front. 13 April 1917
10. Telegram 33178 CIGS To Sir A. Murray (and reply). 21 April 1917
11. The Present Situation In Regard To Military Assistance By the United States. 29 April 1917

12. Operations On West Front. 30 April 1917
13. Forecast Of Arrival Of United States' Troops In France.
14. Addendum To Note By The Chief Of Imperial General Staff, Dated 12 February 1916. 1917
15. Military Effect Of Russia Seceding From The Entente. 9 May 1917

WO 106/1513

1. Summary Of Operations By The Allied Forces At Salonika – May 1917. 26 May 1917
2. GOC Salonika To CIGS. 26 May 1917
3. Defence Against Air Raids – Conference At War Office. 31 May 1917
4. Military Situation In Macedonia. 2 June 1917
5. Military Policy In The Various Theatres Of War. 12 June 1917
6. Field-Marshal Sir Douglas Haig To The Chief Of Imperial General Staff. 22 June 1917
7. Note By The Chief Of Imperial General Staff On The Prime Minister's Memorandum Regarding Future Military Policy. 23 June 1917
8. Causes Of The Lack Of Success In The Recent Italian Operation On The Carso. 24 June 1917
9. Evidence Of War-Weariness And Desire For A Separate Peace In Austria–Hungary. 7 July 1917
10. Note On The Report Of The French Army Commission Upon The French, Colonial And Allied Effectives. 11 July 1917
11. GOC-in-C, Egypt To CIGS. 12 July 1917
12. The Present Military Situation In Russia And Its Effect On Our Future Plans. 29 July 1917

WO 106/1514

1. The Dutch Situation. 7 July 1917
2. The Fighting On The Chemin Des Dames. July 1917
3. Summary Of Operations Of Allied Forces Salonika. July 1917
4. Military Situation In Mesopotamia. 31 July 1917
5. OAD 589 Report On The Battle Of 31st July, 1917, And Its Results. 4 August 1917
6. Ia/38607 Note Regarding German Man-Power, Casualties and 'Moral'. 21 August 1917
7. Examination Of Neutral Press For Information
8. Intercepted Letters
9. Letter From Lloyd George To Macdonagh [sic] and reply. 4 September 1917

WO 106/1515

1. Information On Conditions In Bulgaria
2. Air Raids And The Bombing Of Germany. 6 October 1917
3. OA 216 Comparative Statement Of British And German Wastage By Divisions In The Flanders Battle. 16 October 1917
4. Letter From Lieutenant-General Macdonogh To Lady Booth. 17 October 1917
5. OAD 679 Field-Marshal Sir Douglas Haig To The Chief Of Imperial General Staff. Paper On Possibility of Taking Over More French Line. 17 October 1917

6. OAD 678 Letter From Sir Douglas Haig To General Pétain. 19 October 1917
7. CIGS To Secretary War Cabinet. Observations By CIGS On Reports By Lord French And Sir Henry Wilson Regarding Formation Of Supreme War Council
8. Report From Brigadier-General Delme-Radcliffe No. 1442A. 21 October 1917. On Italian Situation Prior To Present Offensive
9. OAD 688 Field-Marshal Sir Douglas Haig To The Chief Of Imperial General Staff. 31 October 1917
10. Summary Of Work Carried Out By The Royal Flying Corps In The Field During The Month Of October, 1917. 5 November 1917

WO 106/1516

1. Situation In Macedonia. 12 November 1917
2. OAD 702 Field-Marshal Sir Douglas Haig To The Chief Of The Imperial General Staff On Future Action Of British Forces In View Of Reports By Lord French And Sir Henry Wilson. 13 November 1917
3. Note By DMI [on military action to be taken in 1918]. 17 November 1917
4. Note On Cambrai
5. Future Military Policy. 19 November 1917
6. The Postal Censorship

WO 106/1517

1. OAD 644/12 Field-Marshal Sir Douglas Haig To CIGS. Report On Operations Of The Royal Flying Corps In November 1917. 5 December 1917
2. Man-Power Committee: Statement Of Strengths Of Enemy And Allied Forces On The Western Front. 5 December 1917
3. Correspondence On Extension Of British Front. CIGS To Secretary War Cabinet. 6 December 1917
4. Memorandum On Defensive Measures. 14 December 1917
5. CIGS Memorandum On Alleged Breakdown Of The Egyptian Intelligence Branch. 14 December 1917
6. Future Operations In Palestine
7. Sir Douglas Haig's Memorandum On The Question Of An Extension Of The British Front. 15 December 1917
8. OAD 7311/1 Commander-in-Chief, France To CIGS Telegrams Chief Of Imperial General Staff/Field-Marshal Haig On Events Of 30 November 1917. 19 December 1917

The War Office List, And Administrative Directory For The British Army, 1918

By J. R. Wade, BA Of The War Office. HMSO, London, 1918

Royal Air Force Museum, Hendon, Aviation Records Department

Papers of Marshal of the Royal Air Force The Viscount Trenchard
Papers of Major-General Sir Frederick H. Sykes

Hertfordshire County Record Office, Hertford

Letters of Lieutenant-General Sir William Pulteney to Lady Desborough (Mrs Grenfell) D/ERv C2129, C2130/1–170

Royal Free Hospital, Hampstead

Council Minutes 1908–1922
Agenda Books 1916–1920
Hampstead General Hospital House Committee 1909–1922
Annual Reports 1911–1923

Royal Archives, Windsor Castle

Prince Arthur of Connaught's Mission, 1918. RA GV PS 24190

II. THESES, PUBLISHED BOOKS AND JOURNALS

Ackerman, C. *Trailing the Bolsheviki*, New York 1919

Anon. *Colorado Potato Beetle in France – Journal Of The Ministry of Agriculture*, Vol. 29, London 1923, pp. 1053–6

Anon. *Intelligence – The Army Quarterly*, Vol. I, London 1920–21, pp. 327–345

Ardrey, R. *The Territorial Imperative*, London 1969

Ashworth, T. *Trench Warfare 1914–1918: the live and let live system*, London 1980

Aston, Sir George G. *Secret Service*, London n.d.

Barker, A. J. *The Neglected War, Mesopotamia 1914–1918*, London 1967 (The most modern study of the campaign in Mesopotamia which proved very valuable.)

Barnett, C. *The Swordbearers*, London 1963

________ *The Collapse of British Power*, London 1972 (A thought-provoking study by a master historian, providing a stimulating and perceptive analysis of the weaknesses in the British governing classes in the late nineteenth and twentieth centuries.)

Baynes, J. *Morale: a study of men and courage*, London 1967

Beaverbrook, Lord. *Men and Power 1917–1918*; London 1956

Birdwood, Field-Marshal Lord. *Khaki and Gown: an autobiography*, London 1941

Blake, R. (ed.). *Private Papers of Douglas Haig 1914–1919*, London 1952 (Can be misleading on account of the large mass of material omitted. Should have been at least twice as long and accompanied by a volume of appendices.)

Bloch, I. S. *Modern Weapons And Modern War, Being An Abridgement Of 'The War Of The Future In Its Technical, Economic And Political Relations', With Prefactory Conversation with W. T. Stead*, London 1900 (A vital book. The pity is that the politicians and General Staffs of the old world neglected to read it.)

Blunden, E. *Undertones of War*, London 1978 (A subtle, ironic and compelling book by one of the greatest of the war poets.)

Bonham-Carter, V. *Soldier True: the life and times of Field-Marshal Sir William Robertson, Bart., GCB, GCMG, KCVO, DSO*, London 1963

Select Bibliography

Boraston, J. H. *Sir Douglas Haig's Despatches*, London 1919 (Crucial to understanding how the Field-Marshal saw the war developing.)

Boyle, A. *Trenchard, Man of Vision*, London 1962 (The only biography of the 'father of the RAF'. Entertaining, with some valuable insights.)

Brabazon, Lord. *The Brabazon Story*, London 1956

Bray, N. N. E. *Shifting Sands*, London 1934

________ *A Paladin of Arabia*, London 1936 (A laudatory biography of Lieutenant-Colonel Leachman.)

Brinton, C. *The Anatomy of Revolution*, New York 1965. (A stimulating study of revolution which sheds useful light on the morale of large groups.)

Brophy, J. and Partridge, E. *The Long Trail*, New York 1965 (Valuable insights into the morale of the British soldier and some interesting details about items of equipment.)

Bruckshaw, H. (ed. M. Middlebrook). *The Diaries of Private Horace Bruckshaw, Royal Marine Light Infantry 1915–1916*, London 1979

Bruntz, G. G. *Allied Propaganda and the Collapse of the German Empire in 1918*, California 1938. (A valuable work with important ramifications in fields other than propaganda.)

Callwell, Major-General Sir Charles E. *Experiences of a Dug-Out*, London 1920

________ *Field Marshal Sir Henry Wilson* (2 volumes), London 1927

Canetti, E. *Crowds And Power*, London 1962

Carrington, C. *Soldier from the Wars Returning*, London 1965

Chambers, F. P. *The War behind the War 1914–1918*, London 1939

Charteris, Brigadier-General J. A. *At GHQ*, London 1931. (Important, but there is an element of covering-up with some distortion of facts, omissions and the insertion of opinions which were not held at the time; this combination has misled several biographers and historians. To be read very guardedly.)

________ *Field-Marshal Earl Haig*, London 1929. (This book angered the Countess Haig. The above comments apply to this book too, with the added drawback that Charteris was out of his depth when dealing with Haig's early life.)

Churchill, R. S. *Lord Derby 'King of Lancashire'*, London 1959. (The only biography of the influential Secretary of State. Deserves to be more widely read.)

Churchill, W. L. S. *The World Crisis* (5 volumes), London 1923–9. (Contentious. Extremely partisan but beautifully writen. Inspired a memorable response from Nancy, Lady Astor: 'Winston has written a book about himself and called it *The World Crisis*.')

Coppard, G. *With a Machine Gun to Cambrai*, London and Basingstoke 1986 (One of the best accounts of life in the front-line. Superbly written.)

Dallas, G. and Gill, D. *The Unknown Army: mutinies in the British Army in World War I*, London 1985

Davidson, Major-General Sir John. *Haig, Master of the Field*, London 1953

Deacon, R. *A History of the British Secret Service*, London 1969. (Advantageous in that it covers much ground in a single volume, but relies too heavily on undigested and often unreliable secondary sources.)

Demeter, K. (trans. A. Malcolm). *The German Officer Corps in Society and State, 1650–1945*, London 1962

Duff-Cooper, A. *Haig* (2 volumes), London 1935–6

Dupuy, Colonel T. N. *A Genius for War*, London 1977 (An excellent account of the Prusso-German General Staff which made the Prussian and German armies so formidable.)

Edmonds, Brigadier-General Sir James E. (and others). *Military Operations, France and Belgium* (16 volumes), London 1922–49 (The official history of the war on the Western front. In many respects very scholarly, but so far as Intelligence is concerned the authors' field was heavily restricted.)

Elliot, Major S. R. *Scarlet to Green*, Toronto 1981 (A thorough history of Canadian Military Intelligence.)

Ellis, J. *Eye Deep in Hell: the Western Front 1914–1918*, London 1976

_______ *The Sharp End of War*, London 1982 (A graphic account of life and death as experienced by the soldiers of western armies in the front line during the Second World War. Much of what is recorded here applies equally well to the First World War.)

Elton, O. *C. E. Montague: a memoir*, London 1929

Everitt, N. *British Secret Service during the Great War*, London, n.d. (Fiction – and poor fiction too.)

Extracts From General Routine Orders Issued To The British Armies In France By Field-Marshal Sir Douglas Haig, KT, GCB, GCVO, KCIE, London 1918

Facey, A. B. *A Fortunate Life*, Ringwood, Australia 1985

Farrar-Hockley, A. *Goughie*, London 1975. (A favourable biography of General Sir Hubert Gough with some helpful insights about Haig and decision making, but one-sided in that it plays down or ignores Gough's faults.)

Feldman, G. D. *Army, Industry and Labor in Germany 1914–1918*, Princeton (New Jersey) 1966 (A seminal work on the German Home Front.)

French, Major the Hon. E. G. *Field-Marshal Sir John French, First Earl of Ypres*, London 1931 (Hopelessly biased. Not recommended.)

Fussell, P. *The Great War and Modern Memory*, London 1975

Gerard, J. W. *My Four Years in Germany*, London 1917

Gibbs, P. *Now It Can Be Told*, London 1920

Gray, P. *The Grand Duke's Woman: the story of the morganatic marriage of the brother of Tsar Nicholas II*, London 1976

Haig, D., Countess. *The Man I Knew*, Edinburgh and London 1936

Hamilton, General Sir Ian. *Gallipoli Diary* (2 volumes), London 1920

Harington, General Sir Charles. *Plumer Of Messines*, London 1935

_______ *Tim Harington Looks Back*, London 1940

Haswell, J. *British Military Intelligence*, London 1973

_______ *Military Intelligence and the Intelligence Corps*, An Outline History, Ashford 1978

Herbert, A. P. *The Secret Battle*, London 1936

Herbert, D. *Second Son: an autobiography*, London 1972

Hopley, D. *John Ward and the Russian Civil War*, Dissertation for B.A. (Hons.), University of Keele, 1986

Horne, A. *The Fall Of Paris: the siege and the commune 1870–71*, London 1967 (A very good account of the influences which affect the morale of groups in siege conditions. Several parallels with the First World War.)

_______ *The Price of Glory: Verdun 1916*, London 1962 (Magnificent.)

Jerrold, D. *The Royal Naval Division*, London 1923 (A good account of a successful raid by the Drake Battalion in July, 1918, is to be found here.)

Jones, H. A. and Raleigh, W. *Official History of the War: the war in the air* (6 volumes), Oxford 1922–37

Keegan, J. *The Face of Battle*, London, 1976 (A magisterial work on what happens to men in combat. Ought to be compulsory reading.)

Kirkpatrick, Sir Ivone. *The Inner Circle*, London 1959 (Contains a brief but useful account of Secret Service work for GHQ, but one which tends to play down the work of S. P. Best.)

Knightley, P. and Simpson, C. *The Secret Lives of Lawrence of Arabia*, London 1969

Knightley, P. *The Second Oldest Profession: the spy as bureaucrat, patriot, fantasist and whore*, London 1986 (Falls into the trap of relying almost exclusively on published memoirs and reflects the fact that most of those were written for public consumption with the intention of misleading.)

Landau, H. *Spreading the Spy Net*, London 1938

Lasswell, H. D. *Propaganda Technique in the World War*, London 1927

Lied, J. *Return to Happiness*, London 1943

Liddell Hart, Sir Basil H. *History of the First World War*, London 1973 (Eminently readable, but much of the information and many of the conclusions have been rendered unsound by more recent research. To be treated with extreme caution.)

Linebarger, P. M. A. *Psychological Warfare*, Washington 1948

Lloyd George, D. *War Memoirs* (6 volumes), London 1933–6 (Some very good insights which do not alter the fact that there are so many half-truths, omissions, outright lies and twisted facts that the title might be better expressed 'War Lies'. Some might say it is a typical politician's book.)

_______ *War Memoirs* (2 volumes), London 1938

Lockhart, R. B. *Comes the Reckoning*, London 1947

_______ *Ace of Spies*, London 1967 (The best account of the life of the incredible Sidney Reilly. Well written with some fascinating detail.)

Lord, J. *Duty, Honour, Empire: life and times of Colonel Richard Meinertzhagen*, London 1971 (The only biography of Meinertzhagen to date. Captures the essence of his character very well.)

Ludendorff, General E. *My War Memories* (2 volumes), London n.d.

Lutz, R. H. *The Causes of the German Collapse in 1918. Sections of the officially authorized report of the Commission of the German Constituent Assembly and of the German Reichstag, 1919–1928*, California 1934 reprinted 1969

Mackenzie, Sir Compton. *Greek Memories*, Maryland 1987 (Valuable reprint of the suppressed first edition, complete with all the extracts Mackenzie was forced to delete. To be warmly welcomed.)

MacPherson, H. *Scotland's Debt to Protestantism*, Edinburgh and London 1912 (Illustrates what some elements of the Scots Presbyterian Church thought of Roman Catholics at this time.)

Mansfeld, Dr. K. *Der Koloradokartoffelkäfer im Klima Deutschlands Nachrichtenblatt Fur Den Deutschen Pflanzenschutzdienst*, Vol. 4, Part 7, Berlin 1924, pp. 45–46

Marshall-Cornwall, General Sir James. *Haig as Military Commander*, London 1973 (Displays considerable understanding of the difficulties under which Haig had to labour. Argues that Haig was a very capable commander, but was seriously deceived by Charteris.)

_______ *A Memoir: wars and rumours of wars*, London 1984

Martineau, G. D. *History of the Royal Sussex Regiment, 1701–1953*, Chichester 1953

Mead, P. *The Eye in the Air: history of air observation and reconnaissance for the Army 1875–1945*, London 1983 (A most valuable book. The standard history of aerial reconnaissance in the British Army.)

Meinertzhagen, Colonel R. M. *Army Diary 1899–1926*, Edinburgh and London 1960 (A splendid account of Meinertzhagen's work. Well-written and Meinertzhagen is honest in his opinions.)

_______ *Middle East Diary, 1917–1956*, London 1959

Meerloo, J. A. M. *Mental Seduction and Menticide*, London 1957

Middlebrook, M. *The First Day on the Somme*, London 1971

_______ *The Kaiser's Battle*, London 1978 (From an Intelligence perspective this is easily the most important of Middlebrook's books. This is chiefly because of his perceptive insights into morale for there seems to be a degree of uncertainty here about precisely what the British knew about the coming offensive.)

Ministry of Agriculture, Fisheries and Food. *Colorado Beetle* – MAFF Leaflet 71 (revised 1982)

Moran, Lord. *The Anatomy of Courage*, London 1966

Murray, J. *Call To Arms: from Gallipoli to the Western Front*, London 1980

_______ *Gallipoli as I Saw It*, London 1965 (Both books by Joseph Murray stand among the best front-line accounts of the war.)

Nash, D. B. *Imperial German Army Handbook, 1914–1918*, London 1980

Nicolai, Colonel W. (trans. G. Renwick). *The German Secret Service*, London 1924 (A totally misleading book according to which the Germans had no Secret Service worth mentioning and had to battle with Allied Services which were far better funded! Purports to say more about the Allied services than the German, but upon investigation too much of what Nicolai says has little or no foundation. Unreliable and clearly written to persuade the German people and government to devote more funds to their secret intelligence.)

Null, G. *The Conspirator Who Saved The Romanovs*, New Jersey 1971 (Fictitious rubbish.)

'Obituary of Lieutenant-General Sir George Macdonogh, GBE, KCB, KCMG', Royal Engineers Journal, September 1942

Occleshaw, M. E. *British Military Intelligence in the First World War*, University of Keele Ph. D. thesis 1984 (Badly in need of developing in the light of further information.)

Official. *Field Service Pocket Book (1914)*, Originally London 1914, reprinted Newton Abbot 1971

Oman, C. U. C. *The German Losses on the Somme* – The Nineteenth Century, Vol. 101, London 1927, pp. 694–705

Palmer, A. *The Gardeners of Salonika*, New York 1965

Partridge, E., Mottram, R., Easton, J. *Three Personal Records of the War*, London 1929

Pattison, M. *The Munitions Inventions Department: a case study in the state management of military science 1915–1919*, CNAA Thesis, Teesside Polytechnic, November 1981

Prochansky, H. and Seidenberg, B. *Basic Studies in Social Psychology*, London 1969

Rawlinson, A., Lieutenant-Colonel RGA and Commander RNVR. *Adventures on the Western Front, August 1914 – June 1915*, London and New York 1925

Read, A. and Fisher, D. *Colonel Z: the secret life of a master of spies*, London 1984

Reh, L. *Der Kartoffelkäfer bei Stade, Juli 1914 – Zeitschrift Für Angewandte Entomologie*, Vol. 2, Part 1, Hamburg 1914, pp. 213–219

Repington, C. À. C. *The First World War 1914–1918: personal experiences of Lieut.-Colonel C. À. Court Repington C.M.G.* (2 volumes), London 1920

Richards, G. *The Hunt for the Czar*, London 1972 (A tall story founded on an unconvincing 'diary'.)

Richardson, Major-General F. M. *Fighting Spirit: a study of psychological factors in war*, London 1978

Richardson, S. (ed.) *The Recollections of Three Manchesters in the Great War*, Manchester 1985

_______ *Orders Are Orders: a Manchester pal on the Somme*, Manchester 1987

Rickards, M. and Moody, M. *The First World War Ephemera, Mementoes, Documents*, London 1975 (An illuminating book that is well worth consulting.)

Roetter, C. *Psychological Warfare*, London 1974

Rogerson, S. *Propaganda in the Next War*, London 1938

Sander, A. *Deutschlands Kampf Mit Dem Kartoffelkäfer*, Munchen-Gladbach, Ed. 1, 1914

Sargant, W. *Battle for the Mind*, London 1959

Saxe, Maurice, Marshal Comte de. *Reveries, or Memoirs upon the Art of War*, Westport (Connecticut) 1971

Schablowski, H. *Der Koloradokäfer (Leptinotarsa decemlineata) Say – Zeitschrift für Pflanzenkrankenheiten*, Vol. 25, Part 4, 1915, pp. 193–203 and pp. 398–400

Scotland, Lieutenant-Colonel A. P. *The London Cage*, London 1957

Sixsmith, General E. K. G. *Douglas Haig*, London 1976

Sparrow, G. and McBean Ross, J. N. *On Four Fronts with the Royal Naval Division*, London 1918

Spears, General Sir Edward. *Liaison 1914*, London 1968

_______ *Two Men who Saved France: Pétain and de Gaulle*, London 1966

Storrs, Sir Reginald. *Orientations*, London 1939

Stuart, Sir Campbell. *Secrets of Crewe House*, London 1920 (Misleading. Unhappily this became the standard history of the propaganda campaign against Germany and its views exerted an unhealthy influence over the organization and conduct of the Second World War counterpart.)

Summers, A. and Mangold, T. *The File on the Tsar*, London 1976, 1978 and 1987 (Three editions of a most important book. Beautifully written, it reveals much about what rulers, governments and generals do behind closed doors and the extraordinary lengths to which they go to keep it all secret. Effectively demolishes the notorious myth about the alleged massacre at Ekaterinburg. This book performs a valuable public service.)

Sumner, W. G. *Folkways*, New York 1959

Terraine, J. *Douglas Haig: the educated soldier*, London 1963 (The best biography of Haig to date, but tends to overdo the praise.)

_______ *The road to Passchendaele: the Flanders Offensive of 1917, a study in inevitability*, London 1977

_______ *The Smoke and the Fire: myths and anti-myths of war 1861–1945*, London 1980

_______ *White Heat: the new warfare 1914–1918*, London 1982

Tiger, L. *Men in Groups*, London 1970

Thomas, E. C. and Attenborough, C. L. *Leading Cases in Constitutional Law*, London 1908

Trew, S. T. *The Czechoslovak Army Corps ('The Czech Legion') in Russia 1914–1920*, Dissertation for BA (Hons.), University of Keele 1986

Tuchman, B. W. *The Guns of August*, New York 1979

Tuohy, F. *The Secret Corps: a tale of 'Intelligence' on all fronts*, London 1920

Viereck, G. S. *Spreading Germs of Hate*, London 1931

Von Winning, Dr E. *Der Kartoffelkäfer – Festschrift '50 Jahre deutsche Pflanzenschutzforschung'*, Part 3, Berlin 1930, pp. 112–115

_______ *Stand der Kartoffelkäferfrage in Frankreich zu Beginn des Sommers 1930 – Nachrichtenblatt Für den Deutschen Pflanzenschussdienst*, Vol. 10, No. 11, November 1930, pp. 91–94

Watson, P. *War on the Mind*, London 1978 (Easily the best book on psychological warfare. Compulsive reading.)

Wavell, General Sir Archibald. *Allenby, a Study in Greatness: the biography of Field-Marshal Viscount Allenby of Megiddo and Felixstowe, GCB, GCMG*, (2 volumes), London 1940–3

West, N. *MI6 British Secret Intelligence Service Operations 1909–45*, London 1983

Williams, M. J. 'Thirty Per Cent: a study in casualty statistics' – Journal of the Royal United Services Institute, London February 1964, pp. 51–5

_______ 'The Treatment of the German Losses on the Somme in the British Official History: Military Operations France & Belgium, 1916' Volume II – Journal Of The Royal United Services Institute, London February 1966, pp. 69–74

Wilson, Lieutenant-Colonel Sir Arnold T. *Loyalties Mesopotamia 1914–1917: a personal and historical record*, London 1930

Winstone, H. V. F. *Leachman: 'O.C. Desert': the life of Lieutenant-Colonel Gerard Leachman DSO*, London 1982

_______ *The Illicit Adventure: the story of political and military Intelligence in the Middle East from 1898 to 1926*, London 1982

Winter, D. *Death's Men*, London 1978

Woodham-Smith, C. *Queen Victoria, Her Life and Times*, Vol. I, 1819–1861, London 1972

Wrench, J. E. *Geoffrey Dawson and our Times*, London 1955

Index

Ranks and titles are generally the highest mentioned in the text.

Index

Index

Index

Index